Entrepreneurship, Innovation and Sustainability

Entrepreneurship, Innovation and Sustainability

EDITED BY MARCUS WAGNER

LONDON AND NEW YORK

Cover by LaliAbril.com

First published in paperback 2024

First published 2012 by Greenleaf Publishing Limited

Published 2017 by Routledge
4 Park Square, Milton Park, Abingdon, Oxon OX14 4RN

and by Routledge
605 Third Avenue, New York, NY 10158

Routledge is an imprint of the Taylor & Francis Group, an informa business

Copyright © 2012, 2017, 2024 Taylor & Francis

Publisher's Note
The publisher has gone to great lengths to ensure the quality of this reprint but points out that some imperfections in the original copies may be apparent.

British Library Cataloguing in Publication Data:
A catalogue record for this book is available from the British Library.

ISBN: 978-1-906093-73-0 (hbk)
ISBN: 978-1-03-292231-7 (pbk)
ISBN: 978-1-351-27776-1 (ebk)

DOI: 10.4324/9781351277761

Contents

Foreword

Susan E. Jackson
Distinguished Professor, Rutgers University, USA; Past President, Academy of Management

As the world's population continues to climb, along with aspirations for lifestyles that require increasing amounts of energy, the need for new approaches to energy production and use has become increasingly evident. Attempts to change the environmental attitudes and everyday environmentally relevant behaviours of people around the world continue to be worthy goals for reducing the negative effects of modern lifestyles. Nevertheless, changes in everyday attitudes and behaviour are not likely to be sufficient to achieve the scale of change needed if we are to succeed in saving the planet from our unsustainable consumption of natural resources and the accumulation of various types of toxic waste that are associated with such consumption. In addition, the planet's future depends on our success in achieving large-scale, discontinuous changes in the way people live. Such change will come about in response to the creation of new technologies that alter the way people live. Innovations can restructure the social and technical infrastructures that support everyday life at work and at home in ways that reduce the need for individuals to make choices that pit personal gratification against environmental protection. But how can such innovation be achieved? What factors influence whether new innovations will be adopted initially, and eventually be disseminated widely? In this volume, authors with expertise in a variety of fields discuss the challenges that must be met in order to successfully develop and deploy innovations that promote sustainable economic and social development worldwide.

Corporate strategies, management practices, government policies, cultural norms and values, as well as individual decisions and actions all influence the speed and nature of innovations that support sustainable development. Readers of this volume will gain new insights into the dynamics at each of these levels of analysis and gain new appreciation of the interconnectedness of these many determinants of successful innovation. At the level of the firm, strategic decisions about whether to address sustainable development by making it a central pillar of the organisational mission or by positioning it as just another one of many objectives to be considered may determine the likelihood of achieving breakthrough innovations and the speed with which innovations spread. When sustainability is central to a firm's strategy, innovations are more likely within the firm but also throughout the firm's entire supply chain. Within industries, competition among firms may sometimes spur innovations that support sustainable development, but competitive dynamics also introduce uncertainty that can slow changes across an industry. Thus, new means for achieving appropriate cooperation among members of an industry are needed to give individual firms the confidence they need to take the risks required for successful innovation. Government actions can support or hinder innovation, also. Government policies that act as barriers to sustainable development may go unnoticed unless decision-making aids ensure that potential unintended consequences are identified when new policies are being discussed. On the one hand, government policies can spur innovation by providing incentives for corporate actions—including the entrepreneur's decision to start a new business—that are consistent with sustainable development goals. On the other hand, government policies can help shape consumer behaviour and thereby build a customer base for sustainable products and services.

Is sustainable development possible? Ultimately, the answer must be: yes. By developing a deeper understanding of the multitude of factors that can speed sustainable development, we can surely achieve it more quickly.

1

Entrepreneurship, innovation and sustainability
An introduction and overview[1]

Marcus Wagner
Julius-Maximilians-University of Würzburg, Germany

This volume addresses the intersection of entrepreneurship, innovation and sustainability, aiming at the provision and presentation of high-quality research illuminating the relationship between the three fields. The nexus of entrepreneurship, innovation and sustainability is particularly relevant from a European point of view given the focus of the European Commission on corporate social responsibility (CSR) and sustainability as well as the prominent role of the latter in the Framework Programme of the EU (e.g. European Commission 2008). Also the Lisbon Agenda, with its focus on the quality of life of European citizens, requires that firms reconcile sustainability aspects with profitability, and innovation and entrepreneurship have been identified as key to defuse sustainability demands, which immediately leads on to the question of how innovation can be directed to specific forms of technological progress (beyond policy-makers attempting to merely influence the rate of innovation).

Important starting and reference points in this respect are the entrepreneurship and innovation management and economics literatures. Notably these distinguish

1 Much of the content and the conceptual underpinnings and ideas for this edited book were developed during a Marie Curie Fellowship (SUS-PRO Innovation) which I held in 2006–2008, and financial support by the European Commission is gratefully acknowledged.

between radical and incremental innovation (Arrow 1962; Henderson and Clark 1990) on the one hand and into product, process, service (e.g. car sharing), organisational (e.g. environmental management systems), institutional (e.g. eco-clubs), system-oriented (e.g. industrial ecosystems) and function-oriented innovation (Afuah 1998; Kirschten 2005) on the other.[2] Furthermore, the product innovation literature increasingly distinguishes discrete and complex product architectures because the appropriation of profits from innovation differs between these two types with implications especially for business model choices (Davies and Brady 2000; Hall and Martin 2005).

Sustainability-improving innovation seems to require both (technologically) radical innovations that massively improve the environmental or social performance of goods or production processes while not altering consumer benefits, and utility and incremental (product- and process-related) innovations in the existing production and consumption systems due to (partly irreversible) path dependencies causing at least temporal lock-in and inertia. Under these conditions incremental innovation can make an important contribution by improving the eco-efficiency of production processes and environmental performance of goods in the short term at least to some degree. Yet incremental innovation is frequently unable to realise a globally optimal system configuration in a multi-dimensional production and consumption system space (Larson 2000; Frenken *et al.* 2007).

This raises the question as to what the conditions are for spontaneous emergence of sustainable entrepreneurship or sustainability-improving innovation (be it in larger or smaller firms or for the mass market or an initial niche, respectively) and a key requirement for such spontaneous emergence seems to be indeed the existence of a business case. Table 1.1 summarises different realisable combinations with regard to a business case and the type of innovation and also relates these to the seminal paper of Teece (1986), who argues that profiting from an innovation ultimately depends on the interplay of complementary assets, appropriability regimes and the existence of a dominant design (Utterback 1994).[3]

---

2 The last three types of innovation listed seem to include a large component of difficult-to-appropriate benefits because they extend beyond organisational boundaries.

3 Note that, in the case of a weak appropriability regime and the need for complementary assets, entrant innovation is hardly possible because incumbents know they can eventually block further diffusion and entrants anticipate that incumbents will deny them access to complementary assets (except for the case where an entrant acquires access to complementary assets).

Table 1.1 **Relationship between business cases based on Teece 1986 and innovation**

Type of innovation/ phase	Appropriability regime strong and no complementary assets needed	Appropriability regime strong and complementary assets needed	Appropriability regime weak and no complementary assets needed
Product innovation before dominant design	Eco-entrepreneur or social entrepreneur (e.g. Tesla, Ballard Power, Shai Agassi)	Incumbent managing or administrating sustainability or eco-entrepreneur	Social entrepreneur or lead user (e.g. car-sharing, especially relevant in case of service innovation), less strong incentives for eco-entrepreneur
Process innovation after dominant design	Incumbent can take over innovation lead (e.g. Honda, GM Volt, Smart)	Incumbent takes over innovation lead (e.g. photovoltaics, wind energy)	Incumbents can take over, but more difficult than with complementary asset need
Early diffusion	Regulation to push/ accelerate diffusion (e.g. feed-in tariffs for renewable energies) has strongest impact because entrant does not depend on negotiations to access complementary assets	Regulation to push/ accelerate diffusion but problematic because mainly incumbents would benefit (may acquire eco-entrepreneur)	Regulation to push/ accelerate diffusion but problematic because entrants and incumbents both can imitate more easily
Advanced diffusion	Entrant or incumbent can take over market, but may not be achieved if process innovation does not reduce cost to commodity level (vertical product differentiation or market segmentation in 'light' green mass and 'dark' green niche suppliers is a likely result)	Innovation takes over the complete market (if process innovation brings down cost to commodity level without compromising sustainability benefits) and incumbent takes over full market	Diffusion less often pushed/accelerated by regulation because imitation is very easy (high potential that takes over the complete market but also prices quickly move to commodity level and profits are low)

Sustainability-improving innovation that is suitable for the mass market is often system- or function-oriented innovation. However, such system- or function-oriented innovation often builds on more basic product and process innovations (e.g. new forms of data available at reasonable cost in the case of car-sharing) and on a sequence of more radical and more incremental innovation (Utterback 1994; Hall and Vredenburg 2003).

Importantly, in the context of this volume, many sustainability-improving innovations (which tend to require some level of technological radicalness) are carried out by smaller firms, reflecting the theoretically and empirically well-established negative association between firm size and the level of technological radicalness of an innovation (Schumpeter 1934; Markides and Geroski 2005; Harms *et al.* 2010; Schaltegger and Wagner 2011). This implies a significance of entrepreneurship for the nexus of sustainability and innovation. Therefore addressing the entrepreneurship–innovation–sustainability nexus from the point of view of small and medium-sized firms is an important contribution.

Concerning innovations that are not suitable for the mass market, but can survive in a niche, these frequently go along with providing supply for a peer group initially, and this is especially related to startups. For example, the supply of ecological food products can often be traced back to founders emerging from the green movement that start out their activities with customers from a specific milieu/peer community.

This coincides with an interesting logical paradox: namely, the question of whether there can really be a business case.[4] Defining sustainability as bundle of public goods (intra- and inter-generational equity, improvement or preservation of environmental quality, and protection of human health), if a firm pursues a sustainability-oriented or socially responsible activity with the intention to profit economically or financially from it, then that would imply that stakeholders (especially critical ones, see Mitchell *et al.* 1997; Phillips *et al.* 2003) voice concerns about the true social benefit of this. As a result, the reputation of the firm may be tarnished, leading to lower sales volumes and/or lower price levels. Thus such activities, if initially pursued with an instrumental stance aiming for economic benefit to the firm, rather than out of altruistic motives, would ultimately lead to just the opposite situation. The firm will experience difficulties in benefiting economically from these activities because they are not perceived to be very socially beneficial but rather driven by enlightened self-interest and hence the initial assumption is contradicted.

Conversely if a firm pursues sustainability-oriented or socially responsible activities initially with altruistic motives in mind, the improved product or corporate image resulting from this can result (even if not at all intended by the firm) in higher sales volumes or prices (assuming that at least some customers have a positive willingness to pay for certain reputational characteristics of a product or service) which may again cause concern (subsequently voiced) for some stakeholder groups. The same applies to a sustainability-improving innovation that is pursued by a firm on purely altruistic grounds: that is, beyond any enlightened self-interest and without any short- or longer-term economic benefit. Again such action could enhance the (product or corporate) image of the firm, leading to higher sales which

---

4 The notion that there is no such thing as a business case was introduced early on by the late Sir Geoffrey Chandler many years before sustainable development came into fashion as a concept (Davison 2011).

would logically contradict the basic assumption that the firm acts altruistically and without own benefit.

In summary, adapting the well-known economist's saying, there is no such thing as a business case for sustainability, at least *ex ante*: paradoxically sustainability-oriented or socially responsible activities that are largely altruistic should result in higher reputation gains and hence economic benefits whereas if such activities are motivated by self-interest precisely this will likely reduce economic benefits or even cause disbenefits.

From this perspective it seems that the notion that corporate social responsibility is a moral imperative, and not an element of the tactics toolbox of companies to maximise profits, is in some way reconciled with Milton Friedman's famous quip. This is what can be called the paradox of the business case for social responsibility and also sustainability at large and sustainability-improving entrepreneurship and innovation are crucial to resolve it. This is because innovation and entrepreneurship, leading to new combinations in the sense of Schumpeter (1934), are likely the best means to, at least to some degree, surmount the above paradox. Hence any (*ex post*) business case for sustainability needs to be based on sustainability-improving entrepreneurship and innovation as a necessary precondition, which is why the topic of this volume is highly relevant also in this context.

While the original call for this edited volume was rather broad, inviting original research contributions (both empirical and conceptual) in areas as diverse as innovation and sustainable enterprise performance, the role of entrepreneurship for sustainability, integration of sustainability into innovation routines and innovation strategies, the analysis of capabilities required for sustainable innovation, linkages of open innovation and user innovation to sustainability and entrepreneurship, the role of policy instruments and regulation for fostering sustainability-improving innovation and sustainable entrepreneurship, sustainability-improving innovations in specific industries, diffusion aspects of sustainability-improving innovation and sustainable entrepreneurship, and innovation and entrepreneurship for sustainable business models and product-service systems, the ultimate outcome has interestingly narrowed down to a more focused set.

Specifically, the ultimate set of contributions in this edited volume fills an important gap by focusing on less studied areas at the nexus of entrepreneurship, innovation and sustainability. These concern especially the fringes of this nexus: namely, small and medium-sized firms, developing countries, weaker stakeholders and mature industries. While comparatively more has been written, for example, about high-technology startups and industries, the areas addressed in the chapters to follow help to provide a more complete picture of the field. Having defined and discussed different types of sustainable innovation and their relationships to sustainable entrepreneurship, next an overview of the different chapters is provided, putting these into an overall context.

The first section of this edited volume comprises two chapters dealing with integrative views at the nexus of innovation, entrepreneurship and sustainability (EIS). In Chapter 2, Dyerson and Preuss make a case for a multi-level approach to analysing this nexus in order to reveal a connectivity that operates at the level of the individual, the level of the firm, the level of the infrastructure that surrounds innovations and the level of society. This call is in fact supported by empirical research that shows how different levels interact in bringing about entrepreneurial action with high societal benefits (Wagner 2011). Chapter 3 by Verhulst *et al.* similarly addresses from a conceptual point of view the implementation of sustainable product innovations, with a focus on human factors that influence this implementation process, and the emergence of sustainable business models. In doing so, it stresses the relevance of value propositions, the organisation of the upstream and downstream value chains, and the revenue model for developing successful activities at the EIS nexus (Halme *et al.* 2008; Doganova and Eyquem-Renault 2009). The first section overall stresses the role of system- and function-oriented approaches for realising sustainability-improving innovation and entrepreneurship.

The second section of this volume takes established firms and corporate entrepreneurship for sustainability-improving innovation as a reference point. In Chapter 4, Galpin and Whittington derive a number of propositions on how to create a culture of sustainability in companies. Then, Chapter 5 by Wagner builds on this and goes some way in empirically testing and confirming these propositions. Specifically, he confirms a positive association of workforce engagement and job satisfaction with sustainability performance for the case of environmental management system implementation and also addresses ideas developed in the conceptual overview by Dyerson and Preuss in Section 1. In summary, the second section confirms and highlights the role of organisational innovation beyond the role and relevance of product, process and service innovation.

The nexus of EIS in mature industries is the theme of the third section. One important focus here is the automotive industry as a prime example of a mature industry in need of improvements in terms of innovativeness and sustainability potential. Chapter 6 by Banerjee and Preskill focuses specifically on this industry by looking at the role of new environmentally sustainable innovation policies for shifts in the innovation focus of the automotive industry. Using a multi-method approach, they analyse shifts towards hybrid vehicles across common stages of product development. They show that carefully combined policy initiatives can indeed accelerate the shift towards environment-friendly automobiles. In Chapter 7, Llerena and Wagner put the theme of the third section in a broader comparative perspective by analysing, in addition to the automotive industry, the chemicals and electronics industries as well as the service sector. Based on exploratory interviews, they identify critical elements in corporate structures, and processes are identified that lead to the integration of sustainability aspects into innovation processes and strategising and show that market demand and regulation are pivotal factors that limit or push suppliers particularly in business-to-business.

While the third section on EIS in mature industries coincides strongly with a geographical focus on industrialised countries, the fourth section of this volume specifically addresses a logical counterpart, namely the EIS nexus in developing countries. Even before Prahalad's (2005) work on the base of the pyramid, newly industrialising and developing regions beyond the BRIC (Brazil, Russia, India and China) states have been identified as key to the question of how to ensure global and long-term sustainability, and the three chapters of this section testify to this. Mensah-Bonsu and Jell in Chapter 8 analyse obstacles to innovation and entrepreneurship in Ghana (which in various ways is representative of many African countries) with a special focus on sustainability-improving entrepreneurial opportunities. Building on qualitative interviews with entrepreneurs and experts they identify insufficient infrastructure, corruption, limited access to financing and loose regulations, as well as limited human capital as important obstacles and show that new markets can break down because of the quick entry of low-quality imitators—an insight that seems to deserve more attention in the design of policy and aid measures and activities. In Chapter 9, Bjerregaard and Lauring take a slightly different perspective by analysing the social sustainability of entrepreneurship. Based on an ethnographic study in Malawi, their findings complement the more micro-level focus of Chapter 8 by suggesting that entrepreneurship in developing countries often develops in parallel with democratisation processes and moves towards market economies. As they show, entrepreneurs under these conditions need to remain coherent with societal structures while at the same time also become involved in activities aimed at institutional change. Chapter 9 illustrates how entrepreneurs in this respect pursue different courses of action in the face of various institutional logics operating simultaneously and in doing so provides a complementary macro-level perspective. In the final chapter of this section, Chapter 10, Vastbinder *et al.* take up the sustainable business model considerations of Chapter 3 in the context of developing countries. Distinguishing different approaches to development in Africa, they argue that sustainable entrepreneurship is the most promising way to achieve this. They illustrate this with the case of the Ubuntu Company, a socially responsible business active on the international market.

The fifth section of the volume is on EIS in small firms and features two complementary chapters. First, in Chapter 11, Musso and Risso analyse the corporate social responsibility (CSR) relationships between large retailers and small and medium-sized food suppliers in Italy. In particular they analyse the effects of the large retailers' CSR initiatives on the suppliers involved from a supply chain management perspective. They find that small and medium Italian suppliers adapt their processes and tools to the CSR requirements of large retailers and that when small and medium-sized enterprises (SMEs) are involved as suppliers of international large retailers, they are more capable of managing CSR activities by adopting standards and certification systems.

While the results in Chapter 11 are very much in line with the standard paradigm about SMEs and their environmental performance and management (and in fact are found in very similar fashion in other industries such as automotives, electronics or chemicals), Katsikis in Chapter 12 provides, for a very similar industry setting, rather different results that show how co-evolution between demand and new product development can quite significantly alter an established paradigm. His chapter analyses the demand and sectoral characteristics interactions in the cosmetics sector in Greece and the formation of an eco-cosmetics segment using a case study example of eco-entrepreneurial activities based on the ability to adapt to public demand for ecological products. The case also shows that entrepreneurial action can lead to development and positive distributional effects that stabilise local economic growth.

The sixth and final section of this volume approaches the EIS nexus from a network perspective. Chapter 13 by Hansen and Klewitz builds on the famous and fundamental distinction between the rate and the direction of technological progress by Arrow (1962), by introducing the notion of sustainability-oriented innovation and apply this to SMEs. They develop a framework that reveals an important role of publicly mediated inter-organisational networks to support such innovation. Specifically, networks are shown to help share or reduce risks related to sustainability-oriented innovation and to support access to external expertise. The analysis also reveals a special role of public–private partnerships and university–industry relationships in this. Finally, in Chapter 14, Wagner and Lutz confirm some of these insights on an empirical basis, especially as concerns environmental aspects. They provide complementary evidence confirming especially the role of publicly supported incubators and cluster policies. They also move beyond description by suggesting an evaluation system for sustainability-oriented entrepreneurship and innovation and hence provide an integrative endpoint to this edited volume that also points to the relevance of the level of the individual (Wagner 2011).

This edited volume set at the nexus of EIS illustrates the potential and scope that entrepreneurship and innovation hold for fulfilling the promise of sustainable development. Hopefully, therefore, it will assist in managerial and political decision-making and the activities of policy-making bodies within and beyond the European Union.

References

Afuah, A. (1998) *Innovation Management Strategies: Implementation and Profits* (Oxford, UK: Oxford University Press).

Arrow, J.K. (1962) 'The Economic Implications of Learning by Doing', *Review of Economic Studies* 29: 155-73.

Davies, A., and T. Brady (2000) 'Organisational Capabilities and Learning in Complex Product Systems: Towards Repeatable Solutions', *Research Policy* 29.7–8: 931-53.

Davison, P. (2011) 'A stalwart of capitalism who pushed for ethical business', *Financial Times*, 16–17 April 2011: 6.

Doganova, L., and M. Eyquem-Renault (2009) 'What Do Business Models Do? Innovation Devices in Technology Entrepreneurship', *Research Policy* 38.10: 1,559-70.

European Commission (2008) *Progress on EU Sustainable Development Strategy (Final Report)* (Brussels: European Commission).

Frenken, K., M. Schwoon, F. Alkemade and M. Hekkert (2007) 'A Complex Systems Methodology to Transition Management', paper presented at the *DRUID Summer Conference 2007*, Copenhagen, CBS, 18–20 June 2007.

Hall, J., and M. Martin (2005) 'Disruptive Technologies, Stakeholders and the Innovation Value Chain: A Framework for Evaluating Radical Technology Development', *R&D Management* 35.3: 273-84.

Hall, J., and H. Vredenburg (2003) 'The Challenges of Sustainable Development Innovation', *MIT Sloan Management Review* 45.1: 61-68.

Halme, M., M. Anttonen and M. Kuisma (2008) 'Exploration of Business Models for Material Efficiency Services', in S. Sharma, M. Starik, R. Wüstenhagen and J. Hamschmidt (eds.), *Advances on Research in Corporate Sustainability* (Boston, MA: Edward Elgar): 71-96.

Harms, R., M. Wagner and W. Glauner (2010) 'Relating Personal, Firm Based and Environmental Factors to CSR Activities in Owner-Managed SME', *Journal of Small Business and Entrepreneurship* 23.2: 195-210.

Henderson, R., and K. Clark (1990) 'Architectural Innovation: The Reconfiguration of Existing Product Technologies and the Failure of Established Firms', *Administrative Science Quarterly* 35: 9-30.

Kirschten, U. (2005) 'Sustainable Innovation Networks: Conceptual Framework and Institutionalisation', *Progress in Industrial Ecology: An International Journal* 2.1: 132-47.

Larson, A.L. (2000) 'Sustainable Innovation through an Entrepreneurship Lens', *Business Strategy and the Environment* 9: 304-17.

Markides, C., and P. Geroski (2005) *Fast Second: How Smart Companies Bypass Radical Innovation to Enter and Dominate Markets* (San Francisco: Jossey-Bass).

Mitchell, R., B. Agle and D. Wood (1997) 'Toward a Theory of Stakeholder Identification and Salience: Defining the Principle of Who and What Really Counts', *Academy of Management Review* 22.4: 853-86.

Phillips, R., R. Freeman and A. Wicks (2003) 'What Stakeholder Theory is Not', *Business Ethics Quarterly* 13.4: 479-502.

Prahalad, C.K. (2005) *The Fortune at the Bottom of the Pyramid: Eradicating Poverty through Profits* (Upper Saddle River, NJ: Wharton School Publishing).

Schaltegger, S., and M. Wagner (2011) 'Sustainable Entrepreneurship and Sustainability Innovation: Categories and Interactions', *Business Strategy and the Environment* 20.4: 222-37.

Schumpeter, J. (1934) *The Theory of Economic Development: An Inquiry into Profits, Capital, Credit, Interest, and the Business Cycle* (Cambridge, MA: Harvard University Press).

Teece, D.J. (1986) 'Profiting from Technological Innovation: Implications for Integration, Collaboration, Licensing and Public Policy', *Research Policy* 15: 285-305.

Utterback, J. (1994) *Mastering the Dynamics of Innovation* (Boston, MA: Harvard Business School Press).

Wagner, M. (2011) 'Effects of Innovativeness and Long-term Orientation on Entrepreneurial Intentions: A Comparison of Business and Engineering Students', *International Journal of Entrepreneurship and Small Business* 12.3: 300-13.

Section I
Integrative views of the EIS nexus

2

The nexus of innovation, entrepreneurship and sustainability

Making the case for a multi-level approach

Romano Dyerson and Lutz Preuss
Royal Holloway University of London, UK

Over the last century humanity has experienced an unprecedented growth in economic wealth and standards of living. Yet this has been accompanied by an equally growing concern for a wide range of externalities of economic activity, whether climate change or soil erosion, labour standards in supplier plants or a widening gap between rich and poor (Hart 1997; Zadek 2001). The magnitude of these environmental and social challenges has prompted a reinvestigation of the role of industry in the struggle for sustainable development, in particular concerning the role of innovation in this process. Just as it has been called, at societal level, the engine of growth and, at firm level, a source of sustained competitive advantage, innovation now seems to offer the opportunity to decouple economic growth from environmental and social externalities (Lovins *et al.* 1997; Senge and Carstedt 2001). In a related fashion, a realisation has gained ground that entrepreneurship, rather than being synonymous with private wealth generation and increased resource consumption, may actually become 'a panacea for many social and environmental concerns' (Hall *et al.* 2010: 439).

Following such wake-up calls, both the innovation and the entrepreneurship literature have made huge strides to address the challenges of sustainable development. With regard to innovation, it has been recognised that key environmental factors of a novel product can be optimised during the design phase through concepts such as design-for-environment (Lenox *et al.* 2000). Innovation in production processes has pointed to the waste reduction potential of closed loop manufacturing (Jayaraman *et al.* 1999; Braungart and McDonough 2002), while innovation in business models encourages firms to move from selling discrete products to offering integrated solutions, such as offering a 'mobility service' rather than selling a car (Tukker and Tischner 2006). Entrepreneurship scholars, in turn, have focused on market imperfections to argue that sustainability-related market failures actually present opportunities for entrepreneurs to obtain entrepreneurial rents while simultaneously improving social and environmental conditions (Cohen and Winn 2007; Dean and McMullen 2007; York and Venkataraman 2010). The entrepreneurship literature has furthermore researched motivational issues to establish why some individuals set up their own businesses to address sustainability challenges when others do not (Choi and Gray 2008).

Useful as these developments are, they are nonetheless limited in two crucial ways. First, sustainability in innovation and sustainability in entrepreneurship are, more often than not, discussed in isolation from each other. This is perhaps not surprising as they come from two distinct research traditions, an essentially technological/economic aspect in the former and a focus on the enterprising individual in the latter. However, the design, selection and implementation of a technical innovation are all shaped by profoundly human processes, such as individual preferences, peer behaviour or social recognition. Entrepreneurship, in turn, finds its expression through novel products, processes or business models. Hence it is one central argument of this chapter that closely examining the interaction of the two fields would be most fruitful, not least for sustainable development. Second, and perhaps more importantly, both innovation and entrepreneurship are shaped, in the final analysis, by processes that operate at multiple levels. With regard to innovation, it has been recognised, for example, that 'new technologies have a hard time to break through, because regulations, infrastructure, user practices, maintenance networks are aligned to the existing technology' (Geels 2002: 1258). Similarly, scholars of entrepreneurship have stressed the wider nature of their field, where entrepreneurs operate 'through both political and technological mechanisms' (Dean and McMullen 2007: 60).

In order to fully understand the contributions that innovation and entrepreneurship can make to sustainable development, both subjects hence need to be studied in their interaction at and between several levels. Sustainability innovation certainly happens at the firm level, yet firm-level processes are embedded in wider institutional and societal process on the one hand and are driven or hampered by individual level processes on the other (Starik and Rands 1995; Hellström 2007; Wüstenhagen *et al.* 2008). In the same fashion, processes of sustainability-driven entrepreneurship certainly have their starting point in the enterprising individual, but they also occur in established organisations. In either case, their efforts are supported or hampered by societal level factors in both formal aspects, such as public policy, and informal dynamics, such as social norms (Meek *et al.* 2010). This chapter will thus make a case for a multi-level approach to sustainable entrepreneurship and innovation and then examine the nature of sustainability entrepreneurship and innovation as operating at four interlinked levels: (1) the level of the individual who undertakes innovative or entrepreneurial activities; (2) the level of the firm within which the individual operates; (3) the level of the infrastructure that surrounds a particular innovation or technology; and (4) the level of society. Finally, the conclusions will round off the discussion by pointing to limitations and potential future applications of the framework.

Levels of innovation and entrepreneurship

Both innovation (Geels 2002; Markard and Truffer 2008) and entrepreneurship studies (Thornton 1999; Davidsson and Wiklund 2001) have increasingly recognised a similar, essentially symbiotic, characteristic shared between the individual, the organisation and society. That is, both innovation and entrepreneurship are driven by individuals but at the same time are embedded in particular organisations and particular societies. In the words of Geels (2002: 1,257), 'technology, of itself, has no power, does nothing. Only in association with human agency, social structures and organisations does technology fulfil functions'. Interlinkages between the various levels mean that changes at one level can trigger changes at other levels. The growing interest among public policy-makers in actively fostering entrepreneurship is a case in point (Stevenson and Lundström 2007). Entrepreneurship has been widely recognised as an important engine of economic and employment growth; hence attempts to shape the institutional environment in which entrepreneurs operate have an impact on micro-level issues, such as the likelihood for someone to set up their own business, as well as macro-level issues, such as GDP growth in a particular country (Minniti 2008).

To start with innovation, innovative processes are, of course, undertaken, fostered or prevented by individuals. The creative act of invention is resistant to precise analysis but typically requires the combination of differing knowledge sets within the individual, together with the time to experiment and a willingness to tolerate failure (Dodgson 1993; Lester and Piore 2004). Hence the impacts of both individual characteristics, such as gender, age or personal attitudes, as well as organisational positions and roles on innovative behaviour have been studied (Baldridge and Burnham 1975). Owing to the complexity of modern technologies and the increasingly globalised nature of production and distribution, innovation is increasingly becoming characterised by a move towards project-based teamworking, decentralisation and matrix-style structures. Innovation within the firm is thus encouraged to spill over from the traditional, internally localised departments, such as R&D, to embrace the whole firm (Christensen 1997; Teece 2000). This moves the locus of innovation from something arcane, practised and shaped by an elite, to routines practised by the many. Its management thus requires a more entrepreneurial orientation and the ability to make connections out of disparate elements—this places the emphasis at the individual level not just on creativity but also on social intelligence and organisational knowledge (Clark and Wheelwright 1992).

Organisations typically provide the enabling infrastructure and resources within which individuals are encouraged to innovate (Freeman 1982). Consequently, innovation scholars have paid attention to the structural characteristics of organisations, such as size and complexity (Baldridge and Burnham 1975). However, the significance of the organisation as a vessel for innovation is perhaps best captured through concepts such as Prahalad and Hamel's (1990) core competences: that is, the ability of a firm to consolidate technologies and production skills companywide so that individual businesses can quickly adapt to new opportunities. Of similar importance is a firm's absorptive capacity, its ability to recognise the value of external knowledge, assimilate this with existing internal knowledge and then apply it commercially (Cohen and Levinthal 1990). The ambiguity that is located within such patterns of reiterative coordination and learning across the complex web (or 'architecture') of relational or open-ended contracts protects the firm from the duplication of its innovative efforts (Kay 1993). These ideas build on Penrose who argues: 'The general direction of innovation in the firm . . . is not haphazard but is closely related to the nature of existing resources . . . and to the type and range of productive services they can render' (Penrose 1959: 84). Similarly, Pavitt (1986) suggests that the innovative patterns of individual firms are closely aligned to their existing stock of knowledge and technologies (see also Nelson and Winter 1982). This conclusion could also be extended to the behaviour of entrepreneurs (Ács and Varga 1998; Casper and Whitley 2004; Minniti 2005).

Beyond the individual firm, innovation processes also depend on successful coalition building of actors and institutions in the narrow context of the innovation (Garud and Karnøe 2003). At this level, the various impacts on innovation can meaningfully be discussed in terms of technological systems built on a distinct technology, such as electric power (Hughes 1983) or robotics (Fleck and Howells 2001). Such a technological system can be defined as 'network(s) of agents interacting in a specific technology area under a particular institutional infrastructure to generate, diffuse, and utilize technology' (Carlsson and Stankiewicz 1991: 111). Typically, at the intermediate level, bottlenecks, or what Hughes (1983) terms reverse salients, in the system help to develop the technology along critical emergent paths that may be context-specific. As the concept of open innovation systems (Chesbrough 2003) emphasises, innovation is no longer restricted to the industrialised labs of the large corporation, rather it has become a collaborative process that requires the input of many specialised actors or institutions both within and beyond the firm. Building open innovation systems requires a willingness to engage in dialogue with the external environment. Firms have to agree to cooperate and integrate knowledge and resources to successfully commercialise inventions. This requires the development of trust- and alliance-building capabilities so that firms share their knowledge and skills through cooperative relationships.

Framing innovation at the individual, firm and infrastructure levels is the national innovation system that operates at a societal level to shape and motivate innovative acts. Innovation is enacted through the interplay of a number of different institutions, such as the education system, government policy, the legal system and consumers and producers in general (Dosi 1984; Nelson 1992; Freeman 1994; Balzat and Hanusch 2004). From this perspective, technology is not only non-neutral but eminently negotiable and amenable to being shaped by different societal groups. At its heart, technology thus embodies the political choices made by different interested parties. In other words, society encounters choices (consciously or not) over differing innovation paths, subsequent embodiment and utilisation of technology as well as the impact of technological change on different societal groupings (Hughes 1983; Molina 1990; Liebowitz 1995). These interactions, however, are fragile and easily disrupted; without constant renewal and adaptation a once thriving set of interactions can quickly become reduced to routine and habit. Critically, to remain competitive in a dynamic global environment, these national systems are expected to display characteristics of co-evolution and self-organisation (Lundvall 2007).

In a similar fashion, Davidsson and Wiklund (2001: 81) argue: 'Entrepreneurship takes place and has effects on different societal levels simultaneously.' A key level in entrepreneurship is, of course, the individual; as Schumpeter (1934) stresses, it is the individual who engages in entrepreneurial activities. Entrepreneurship scholars have thus shown a keen interest in differences between individuals in terms of how they recognise and exploit opportunities (Lumpkin and Dess 1996; Choi and Shepherd 2004). These differences include cognitive aspects, such as the mechanisms individuals use to deal with uncertainty (Hill and Levenhagen 1995), as well as motivational ones, such as an individual's need for achievement, his or her locus of control or desire for independence (Shane et al. 2003). Some of these motivations may also be external to the individual, where a perceived 'social marginality' may encourage an individual to become an entrepreneur rather than pursue other careers (Stanworth et al. 1989). Another key theme at the individual level concerns decision-making by entrepreneurs, where entrepreneurs were found to adopt a much wider conceptualisation of their responsibilities than, for example, bankers (Sarasvathy et al. 1998).

Although primarily concerned with the discovery and exploitation of opportunities irrespective of any organisational context, entrepreneurship scholars acknowledge that such opportunities may be exploited through newly created firms as much as within existing ones (Davidsson and Wiklund 2001). Often grouped together under the term 'corporate entrepreneurship', enterprising acts within the organisation can lead to the creation of new businesses within an existing firm and to its transformation or renewal as well as to changes in the competition rules for its industry (Guth and Ginsberg 1990; Stopford and Baden-Fuller 1994). Elements of corporate entrepreneurship can include the introduction of new products or services (organisational regeneration), an ongoing alteration of internal processes, structures and capabilities (organisational rejuvenation), a redefinition of its relationship with its markets or competitors (strategic renewal) or a proactive creation of a new arena for its products (redefinition of its domain) (Covin and Miles 1999). Where applied successfully, even troubled firms operating in a hostile context may shed past ways of doing things and adopt more promising strategies (Morris and Trotter 1990). More recently, corporate entrepreneurship has gained an international dimension: for example, with regard to risk management in decisions on foreign market entry (Shrader *et al.* 2000).

The intermediate level has attracted attention in the entrepreneurship literature, too. Schumpeter (1934) linked entrepreneurial initiatives of individuals to the creation and destruction of entire industries. Empirical work has established that many industries go through a life-cycle with distinct phases of entry, survival or exit (Klepper 1997). The intermediate level has furthermore been conceptualised in geographical terms, as new industries have often developed in geographically defined clusters, typified in the concept of the industrial district (Marshall 1920; Piore and Sabel 1984; Porter 1998; Carbonara 2002). At the regional level, cultural differences have been found to be more or less supportive of entrepreneurial activities (Davidsson and Wiklund 1997; Frederking 2004). Density and proximity of venture capital firms are other spatial factors that have a bearing on the likelihood of new ventures emerging (Florida and Kenney 1988). The intermediate level has additionally been perceived in terms of the network of contacts to which an individual entrepreneur has access. Here the concept of social capital indicates the amount of resources an entrepreneur can mobilise through his or her network of social relationships (Davidsson and Honig 2003).

At the societal level, the significant contributions entrepreneurship can make to employment, economic growth and technological progress become particularly visible (Schumpeter 1934; Davidsson and Wiklund 2001; Ireland and Webb 2007). However, entrepreneurial activities, just like innovation, are not automatically beneficial to society, as they may include unproductive rent-seeking behaviour and even destructive activities (Baumol 1990). At societal level, entrepreneurship can also be seen as an expression of societal values: 'Entrepreneurship is unique, because entrepreneurship is the only business form which can directly incorporate and consolidate the value perceptions of the individual' (Anderson 1998: 139). However, there may be more than one conceptualisation of the entrepreneur in any one society, as for example gender-based stereotypes of male and female entrepreneurs indicate (Gupta *et al.* 2009). The societal level, too, has thus sparked a systematic study of the impact on the development of entrepreneurial behaviour of such diverse factors as government policies to foster entrepreneurial activities (Stevenson and Lundström 2007; Minniti 2008), national culture (Shane 1992) or socioeconomic factors, such as consumer spending power, urbanisation or levels of unemployment (Reynolds *et al.* 1994).

The embeddedness of innovation and entrepreneurship is of particular relevance for sustainable development, as this is by definition a multi-level concept. Businesses represent the productive resources of the economy; hence society cannot achieve sustainable development without business support (Bansal 2002). Yet 'individual organisations cannot become sustainable: Individual organisations simply contribute to the large system in which sustainability may or may not be achieved' (Jennings and Zandbergen 1995: 1,023). In other words, it is only at the higher levels where individual innovative and entrepreneurial acts can be evaluated as having achieved a contribution to sustainable development or as having failed to do so. Having made the case that it does make sense to discuss both innovation and entrepreneurship at the individual, organisational, intermediate and societal levels, the following sections will discuss in more detail what key themes emerge at the respective levels in terms of the contribution of innovation and entrepreneurship to sustainable development.

The individual level

Individuals have a number of differing roles to play in innovation and entrepreneurship, from the imaginative act of setting up a new venture to the more pragmatic function of innovation management. The discussion above of individual-level themes in entrepreneurship pointed to cognitive and motivational characteristics of entrepreneurs (Lumpkin and Dess 1996; Shane *et al.* 2003; Choi and Shepherd 2004) as well as to differences in decision-making between entrepreneurs and other people (Sarasvathy *et al.* 1998). From an innovation perspective, the individual level has been concerned with varying combinations of creativity, experience and knowledge sets within the individual, together with the time to experiment and a willingness to tolerate failure (Dodgson 1993; Lester and Piore 2004). As innovation moves from being the activity of an individual to becoming based on teamwork (Teece 2000), learning and knowledge transfer processes become something for all organisational members to engage with rather than just the esoteric few (Christensen 1997).

The role of personal values has been documented in a number of studies into sustainability innovation and entrepreneurship, too (Young and Tilley 2006; Tilley and Young 2009). For example, Dixon and Clifford (2007) report a strong link between entrepreneurialism and environmentalism; rather than hindering entrepreneurialism, idealistic values regarding environmental and social goals can translate into valuable economic assets. Similarly, most of the sustainability-driven ventures identified by Choi and Gray (2008) were built on founder idealism rather than extensive business experience. Contrasting conventional with sustainability entrepreneurs, Parrish (2010: 511) found a crucial difference in their respective approach to reconciling sustainability-driven values with their organisation's need to survive: 'Conventional entrepreneurs view enterprises as a means of profiting from the exploitation of resources . . . In contrast, sustainability entrepreneurs view enterprises as a means of perpetuating resources.' Instead of utilising resources for their own advantage to generate maximum financial returns in the short run, sustainability entrepreneurs aim to use resources in a way that enhances them in the long run.

The literature on sustainability innovation has also stressed the importance of individuals' knowledge, skills and training, as without these the individual is unlikely to engage with sustainability challenges (Van Kleef and Roome 2007). Sustainability entrepreneurs hence need the skills to manage not only the conventional challenges of fluctuations in demand and supply, but novel ones, such as their company's reputation in the light of shifts in popular perceptions of 'sustainable' or 'green' or the balancing of competing demands by a wide variety of stakeholders (Hall and Vredenburg 2003; Dixon and Clifford 2007). The latter points to the need for managerial leadership in addition to sustainability-related knowledge. Again, the challenge is different from the traditional management one (Shrivastava 1994), as sustainability leaders need to display both transactional leadership behaviour—guide and steer the innovation and entrepreneurial processes around sustainability—as well as transformational leadership behaviour—inspire and guide the fundamental transformation that sustainability requires (Egri and Herman 2000; Angus-Leppan *et al.* 2010). More disturbing perhaps is recent work that suggests an individual's orientation towards sustainability may decline as business experience increases (Kuckertz and Wagner 2010).

The firm level

Both the innovation and the entrepreneurship literature readily acknowledge that individuals, and their innovative and enterprising activities, act from within organisations. From an innovation perspective, an initial focus was on structural characteristics, such as an organisation's size and complexity (Baldridge and Burnham 1975). This was followed by emphases on the organisation's core competences (Prahalad and Hamel 1990) and its 'architecture' of firm-specific relational contracts (Kay 1993) as well as its absorptive capacity (Cohen and Levinthal 1990). These concepts dock well with a stress in corporate entrepreneurship on organisational regeneration, organisational rejuvenation, strategic renewal or a redefinition of its domain (Covin and Miles 1999), which may not only contribute to ongoing or regained firm success but may also instigate changes in industry rules (Guth and Ginsberg 1990; Stopford and Baden-Fuller 1994). The question again is to what extent these concepts have been used to illuminate how innovation and entrepreneurship can influence developments with regard to sustainability.

The impact of organisational structure on the ability of a firm to address its sustainability challenges has been highlighted by Atkinson *et al.* (2000). Investigating how electricity providers grew into multi-utility firms, they found that this progression also affected the way in which environmental management was organised in these firms. According to Griffiths and Petrick (2001), current corporate architecture can hamper firms in their engagement with sustainability in three significant ways: a lack of structural elements through which the organisation can address sustainability; systems and routines that protect the status quo; and a denial of access to crucial external stakeholders that are seen as being disruptive. The concept of a firm's absorptive capacity has been extended into sustainability innovation too. Pinkse *et al.* (2010) argue that, while knowledge required for technological innovation may come from internal sources or value chain members, sustainability-specific knowledge is much more likely to reside outside the firm, for example in local communities, NGOs and regulatory bodies (see also Hart and Milstein 1999). Consequently, this type of knowledge is more likely than technical knowledge to require active assimilation into the organisation. For multinational enterprises, this situation may lead to tensions between location-specific knowledge on sustainability and the implementation of a global sustainability strategy.

Extending the concept of corporate entrepreneurship into sustainability, Miles *et al.* (2009: 69) define sustainable corporate entrepreneurship as 'the process of leveraging innovation of an organisation's products, processes, strategies, domain, or business models to discover, assess and ultimately exploit attractive economic opportunities created by latent and manifest environmental problems and/ or social responsibility issues'. In turn, these processes may requires changes to organisational decision-making, as more collaborative decision-making may lead to more robust decision outcomes that enhance corporate performance (Holloway 2010). Sustainable corporate entrepreneurship also depends on learning processes within the firm. It has, for example, been suggested that firms that are good at learning, such as large research-based pharmaceutical companies, are also good at learning from past steps in sustainability innovation (Blum-Kusterer and Hussain 2001). Learning with regard to sustainability is likely to benefit from an organisational capability to foster the development of both explicit sustainability-related knowledge and tacit knowledge needed to generate support from key internal and external stakeholders (Preuss and Cordoba-Pachon 2009).

The intermediate level

Innovation has been characterised, at the intermediate level, as a technology-specific innovation system that is based on successful coalition-building of actors and institutions in the narrow context of the particular innovation (Carlsson and Stankiewicz 1991; Garud and Karnøe 2003). Here the concept of an open innovation system (Chesbrough 2003) characterised innovation as having become a collaborative process involving many specialised actors or institutions within and beyond the firm. In geographical terms, entrepreneurship and inter-firm innovation have been explained through references to clusters, such as industrial districts (Marshall 1920; Piore and Sabel 1984; Porter 1998; Carbonara 2002). Such clusters consist not only of innovating firms but also of linked industries and other entities, such as governmental institutions, vocational training providers or trade associations. Geographic concentration may, in addition, support the formation of social capital (Coleman 1988; Davidsson and Honig 2003).

Perhaps the best-known example of a technology-specific innovation system with regard to sustainability is the Responsible Care Programme of the chemical industry, which was set up in the wake of major accidents, such as the explosion at the Union Carbide plant in Bhopal, India, in 1984 (King and Lenox 2000; Delmas and Montiel 2008). Since then, a whole raft of other industry-level initiatives have come into being, including the Ethical Trading Initiative, the standards for responsible forest management by the Forest Stewardship Council, the Extractive Industries Transparency Initiative, the International Cocoa Initiative on labour standards for cocoa growing or the Equator Principles, a framework for banks to manage environmental and social issues in project financing (Leipziger 2010). Many of the industry-level attempts to create global rules for responsible business have emerged through the interaction of multiple stakeholders, demonstrating the potential of such initiatives for effective consensus-building, knowledge-sharing and interest representation (Fransen and Kolk 2007). While traditional approaches to innovation highlighted the need for interaction with a relatively narrow range of stakeholders, such as suppliers, complementary innovators, customers or regulators, sustainability innovation needs to consider a much wider range of stakeholders, including environmental and social activists (Hall and Vredenburg 2003).

An ideal type of a geographic cluster approach to sustainability innovation and entrepreneurship is represented by the concept of industrial ecology. Analogous to a natural ecosystem, an industrial ecology system organises material and energy flows among multiple organisations in a location in such a way that they use each other's waste and by-products as input to collectively reduce their environmental footprint (Frosch 1992; Graedel 1994). In a related vein, clusters of small firms may be a major source of innovation with regard to the development of green technology. In addition, the emphasis on a free flow of information in such networks provides an appropriate structure to diffuse sustainability innovation quickly (Griffiths and Petrick 2001). Geographic concentration is also likely to promote the formation of social capital, which can not only aid the dissemination of scarce information but also reduce transaction costs through the creation of trust as well as help enforce norms and sanctions (Coleman 1988). In the context of the wind energy sector in California, social capital has indeed been found to be an important factor in the development of the industry, as informal networks aided information exchange, provided better access to skills locally and not least helped generate legitimacy for the emerging industry (Russo 2003).

The societal level

The societal level emphasises that innovation does not exist in a vacuum but is shaped and moulded by a complex myriad of societal pressures reflecting varying perceptions, interactions and power relations (Williams and Edge 1996), which together form a national innovation system (Nelson 1992; Freeman 1994). The interplay of the different institutions is, however, easily disrupted again (Lundvall 2007). This social emphasis on the process of innovation and technology development also suggests that innovation and technology development are not pre-determined, programmed in, as it were, by inviolable characteristics, but are rather open-ended, shaped and constructed by society as a whole (MacKenzie and Wajcman 1985; Bijker and Law 1992). With regard to entrepreneurship, the societal perspective highlights first the enormous contributions new venture creation can make to economic growth, employment and technological progress (Schumpeter 1934; Davidsson and Wiklund 2001; Ireland and Webb 2007). Entrepreneurship has moreover been characterised as being an outflow of societal values (Anderson 1998). This is reflected in Stirling's (2007: 297) plea for a discussion on the 'missing politics of technology'.

The emphasis in entrepreneurship and innovation on contributions to growth, employment and technological progress has led to the hope that business can contribute to 'a new environmentalism . . . driven by innovation, not regulation—radical new technologies, products, processes *and* business models' (Senge and Carstedt 2001: 26; emphasis in the original). However, the existing foci within large firms on process innovation and efficiency gains and beyond the firm on industry-wide collaboration in pollution prevention and product stewardship have predominantly fostered incremental innovation (Hellström 2007; Murphy and Gouldson 2000). Yet the stress in the innovation literature on the opportunities for locked-out parties to threaten the established sociotechnical regime through radical innovations (Geels 2010) has been picked up enthusiastically in the sustainability innovation literature: 'competency-enhancing incremental innovation is insufficient to meet sustainable development pressures. Instead, competency-destroying radical innovation is needed' (Hall and Vredenburg 2003: 62).

Seeing innovation as a political process leads to the question of democratic governance for sustainability. The increasingly global nature of many environmental problems, such as transboundary pollution, has raised awareness of situations where societal actors may be responsible for environmental damage but cannot be held accountable, for instance because they reside in a different jurisdiction (Dobson 1998). Extending this asymmetry of causation and accountability to the role of business in sustainability innovation, a similar concern has been voiced that the private sector must not drive out alternative forms of sustainability innovation, in particular bottom-up solutions for sustainable development (Seyfang and Smith 2007). Perhaps surprisingly at a first glance, such calls receive support from the conceptualisation of entrepreneurship as reflecting societal values. Given the

Table 2.1 Key themes on the nexus of innovation, entrepreneurship and sustainability

Level	Innovation research	Entrepreneurship research	Sustainability innovation and entrepreneurship research
Individual	• Learning and knowledge transfer as challenge for all organisational members • Impact of demographic and hierarchical position on innovative behaviour	• Identification and exploitation of entrepreneurial opportunities • Unique traits that cause individuals to pursue entrepreneurship • Entrepreneurial decision-making	• Importance of personal values and personal convictions about sustainability • Knowledge, skills and training on sustainability • Managerial skills
Firm	• Core competences of the firm; its absorptive capacity; architecture of relational contracts • Innovation as proceeding into 'zones' akin to existing knowledge and technologies • Impact of structural characteristics of organisations on innovative behaviour	• Corporate entrepreneurship: creation of new businesses within the organisation, renewal of an existing organisation or change to industry rules • Organisational regeneration; organisational rejuvenation; strategic renewal; redefinition of firm domain • Importance of networking/alliance development	• Alignment of general and sustainability management structures • Corporate sustainability architecture: impact of structural elements, desire to protect the status quo, denial of access to crucial but potentially disruptive stakeholders • Absorptive capacity for sustainability innovation • Sustainable corporate entrepreneurship: leveraging sustainability-related innovation in a firm's products, processes, strategies, domain or business models • Organisational learning with regard to sustainability

Level	Innovation research	Entrepreneurship research	Sustainability innovation and entrepreneurship research
Intermediate	• Coalition building of actors and institutions • Technological systems built on distinct technology • Open innovation systems, requiring development of trust- and alliance-building capabilities	• Role of entrepreneurship in creation and destruction of industries • Clusters, industrial district • Impact of norms and values of a region on entrepreneurship • Networking skills of individual entrepreneurs, social capital	• Technology-specific innovation system for sustainability at industry level, e.g. Responsible Care • Need for interaction with wide range of stakeholders • Cluster as particularly appropriate form for sustainability innovation and diffusion • Social capital aids information flows, identification of skills and generation of legitimacy
Society	• National innovation systems • Technology as political/social choice and the importance of coalition building • Path dependency of innovations • Interactions are fragile and easily disrupted	• Contribution to wealth creation, economic growth, employment creation and technological progress • Entrepreneurship as expression of societal values • Impact on entrepreneurship of government policies, national culture or socioeconomic factors	• Limitations of incremental innovation and opportunities in radical innovation • Sustainability as basis for alternative conceptualisation of entrepreneurship • Democratic governance of sustainability • Concern over private sector crowding out bottom-up solutions to sustainability

plurality of values in modern societies, this opens up the distinct possibility that there is more than one type of entrepreneur (Tilley and Young 2009). Building on societal shifts towards greater concern for the natural environment, alternative forms of entrepreneurship are thus feasible that aim 'to "fix" environmentalism within new businesses' (Anderson 1998: 135).

Conclusions

In this chapter we have argued that corporate sustainability, innovation and entrepreneurship are symbiotically connected and together form a nexus of linkages that can be analysed at varying levels of micro- and macro-engagement (see Table 2.1 for the key themes arising from innovation, entrepreneurship and sustainability innovation and entrepreneurship). This multi-level analysis is important in building a nuanced view of sustainability; one that depicts more thoroughly the interrelated connections made between the individual and the firm, the position of the firm inside an industrial infrastructure and ultimately the processes of innovation, entrepreneurship and sustainability bounded within a societal context. Exploring sustainability in this way also exposes the inherent fragility of the connections established, subject as they are to varying drivers of change from shifting political coalitions, competition over technological systems, changing market imperatives and evolving individual motivations.

Adopting this more holistic approach, as opposed to the closer scrutiny of individual components, has forced a necessarily broad, if not sweeping, examination of the available literature. At each level of analysis, we have sought to pick out drivers that are important to both innovation and entrepreneurship in the pursuit of sustainability. Inevitably this has led to the omission of other aspects, such as culture, market power and legitimacy, from this chapter. Similarly, we have not attempted here to attach relative weights to the drivers that we have discussed. While we recognise that these are limitations in the current analysis, the general insights that a multi-level analysis offers remain. Namely, that the processes at the nexus of innovation, entrepreneurship and sustainability are far from dispassionate; rather they help shape and frame sustainability outcomes that are the—quite possibly biased—culmination of interactions between different societal groups. Furthermore, these outcomes are not fixed or path-dependent in their trajectories, but instead are subject to periods of flux and stasis.

This conclusion has a number of implications for scholars and practitioners of sustainability innovation. From an academic perspective, the interrelated nature inherent in the nexus of sustainability, innovation and entrepreneurship suggests that attempts to view sustainability as a neutral, almost benign concept are likely to be illusionary, if not, more provocatively, ideological. Rather, our analysis suggests that sustainability is socially constructed and as such arrives reflective of dominating coalitions' expressions of power and influence. Concurrently, the dynamism inherent in these processes also indicates a fractured and disrupted view of sustainability over time. How, then, should corporate managers adapt themselves to this uncertain and changing state of affairs? One implication is that practitioners should keep their options open with a pluralistic approach that stresses flexibility as opposed to dedication to a particular type or mode of corporate sustainability. Here dedication should be to the processes of education and learning about sustainability options through entrepreneurship and innovation as opposed to concentrating on the (fixed) outputs of such options. In the final analysis, sustainability innovation emerges as being saturated with ethical challenges: which projects to promote, which values to foster in employees, how to handle conflict, what amount of risk to take, which stakeholders to engage with and so on. However, the ethical nature of these issues is rarely discussed in the innovation literature (Baucus *et al.* 2008).

References

Ács, Z.J., and A. Varga (1998) 'Entrepreneurship, Agglomeration and Technological Change', *Small Business Economics* 24.3: 323-34.

Anderson, A.R. (1998) 'Cultivating the Garden of Eden: Environmental Entrepreneuring', *Journal of Organisational Change Management* 11.2: 135-44.

Angus-Leppan, T., L. Metcalf and S. Benn (2010) 'Leadership Styles and CSR Practice: An Examination of Sensemaking, Institutional Drivers and CSR Leadership', *Journal of Business Ethics* 93.2: 189-213.

Atkinson, S., A. Schaefer and H. Viney (2000) 'Organizational Structure and Effective Environmental Management', *Business Strategy and the Environment* 9.2: 108-20.

Baldridge, J.V., and R.A. Burnham (1975) 'Organizational Innovation: Individual, Organizational, and Environmental Impacts', *Administrative Science Quarterly* 20.2: 165-76.

Balzat, M., and H. Hanusch (2004) 'Recent Trends in the Research on National Innovation Systems', *Journal of Evolutionary Economics* 14.2: 197-210.

Bansal, P. (2002) 'The Corporate Challenges of Sustainable Development', *Academy of Management Executive* 16.2: 122-31.

Baucus, M., W. Norton, D. Baucus and S. Human (2008) 'Fostering Creativity and Innovation without Encouraging Unethical Behavior', *Journal of Business Ethics* 81.1: 97-115.

Baumol, W.J. (1990) 'Entrepreneurship: Productive, Unproductive, and Destructive', *Journal of Political Economy* 98.5: 893-921.

Bijker, W., and J. Law (eds.) (1992) *Shaping Technology/Building Society: Studies in Socio-technical Change* (Cambridge, MA: MIT Press).

Blum-Kusterer, M., and S.S. Hussain (2001) 'Innovation and Corporate Sustainability: An Investigation into the Process of Change in the Pharmaceuticals Industry', *Business Strategy and the Environment* 10.5: 300-16.

Braungart, M., and W. McDonough (2002) *Cradle to Cradle: Remaking the Way We Make Things* (New York: North Point Press).

Carbonara, N. (2002) 'New Models of Inter-firm Networks within Industrial Districts', *Entrepreneurship and Regional Development* 14.3: 229-46.

Carlsson, B., and R. Stankiewicz (1991) 'On the Nature, Function and Composition of Technological Systems', *Journal of Evolutionary Economics* 1.2: 93-118.

Casper, S., and R. Whitley (2004) 'Managing Competences in Entrepreneurial Technology Firms: A Comparative Institutional Analysis of Germany, Sweden and the UK', *Research Policy* 33.1: 89-106.

Chesbrough, H. (2003) *Open Innovation: The New Imperative for Creating and Profiting from Technology* (Boston, MA: Harvard Business School Press).

Choi, D.Y., and E.R. Gray (2008) 'The Venture Development Processes of 'Sustainable' Entrepreneurs', *Management Research News* 31.8: 558-69.

Choi, Y.R., and D.A. Shepherd (2004) 'Entrepreneurs' Decisions to Exploit Opportunities', *Journal of Management* 30.3: 377-95.

Christensen, C.M. (1997) *The Innovator's Dilemma: When New Technologies Cause Great Firms to Fail* (Boston, MA: Harvard Business School Press).

Clark, K.B., and S. Wheelwright (1992) 'Organizing and Leading "Heavyweight" Development Teams', *California Management Review* 34.3: 9-28.

Cohen, B., and M.I. Winn (2007) 'Market Imperfections, Opportunity and Sustainable Entrepreneurship', *Journal of Business Venturing* 22.1: 29-49.

Cohen, W., and D. Levinthal (1990) 'Absorptive Capacity: A New Perspective on Learning and Innovation', *Administrative Science Quarterly* 35.1: 128-52.

Coleman, J.S. (1988) 'Social Capital in the Creation of Human Capital', *American Journal of Sociology* 94 (Supplement): S95-S120.

Covin, J.G., and M.P. Miles (1999) 'Corporate Entrepreneurship and the Pursuit of Competitive Advantage', *Entrepreneurship Theory and Practice* 23.3: 47-63.

Davidsson, P., and B. Honig (2003) 'The Role of Social and Human Capital among Nascent Entrepreneurs', *Journal of Business Venturing* 18.3: 301-31.

Davidsson, P., and J. Wiklund (1997) 'Values, Beliefs and Regional Variations in New Firm Formation Rates', *Journal of Economic Psychology* 18.2–3: 179-99.

Davidsson, P., and J. Wiklund (2001) 'Levels of Analysis in Entrepreneurship Research: Current Research Practice and Suggestions for the Future', *Entrepreneurship Theory and Practice* 25.4: 81-100.

Dean, T.J., and J.S. McMullen (2007) 'Toward a Theory of Sustainable Entrepreneurship: Reducing Environmental Degradation through Entrepreneurial Action', *Journal of Business Venturing* 22.1: 50-76.

Delmas, M., and I. Montiel (2008) 'The Diffusion of Voluntary International Management Standards: Responsible Care, ISO 9000, and ISO 14001 in the Chemical Industry', *Policy Studies Journal* 36.1: 65-93.

Dixon, S.E.A., and A. Clifford (2007) 'Ecopreneurship: A New Approach to Managing the Triple Bottom Line', *Journal of Organizational Change Management* 20.3: 326-45.

Dobson, A. (1998) 'Representative Democracy and the Environment', in W.M. Lafferty and J. Meadowcroft (eds.), *Democracy and the Environment: Problems and Prospects* (Cheltenham, UK: Edward Elgar): 124-39.

Dodgson, M. (1993) 'Organizational Learning: A Review of Some Literatures', *Organisation Studies* 14.3: 375-94.

Dosi, G. (1984) *Technical Change and Industrial Transformation* (London: Macmillan).

Egri, C.P., and S. Herman (2000) 'Leadership in the North American Environmental Sector: Values, Leadership Styles and Contexts of Environmental Leaders and their Organizations', *Academy of Management Journal* 43.4: 571-604.

Fleck, J., and J. Howells (2001) 'Technology, the Technology Complex and the Paradox of Technological Determinism', *Technology Analysis and Strategic Management* 13.4: 523-53.

Florida, R.L., and M. Kenney (1988) 'Venture Capital, High Technology and Regional Development', *Regional Studies* 22.1: 33-48.

Fransen, L.W., and A. Kolk (2007) 'Global Rule-setting for Business: A Critical Analysis of Multi-stakeholder Standards', *Organization* 14.5: 667-84.

Frederking, L.C. (2004) 'A Cross-national Study of Culture, Organization and Entrepreneurship in Three Neighbourhoods', *Entrepreneurship and Regional Development* 16.3: 197-215.

Freeman, C. (1982) *Economics of Industrial Innovation* (London: Macmillan).

Freeman, C. (1994) 'Continental, National and Sub-national Innovation Systems: Complementarity and Economic Growth', *Research Policy* 31.2: 191-211.

Frosch, R.A. (1992) 'Industrial Ecology: A Philosophical Introduction', *Proceedings of the National Academy of Sciences of the United States of America* 89.3: 800-803.

Garud, R., and P. Karnøe (2003) 'Bricolage versus Breakthrough: Distributed and Embedded Agency in Technology Entrepreneurship', *Research Policy* 32.2: 277-300.

Geels, F.W. (2002) 'Technological Transitions as Evolutionary Reconfiguration Processes: A Multi-level Perspective and a Case Study', *Research Policy* 31.8/9: 1257-74.

Geels, F.W. (2010) 'Ontologies, Socio-technical Transitions (To Sustainability) and the Multi-level Perspective', *Research Policy* 39.10: 495-510.

Graedel, T. (1994) 'Industrial Ecology: Definition and Implementation', in R. Socolow, C. Andrews, F. Berkhout and V. Thomas (eds.), *Industrial Ecology and Global Change* (Cambridge, UK: Cambridge University Press): 23-42.

Griffiths, A., and J.A. Petrick (2001) 'Corporate Architectures for Sustainability', *International Journal of Operations & Production Management* 21.12: 1573-85.

Gupta, V.K., D.B. Turban, S.A. Wasti and A. Sikdar (2009) 'The Role of Gender Stereotypes in Perceptions of Entrepreneurs and Intentions to Become an Entrepreneur', *Entrepreneurship Theory and Practice* 33.2: 397-417.

Guth, W.D., and A. Ginsberg (1990) 'Guest Editors' Introduction: Corporate Entrepreneurship', *Strategic Management Journal* 11 (Special Issue): 5-15.

Hall, J., and H. Vredenburg (2003) 'The Challenges of Innovating for Sustainable Development', *MIT Sloan Management Review* 45.1: 61-68.

Hall, J.K., G.A. Daneke and M.J. Lenox (2010) 'Sustainable Development and Entrepreneurship: Past Contributions and Future Directions', *Journal of Business Venturing* 25.5: 439-48.

Hart, S.L. (1997) 'Beyond Greening: Strategies for a Sustainable World', *Harvard Business Review* 75.1: 66-76.

Hart, S.L., and M.B. Milstein (1999) 'Global Sustainability and the Creative Destruction of Industries', *Sloan Management Review* 41.1: 23-33.

Hellström, T. (2007) 'Dimensions of Environmentally Sustainable Innovation: The Structure of Eco-innovation Concepts', *Sustainable Development* 15.3: 148-59.

Hill, R.C., and M. Levenhagen (1995) 'Metaphors and Mental Models: Sensemaking and Sensegiving in Innovative and Entrepreneurial Activities', *Journal of Management* 21.6: 1,057-74.

Holloway, D.A. (2010) 'Ecopreneurship, Corporate Citizenship and Sustainable Decision-Making', in M. Schaper (ed.), *Making Ecopreneurs: Developing Sustainable Entrepreneurship* (Farnham, UK: Gower, 2nd edn): 207-22.

Hughes, T. (1983) *Networks of Power* (Baltimore, MD: Johns Hopkins University Press).

Ireland, R.D., and J.W. Webb (2007) 'A Cross-disciplinary Exploration of Entrepreneurship Research', *Journal of Management* 33.6: 891-927.

Jayaraman, V., V.D.R. Guide and R. Srivastava (1999) 'A Closed-Loop Logistics Model for Remanufacturing', *Journal of the Operational Research Society* 50.5: 497-508.

Jennings, P.D., and P.A. Zandbergen (1995) 'Ecologically Sustainable Organizations: An Institutional Approach', *Academy of Management Review* 20.4: 1,015-52.

Kay, J.A. (1993) *Foundations of Corporate Success* (Oxford, UK: Oxford University Press).

King, A.A., and M.J. Lenox (2000) 'Industry Self-regulation without Sanctions: The Chemical Industry's Responsible Care Program', *Academy of Management Journal* 43.4: 698-716.

Klepper, S. (1997) 'Industry Life Cycles', *Industrial and Corporate Change* 6.1: 145-81.

Kuckertz, A., and M. Wagner (2010) 'The Influence of Sustainability Orientation on Entrepreneurial Intentions: Investigating the Role of Business Experience', *Journal of Business Venturing* 25.5: 524-39.

Leipziger, D. (2010) *The Corporate Responsibility Code Book* (Sheffield, UK: Greenleaf Publishing, 2nd edn).

Lenox, M., A. King and J. Ehrenfeld (2000) 'An Assessment of Design-for-Environment Practices in Leading US Electronics Firms', *Interfaces* 30.3: 83-94.

Lester, R.K., and M.J. Piore (2004) *Innovation: The Missing Dimension* (Boston, MA: Harvard Business School Press).

Liebowitz, S.J. (1995) 'Path Dependence, Lock-in, and History', *Journal of Law, Economics and Organization* 11.1: 205-26.

Lovins, A.B., L.H. Lovins and E.U. von Weizsäcker (1997) *Factor Four: Doubling Wealth, Halving Resource Use* (London: Earthscan).

Lumpkin, G.T., and G.G. Dess (1996) 'Clarifying the Entrepreneurial Orientation Construct and Linking it to Performance', *Academy of Management Review* 21.1: 135-72.

Lundvall, B.-A. (2007) 'National Innovation Systems: Analytical Concept and Development Tool', *Industry and Innovation* 14.1: 95-119.

MacKenzie, D., and J. Wajcman (eds.) (1985) *The Social Shaping of Technology: How the Refrigerator Got Its Hum* (Milton Keynes, UK: Open University Press).

Markard, J., and B. Truffer (2008) 'Technological Innovation Systems and the Multi-level Perspective: Towards an Integrated Framework', *Research Policy* 37.4: 596-615.

Marshall, A. (1920) *Principles of Economics* (London: Macmillan, 8th edn).

Meek, W.R., D.F. Pacheco and J.G. York (2010) 'The Impact of Social Norms on Entrepreneurial Action: Evidence from the Environmental Entrepreneurship Context', *Journal of Business Venturing* 25.5: 493-509.

Miles, M.P., L.S. Munilla and J. Darroch (2009) 'Sustainable Corporate Entrepreneurship', *International Entrepreneurship and Management Journal* 5.1: 65-76.

Minniti, M. (2005) 'Entrepreneurship and Network Externalities', *Journal of Economic Behavior & Organization* 57.1: 1-27.

Minniti, M. (2008) 'The Role of Government Policy on Entrepreneurial Activity: Productive, Unproductive, or Destructive?' *Entrepreneurship Theory and Practice* 32.5: 779-90.

Molina, A. (1990) 'Transputers and Transputer-Based Parallel Computers: Socio-technical Constituencies and the Build-up of British-European Capabilities in Information Technologies', *Research Policy* 19.4: 309-33.

Morris, M.H., and J.D. Trotter (1990) 'Institutionalizing Entrepreneurship in a Large Company: A Case Study at AT&T', *Industrial Marketing Management* 19.2: 131-39.

Murphy, J., and A. Gouldson (2000) 'Environmental Policy and Industrial Innovation: Integrating Environment and Economy through Ecological Modernisation', *Geoforum* 31.1: 33-44.

Nelson, R., and S. Winter (1982) *An Evolutionary Theory of Economic Change* (Boston, MA: Harvard University Press).

Nelson, R.R. (1992) 'National Innovation Systems: A Retrospective on a Study', *Industrial and Corporate Change* 1.2: 347-74.

Parrish, B.D. (2010) 'Sustainability-Driven Entrepreneurship: Principles of Organization Design', *Journal of Business Venturing* 25.5: 510-23.

Pavitt, K. (1986) 'Technology, Innovation and Strategic Management', in J. McGee and H. Thomas (eds.), *Strategic Management Research* (Chichester, UK: Wiley).

Penrose, E. (1959) *The Theory of the Growth of the Firm* (London: Blackwell).

Pinkse, J., M.J. Kuss and V.H. Hoffmann (2010) 'On the Implementation of a "Global" Environmental Strategy: The Role of Absorptive Capacity', *International Business Review* 19.2: 160-77.

Piore, M., and C. Sabel (1984) *The Second Industrial Divide: Possibilities for Prosperity* (New York: Basic Books).

Porter, M.E. (1998) 'Clusters and the New Economics of Competition', *Harvard Business Review* 76.6: 77-90.

Prahalad, C.K., and G. Hamel (1990) 'The Core Competence of the Corporation', *Harvard Business Review* 68.3: 79-91.

Preuss, L., and J.-R. Cordoba-Pachon (2009) 'A Knowledge Management Perspective of Corporate Social Responsibility', *Corporate Governance: The International Journal of Business in Society* 9.4: 517-27.

Reynolds, P.D., D.J. Storey and P. Westhead (1994) 'Cross-national Comparisons of the Variation in New Firm Formation Rates', *Regional Studies* 28.4: 443-56.

Russo, M.V. (2003) 'The Emergence of Sustainable Industries: Building on Natural Capital', *Strategic Management Journal* 24.4: 317-31.

Sarasvathy, D.K., H.A. Simon and L. Lave (1998) 'Perceiving and Managing Business Risks: Differences between Entrepreneurs and Bankers', *Journal of Economic Behavior & Organization* 33.2: 207-25.

Schumpeter, J. (1934) *The Theory of Economic Development* (Cambridge, MA: Harvard University Press).

Senge, P.M., and G. Carstedt (2001) 'Innovating Our Way to the Next Industrial Revolution', *MIT Sloan Management Review* 42.2: 24-38.

Seyfang, G., and A. Smith (2007) 'Grassroots Innovations for Sustainable Development: Towards a New Research and Policy Agenda', *Environmental Politics* 16.4: 584-603.

Shane, S.A. (1992) 'Why Do Some Societies Invent More Than Others?' *Journal of Business Venturing* 7.1: 29-46.

Shane, S., E.A. Locke and C.C. Collins (2003) 'Entrepreneurial Motivation', *Human Resource Management Review* 13.2: 257-79.

Shrader, R.C., B.M. Oviatt and P.P. McDougall (2000) 'How New Ventures Exploit Trade-offs among International Risk Factors: Lessons for the Accelerated Internationalization of the 21st Century', *Academy of Management Journal* 43.6: 1227-47.

Shrivastava, P. (1994) 'Ecocentric Leadership in the 21st Century', *Leadership Quarterly* 5.3–4: 223-26.

Stanworth, J., C. Stanworth, B. Granger and S. Blythe (1989) 'Who Becomes an Entrepreneur?' *International Small Business Journal* 8.1: 11-22.

Starik, M., and G.P. Rands (1995) 'Weaving an Integrated Web: Multilevel and Multisystem Perspectives of Ecologically Sustainable Organizations', *Academy of Management Review* 20.4: 908-35.

Stevenson, L., and A. Lundström (2007) 'Dressing the Emperor: The Fabric of Entrepreneurship Policy', in D.B. Audretsch, I. Grilo and A.R. Thurik (eds.), *Handbook of Research on Entrepreneurship Policy* (Cheltenham, UK: Edward Elgar): 94-129.

Stirling, A. (2007) 'Deliberate Futures: Precaution and Progress in Social Choice of Sustainable Technology', *Sustainable Development* 15.5: 286-95.

Stopford, J.M., and C.W.F. Baden-Fuller (1994) 'Creating Corporate Entrepreneurship', *Strategic Management Journal* 15.7: 521-36.

Teece, D.J. (2000) *Managing Intellectual Capital: Organizational, Strategic, and Policy Dimensions* (Oxford, UK: Oxford University Press).

Thornton, P.H. (1999) 'The Sociology of Entrepreneurship', *Annual Review of Sociology* 25: 19-46.

Tilley, F., and W. Young (2009) 'Sustainability Entrepreneurs: Could They Be the True Wealth Generators of the Future?' *Greener Management International* 55: 79-92.

Tukker, A., and U. Tischner (2006) *New Business for Old Europe: Product-Service Development, Competitiveness and Sustainability* (Sheffield, UK: Greenleaf Publishing).

Van Kleef, J.A.G., and N.J. Roome (2007) 'Developing Capabilities and Competence for Sustainable Business Management as Innovation: A Research Agenda', *Journal of Cleaner Production* 15.1: 38-51.

Williams, R., and D. Edge (1996) 'The Social Shaping of Technology', *Research Policy* 25.6: 865-99.

Wüstenhagen, R., S. Sharma, M. Starik and R. Wuebker (2008) 'Sustainability, Innovation and Entrepreneurship: Introduction to the Volume', in R. Wüstenhagen, J. Hamschmidt, S. Sharma and M. Starik (eds.), *Sustainable Innovation and Entrepreneurship: New Perspectives in Research on Corporate Sustainability* (Cheltenham, UK: Edward Elgar): 1-23.

York, J.G., and S. Venkataraman (2010) 'The Entrepreneur–Environment Nexus: Uncertainty, Innovation, and Allocation', *Journal of Business Venturing* 25.5: 449-63.

Young, W., and F. Tilley (2006) 'Can Businesses Move beyond Efficiency? The Shift toward Effectiveness and Equity in the Corporate Sustainability Debate', *Business Strategy and the Environment* 15.6: 402-15.

Zadek, S. (2001) *The Civil Corporation: The New Economy of Corporate Citizenship* (London: Earthscan).

3

Implementation of sustainable innovations and business models[1]

Elli Verhulst
Artesis University College Antwerp, Belgium;
Norwegian University of Science and Technology, Norway

Ivo Dewit
Artesis University College Antwerp, Belgium

Casper Boks
Norwegian University of Science and Technology, Norway

Changing customer demands, upcoming legislation and other types of pressure from various stakeholders make many firms realise that action is needed in order to follow current developments towards sustainable product innovations (Sarkis *et al.* 2010) and subsequently take action within product development and production. However, incorporating sustainability criteria in product innovations in a firm is not something that happens overnight. Transitions are necessary in order to make product innovations sustainable, particularly when it concerns the implementation of sustainability criteria in a firm's product development process. Several frameworks, models and strategies towards sustainable product innovations are presented in the literature on sustainable product innovations with the aim of practical application by a wide range of firms (UNEP DTIE and DfS 2009).

---

1 The authors would like to thank the companies and interviewees for their cooperation in the project and the Norwegian Research Council for financial support.

Motives to study the implementation process of a strategy for sustainable product innovations are given by different scholars, who articulate that the challenging part of applying sustainable product innovations does not occur during the development and formulation of a sustainable strategy and vision, but during the implementation of this new strategy in a firm (Tukker *et al.* 2001; Baumann *et al.* 2002; McAloone *et al.* 2002). During this implementation process, the theoretical strategy needs to be translated into practice. A well-developed approach can support this translation process, but the individual changes need to be made by the people within the firm. However, the position and strength of the employees in this process is often neglected within the field of sustainable product innovations, but it is considered as being of great significance within the field of change management (Verhulst *et al.* 2007). Different aspects related to the implementation of sustainable product innovations, with a strong focus on the human aspects that influence the progress of this implementation process, are discussed in the first part of this chapter. Moreover, as a result of the incorporation of sustainable product innovations, sustainable business models are found to emerge in practice. Lüdeke-Freund (2009) indicates that the introduction of such a strategy in the firm—by the occurrence of different activities—can grow in time and finally result in an (un)intended (sustainable) business model. Insight into the emergence of these business models is further explored in the last part of this chapter.

Insights from theory and practice: literature and business cases

In this chapter, available knowledge from the literature is combined with newly gathered knowledge from practice. The literature provides theoretical insights into sustainable product innovation strategies, the implementation process of sustainable product innovations, influencing human factors on this implementation process and sustainable business models. Eight business cases provide qualitative data and profound insights into these issues that can offer support to firms that are at the start of implementing sustainability criteria. In order to select appropriate business cases that make possible a good understanding of the phenomenon under study (Patton 1990), three criteria have been used.

A business case needs to:

- Be a firm with its own product development department and activities

- Have taken at least the first steps towards the integration of sustainability criteria in the firm and in product development (this is the main selection criterion in the study)

- Have its headquarters located in Belgium (Flanders) or the Netherlands. This geographical boundary limits differences in legislation and national culture, while it simultaneously increases the accessibility of the sites to be visited

Combined qualitative data from a set of data sources (Yin 2003) is used to analyse and study the business cases: interviews, archives and documentation and observations, of which the interviews form the main data source. In each business case, employees were addressed that are involved in both product development and the process of implementing sustainability criteria in product development or in the firm. The analysis of the empirical data has been done in two main stages, of which the first has a descriptive nature, whereas the latter is explanatory. In a first step, different topics that have been touched on in the data set are coded and subsequently clustered. A second part of this step contained the description of the phenomenon under study; that is, the implementation process of sustainability in product development, subsequently followed with an analysis of each case. This step provides insights into the followed strategy, steps and activities a firm has gone through in the implementation process and human factors that occurred during this process. In a last step, a cross-case analysis between the different business cases has been made.

In the research, 14 people cooperated from eight different firms (see Table 3.1) spread over 16 interviews and observations during work sessions. Five of the firms have their headquarters in Belgium; the three other firms are situated in the Netherlands. From the people that cooperated, there are eight respondents that 'pull' the incorporation of sustainability within the firm and the product development process, either through personal commitment, or by having a clearly defined responsibility in implementing sustainability. The functions of these people vary between the different firms: coordinator of corporate social responsibility (CSR); coordinator of quality, health and environment; communication manager; or R&D manager. The business cases do not necessarily have the same level of maturity in implementing sustainability in their business innovations; a distinction is made between starters and experienced firms. The starters are considered as firms that recently commenced their explorative trajectory, trying to find out what fits best to the firm and its products, which should lead them towards more sustainable products. The 'experienced' firms have been incorporating and reporting on sustainability aspects for more than ten years. This does not mean that all the work has been done, as all of them are currently working on improvements in order to reach a higher level of maturity with respect to sustainability.

Table 3.1 **Overview of cooperating firms**

Case	Product	Product sector	Firm's size	Experience with sustainability issues
Case 1	Creation of durable working, learning and living environments	Furniture	Large	Experienced Since 1990
Case 2	Display and visualisation solutions	Electronics	Large	Starter Since 2009
Case 3	Ergonomic office chairs	Furniture	Medium	Experienced Since 1997
Case 4	Space-saving, functional and modular furniture	Furniture	Medium	Starter Since 2007
Case 5	Sheets and films	Chemical industry	Large	Starter Since 2007
Case 6	Electronic consumer goods	Consumer goods	Large	Experienced Since 1994
Case 7	Quality aluminium systems for external use	Construction industry	Large	Starter Since 2006
Case 8	Public lighting systems	Lighting equipment and traffic signalisation	Large	Starter Since 2008

Implementing sustainable product innovations

Strategies for sustainable product innovation

Strategies that are directed towards sustainability and sustainable product innovations range from methods and tools directed at a specific part of the life-cycle of a product, for example energy-efficiency, focus on low-impact materials or end-of-life design strategies, to more holistic approaches such as corporate social responsibility (CSR), product-service systems, or cradle-to-cradle (C2C) (Van Hemel 1998; Tischner and Charter 2001; McAloone *et al.* 2002; Braungart *et al.* 2007; McAloone and Bey 2009; Suttclife *et al.* 2009; UNEP DTIE and DfS 2009; Carroll and Shabana 2010). The availability of this vast number of strategies and frameworks in the literature shows that there are many different roadmaps available to a firm for moving towards more sustainable product innovations. Many of these existing roadmaps however offer support on pilot initiatives, while Wilson *et al.* (2009) indicate a bottleneck between (a significant number of) successful pilot initiatives and the conversion into recurring initiatives that lead to long-term sustainability.

The business cases' strategies for sustainable product innovation

Table 3.2 shows the different strategies that are selected and being incorporated on a general and a product level in each of the business cases that cooperated in the study. The table indicates that not all firms already have a clear vision, mission and general strategy on both the social and environmental aspects of sustainability on a general firm level. However, all of them have formulated a strategy for improving their products on (mostly) environmental aspects.

Table 3.2 **Strategies on general sustainability issues (people and planet) in business cases**

Case	General strategy for social sustainability	General strategy for environmental sustainability	Strategy for sustainable product innovations
Case 1	CSR, ISO 26000	Closed loops (C2C) and CO_2-neutral production by 2020	PSS, closed material loops
Case 2	Environment, Health, Safety & Security pledge Corporate Governance Charter	–	Materials (REACH, WEEE)
Case 3	CSR	–	Materials, recycling, closed loop
Case 4	–	–	Material and weight reduction
Case 5	Environment, Health, Safety & Security Policy	Reduction of energy use, ecological products, less waste and care of the environment, clean products	Materials (REACH)
Case 6	Occupational Health & Safety Policy	A new set of sustainability targets for 2012: improve operational energy efficiency, reduce CO_2 emissions	Life-cycle thinking, materials, lower energy consumption, packaging
Case 7	CSR, recurrent social initiatives	–	Energy efficiency of products
Case 8	–	Improve energy consumption according to legislation and competitors	Lower energy consumption

Implementing strategies for sustainable product innovation

The choice of an appropriate strategy towards sustainable product innovations forms the beginning of a longer trajectory. The next step is to implement this strategy in the product innovation process and the other departments and levels within the firm; in other words, to switch from a theoretical or ad hoc perspective into practical, tangible actions and results. In order to reach such a level of integration, a firm may pass different phases: rejection, non-responsiveness, compliance, efficiency, strategic proactivity and the sustaining corporation (Dunphy *et al.* 2007). In order to reach the last stage, a firm needs an implementation approach that ensures a practical application of a selection of available or developed tools and methods. Much attention is often given to this process and the methodologies used, but less research has been performed on the human side of this implementation process. Zilahy (2004) for example studies restrictive and incentive motivational factors for employees that can hinder the implementation of energy-related measures, whereas Cohen-Rosenthal (2000) approaches the human dimension and its role as a success factor. Social-psychological factors have been suggested by Boks (2006) as a factor of influence for adoption that needs further study. The main focus thereby was on a departmental level, which has been confirmed by Driessen (2005). Humans and their interactions may thus have a significant impact on the course and progress of implementation processes, also on sustainability issues (Verhulst and Boks 2010b). The different factors related to people that interact and influence the integration of sustainable product innovations in firms are referred to as **human factors** and are studied in more depth in the field of change management. Insights from this adjacent discipline are gathered in the light of this study and again combined with empirical data assembled from the business cases. The findings on human factors are described in the following section.

Human factors in the implementation process of sustainable product innovations

Human factors in the implementation process

Change management literature states that an elaborate set of factors can support or hamper change processes (Pettigrew and Whipp 1991; de Caluwé and Vermaak 2006). Many of these factors that are generally accepted as necessary to emphasise in a change process are related to people and are classified in a number of human-related concepts: participation and empowerment, organisational culture, communication and resistance to change (Lewin 1951; Beckhard and Harris 1987; Kanter *et al.* 1992; Garside 1998). Some recent literature is available on change specifically oriented towards sustainability issues, in which different authors incorporate some of the knowledge of change management in newly proposed approaches towards sustainability. An example thereof is Dunphy *et al.* (2007), who translated a generic change approach into a change approach for incorporating sustainability in business. However, the authors state that this approach by itself cannot guarantee the success of an incremental change programme, but that a great deal depends on the support given by senior management to the changes, the readiness for change on the part of the workforce and the skills of change agents. These can all be considered 'human factors'. These human factors are also mentioned by Doppelt (2003), who defines seven sustainability blunders of which more than half are people-related issues, such as the firm's culture, learning mechanisms and internal communication. Other authors specifically focus on sustainability criteria within the product development process, such as Le Pochat *et al.* (2007), who incorporate factors from change management into their proposed implementation approach, such as the formation of a project team, building awareness and strategy definition. Schiavone and Pierini (2008) on the other hand emphasise the importance of creating a new culture inside an organisation. Reyes (2009) proposes an integration trajectory that combines three complementary mechanisms: methodological aspects, relational aspects and decision-making and informational aspects.

The implementation process and human factors in practice

This section provides a brief illustration of how the implementation process and human factors within this process have occurred in practice in two of the eight business cases: Case 2 recently started its implementation of sustainability criteria in product innovations, whereas Case 3 has already passed different stages in its implementation process. The descriptions provide insights on which human factors occurred in these firms and how they are accounted for during the implementation of strategies for sustainable product innovations. The description of the other cases can be found in Appendix I.

Case 2

Implementation process

This firm recently (2009) started incorporating sustainability issues in its product development process. A standardised change management procedure that is applied in the case for several changes in the firm, is also used for the specific case of sustainability criteria in product development. In general, this way of working was described by the respondent as: 'it's always the same way of working: identify it, find a solution and document it, and try it. It's always going through that circle. Identify the issue, find a solution, document a solution and then train the people'. The approach used entails three aspects: the process itself; the organisation of different functionalities and process activities; and the monitoring and steering of the process with meetings and decision processes.

The focus is put on green requirements for materials and parts of products, with the aim 'to drive the development process in such a way that the designers do not use those parts which have some forbidden substances'. The different steps as described above are performed subsequently in this case. First a burning platform is created to get sustainability on the agenda of the firm. A pilot project has been set up, in which a product development process has been completed with environmental issues included. The pilot project was planned to finish in March 2010 and resulted in a completely documented process, validated and improved templates and tooling, and a high level of information. As a part of the pilot, a green material database is developed and tested by external experts, and will be further implemented in the product development process to a broader group; that is, to the product development departments in the different divisions after completion of the pilot. Guidelines are also developed to support product developers during the process, and training is provided for this same group to take place after completion of the pilot. A next step is to provide clear communication on the efforts that are made, the approaches followed, the training, templates and tools that are provided and the future goals of the firm. This will be done by the development of a brochure that explains what the firm does in an accessible way. Responsibility for further implementation will thereby be transferred to the divisions.

Human factors during implementation

Education of employees, well-tested tools and clear division of responsibility. In this firm, training is seen as a crucial aspect for attaining competitiveness and innovation and all changes that come with it. Tools are developed and tested in order to support new methods that come together with the change (e.g. database support for green material selection). Responsibility is clearly defined and assigned to certain people in specific projects. Resistance is expected and seen as natural, and (middle) management employees are trained to deal with it.

Case 3

Implementation process

This company changed its core business in 1996 from consultancy towards the development of its own ergonomic office furniture. In 1997, a new product was developed with the principles of design for disassembly in mind. Recycling was thus already considered as an important aspect of the firm's products. In 2000, the first environmental report was published, in which the energy content of the chair throughout its complete life-cycle was mapped and explained. More projects with the focus on design for disassembly occurred in the following years. In 2007, a disassembly line was constructed in the main office of the firm. This line was constructed with the idea to close the material loop of the products. A redefinition of the strategy was made in 2008, in which the focus on materials was split into several more specific directions of material improvements including the use of recycled materials, the banning of hazardous materials and the minimising of the gross energy requirement (GER), the total energetic value of a product, and optimisation of recycling opportunities. A new environmental report was composed in the same year, in which the new directions were presented, together with the results attained so far. In 2009, different exploratory studies were done that are aimed at the goals that were formulated in the new strategy. External studies, for example a life-cycle analysis and a study on the opportunities for cradle-to-cradle thinking for the firm, have been carried out. In addition, a leasing system for the office chairs was developed and launched in that year. New elements that need to be taken into account from 2010 are the governmental guidelines on sustainable purchasing, as governmental tenders form a significant portion of the contracts of the firm. In 2010, the firm organised a seminar in Belgium on CSR in the firm, in which aspects of the social, environmental and economic sides of sustainability were considered in different presentations by people from business and research institutes. A goal for future product development is the design and production of a 100% recyclable product.

The progress of the implementation process shows that most interventions, if not all, start from within the product development department. Most interventions mentioned by the firm are directed towards environmental improvements. However, social issues are inherent in the core business and culture of the firm, as they focus on ergonomics within their product innovations. Providing an ergonomic environment and pleasant working conditions for the employees that promote vitality are aspects that were incorporated in the firm's mission from start-up.

Human factors during implementation

Empowerment and responsibility within the product development department. The product development department pulls sustainability issues forward in this firm, not only in their products, but also in production, marketing and sales. This implies that employees in other departments (e.g. in production) are less empowered and involved. Internal communication on sustainability issues is present, mostly on a personal level (one-to-one) and directed to a limited group of appropriate employees and other 'believers' in the firm.

Resistance, communication, empowerment and organisational culture

A description of the implementation processes of the eight business cases was given in the previous section. The data indicates that progress in the different cases follows a rather similar trajectory, in which—most often—a first stage entails several independent projects that are linked to specific aspects of sustainability, subsequently followed by the development of a general vision and strategy for sustainability for the whole firm. A next stage is a broader integration of this general vision and strategy, whereby internal and external communication, as well as cooperation with external partners is further extended. These stages match with the middle part of the trajectory as presented by Dunphy *et al.* (2007). Although a similarity in progress occurs in the different business cases, different approaches have been taken to follow the path towards sustainable product innovations. These approaches represent the culture and environment of a firm, as well as the way human-related factors such as communication or participation of employees is realised and supported. The manner in which these human factors occur and are dealt with was also described in the previous section for each of the business cases. In this section, four groups of human factors are described that were indicated in the literature and in the empirical data as most significant and recurrent. These are resistance, communication, empowerment and organisational culture. Each of these factors is discussed in the subsequent sections.

Resistance to change

An important human factor which is often mentioned in the literature as an obstacle to successful implementation of change is resistance against the change (Lewin 1951; Dent and Goldberg 1999).

The following quotation by the coordinator for incorporating environmental issues in product development in Case 6 represents responses that were given in five of the business cases on (the absence of) resistance to the introduction of sustainability: 'In general, 95% of the people [inside the firm] have a positive attitude when it concerns environmental and sustainable issues, even people that know nothing about the occupation'.

Although the interviewees were asked about resistance to the introduction of sustainability issues in all interviews, the data suggests that, in contrast, enthusiasm is often present on a general level, especially when employees see the value added by incorporating sustainability issues within the firm. This positive attitude seems to change in the next stage of the implementation process, when people have to start adapting their daily habits and working procedures. But by studying the time and place of occurrence of resistance to incorporating sustainability criteria within the working procedures, the data suggests that a distinction can be made between employees from product development and R&D, and employees from other departments such as sales or production (Verhulst and Boks 2010b). A proactive attitude of the product developers was pointed out in half of the cases, but also several obstacles were mentioned by the respondents:

- **Practical and organisational factors.** Time limits, trade-offs, legislation, new (external) data and information needed, much time and energy needed

- **Personal factors.** Other (personal) threats, no responsibility, lack of involvement, fear of work overload, fear of limitation of creativity, fear of losing flexibility, lack of ownership of procedures

- **Factors related to sustainability.** Intangible subject, complexity of the topic

The data suggests that two main groups of factors of resistance occur in the product development department: practical and personal factors of resistance. A third group of factors is related to the subject of the implementation process (i.e. sustainability) whereas the other factors are linked to the change, but not necessarily to sustainability. The three types of resistance came forward in the different business cases as significant factors that need to be monitored and taken account of when implementing the changes towards sustainable innovations.

These different sorts of resistance to change are considered to hamper the implementation process. Although some resistance will always be present when changes occur, the resistance to change can become stronger when too little attention is given to other human-related aspects during the implementation process, such as empowerment and involvement of employees. Therefore, three human-related concepts have also been studied in the business cases that can provide solutions for supporting the implementation process and that can lower the resistance, provided that these concepts are dealt with in an appropriate way.

Internal communication

Many different communication methods and tools have been mentioned in the different business cases that are used in order to structure internal communication on sustainability issues. Table 3.3 shows the variety of applied methods and tools.

Table 3.3 **Overview of communication methods and tools**

Empowerment and participation
• Believers
• Core team
• Direct communication in internal network
• Steering committee
• Regular meetings of committee
• Ambassadors
• Adapted information or communication style per department
• Dedicated training
• Dedicated workshops sessions

Process supporting tools
• Example products or projects
• Pilot projects
• Guidelines, checklists, templates, etc.
• Database
• External consultant

➔

Spreading of information

- Own label
- Existing labels and framework
- Item in internal firm magazine
- Item on intranet
- Dedicated mailings
- Dedicated presentation or seminars
- Dedicated brochure

Four individual communication methods and tools are employed in most of the business cases (in six or more cases), which makes those the most frequently utilised methods and tools for communication on sustainability issues: the presence of strong believers in the ideas behind sustainability; the presence of a core team; sustainable product or project examples; and guidelines and checklists. Moreover, nine other methods are carried out in practice in more than half of the firms. These are: use of the personal and internal network; use of ambassadors; pilot projects; information database; development of an own label; use of an existing label and framework; employment of intranet; spreading of dedicated presentations and seminars; and provision of training sessions that focus on sustainability issues. This indicates that various methods and tools are applied in practice to support the implementation process of sustainability criteria in product development. Some of these communication channels were also mentioned to be present in the firm to manage and support daily business processes without a further link with sustainability. The latter group includes the employment of an intranet, training sessions, the use of databases and the use of the internal network, among others. The different communication methods and tools presented in Table 3.3 can be grouped in three types of communication:

- **Spreading of information on sustainability** is important in order to inform the employees about the 'why' of incorporating sustainability, but also about 'how' this will happen, 'when' and by 'whom'

- Using **methods and tools that support the product development process** is important in order to streamline the process, to make it possible for the product developers to focus on the content, to make the changes measurable and to provide examples from practice

- A focus on **involvement and empowerment** is important in order to get a growing group of employees enthusiastic about the changes, to make employees participate actively and to let a new (sustainable) culture grow inside the firm

The applied communication types in the business cases indicate that all three types are needed to support the implementation process, but that the distribution of the type of communication differs throughout the process. In the early stages of the implementation process, more attention is given to methods and tools that support the sustainable product innovation process, while communication on empowerment and involvement was indicated to be underexposed. This communication type gains importance once a larger group of employees needs to get involved in the change process; that is, after the development of a general vision and strategy on sustainable (product) innovations. Communication that is aimed at informing internal and external stakeholders was indicated to occur during the whole implementation process.

Empowerment and involvement

Involvement and empowerment was emphasised in six business cases, in which employees are empowered on several levels and in different departments inside the firm. The empirical data suggests that empowering and involving people can be achieved in different ways, depending on the experience of the firm on sustainability issues: giving responsibility to employees in projects; appointing ambassadors; forming committees; or creating a job function directed towards sustainability. Empowerment of a growing group of employees is suggested to gain importance from the moment when employees have to start changing their daily working habits in order to reach sustainability goals. Another aspect that came forward in the business cases is the importance of *training* the appropriate employees on sustainability issues. Training and education of the employees is a meaningful aspect of empowerment. This is especially the case for complex subjects, as training can support the employees in grasping the context around sustainability and sufficiently understanding the content. However, individual ability and willingness to learn these new, complex concepts, methods and tools that support the consideration of sustainability criteria in the product development process also need to be considered. Internal champions that have a personal belief in the story behind sustainability were indicated as the people that pull the implementation of sustainable product innovations in six of the business cases: 'in an organisation you always need a few people that very strongly believe in it' (respondent from Case 1). These employees play a vital role in making the implementation process succeed, for which they need a high degree of autonomy to fulfil their function, as well as sufficient support from the management and other employees.

Indications are given in the business cases that different aspects of empowerment and involvement of employees were present in the firms; however this did not always happen consciously or as a function of the implementation process of sustainable product innovations. A company should thus consider how it can employ empowerment and involvement of employees in the implementation process right at the beginning: at the moment that a small group of employees is involved in the changes towards sustainability.

Organisational culture

A last aspect that came forward as an element that can influence the incorporation of sustainability criteria in product innovations is the culture in the firm and the different departments within it. Although the data suggests that sustainability is accepted by most employees on a general level in the business cases, the same data also suggests that a new 'sustainable' way of thinking and behaviour—a new culture—needs to be introduced in the firm in order to incorporate sustainability criteria to a sufficient extent. In the cases, different organisational cultures were recognised, as well as different approaches that were used for the implementation of sustainable product innovations. The type of culture thereby was also observed to influence the way a firm deals with sustainability criteria in the design process. In some business cases, the employees are considered as a central element in the process, whereby change is seen as a shift in human behaviour (Cases 1 and 3). In half of the cases, change is considered mostly as a learning process, whereby the motivation and learning capacity of the employees is seen as an important element that can provide the changes needed (Cases 2, 6, 7 and 8). The empirical data thus indicates that different approaches can lead towards sustainability in product development, depending on the culture of a firm. On the other hand, the subject of change—sustainability criteria in product development—also implies specific points of interest that need attention during the implementation process, such as the complexity of the subject, a lack of clarity on the concept of sustainability and a lack of clear and uniform measurement systems. This can be attained in an organisational culture where there is sufficient openness for new knowledge, customised and dedicated internal communication towards different layers in the firm and a minimum of structure and methods within the processes in order to support the employees in the new process. In a firm where these aspects are not present or only present to a small degree in the current culture of the firm, a larger shift in culture will be needed in that firm.

Conclusion on human factors

Four groups of human factors, how they occur and how they influence the implementation process of sustainable product innovations have been discussed: resistance, internal communication, empowerment and organisational culture. Based on the literature and on an empirical study, indications are given that aspects of the different human factors are somehow taken account of during the implementation process. However, this is often unconscious and not or seldom as a function of implementing sustainable product innovations. A higher awareness of the possible factors and a better integration of them in current implementation methodologies might support the integration of strategies for sustainable product innovations in practice. Recommendations on how these human factors can be taken into account during this process are formulated at the end of this chapter.

Emergence of sustainable business models

The implementation process of sustainable product innovations has been described based on the literature and on an empirical study, with a specific focus on human-related factors that—positively or negatively—influence the implementation process in firms. Based on the empirical data provided by the eight business cases that were studied, the data indicates that throughout the implementation process of strategies for sustainable product innovations, new and sustainable business models emerge. This has also been indicated by Lüdeke-Freund (2009), who shows how the introduction of a strategy in the firm—by the occurrence of different activities—can grow in time and finally result in an (un)intended (sustainable) business model. This is strengthened by Zott and Amit (2008), who emphasise that the order of developing and implementing a product strategy or a business model can be interchanged. The next section goes deeper into this subject, first describing the literature on (sustainable) business models and subsequently describing the changes that emerge in the business models in the cases. A last part introduces an example of a sustainable business model that emerged in one of the business cases.

Innovation through (sustainable) business models

Past and recent product innovations often occur on a technical level, whereas innovation of the business model happens at a higher level in the firm and may add value for all departments in the firm. Business models therefore link technical inputs and economic outputs of a firm, in other words converting new technology into economic value. The value of products and services is thereby considered as crucial to firms providing all types of goods (Johansson and Mollstedt 2006). The **creation of value** forms a central element in a business model. Amit and Zott (2001) define a business model as a depiction of the content, structure and governance of transactions designed so as to create value through the exploitation of business opportunities. The value thereby refers to the total value that is created in the transactions, regardless of whether it is the firm, the customer or any other participant in the transaction who appropriates that value. The latter authors describe content, structure and governance as the three constructs of a business model. Several other authors consider four main areas in business that need to be covered in a business model, which are further divided into six to ten attributes (Chesbrough and Rosenbloom 2002; De Mey and De Ridder 2009; Osterwalder and Pigneur 2010). The four main areas are given in Figure 3.1.

Figure 3.1 **Four main areas in business models**

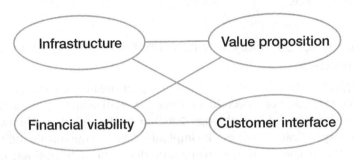

A sustainable business model (SBM) should show how sustainability is embedded in these four main areas, related to content, structure and governance of a firm and its partners. The SBM can thereby 'tell the story of sustainability' within this firm. Incorporating sustainability criteria in a firm's business model is mentioned as another way to support eco-innovations (Lüdeke-Freund 2010). However, according to Lüdeke-Freund, few theoretical frameworks and empirical cases serve as an example for the development of sustainable business models.

Some authors see the incorporation of sustainability criteria in the business model as separate attributes next to the four main attributes: social and environmental costs and social and environmental benefits form two supplementary attributes (Osterwalder 2009; Dewulf 2010). However, adding these attributes separately might restrict a full integration of sustainability criteria in the business model and thus also in the firm. This partial integration is also mentioned by Wilson *et al.* (2009) as a restriction of traditional approaches such as CSR, where environmental and social issues often get relegated to the margins of company activity, thereby staying unrelated to the core activities of the company and thus not seen as an integral of the business. Other authors propose a more holistic approach, such as Lüdeke-Freund (2010) who proposes a conceptual framework of business model eco-innovation. The business model canvas of Osterwalder and Pigneur (2010) is thereby incorporated in a broader framework that includes the development side of marketable eco-innovations, the incorporation of economic, ecological and social aspects in the model as well as marketing and successful implementation of the eco-innovations. Stubbs and Cocklin (2008) propose a system-based sustainable business model based on two company cases, in which both the socioeconomic as well as the natural environment are included.

In their sustainable value framework, Hart and Milstein (2003) combine sustainability drivers and opportunities with four basic components that create value for the shareholders, which are mapped according to two dimensions: time and activity boundaries (internal versus external). The four components are innovation and repositioning, cost and risk reduction, growth trajectory, and reputation and legitimacy. Although the availability of these, mostly conceptual, models and frameworks may turn out to be of great value, they need further development and verification in practice.

From strategy for sustainable innovations towards sustainable business models

Appendix II gives an overview of how different aspects related to strategies for sustainable product innovation affect the four main areas of a business model as proposed by Chesbrough and Rosenbloom (2002) and other scholars. The overview gives preliminary indications of how the implementation of the sustainability strategies influences the content of the business model in the eight business cases. A first indication that comes forward is a variation in impact between the business cases depending on the strategy and the experience of the firm: for example, firms that incorporate a product-service system (PSS) versus firms that focus merely on material improvements, eco-efficiency or legislation. The data indicates that product-service systems have a larger impact on a sustainable business model. In two of the case firms, a transition towards a PSS is made. This seems to have a larger impact on customer interface, infrastructure and financial viability than is the case with, for example, eco-efficiency. The data also indicates a difference in impact on the business model between cases that have a common vision on and framework for sustainability and cases that do not. In the latter group of firms, adaptations in the sustainable business model stay limited to the margins of the company's activities (e.g. Cases 2, 4 and 7), which was also indicated by Wilson *et al.* (2009) as a restriction of traditional approaches. The integration of the strategies changes some internal elements of the firm, including an improved value proposition and an adaptation of the key activities. However, in the other firms, the presence of a general vision affects all four areas of the business model. The overview, however, does not indicate the degree of adaptation that is caused in the business models.

Value proposition

The integration of a strategy for sustainable product innovation leads to a new and (more) sustainable value proposition in all the business cases. However, this adaptation or change of the value proposition does not equally influence the value creation in the different transactions in the other main areas of the business model (infrastructure, customer interface and financial viability) or towards the different stakeholders (firm, customer, other partners) (cf. Amit and Zott 2001). However, the data offers some interesting indications of how the other main areas can be affected.

Infrastructure

Cooperation in sustainability networks was mentioned in all firms, independent of the experience of the firm. External experts on sustainability occur in many of the cases, mostly in those that have little experience of sustainability issues, whereas in-house expertise occurs only in firms with significant experience, as well as cooperation with universities and research institutes, and influence in the supply chain. The data suggests that the business cases that do not have a common vision mostly cooperate with external experts and partners in order to assemble and gain knowledge on sustainability issues. In the other firms, however, sustainability experts are regarded as key resources, and a sustainability network rather has a strategic function with the aim of finding allies on the same sustainability level. More and different partnerships thus arise as a result of the integrated strategy for sustainable innovation.

Next to a larger number and different types of key partner, the key activities are also indicated in the eight business cases to be affected by the implementation of sustainability criteria in product innovations: for example, the integration of eco-efficiency in product development, production or marketing. Other, new activities occurred in some of the business cases, such as the development of new in-house expertise and the development and management of leasing and take-back systems.

Customer interface

Less attention to the customer interface comes forward from the data in Appendix II from the different business cases. In some of the cases, sustainability is not considered to add value to the customer, whereas in other cases, some elements related to sustainability are identified that can support and strengthen customer relations and customer channels. This occurs mostly in the firms that offer a PSS, or in the cases that are very customer-oriented, regardless of the presence of sustainability issues. These insights suggest that, so far, the customer side of the (sustainable) business model is barely influenced by the implemented strategies, or rather, that the current strategies for sustainable product innovations take insufficient account of this customer side.

Financial viability

The data suggests that low revenue streams are present in the business cases, especially in the early stage of implementing strategies for sustainable product innovations. Although the incorporation of sustainability criteria does not immediately lead to direct revenues for a firm, it might lead to cost reduction and efficiency, which is the financial viability that was most often indicated in the business cases. This cost efficiency can also be considered as a part of the value proposition. It should also be noted that the data in this study only provided limited information on the financial viability as an aspect of the emerging sustainable business models from the integrated strategies.

Business cases: example of an emerging sustainable business model

An example of an emerging sustainable business model is given in this section, based on business case 3. This firm followed an interesting trajectory towards sustainable product innovations, whereby different strategies were applied consecutively; from a focus on design for disassembly, the firm broadened its sustainable activities to an own internal disassembly line and a corresponding take-back system. However, in order to complete and ensure the closed material loop of its products, a new strategy was introduced: the leasing of products. Although leasing is not new as a concept (i.e. for cars), it is an innovative approach in the furniture sector.

The changes that are induced by the implementation of these strategies in the firm and that affect the business model of the firm are shown in Figure 3.2. The canvas as proposed by Osterwalder and Pigneur (2010) is used for this visual representation, as it offer a clear visualisation of the four main areas of a business model, further divided into nine building blocks.

In this business case, the value proposition changed significantly: by introducing a system to lease its products (i.e. office chairs), the company switches from offering a product towards a product-service system (PSS). For both the firm and the customer, this creates interesting opportunities, but also a new way of working, selling, distributing, maintenance and usage.

For the company, it closes the material loop, because by offering the products as a service, the firm is guaranteed that it will get all the leased chairs back. These can subsequently be disassembled, reused (parts) or recycled (materials) and manufactured into new chairs or other products. However, it also demands new methods and approaches for the sales department, as well as for distribution, maintenance and take-back.

This indicates significant changes in the customer relationships, whereby much energy and time needs to be invested by the sales department to explain the new product-service combination to possible customers, the benefits of the system for the customers, the environmental gains from the system, and an explanation on the pricing of product and service that shows the financial consequences of the system in comparison to the traditional way of buying office chairs. However, no new channels for sales and distribution were approached and the company stayed with its current customer segments.

The infrastructure of the business case is also indicated to be affected significantly, as substantial changes are needed in the key activities, key resources and the key partners, as shown in Figure 3.2. New key activities are linked to the leasing and take-back system, whereby the sales, maintenance and service and collection of the products needs to be well-organised. Moreover, the disassembly of the products happens in-house, which means that the infrastructure has been adapted (assembly line), but also the employees needed education on the purpose and the procedure to follow. New partners entail recycling companies, suppliers of recycled materials and other sustainable materials, as well as other partners with which the

Figure 3.2 **Emerging sustainable business model of business case 3**

Source: based on canvas as proposed by Osterwalder and Pigneur (2010: www.businessmodelgeneration.com)

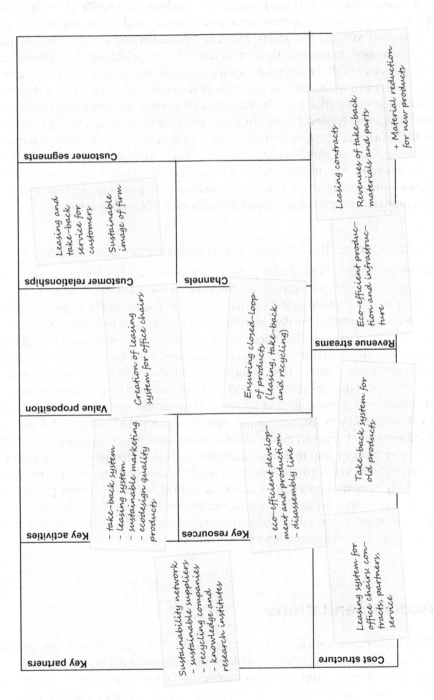

business case cooperates in research and other projects concerning sustainable innovations.

All these changes also have repercussions on financial viability; leasing contracts create constant and long-term revenue streams, as well as a strong and long-term connection with the customers. Moreover, the collection and recycling of materials saves (new) material costs and an eco-efficient production and infrastructure lowers costs. On the other hand, the organisation and fulfilment of the leasing system with extra maintenance and collection requires an adapted cost structure in which additional efforts and investments are needed for personnel, infrastructure and education. However, in this business case, the financial advantages are merged with the other advantages that are created for the customers, the firm and the environment, which makes it a viable and attractive sustainable business model.

In this company, the integration of the applied strategies for sustainable product innovations clearly led to a new and sustainable business model that strengthens its approach and the value created throughout the complete value chain.

Conclusion on the emergence of sustainable business models

When strategies for sustainable product innovations are implemented, this leads to changes in the business model, whereby the changes are either rather limited and sustainability is added to the standard business model, or the implementation of the strategies leads to the development of a new business model that delivers more sustainable outcomes. The difference in type of sustainable business model seems to depend on the maturity level of sustainability of the firm, and/or to the chosen strategy for sustainable product innovations. Product-service systems thereby have a large impact on the business model and can thus lead to a newly well-integrated sustainable business model, as shown in the example case. Other strategies, such as eco-efficiency or material improvements, do not lead to large changes in the business model. The incorporation of sustainability issues was indicated in all the business cases to lead to a new value proposition, a change in key activities and more and new key partners. External experts as new partners seem to occur more regularly in inexperienced firms, whereas more in-house experts are present in the more experienced firms. The customer side of the business model is indicated to be underexposed in several of the business cases and merits more attention in order to raise the total value creation of the business.

Recommendations

This chapter deals with two main subjects. In the first part, different aspects related to the implementation of sustainable product innovations were discussed, with a strong focus on the human aspects that influence the progress of this implementation process. The second part of the chapter concentrated on the way sustainable business models emerge during and after the implementation of the strategies for sustainable product innovations. Insights from the literature and an empirical study of business cases were combined. The insights assembled are formulated as recommendations.

Box 3.1 **Recommendations on implementing strategies for sustainable product innovations**

- Incorporate the following human factors in the implementation approach supporting sustainability: resistance, internal communication, empowerment and organisational culture

Resistance

- Keep in mind that sustainability as the subject of change seldom creates resistance
- Try to get insights into the sorts of resistance (practical and organisational factors, personal factors or factors related to sustainability) and the underlying reasons
- Think of possible ways to deal with the resistance before the resistance occurs
- Try to adapt the implementation approach, communication and participation to the needs, knowledge, skills and culture of the affected departments and individuals. This lowers resistance

Internal communication

- Combine three types of communication tools and methods:
  - Spreading of information on sustainability
  - Methods and tools that support the product innovation process
  - Communication supporting involvement and empowerment
- Focus more on methods and tools that support the product innovation process in the beginning of the implementation process (e.g. pilot projects)
- Focus more on communication supporting involvement and empowerment from the moment a larger group gets involved
- Focus on added value, opportunities and (provisional) results from sustainable innovations

Empowerment and participation

- Give responsibility to different layers:
  - Appoint employees in projects
  - Appoint ambassadors
  - Form committees
  - Create a job function directed towards sustainability

- Start the implementation process with a limited group of motivated employees (i.e. in pilot projects)
- Make sure there are internal champions that personally believe in the need for sustainability
- Support these internal champions

Organisational culture

- Adapt the implementation approach to the culture of your firm at the start of the implementation process
- During the implementation process, adapt the organisational culture to the specific needs of sustainability, such as:
  - Openness to need for education
  - Presence of structure and methods for processes that involve sustainability issues
  - Sufficient training and internal communication on sustainability

---

Box 3.2 **Recommendations on the development of a sustainable business model**

Choice of strategy or sustainable business model

- First, consider which approach might be most appropriate for your company and the current situation it is in. Will you rather:
  - Choose a strategy for sustainable product innovation, and implement it?
  - Develop a sustainable business model, and implement it?
- For firms that lack maturity on sustainability issues, developing a sustainable business model can offer a good starting point for finding a new way to create (sustainable) value for customer, firm and other partners, whereby sustainability goals are linked with economic value for the firm
- For firms that already have sufficient maturity on sustainability, the definition of a sustainable model can visualise, communicate and reinforce the current sustainability strategy in the firm
- Consider the degree of innovation you want to put into the sustainable business model. Is it the aim to:
  - Add sustainability to the standard business model?
  - Develop a new business model that delivers more sustainable outcomes?

Implementation of the sustainable business model

- When implementation of a sustainable business model in a firm starts, also consider the different human factors as described above to support the implementation process

References

Amit, R., and C. Zott (2001) 'Value Creation in e-Business', *Strategic Management Journal* 22: 493-520.

Baumann, H., F. Boons and A. Bragd (2002) 'Mapping the Green Product Development Field: Engineering, Policy and Business Perspectives', *Journal of Cleaner Production* 10: 409-25.

Beckhard, R., and R. Harris (1987) *Organizational Transitions* (Reading, MA: Addison Wesley, 2nd edn).

Boks, C. (2006) 'The Soft Side of Ecodesign', *Journal of Cleaner Production* 14: 1,346-56.

Braungart, M., W. McDonough and A. Bollinger (2007) 'Cradle-to-Cradle Design: Creating Healthy Emissions—A Strategy for Eco-effective Product and System Design', *Journal of Cleaner Production* 15.13–14: 1,337-48.

Carroll, A., and K. Shabana (2010) 'The Business Case for Corporate Social Responsibility: A Review of Concepts, Research and Practice', *International Journal of Management Reviews* 12.1: 85-105.

Chesbrough, H., and R.S. Rosenbloom (2002) 'The Role of the Business Model in Capturing Value from Innovation: Evidence from Xerox Corporation's Technology Spin-off Companies', *Industrial and Corporate Change* 11.3: 529-55.

Cohen-Rosenthal, E. (2000) 'A Walk on the Human Side of Industrial Ecology', *American Behaviour Scientist* 44.2: 245-64.

De Caluwé, L., and H. Vermaak (2006) *Leren veranderen. Een handboek voor de veranderkundige* (Deventer, Netherlands: Kluwer).

De Mey, N., and P. De Ridder (2009) 'Business Model Framework', tbmdb.blogspot.com/2010/12/de-mey-and-de-ridders-business-model.html, accessed 13 September 2011.

Dent, E.B., and S.G. Goldberg (1999) 'Challenging "Resistance to Change" ', *Journal of Applied Behavioral Science* 35.1: 25-41.

Dewulf, K. (2010) 'Play it Forward: A Game-Based Tool for Sustainable Product and Business Model Innovation in the Fuzzy Front End', online *Proceedings of ERSCP-EMSU 2010 Conference: Knowledge Collaboration & Learning for Sustainable Innovation*, Delft, The Netherlands.

Doppelt, B. (2003) 'Overcoming the Seven Sustainability Blunders', *The Systems Thinker* 14.5: 2-7.

Driessen, P.H. (2005) *Green Product Innovation Strategy* (PhD thesis, CentER Dissertation Series; Tilburg, Netherlands: Tilburg University).

Dunphy, D., A. Griffiths and S. Benn (2007) *Organizational Change for Corporate Sustainability: A Guide for Leaders and Change Agents of the Future* (New York: Routledge, 2nd edn).

Garside, P. (1998) 'Organisational Context for Quality: Lessons from the Fields of Organisational Development and Change Management', *Quality in Health Care* 7 (Suppl.): S8-S15.

Hart, S.L., and M.B. Milstein (2003) 'Creating Sustainable Value', *Academy of Management Executive* 17.2: 56-67.

Johansson, N., and U. Mollstedt (2006) 'Revisiting Amit and Zott's Model of Value Creation Sources: The SymBelt Customer Center Case', *Journal of Theoretical and Applied Electronic Commerce Research* 1.3 (December 2006): 16-27.

Kanter, R. M., B. Stein and T.D. Jick (1992) *The Challenge of Organizational Change: How Companies Experience It, and Leaders Guide It* (New York: Free Press).

Lewin, K. (1951) *Field Theory in Social Science* (New York: Greenwood Press).

Le Pochat, S., G. Bertolucci and D. Froelich (2007) 'Integrating Ecodesign by Conducting Changes in SMEs', *Journal of Cleaner Production* 15: 671-80.

Lüdeke-Freund, F. (2009) *Business Model Concepts in Corporate Sustainability Contexts: From Rhetoric to a Generic Template for 'Business Models for Sustainability'* (Lüneburg, Germany: Centre for Sustainability Management).

Lüdeke-Freund, F. (2010) 'Towards a Conceptual Framework of Business Models for Sustainability', online *Proceedings of ERSCP-EMSU 2010 Conference: Knowledge Collaboration & Learning for Sustainable Innovation*, Delft, The Netherlands.

McAloone, T., and N. Bey (2009) *Environmental Improvement through Product Development: A Guide* (Copenhagen: Danish Protection Agency).

McAloone, T., N. Bey, C. Boks, M. Ernzer and W. Wimmer (2002) 'Towards the Actual Implementation of Ecodesign in Industry: The Haves and Needs Viewed by the European Ecodesign Community', in *Proceedings of CARE Innovation 2002*, Vienna, Austria.

Osterwalder, A. (2009) 'How to Systematically Build Business Models Beyond Profit', presentation at *impACT³*, Jacobs University, Bremen, Germany, www.slideshare.net/Alex. Osterwalder/business-models-beyond-profit-social-entrepreneurship-lecture-wise-etienne-eichenberger-iqbal-quadir-grameen-bank-grameen-phone, accessed 14 September 2011.

Osterwalder, A., and Y. Pigneur (2010) *Business Model Generation* (Hoboken, NJ: John Wiley & Sons).

Patton, M.Q. (1990) *Qualitative Evaluation and Research Methods* (Thousand Oaks, CA: Sage).

Pettigrew, A.M., and R. Whipp (1991) *Managing Change for Competitive Success* (Oxford, UK: Blackwell).

Reyes, T. (2009) 'Ecodesign Trajectories: A Strategy for Integration of Environmental Consideration in the Design Process at SMEs', in *Proceedings of the 16th CIRP International Conference in Life Cycle Engineering*, Cairo, Egypt: 118-24.

Sarkis, J., P. Gonzalez-Torre and B. Adenso-Dias (2010) 'Stakeholder Pressure and the Adoption of Environmental Practices: The Mediating Effect of Training', *Journal of Operational Management* 28: 163-76.

Schiavone, F., and M. Pierini (2008) 'Strategy-based Approach to Eco-design: An Innovative Methodology for Systematic Integration of Ecologic/Economic Considerations into Product Development Process', *International Journal of Sustainable Design* 1.1: 29-44.

Stubbs, W., and C. Cocklin (2008) 'Conceptualizing a "Sustainability Business Model"', *Organization & Environment* 21.2: 103-27.

Suttcliffe, L.F.R., A.M. Maier, J. Moultrie and P.J. Clarkson (2009) 'Development of a Framework for Assessing Sustainability in New Product Development', in *Proceedings of the 17th International Conference on Engineering Design (ICED'09), Design for X, Design to X* (vol. 7; Stanford, CA: Stanford University): 289-300.

Tischner, U., and M. Charter (2001) *Sustainable Solutions: Developing Products and Services for the Future* (Sheffield, UK: Greenleaf Publishing).

Tukker, A., P. Eder, M. Charter, E. Haag, A. Vercalsteren and T. Wiedmann (2001) 'Eco-design: The State of Implementation in Europe', *Journal of Sustainable Product Design* 1: 147-61.

UNEP DTIE and DfS TU Delft (2009) *Design for Sustainability: A Step-by-Step Approach* (Paris: UNEP).

Van Hemel, C. (1998) *EcoDesign Empirically Explored: Design for Environment in Dutch Small and Medium Sized Enterprises* (PhD dissertation; Delft, Netherlands: TU Delft).

Verhulst, E., and C. Boks (2010a) 'The Role of Human Aspects in Design for Sustainability Strategies and Approaches', in *Proceedings of APMS2010 International Conference on Competitive and Sustainable Manufacturing, Products and Services*, Cernobbio, Italy, October 2010.

Verhulst, E., and C. Boks (2010b) 'The Role of Human Factors in the Adoption of Sustainable Design Criteria in Business: Experiences from Practice', *Electronic Proceedings of ERSCP-EMSU Conference on Knowledge Collaboration & Learning for Sustainable Innovation*, Delft, The Netherlands, October 2010.

Verhulst, E., C. Boks, M. Stranger and H. Masson (2007) 'The Human Side of Ecodesign from the Perspective of Change Management', in *Advances in Life Cycle Engineering for Sustainable Manufacturing: Proceedings of the 14th CIRP Life Cycle Engineering Conference*, Tokyo (London: Springer): 107-12.

Wilson, E., G. MacGregor, D. MacQueen, S. Vermeulen, B. Vorley and L. Zarsky (2009) 'Innovating for Environment and Society: An Overview', IIED Briefing Business Models for Sustainable Development, pubs.iied.org/17056IIED.html, accessed 14 September 2011.

Yin, R.K. (2003) *Case Study Research: Design and Methods* (Applied Social Research Methods Series, Vol. 5; Thousand Oaks, CA: Sage, 3rd edn).

Zilahy, G. (2004) 'Organisational Factors Determining the Implementation of Cleaner Production Measures in the Corporate Sector', *Journal of Cleaner Production* 12: 311-19.

Zott, C., and R. Amit (2008) 'The Fit between Product Market Strategy and Business Model: Implications for Firm Performance', *Strategic Management Journal* 29: 1-26.

Appendix I **Description of the implementation process and the human factors (Cases 1, 4–8)**

Case 1

Implementation process

Case 1 started by taking account of environmental improvements in its production facilities in the 1980s. Different projects have been performed that were aimed at raising eco-efficiency on a production level. Over the years, these projects evolved towards projects that focus on the prevention of, for example, waste and energy use. A first ecodesign project was performed in 1992 as part of a demonstration project from the Dutch government. This led to the first ecodesign product of Case 1. In 1995 the firm joined another national research programme that was aimed at an evaluation of the current product portfolio of different companies in the Netherlands, in order to measure the environmental impact of the products and to trigger firms to improve their products from an environmental perspective. A shift in focus took place between 1995 and 2003, a period in which different projects and researches focused on the development and implementation of an integrated approach that mapped the costs and environmental impacts throughout the whole life-cycle of interior concepts for the different markets of Case 1. This life-cycle approach was further integrated into the firm at a product level from 2004 on. Furthermore, past developments were combined into a product-service combination that provides an interesting package for the customers and that can further improve the sustainable profile of the company. Case 1 cooperated in the development and pre-testing of the new ISO26000 standard on social responsibility, which was launched in 2010. The aim is to integrate this standard in all departments and divisions of the firm. Other recent activities entail the involvement of stakeholders in the firm's sustainability efforts, and a more profound communication strategy on the firm's sustainability efforts such as the website, a yearly sustainability report and regular items in the news. In 2009, Case 1 started to streamline its business operations with the cradle-to-cradle principles (Braungart et al. 2007).

Human factors during implementation

Customised and elaborate communication, key believers. In order to spread a 'sustainable' culture in a steady manner throughout the whole firm (including all employees), internal communication has been specifically developed and customised for each targeted department and its employees. Ambassadors are appointed in different departments in order to obtain a commensurate spread through the firm. Cooperation and discussions with key partners and sustainability networks are a key element of external communication. Sustainability in the firm started with a few sustainability pioneers by performing different, sometimes independent initiatives. This has been turned into one general vision on sustainability.

Case 4

Implementation process

Case 4 approaches sustainability by participating in several projects that comprise environmental and social elements in the project targets. This means that no preparatory work has been done on the formulation of a general mission or vision on sustainability, or on the planning of interventions and implementation steps. In this firm, the focus immediately went on practical interventions at a product innovation level. Independent projects with a different focus, for example on sustainability criteria at the front end of innovation or the patient room of the future, are performed, each offering opportunities for the firm, but simultaneously broadening the understanding of the employees on sustainability issues in product development, as well as on incorporating these aspects in the firm's new products. Moreover, these cooperation projects broaden the partner network that is active in the niche markets of Case 4. Depending on the project, more attention is given to the social or environmental aspects of sustainability: for example in a project that studies interactions between nurses, patient and the room environment in healthcare, where the focus is on the social aspects of these interactions. The firm at first participated in some projects that needed companies as examples and test cases, while later on, the owner himself took the initiative to formulate own projects, to find appropriate partners and financial support for the proposals. Experts on sustainable design have been invited several times to the firm, either to cooperate on one of the projects, or to discuss possible pathways or strategies that could be followed by the firm. Case 4 is a small firm with one in-house product developer who cooperates in all projects, together with the owner/manager. Depending on the project, one of the technical staff (production) is also involved.

Human factors during implementation

Culture of openness for innovative projects and opportunities with management and designers. The entrepreneurial character of the CEO and the product development team opens doors to innovative projects with external partners and experts. Sustainability criteria are considered in some of the projects, dependent on the opportunity for the firm and the enthusiasm of the core team. Further spreading of the information or knowledge that is gathered is not organised, internally or externally. However, internal communication takes place spontaneously and on a personal level.

Case 5

Implementation process

A general vision and strategy towards sustainability has been developed by the parent firm of this company. An adaptation of this vision has been made through the analysis of current activities within the firm, and the current status, demands and future prospects of stakeholders in the value chain and other actors in the firm's environment. Simultaneously, several projects concerning (mostly) environmental innovations have been started and performed by individual employees inside R&D. Communication on the vision and strategy for sustainability—including social aspects—has been presented and spread, first internally in the firm and later also towards external stakeholders and a growing network, with an emphasis on the need for sustainable innovation in the firm. As a next step, priorities have been determined concerning sustainability matters, together with the selection of—ongoing and new—product innovation projects (pilot projects) within product development with a focus on the prioritised areas of sustainability. More activities related to environmental and social issues are planned, with a particular focus on social aspects. Communication on sustainability issues is further developed with folders that provide information on the environmental profile of the firm's products, and a general information folder on the firm's vision, strategy and goals towards sustainability. Currently, the pilot projects are continuing and, simultaneously, a measurement system is being developed in order to be able to follow up the progress in each project, as well as to communicate the environmental profile of the improved products towards customers. Sales representatives have personal support from internal experts on an individual basis. Special meetings with (potential) clients that are also searching for effective ways to deal with sustainability issues are organised. In the current and future stages, formal training of the sales representatives are being planned. The firm aims to launch some of the new environmental products that will result from the pilot projects. These will then serve as demonstration cases for promoting the firm's vision inside and outside the firm.

Human factors during implementation

Combination of factors: culture, methods, empowerment, personal support and communication. An organisational culture of knowledge gathering and sharing supports the openness for sustainability as a new topic. A well-developed change programme is prepared in order to support the different steps that need to be taken. Empowerment and (internal) communication are incorporated in this programme and are dealt with from the beginning of the process towards a well-considered, growing group of employees. Connections with sustainability networks and experts are developed as part of the external communication. Management is conscious about possible resistance and a personal approach is followed to prevent this (by offering personal support) or tackle it when needed.

Implementation process

This firm developed, produced and sold strong, solid products that were sold in equally solid packaging in the 1990s. From 1992 on, a defensive approach was followed by Case 6, in which the awareness of the need for environmental improvements in product development grew. An environmental manager was appointed in that period with the responsibility to gather information on environmental issues in product development. This led to the first improvements (1995–1998) in the packaging of the products from an environmental perspective, but with clear financial advantages: elimination of superfluous packaging and superfluous materials in packaging. These improvements were supplemented with the development of a manual and several tools, and metrics to measure the environmental improvements of products, as well as financial and other benefits. A cost-oriented approach was thereby taken. With the gathered knowledge, the environmental manager supported different divisions (worldwide) that were eager to improve their environmental status. This happened on a voluntary basis by the divisions. The 'green' manual thereby functioned as an educational and informative tool that offers a methodology and several tools that can be used by the employees, supported by the environmental manager. This support took place in the form of sessions in the local division given by the environmental manager to inform employees about the opportunities that lie in environmental improvements, and practical workshops to help the employees understand possible improvements in their products while simultaneously practising the new tools and techniques for ecodesign. In 1998 a need for more research was felt in order to bring environmental sustainability in the firm to a higher level. This led to the appointment of more environmental managers and the start of research projects in cooperation with universities and other knowledge partners. This broadening of the responsibility and the knowledge, as well as the experience gained in the different divisions, has led to the development of an internal benchmarking system, as well as metrics for measuring the environmental performance of divisions, green supply chain management and green marketing (2001). A general vision and strategy for (environmental) sustainability has since been developed for the long, medium and short term in environmental programmes that emphasise specific areas of improvements (periods of 5 years); implementation is now obligatory for all divisions, although with a certain degree of freedom. In this last stage, a proactive approach is taken, whereby the strategy and vision are spread top-down throughout the firm, whereas in the earlier phases— the pioneering years—improvements came from bottom up.

Human factors during implementation

Pioneer with persuasive approach, involvement and empowerment. In this firm, sustainability has been introduced by a 'sustainability champion' with a strong but personal approach to involving and empowering people: 'support the employees with knowledge but they need to do the work themselves'. Supporting tools have been developed in order to make the results measurable and comparable. The latter are still used in order to involve employees by performing internal benchmarking of products between departments.

Case 7

Implementation process

Different independent projects related to sustainability issues have taken place throughout several years in this firm, such as a switch from a technological perspective towards a systems perspective in product development, annual social activities that are linked to an internal CSR programme, different projects in cooperation with universities and external experts on sustainable innovation, an internal project on environmental consciousness and energy reduction, and the installation of a large photovoltaic installation on the firm's infrastructure. However, no clear general vision or strategy on sustainability was present until 2010, when clear sustainability goals were defined and bundled into a general vision, with priorities set out and specific projects planned for the coming years. One of the interviewees even stated that sustainability was considered as the main subject to concentrate on in that year. This informant also indicated that different research and development on sustainability aspects were planned for the coming year: for example a research project on possible opportunities for a closed material loop for the firm's main material.

After the formulation of a general vision and strategy, research projects have been proposed and planned to define opportunities for closing the material loop. Other projects keep the focus on energy-efficiency and thermal insulation. Each of these projects has specific goals towards some sustainability criteria but so far, sustainability criteria have not been incorporated in the generic product development process of the firm. Future projects were mentioned, such as the participation in a solar-powered decathlon with a modular housing project in cooperation with different partner institutes and universities. Other future innovations towards sustainability were indicated in the direction of future thermal improvements towards zero- and even plus-energy housing systems.

Human factors during implementation

Creation of culture on values, involvement by internal benchmarking. Social and environmental values are encouraged in employees by performing benchmarking between departments: for example on energy-use in the office. Different projects are carried out, either internally or with external experts and partners, that have either social or environmental aspects and goals. A culture of openness for change is present and there is a high level of knowledge generation. Limited opportunities for sustainability on product innovations are perceived in this firm, as it is strongly dependent on the use of a specific core material, on competitors and a conservative market, market demands, strict product specifications and competitive pricing.

Case 8

Implementation process

Energy efficiency and a high product quality for durable products have always been the focus in product innovations within this case. A new direction was launched in 2000, when the firm started looking for applications for LEDs. Constant improvements in efficiency are achieved within LED technology, but the efficiency has not reached a level that is high enough to compete with other, current lighting technologies. In 2008, an own environmental product label was presented as a strategy to bring the efforts on environmental product innovations within the firm to a higher level. A broader programme provides guidelines for the product development departments that simultaneously serve as criteria for the granting of the internal label on green product innovations. In order to attain such a label, a number of compulsory criteria need to be fulfilled within a new product, together with some other criteria from the guidelines. After the launch of the programme, it was communicated on the internal website of the group, as well as at an annual gathering with seminars that takes place within the whole business group and where new guidelines, developments, innovations, strategies and so on within the business group are presented to a large number of employees. Different product development projects within several countries have since then been proposed inside the firm. Another programme on sustainability was initiated by the firm in 2009 that awards municipalities and cities for the implementation of exterior lighting systems that minimise the ecological footprint in the most noticeable, exemplary and original way. The firm organises this yearly award with an international community that focuses on lighting in the development of cities. The initiative aims at gathering *best practices* that can inspire and enable other cities to also invest in sustainable lighting. The business group is aiming at the attainment of ISO 14001 certificates in its different production facilities. In the branch of the firm that is the main subject of this study, developments were going on concerning this certification at the time of data gathering.

Human factors during implementation

Involvement by internal benchmarking, communication through internal network. Strong competition and strict specifications and guidelines for products limit the opportunities for sustainable product innovations. However, the aim is to involve employees by encouraging employees and departments to join internal benchmarks at a product and project level. There is relatively little attention to empowerment and involvement; interest for and application of sustainability criteria is dependent on the own interest of the designers and engineers. Encouragement of the employees is therefore accomplished by informing the product developers through the internal website of the group, by presenting the programme to all employees at the annual gathering, and by offering training to product developers who want to improve the environmental profile of their products.

Appendix II Aspects of strategies for sustainable product innovation in the main areas of a business model

Case	Value proposition	Customer interface	Infrastructure	Financial viability
Case 1	Creation of *durable* working, learning and living environments (combination of products and service) Ensuring closed loop of products (take-back and recycling)	Pioneer in sustainable innovations Creators of sustainable vision for governments, customers and industry	Sustainability network: • sustainable suppliers • disassembly and recycling companies • knowledge and research institutes Key activities and resources: • co-development • eco-efficient production • sustainable marketing • ecodesign quality products • eco-efficient and engaging infrastructure • take-back system	Take-back system Eco-efficient production and infrastructure
Case 2	Compliance with current and future international legislations concerning materials		Sustainability network: • external experts and consultancy • strategic alliances Key activities and resources: • use of compliant materials in development	Costs of external knowledge

Case	Value proposition	Customer interface	Infrastructure	Financial viability
Case 3	Creation of leasing system for office chairs Ensuring closed loop of products (leasing, take-back and recycling)	Leasing and take-back services for products	Sustainability network: • sustainable suppliers • recycling companies • knowledge and research institutes Key activities and resources: • take-back system • leasing system • sustainable marketing • ecodesign quality products • eco-efficient development and production • disassembly line	Leasing system Take-back system Material reduction for new products Eco-efficient production and infrastructure
Case 4	Lightweight, space-saving and modular furniture	—	Sustainability network: • external experts • knowledge and research institutes Key activities and resources: • projects in cooperation with partners from network	Cost-efficiency
Case 5	Products with added functionality and/or closed-loop materials	Sustainable image of firm Provider of green value of products for further incorporation in end products Expansion of sales network to new (sustainable) market segments	Sustainability network: • external experts • knowledge and research institutes Key activities and resources: • projects in cooperation with partners from network and with companies with similar sustainability goals • sustainable marketing	Costs of external knowledge Eco-efficient production and infrastructure Sustainable marketing

Case	Value proposition	Customer interface	Infrastructure	Financial viability
Case 6	Products that offer simple ecodesign solutions	Pioneer in ecodesign products Creators of sustainable vision for governments, customers and industry Sustainable image of firm	Sustainability network: • sustainable suppliers • knowledge and research institutes Key activities and resources: • eco-efficient production • ecodesign quality products	Cost-efficiency
Case 7	Eco-efficient and durable building solutions Enduring closed loop of products (recyclable and recycling materials)	–	Sustainability network: • sustainable suppliers • knowledge and research institutes Key activities and resources: • projects in cooperation with partners from network • R&D sustainable innovations • eco-efficient infrastructure	Cost-efficiency
Case 8	Energy-efficient lighting solutions	Best practices of energy-efficient projects and products Sustainable image of firm	Sustainability network: • internal network of group Key activities and resources: • partner projects with communalities • in-house expertise on energy-efficiency	Cost-efficiency

Creating a culture
of sustainability in
entrepreneurial enterprise

Section II
Corporate entrepreneurship for sustainability-improving innovation

4
Creating a culture of sustainability in entrepreneurial enterprises

Timothy J. Galpin
Colorado Mesa University, USA

J. Lee Whittington
University of Dallas, USA

Sustainability has captured the attention of corporations and society at large. Whether identified as sustainability, corporate social responsibility (CSR), corporate social performance (CSP), going green or the 'triple bottom line' (Elkington 1998; Savitz and Weber 2006), it now appears that sustainability is here to stay. Early representations of sustainability were based on the assumption that only large companies had the resource base necessary to pursue sustainability (Jenkins 2004). However, a recent stream of research has proposed that small and medium-sized enterprises (SMEs) can also play a significant role in the sustainability landscape (York and Venkataraman 2010).

Beyond simply being the 'right thing to do', sustainability can be a differentiator and source of competitive advantage for SMEs (Jenkins 2009). The key characteristics of organisations that effectively pursue sustainability include: management espousing sustainability values (Hargett and Williams 2009; Morsing and Oswald 2009); making sustainability a part of firm strategy (Porter and Kramer 2006; Castello and Lozano 2009; Jacopin and Fontrodona 2009); and reinforcing sustainability values and strategy through organisational culture (Grayson and Hodges 2004; Jenkins 2009).

While advice abounds from researchers and practitioners alike regarding *what* an organisation should do to pursue an agenda of sustainability, little information exists about *how* to go about it. In this chapter we address this issue by offering an evidence-based framework of how the leaders of SMEs can create a **virtuous cycle of sustainability**. Our framework is constructed by using a narrative synthesis (Denyer and Tranfield 2006) approach that draws from relevant empirical and practitioner literature spanning various disciplines. In addition to describing the components of the model, this chapter also provides a description of the definitional, theoretical and empirical foundations of the framework.

Sustainability and entrepreneurship

Sustainability has been defined as 'meeting the needs of the present without compromising the ability of future generations to meet their own needs' (Porter and Kramer 2006: 3). Because entrepreneurial ventures do not have to overcome the complacency of organisational inertia often found in large firms, they are particularly well positioned to pursue sustainability agendas (Jenkins 2009; York and Venkataraman 2010). For example, as service providers, entrepreneurs can contribute to solving societal problems by assisting existing institutions in achieving their goals; entrepreneurial ventures can also create new, sustainable products and services (York and Venkataraman 2010). Likewise, Jenkins (2009) identifies three key areas of 'corporate social opportunity' (CSO) that SMEs are well positioned to address: (1) innovative products and services; (2) serving un-served or under-served markets; and (3) building new business models that can replace traditional large-firm business models.

The virtuous cycle of sustainability

The virtuous cycle of sustainability is a multi-level model providing a blueprint for the leaders of entrepreneurial organisations who are attempting to build a culture of sustainability within their organisations. As illustrated in Figure 4.1, the reciprocal nature of sustainability with employee engagement creates a reinforcing virtuous cycle. The cycle occurs as employees become fully engaged in the firm's sustainability efforts, create results and help to shape the firm's future mission, strategy and values setting; thus, beginning the cycle again with even higher levels of public reputation, sustainability expectations and performance. Employee participation in firm direction-setting creates more ideas, fosters organisational innovation, enhances employee buy-in to firm initiatives and improves implementation (Hamel 1996). All of these have important implications for the development, implementation and ultimate success of an SME's sustainability efforts.

Figure 4.1 **Virtuous cycle of sustainability**

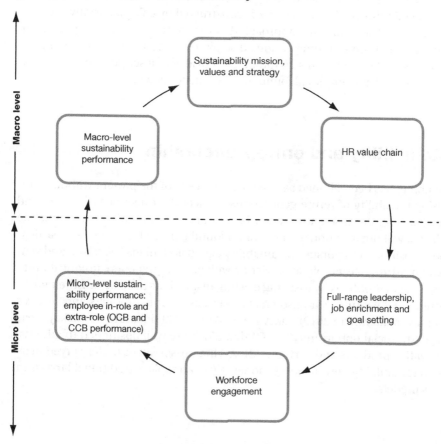

The components of the virtuous cycle presented in Figure 4.1 are interrelated and the process is ongoing; hence, the circular nature of the model. However, our discussion follows a linear flow through the components of the model, including propositions describing the key relationships between each element of the framework, as depicted in Figure 4.2. The process begins with the articulation of sustainability as part of the organisation's mission, values and strategy. Next, an HR value chain should be created that supports the firm's strategic intent. The HR value chain needs to be designed to attract, retain and engage a workforce who possess values and talents that are aligned with the firm's strategic direction. The HR value chain supports the formation of an engaged workforce, but these practices alone are not sufficient to create a culture of sustainability. These macro-level (i.e. organisation-wide) practices must be complemented by a set of micro-level (i.e. manager to employee) practices. Leader behaviour, job characteristics and challenging goals are the necessary antecedents to employee engagement. When employees experience engagement in a firm's sustainability endeavours, there will be positive in-role and extra-role employee performance, as well as positive overall firm performance.

Figure 4.2 **Elements of the virtuous cycle**

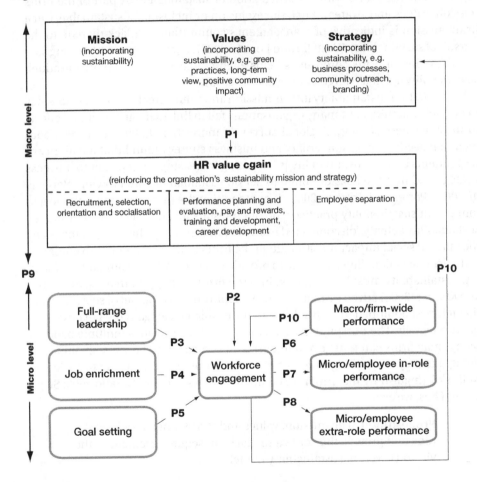

Components of the model and implications for best practice

Sustainability mission, strategy and values

The process of creating a culture of sustainability in SMEs begins at the macro-/ organisation-wide level with the articulation of sustainability as part of the firm's mission, values and strategy. First, the exclusion or inclusion of sustainability in a firm's mission is indicative of management's commitment, or lack thereof, to the pursuit of sustainability (Castello and Lozano 2009). Furthermore, embedding sustainability into a firm's core values helps align employees with the organisation's sustainability agenda (Hargett and Williams 2009).

Incorporating sustainability into its mission and values creates a sense of urgency to just do something, but many organisations fail to link their sustainability efforts to their business strategy. A global survey of more than 1,500 executives about their perspectives on sustainability and business strategy found that a majority of respondents believe sustainability is becoming increasingly important to business strategy and that the risks of failing to act on sustainability are growing (Berns *et al.* 2009). Porter and Kramer (2006: 4) contend that the pressure companies feel to implement sustainability practices too often results in a jumble of uncoordinated sustainability activity, 'disconnected from the firm's strategy, that neither make any meaningful social impact nor strengthen the firm's long-term competitiveness'.

If a firm's sustainability efforts are to provide value to both the company and society, sustainability must be integrated into the firm's strategy. In that regard, Porter and Kramer (2006) advocate that each firm identify the distinct set of societal issues that it is best equipped to help solve, and from which it can gain the greatest competitive benefit. The pursuit of sustainability for SMEs provides multiple benefits. Many small firms can pursue a differentiation strategy based on sustainability. By doing this they are seeking to reap a dual benefit of providing value to society as well as distinguishing the firm from competitors (Castello and Lozano 2009; Siegel 2009). Thus, we expect:

> **Proposition 1.** The mission, values and strategy of an SME set the tone and provide the context for each subsequent element in the virtuous cycle of sustainability model.

The HR value chain

The HR value chain provides a conceptual framework for the connection between a firm's strategy and its human capital practices. The HR value chain is the integrated set of human resource management practices—from the sourcing and hiring of talent, through workforce development and performance management, to employee separation—which engages people in a committed pursuit of a chosen strategy and set of core values. Once the company's sustainability mission, values and strategy are clearly articulated, the first stage of the HR value chain involves finding and hiring people that fit the desired mission, values and strategy. Dessler (1999) suggests companies use value-based hiring practices that screen potential new employees for a commitment to a set of chosen values and reject a large portion of prospective employees. He states, 'In many firms the process of linking employees to ideology begins before the worker is even hired' (Dessler 1999: 23).

A sustainability strategy requires that companies execute their strategy through the firm's human capital (Lacy *et al.* 2009). Yet many firms do a poor job of engaging their workforce in their sustainability efforts through their human capital practices (Porter and Kramer 2006; Lacy *et al.* 2009). In order to build and reinforce a culture of sustainability, SMEs must establish human resource management (HRM) practices which support their desired strategy and core values (Dessler 1999; Grayson and Hodges 2004; Chow and Liu 2009; Jenkins 2009). The organisation's strategy provides a base from which to build human resource practices. The firm's strategy also provides a foundation for management to work from when making day-to-day people management decisions such as hiring and firing, job design, training, promotions, communicating and coaching.

As an SME sets its sustainability strategy, management's approach to human capital must reinforce the achievement of the firm's sustainability aims. Recognising that the chief source of value is a workforce which is knowledgeable, flexible and engaged in a firm's strategy requires a fundamental shift in the concept of value management within a corporation (Bartlett and Ghoshal 2002; Pfeffer 2005).

HRM practices have been shown to have a positive impact on SME performance (Carlson *et al.* 2006), yet there is a great deal of variance in the design and implementation of HRM practices in entrepreneurial ventures (Cassell *et al.* 2002). This variance is due in part to the informal nature of HR practices in young firms (Cardon and Stevens 2004). Cassell *et al.* (2002: 687) summarise the approach to HRM practices within small and medium-sized enterprises by stating that 'key managers within SMEs, rather than taking a coherent, strategy based approach to the implementation of HRM, are taking a more "pick and mix" contingency approach'. This piecemeal approach to human capital management within SMEs is problematic for the reason that early HRM decisions have a significant impact on longer-term firm performance (Cardon and Stevens 2004). Furthermore, Baron (2003: 253) states that:

> Once a new venture is founded, becomes an organization, and hires its first employees, human resource issues and forces that exist in—and influences the success of—all organizations come into play. Indeed, growing evidence suggests that an inability on the part of some founders of new ventures to successfully manage HRM issues is an important factor in their ultimate failure.

In fact, there is substantial evidence of a link between a firm's sustainability practices and its attractiveness as an employer (Turban and Greening 1996; Albinger and Freeman 2000; Greening and Turban 2000; Backhaus *et al.* 2002; Bhattacharya *et al.* 2008). This attractiveness has been explained by the fact that a firm's sustainability practices enhance its reputation and increase the perceived trustworthiness of an organisation for a job seeker who lacks any previous interaction with the organisation (Viswesvaran *et al.* 1998).

This appeal may also be explained using social identity theory. According to this perspective, a firm's sustainability performance sends positive signals to prospective job applicants about what it would be like to work for the company (Greening and Turban 2000). This attractiveness may help to create an *a priori* level of affective commitment to the firm. Beyond potential employees selecting firms that match their personal values, Pfeffer (2005) also advocates selective hiring practices on the part of employers to find employees who 'fit' the organisation's values.

Once new employees are brought onboard that fit the organisation's sustainability mission, strategy and values, a process of continuous reinforcement begins. This stage of the HR value chain involves multiple approaches to reinforce the link between the firm's sustainability strategy and its employees. These approaches include information sharing, empowerment, skill development, performance appraisals, and competitive and incentive compensation (Pfeffer 2005). Similarly, Dessler (1999) identifies training linked to strategy and values, tradition-building symbols and ceremonies, extensive two-way communications, and promoting the right leaders—those who demonstrate a commitment to the firm's strategy and values—as essential elements of employee engagement. SMEs can engage employees in their sustainability efforts by consistently emphasising the sustainability mission, values and strategy of the firm. This can be done by creating community volunteer programmes, providing training in sustainability processes and implementing performance management systems that link the achievement of sustainability goals with compensation (Porter and Kramer 2006; Ahern 2009; Lacy, *et al.* 2009; Morsing and Oswald 2009; Rok 2009).

An often overlooked dimension of the HR value chain involves the way an organisation handles employee separations. How the process of employee separation is handled demonstrates a firm's commitment to being socially responsible through the use of procedures that demonstrate respect for the affected individuals. Every effort should be made to ensure that employee separations are ethical and just. When employee separations take place, it is more than just the exiting employees who are attentive to how the process of separation is being handled. The people remaining in the organisation also view the way separations are addressed as a clear indicator of the value a firm places on its workforce. In this regard, Dessler (1999) stresses the need for management to demonstrate 'organisational justice'. When employee separations are conducted in a manner that demonstrates both respect for the individual and the integrity of the organisation, people leave with a sense of fairness. This also helps foster a sense of engagement and commitment to the firm among those employees who remain in the organisation because they view the separation process as being fair.

As an SME's approach to sustainability evolves, there will be corresponding shifts in the firm's mission, values and strategy (Zadek 2004; Munilla and Miles 2005; Mirvis and Googins 2006; Castello and Lozano 2009). As these shifts occur, the components of the firm's HR value chain must be revisited and revised if necessary. This alignment check ensures that the organisation's HR management practices stay in synch with the evolving sustainability efforts of the firm, and that the organisation will continue to benefit from a knowledgeable and engaged workforce. Thus, we expect that:

> **Proposition 2.** Workforce engagement in an SME's sustainability efforts is positively related to the presence of an integrated HR value chain designed to reinforce the firm's sustainability mission, values and strategy.

Full-range leadership, job enrichment and goal setting

The macro-level organisational practices that make up the HR value chain provide an important dimension to high-performing SMEs. These practices provide the context in which an engaged workforce can develop and they have been associated with organisational success in sustainability efforts (Ahern 2009; Lacy *et al.* 2009; Morsing and Oswald 2009; Rok 2009). But these macro-level practices alone will not create the high levels of employee engagement necessary to achieve an SME's sustainability objectives and may actually lose their impact if they are not supported by a complementary set of micro-level practices. The best-intentioned sustainability strategies may be undermined by day-to-day manager-to-employee interactions. Thus, the manner in which employees perceive and respond to their tasks and interactions with their direct supervisors will ultimately determine the impact of the firm's macro-level HRM practices.

The following discussion presents the micro-level components of the virtuous cycle of sustainability, presented in Figure 4.1, that contribute to high levels of employee engagement in an SME's sustainability efforts.

Full-range leadership

Leaders set the tone for the entire organisation. Indeed, the leader's attitudes and behaviours cascade throughout the entire organisation (Bass *et al.* 1997). There is a strong connection between the leader and the culture of the organisation, since leaders create organisational cultures in their own image and then those cultures reproduce leaders in that image (Schein 2010).

Recent research in the social scientific approach to leadership has been dominated by the 'full-range of leadership' paradigm that encompasses both transactional and transformational leadership behaviours (Avolio 1999; Bass and Riggio 2006). This research emphasis is well deserved because the outcomes associated with full-range leadership are impressive. Transformational leadership has consistently been linked to high levels of in-role performance (Howell and Avolio 1993; Whittington *et al.* 2004) and satisfaction with the leader (Podsakoff *et al.* 1990; Bycio *et al.* 1995). Transformational leadership is positively related to employees' affective commitment to the organisation (Bycio *et al.* 1995; Whittington *et al.* 2004) and trust in the leader (Podsakoff *et al.* 1990). Furthermore, Whittington *et al.* (2004) found that transformational leadership was positively related to a variety of organisational citizenship behaviours (OCBs). Keller (1992) found a positive relationship between transformational leadership and the effectiveness of research and development units. Lowe *et al.* (1996) provide additional support for the strong positive relationship between transformational leadership and work unit effectiveness.

The full-range leadership model is a major way to develop a positive relationship between the company and its employees, and is critical in the process of creating a culture of sustainability throughout the organisation (Kotter and Heskett 1992; Rok 2009). Therefore, it is important to understand each set of leader behaviours that constitute full-range leadership—transactional and transformational—in order to grasp the benefits of the full-range model.

According to the full-range view, transformational leadership may be used either independently from or in conjunction with transactional leadership (Wofford *et al.* 1998). The highest level of effectiveness is achieved when leaders engage in a two-stage process in which transactional leadership provides the basis for the subsequent development of transformational leadership (Avolio 1999).

Transactional leadership behaviour focuses on the leader's efforts to clarify performance expectations and the rewards that may be expected for meeting these expectations. These behaviours contribute to the formulation of a subordinate's explicit psychological contract. Leaders who fail to establish this set of role expectations leave followers with an ill-defined sense of direction and ambiguous task assignments. However, when done correctly the clarification of role expectations provides the basis for more mature relationships between a leader and his or her followers to evolve over time. Transactional leadership behaviours provide a clear sense of the leader's expectations in terms of performance. When the leader consistently follows through with the rewards that are promised in exchange for that performance, trust and commitment are likely to emerge.

Transactional leadership is not enough to develop the full potential of followers, but it is a necessary transitional step in developing the trust between a leader and follower that is required for high levels of employee engagement. In order to maximise employee engagement, leaders must augment their transactional behaviours with the transformational leadership behaviours normally referred to as the '4I's':

idealised vision, inspirational motivation, intellectual stimulation and individualised consideration (Bass and Avolio 1994; Avolio 1999; Bass and Riggio 2006). These behaviours motivate employees to transcend their self-interests for the good of the organisation and have been shown to encourage greater follower creativity and innovation (Bass and Riggio 2006).

Idealised vision refers to the role-modelling behaviour of transformational leaders. These leaders are admired, respected and trusted. Their followers identify with and attempt to emulate them (Bass and Avolio 1994). To earn this credibility, transformational leaders consider the needs of others over their own, share risk with their followers and demonstrate high standards of moral conduct. These leaders engender faith in others by empowering followers and creating a joint sense of mission (Avolio 1999). **Inspirational motivation** occurs through envisioning and articulating an attractive future that provides meaning and challenge for followers (Bass 1985). Clear expectations are communicated with a demonstrated commitment to goals and the shared vision.

Intellectual stimulation is created by the transformational leader's questioning of assumptions, reframing of problems and approaching existing situations from a fresh perspective (Bass 1985). This behaviour set also includes encouraging employees to employ their own intuition in solving problems and entertaining ideas that may on first review seem silly. This behaviour encourages the innovation and creativity of followers rather than creating dependence on the leader to always be the primary source of innovation (Mumford *et al.* 2003). Participation and creative risk-taking are encouraged without the fear of public criticism or penalty for departure from the leader's ideas (Heifetz 1994; Elkins and Keller 2003). Because transformational leaders create a climate of trust, their employees are comfortable with the experimentation and hypothesis testing necessary for the development of new products and services.

Individualised consideration refers to the transformational leader's mentoring role. Through this role, the leader pays special attention to each individual's need for achievement and personal growth (Bass 1985). Delegation is used as a developmental tool to advance followers to successively higher levels of potential. Learning opportunities are created within the context of a supportive environment to further facilitate the development of followers.

In line with the full-range of leadership behaviours, Morsing and Oswald (2009) stress that a central aspect of integrating sustainability into organisations is the importance of leaders' non-coercive influence to direct and coordinate the activities of a group towards its sustainability objectives. They emphasise that an effective leader is one who is perceived by others as having certain attributes or characteristics which enable him or her to exert influence over them. Leaders who exhibit this 'full-range' of behaviours can expect 'performance beyond expectations' (Bass 1985), as well as a wide variety of other positive outcomes in organisational settings. Therefore, we expect that:

Proposition 3. Workforce engagement in an SME's sustainability efforts is positively related to full-range leadership.

Job enrichment

The effects of the full-range leadership model are enhanced by the presence of an enriched job and challenging goals (Whittington *et al.* 2004). Enriched jobs are characterised by five core job dimensions: task variety, task identity, task significance, autonomy, and feedback. Jobs that have these dimensions are said to be enriched and have a high motivating potential (Hackman and Oldham 1976). The presence of these core job dimensions leads to high internal motivation, high quality of work performance and high satisfaction with the work, and low levels of absenteeism and turnover (Griffin 1991).

Saks (2006) found that job characteristics were positively related to workforce engagement. Moreover, Rok (2009: 463) asserts that, 'More and more employees have strong expectations for a meaningful work, particularly for work that makes a positive social and ecological contribution to the society as well as providing an income'. The most effective workforce engagement occurs when people understand how their company's approach to sustainability makes a difference in their day-to-day jobs and in their communities (Rok 2009). Thus, we expect that:

Proposition 4. Workforce engagement in an SME's sustainability efforts is positively related to enriched jobs.

Goal setting

Morsing and Oswald (2009) emphasise that clearly communicating and measuring established goals matters when it comes to employees carrying out sustainability initiatives. Quinn and Dalton (2009: 30) maintain that, 'Having sustainability goals and objectives encourages employees to incorporate sustainability into their day-to-day activities'. Establishing goals at the individual employee level is essential for a sustainability effort to succeed, and should be included in employees' performance development and evaluation plans (D'Amato and Roome 2009).

Goal-setting complements the transactional dimensions of the full-range leadership model by explicitly identifying the performance expectations for employees. When these expectations are coupled with the rewards associated with meeting the expectations, an explicit psychological contract is formed (Goodwin *et al.* 2001). This clarification of performance and reward expectancies both heightens performance and enhances the level of trust between a leader and follower. The climate of trust is a key dimension in creating a culture of sustainability.

Proposition 5. Workforce engagement in an SME's sustainability efforts is positively related to challenging and specific sustainability performance goals.

Workforce engagement

In the context of the virtuous cycle of sustainability presented here, workforce engagement is defined as the workforce's involvement and satisfaction with, as well as enthusiasm for, work and the organisation's sustainability efforts (Harter *et al.* 2002; Whittington and Galpin 2010; Rich *et al.* 2010).Workforce engagement as a general construct has been shown to have a positive relationship with productivity, profitability, employee retention, safety and customer satisfaction (Buckingham and Coffman 1999; Coffman and Gonzalez-Molina 2002). A recent study by The Hackett Group of 60 global companies found that firms which are more effective at engaging employees generated US$673 million more in earnings before interest, taxes, depreciation and amortisation (EBITDA) than their peers (Teng 2010).

Workforce engagement is also a central element of transforming a firm's sustainability mission, values and strategy into measurable results. In fact, many employees now identify a commitment to sustainability among their closest-held values (Lacy *et al.* 2009). A firm's leadership and performance regarding sustainability can motivate employees to go beyond what is expected of them, which in turn can enhance productivity as well as elevate revenues and customer satisfaction. Moreover, the authors assert, 'when employees are engaged with their company's sustainability strategy, they proactively identify, communicate and pursue opportunities to execute the strategy' (Lacy *et al.* 2009: 491). Thus, we expect that:

Proposition 6. Workforce engagement is positively related to an SME's performance.

Micro-level performance

In-role and extra-role performance

The outcome components of the model identify the relationship between workforce engagement and two aspects of individual sustainability performance: **in-role** and **extra-role**.

In-role performance refers to the achievement of those tasks that are explicitly identified in position descriptions and evaluated in the performance appraisal process. The assessment of in-role performance often includes both qualitative and quantitative dimensions. Increasingly, firms are making sustainability a regular component in the performance management process by measuring an individual's performance against sustainability goals (Lacy et al. 2009). Therefore, we expect that:

> **Proposition 7.** Workforce engagement in an SME's sustainability efforts is positively related to in-role employee performance.

A great deal of attention is normally paid to the formal aspects of in-role performance; however, an often neglected dimension of individual performance is the contributions an employee makes to the organisation in the form of extra-role behaviours that exceed the requirements of in-role expectations. These important behaviours are best articulated by the idea of organisational citizenship behaviour (OCB) developed by Organ (1988, 1990). OCBs are organisationally beneficial behaviours that can be neither elicited nor enforced through formal organisational roles. These behaviours are spontaneous. They go beyond the expectations of formal job descriptions and are discretionary on the part of the employee. These behaviours are not rewarded or recognised in an explicit way by the organisation. These voluntary activities tend to promote efficient and effective functioning of the organisation (Organ 1988).

From a sustainability perspective, extra-role performance can also include an employees' community citizenship behaviour (CCB). Community citizenship behaviours include activities such as volunteering for community-outreach programmes and making donations to various causes in the community (Lacy et al. 2009; Hargett and Williams 2009). Thus, we expect that:

> **Proposition 8.** Workforce engagement in an SME's sustainability efforts is positively related to employee extra-role (organisational and community citizenship behaviours) performance.

Macro-level performance

Firm performance

The evidence regarding the relationship between a firm's level of corporate social performance (CSP) and its financial performance is somewhat mixed. In a comprehensive meta-analysis of 52 quantitative studies, the findings of Orlitzky et al. (2003) suggest that corporate social and, to a lesser degree, environmental responsibility result in positive financial performance. On further analysis of the same data, Orlitzky (2005) found that the positive impact of CSP on financial performance appears to be mostly due to effects of firms' sustainability efforts on their reputation. Another meta-analysis conducted by Wu (2006) supports the findings of Orlitzky *et al.* (2003) that CSP and financial performance are positively related, and that reputation had the strongest relationship with firms' financial performance.

As depicted in our model, the relationship between CSP and financial performance is complex. Recent research has identified several intervening variables between CSP and financial performance, including: a firm's sustainability mission, values and strategy (Porter and Kramer 2006; Castello and Lozano 2009; Hargett and Williams 2009; Morsing and Oswald 2009); how a firm operationalises its sustainability strategy (Orlitzky *et al.* 2003; White 2009; Golicic *et al.* 2010); the engagement of employees in the firm's sustainability efforts (Porter and Kramer 2006; Ahern 2009; Lacy *et al.* 2009; Morsing and Oswald 2009; Rok 2009); and the role of employee-to-firm and employee-to-leader trust (D'Amato and Roome 2009; Hind *et al.* 2009; Lacy *et al.* 2009). This multitude of variables supports the need for a comprehensive model of sustainability which takes into account the various, interconnected components of such a complex undertaking. Thus, we expect that:

> **Proposition 9.** Successful sustainability endeavours in SMEs require a multi-level effort, reflecting the complex interplay of both macro- and micro-level leadership elements, in order to result in positive firm performance.

Reinforcing feedback loop

The last stage of the model involves a reinforcing feedback loop, where positive firm performance reinforces the virtuous cycle of sustainability. This occurs for two primary reasons. First, positive firm performance creates more opportunities for employees to advance into larger and more significant roles within the company, providing additional incentives for employees to assist in developing and executing the firm's sustainability efforts (Hausknecht *et al.* 2009). Second, when a firm executes its sustainability strategy well, achieving positive firm performance, a sense of pride in working for a successful company is established among employees, contributing to their further engagement with the firm's sustainability mission, values and strategy (Katzenbach 2003).

As the virtuous cycle depicted in Figure 4.1 takes hold, with input from an engaged workforce, organisations continually adjust their sustainability strategies to reflect the changes encountered in the increasingly complex and dynamic environments in which they operate. Successful navigation in these environments requires a synthesis of both strategic planning and strategic thinking (Mintzberg 1987). Innovative and sustainable SMEs view strategy as a dynamic process that must be crafted. Leaders of these organisations understand that the strategy in action may actually vary from the intended strategy because of unintended fallout from planned efforts, and the successful seizing of unanticipated opportunities that emerge as the strategy unfolds. Therefore, we expect that:

> **Proposition 10.** Positive SME performance reinforces employee engagement in the firm's sustainability mission, values and strategy.

Next steps and recommendations for future research

The model presented puts forward a broad and varied research agenda. The logical next step is to conduct a series of empirical studies in order to validate the propositions identified within each component of the model. Ideally, these studies will be cross-functional in nature and represent the various disciplines of study regarding entrepreneurship and sustainability, including representation from: strategy, finance, accounting, economics, sociology, organisational behaviour, human resources and/or management. Further research should include:

- Identification of SMEs' sustainability missions, values and strategies that are found by employees to be the most compelling

- The relationship between the macro-components (i.e. various elements of the HR value chain) and employee engagement during SMEs' sustainability efforts

- The relationship between the micro-components (i.e. direct supervisory leadership elements) and employee engagement during SMEs' sustainability efforts

- Validation of the purported relationship between employee engagement and the micro- and macro-outcomes of SMEs' sustainability efforts

These propositions can be best investigated in a field study that utilises existing validated instruments. For instance, the full-range of leadership is assessed through the multi-factor leadership questionnaire (MLQ; Bass and Avolio 1994). The central construct, employee engagement, can be measured using the scale developed by Rich *et al.* (2010). A useful measure of in-role performance can be found in Whittington *et al.* (2004). Measures of extra-role performance are best captured through the assessment of organisational citizenship behaviours (Organ 1988).

Conclusions

The evidence-based model developed in this chapter is an important advance in the literature for several reasons. First, the model is applicable to a wide variety of SME sustainability efforts. Second, it may be applied regardless of the industry within which a firm operates. Third, the model enables researchers to frame their focused inquiry within a multi-level perspective and in relation to other disciplines.

In addition to providing guidance for research, the model also provides a road-map that can be used by entrepreneurs to create a culture of sustainability. Despite the observations into what needs to be done around sustainability, many leaders of SMEs do not quite seem to know how to do it. Therefore, our discussion of the virtuous cycle of sustainability also provides guidelines for managers of SMEs seeking to apply identified best practices within their organisations. The best practices at both the macro- and micro-levels of sustainability are summarised in Table 4.1.

Table 4.1 **Example best practices at the macro- and micro-leadership levels**

Macro-level best practices	Micro-level best practices
Establish the firm's mission, values and strategy around the distinct sustainability issues it is best equipped to help solve	Hire and/or promote managers who demonstrate both transactional and transformational (full-range) leadership behaviours, including the '4I's': idealised vision, inspirational motivation, intellectual stimulation and individualised consideration; as well as contingent rewards
Develop and implement HR value-chain practices that support the firm's sustainability mission, values and strategy	Incorporate job enrichment (task variety, task identity, task significance, autonomy and feedback) into all jobs within the firm
Incorporate sustainability in the firm's recruitment, selection, orientation and socialisation processes	Integrate goal setting into roles across the firm
Integrate sustainability into the firm's performance planning and evaluation, pay and rewards, and training and career development processes	Provide opportunities for employees to engage in organisational and community citizenship activities, beyond their immediate job roles
Include sustainability in the firm's separation policies and processes	Involve employees in helping shape the firm's mission, values and strategy as the organisation's sustainability posture evolves

References

Ahern, G. (2009) 'Implementing Environmental Sustainability in Ten Multinationals', *Corporate Finance Review* 13.6: 27-32.

Albinger, H.S., and S.J. Freeman (2000) 'Corporate Social Performance and Attractiveness as an Employer to Different Job Seeking Populations', *Journal of Business Ethics* 28.3: 243-53.

Avolio, B. (1999) *Full Leadership Development* (Thousand Oaks, CA: Sage).

Backhaus, K.B., B.A. Stone and K. Heiner (2002) 'Exploring the Relationship between Corporate Social Performance and Employer Attractiveness', *Business & Society* 41.3: 292-318.

Baron, R.A. (2003) 'Human Resource Management and Entrepreneurship: Some Reciprocal Benefits of Closer Links', *Human Resource Management Review* 13: 253-56.

Bartlett, C., and S. Ghoshal (2002) 'Building Competitive Advantage through People', *MIT Sloan Management Review* 43.2: 34-41.

Bass, B. (1985) *Leadership and Performance beyond Expectations* (New York: The Free Press).

Bass, B., and B. Avolio (1994) *Improving Organizational Effectiveness through Transformational Leadership* (Thousand Oaks, CA: Sage).

Bass, B., and R. Riggio (2006) *Transformational Leadership* (Mahwah, NJ: Lawrence Erlbaum & Associates, 2nd edn).

Bass, B., D. Waldman, B. Avolio and M. Bebb (1997) 'Transformational Leadership and the Falling Dominoes Effect', *Group and Organization Studies* 12: 73-87.

Berns, M., A. Townsend, Z. Khayat, B. Balagopal, M. Reeves, M.S. Hopkins and N. Kruschwitz (2009) 'Sustainability and Competitive Advantage', *MIT Sloan Management Review* 51.1: 19-26.

Bhattacharya, C.B., S. Sen and D. Korschun (2008) 'Using Corporate Social Responsibility to Win the War for Talent', *MIT Sloan Management Review* 49.2: 37-44.

Buckingham, M., and C. Coffman (1999) *First, Break All the Rules: What the World's Greatest Managers Do Differently* (New York: Simon and Schuster).

Bycio, P., R. Hackett and J. Allen (1995) 'Further Assessments of Bass's (1985) Conceptualization of Transactional and Transformational Leadership', *Journal of Applied Psychology* 80: 468-78.

Cardon, M.S., and C.E. Stevens (2004) 'Managing Human Resources in Small Organizations: What Do We Know?' *Human Resource Management Review* 14: 295-323.

Carlson, D.S., N. Upton and S. Seaman (2006) 'The Impact of Human Resource Practices and Compensation Design on Performance: An Analysis of Family-owned SMEs', *Journal of Small Business Management* 44.4: 531-43.

Cassell, C., S. Nadin, M. Gray and C. Clegg (2002) 'Exploring Human Resource Management Practices in Small and Medium Sized Enterprises', *Personnel Review* 31.5–6: 671-92.

Castello, I., and J. Lozano (2009) 'From Risk Management to Citizenship Corporate Social Responsibility: Analysis of Strategic Drivers of Change', *Corporate Governance* 9.4: 373-85.

Chow, I., and S.S. Liu (2009) 'The Effect of Aligning Organizational Culture and Business Strategy with HR Systems on Firm Performance in Chinese Enterprises', *International Journal of Human Resource Management* 11: 2,292-310.

Coffman, C., and G. Gonzalez-Molina (2002) *Follow this Path: How the World's Greatest Organizations Drive Growth by Unleashing Human Potential* (New York: Warner Books, Inc).

D'Amato, A., and N. Roome (2009) 'Toward an Integrated Model of Leadership for Corporate Responsibility and Sustainable Development: A Process Model of Corporate Responsibility beyond Management Innovation', *Corporate Governance* 9.4: 421-34.

Denyer, D., and D. Tranfield (2006) 'Using Qualitative Research Synthesis to Build an Actionable Knowledge Base', *Management Decision* 44.2: 213-27.

Dessler, G. (1999) 'How to Earn Your Employees' Commitment', *Academy of Management Executive* 13.2: 58-67.

Elkington, J. (1998) *Cannibals with Forks: The Triple Bottom Line of 21st Century Business* (Gabriola Island, BC: New Society Publishing).

Elkins, T., and R. Keller (2003) 'Leadership in Research and Development Organizations: A Literature Review and Conceptual Framework', *The Leadership Quarterly* 14: 587-606.

Golicic, S.L., C.N. Boerstler and L.M. Ellram (2010) ' "Greening" Transportation in the Supply Chain', *MIT Sloan Management Review* 51.2: 46-55.

Goodwin, V.L., J.C. Wofford and J.L. Whittington (2001) 'A Theoretical and Empirical Extension of the Transformational Leadership Construct', *Journal of Organizational Behavior* 22: 759-74.

Grayson, D., and A. Hodges (2004) *Corporate Social Opportunity! 7 Steps to Make Corporate Social Responsibility Work for Your Business* (Sheffield, UK: Greenleaf Publishing).

Greening, D.W., and D.B. Turban (2000) 'Corporate Social Performance as a Competitive Advantage in Attracting a Quality Work Force', *Business & Society* 39.3: 254-80.

Griffin, R. (1991) 'Effects of Work Redesign on Employee Perceptions, Attitudes, and Behaviors: A Long-term Investigation', *Academy of Management Journal* 34.2: 425-35.

Hackman, J., and G. Oldham (1976) 'Motivation through the Design of Work: Test of a Theory', *Organizational Behavior and Human Performance* 16: 250-79.

Hamel, G. (1996) 'Strategy as Revolution', *Harvard Business Review* 74.4: 69-82.

Hargett, T.R., and M.F. Williams (2009) 'Wilh. Wilhelmsen Shipping Company: Moving from CSR Tradition to CSR Leadership', *Corporate Governance* 9.1: 73-82.

Harter, J.K., F.L. Schmidt and T.L. Hayes (2002) 'Business-Unit-Level Relationship between Employee Satisfaction, Employee Engagement, and Business Outcomes: A Meta-analysis', *Journal of Applied Psychology* 87.2: 268-79.

Hausknecht, J.P., J. Rodda and M.J. Howard (2009) 'Targeted Employee Retention: Performance-Based and Job-Related Differences in Reported Reasons for Staying', *Human Resource Management* 48.2: 269-88.

Heifetz, R. (1994) *Leadership without Easy Answers* (Cambridge, MA: Harvard University Press).

Hind, P., A. Wilson and G. Lenssen (2009) 'Developing Leaders for Sustainable Business', *Corporate Governance* 9.1: 7-20.

Howell, J., and B. Avolio (1993) 'Transformational Leadership, Transactional Leadership, Locus of Control, and Support for Innovation: Key Predictors of Consolidated-Business-Unit Performance', *Journal of Applied Psychology* 78: 891-902.

Jacopin, T., and J. Fontrodona (2009) 'Questioning the Corporate Responsibility (CR) Department Alignment with the Business Model of the Company', *Corporate Governance* 9.4: 528-36.

Jenkins, H. (2004) 'A Critique of Conventional CSR Theory: An SME Perspective', *Journal of General Management* 9.4: 55-75.

Jenkins, H. (2009) 'A "Business Opportunity" Model of Corporate Social Responsibility for Small- and Medium-Sized Enterprises', *Business Ethics: A European Review* 18.1: 21-36.

Katzenbach, J.R. (2003) *Why Pride Matters More Than Money: The Power of the World's Greatest Motivational Force* (New York: Crown Business).

Keller, R. (1992) 'Transformational Leader and the Performance of Research and Design Project Groups', *Journal of Management* 18: 489-501.

Kotter, J.P., and J.L. Heskett (1992) *Corporate Culture and Performance* (New York: Free Press).

Lacy, P., J. Arnott and E. Lowitt (2009) 'The Challenge of Integrating Sustainability into Talent and Organization Strategies: Investing in the Knowledge, Skills and Attitudes to Achieve High Performance', *Corporate Governance* 9.4: 484-94.

Lowe, K., K.G. Kroeck and N. Sivasubramamianiam (1996) 'Effectiveness Correlates of Transformational and Transactional Leadership: A Meta-analytic Review', *The Leadership Quarterly* 7: 385-425.

Mintzberg, H. (1987) 'Crafting Strategy', *Harvard Business Review*, July–August 1987: 66-75.

Mirvis. P., and B. Googins (2006) 'Stages of Corporate Citizenship', *California Management Review* 48.2: 104-26.

Morsing, M., and D. Oswald (2009) 'Sustainable Leadership: Management Control Systems and Organizational Culture in Novo Nordisk A/S', *Corporate Governance* 9.1: 83-99.

Mumford, M., S. Connelly and B. Gaddis (2003) 'How Creative Leaders Think: Experimental Findings and Cases', *The Leadership Quarterly* 14: 411-32.

Munilla, L., and M.P. Miles (2005) 'The Corporate Social Responsibility Continuum as a Component of Stakeholder Theory', *Business and Society Review* 110.4: 371-87.

Organ, D. (1988) *Organizational Citizenship Behavior: The Good Soldier Syndrome* (Lexington, MA: Lexington Books).

Organ, D. (1990) 'The Motivational Basis of Organizational Citizenship Behavior', *Research in Organizational Behavior* 12: 43-72.

Orlitzky, M. (2005) 'Payoffs to Social and Environmental Performance', *Journal of Investing* 14.3: 48-51.

Orlitzky, M., F.L. Schmidt and S.L. Rynes (2003) 'Corporate Social and Financial Performance: A Meta-analysis', *Organization Studies* 24.3: 403-41.

Pfeffer, J. (2005) 'Producing Sustainable Competitive Advantage through the Effective Management of People', *Academy of Management Executive* 19.4: 95-106.

Podsakoff, P.M., S. MacKenzie, R. Moorman and R. Fetter (1990) 'Transformational Leader Behaviors and their Effects on Followers' Trust in Leader, Satisfaction, and Organizational Citizenship Behaviors', *The Leadership Quarterly* 1: 107-42.

Porter, M.E., and M.R. Kramer (2006) 'Strategy and Society: The Link between Competitive Advantage and Corporate Social Responsibility', *Harvard Business Review* 84.12: 78-92.

Quinn, L., and M. Dalton (2009) 'Leading for Sustainability: Implementing the Tasks of Leadership', *Corporate Governance* 9.1: 21-38.

Rich, B., J. Lepine and E. Crawford (2010) 'Job Engagement: Antecedents and Effects on Job Performance', *Academy of Management Journal* 53.3: 617-35.

Rok, B. (2009) 'Ethical Context of the Participative Leadership Model: Taking People into Account', *Corporate Governance* 9.4: 461-72.

Saks, A.M. (2006) 'Antecedents and Consequences of Employee Engagement', *Journal of Managerial Psychology* 21.7: 600-19.

Savitz, A.W., and K. Weber (2006) *The Triple Bottom Line: How Today's Best-Run Companies are Achieving Economic, Social and Environmental Success— and how you can too* (San Francisco: Jossey-Bass).

Schein, E.H. (2010) *Organizational Culture and Leadership* (San Francisco: Jossey-Bass, 4th edn).

Siegel, D.S. (2009) 'Green Management Matters Only if it Yields More Green: An Economic/Strategic Perspective', *Academy of Management Perspectives* 23.3: 5-16.

Teng, A. (2010) 'The HR Transformation Continuum', *Human Resource Executive* 24.3: 45-47.

Turban, D.B., and D.W. Greening (1996) 'Corporate Social Performance and Organizational Attractiveness to Prospective Employees', *Academy of Management Journal* 40: 658-72.

Viswesvaran, C., S.P. Deshpande and C. Milman (1998) 'The Effect of Corporate Social Responsibility on Employee Counterproductive Behavior', *Cross Cultural Management* 5.4: 5-12.

White: (2009) 'Building a Sustainability Strategy into the Business', *Corporate Governance* 9.4: 386-94.

Whittington, J.L., and T.J. Galpin (2010) 'The Engagement Factor: Building a High-Commitment Organization in a Low-Commitment World', *Journal of Business Strategy* 31.5: 14-24.

Whittington, J.L., V.L. Goodwin and B. Murray (2004) 'Transformational Leadership, Goal Difficulty, and Task Design: Independent and Interactive Effects on Employee Outcomes', *The Leadership Quarterly* 15.5: 593-606.

Wofford, J., V. Goodwin and J. Whittington (1998) 'A Field Study of a Cognitive Approach to Transformational and Transactional Leadership', *The Leadership Quarterly* 9: 55-84.

Wu, M. (2006) 'Corporate Social Performance, Corporate Financial Performance, and Firm Size: A Meta-analysis', *Journal of American Academy of Business* 8.1: 163-71.

York, J., and S. Venkataraman (2010) 'The Entrepreneur–Environment Nexus: Uncertainty, Innovation, and Allocation', *Journal of Business Venturing* 25.5: 449-63.

Zadek, S. (2004) 'The Path to Corporate Responsibility', *Harvard Business Review* 82.12: 125-32.

5

Corporate entrepreneurship and organisational innovation

The case of environmental management system implementation

Marcus Wagner

Julius-Maximilians-University of Würzburg, Germany

Environmental management systems (EMS) are considered as one important means to integrate aspects of environmental management into corporate decision-making. Environmental management is considered to be one cornerstone of sustainability and sustainable development. The World Commission on Environment and Development (WCED 1987: 54) defines sustainable development as 'development that meets the needs of the present without compromising the ability of future generations to meet their own needs'. For corporate sustainability this implies a requirement to perform financially (as traditionally expected from firms) as well as socially and environmentally. Hence EMS implementation is potentially an important means to achieve corporate sustainability (Schaltegger and Burritt 2005). Yet, ever since their conception, the argument of the uncertain benefits of EMS has also been made. In this respect, the mounting evidence of their limited ecological effectiveness (Hertin *et al.* 2008) increasingly suggests that if benefits of EMS implementation exist, then these are probably mainly of (more or less tangible) economic nature. Indeed, cost savings, differentiation potential and more intangible benefits have been frequently suggested in the literature based on circumstantial and case evidence (Hamschmidt and Dyllick 2001). However, it has rarely been confirmed empirically on a larger scale whether such economic benefits are systematic. More specifically, benefits in the context of human resources (HR) have been suggested as a particularly important category of 'softer' benefits resulting from EMS implementation (Wehrmeyer and Parker 1995; Wehrmeyer 1996a). In the remainder, this chapter combines these two last aspects by establishing what determines the consideration of EMS in the personnel function, by developing hypotheses on the link between HR and EMS implementation and by testing these on a larger scale empirically.

Literature review and hypothesis development

Current issues in personnel and development can only be seen against the background of recent and emerging global and environmental trends forming a framework for business activities. Changes on the agenda are, for example, increasing consumer individualism, higher quality and service demands, teleworking towards the 'virtual' firm, growing global competition, shorter product life-cycles and public awareness of social and environmental responsibility (Emerson 1996; Wehrmeyer 1996b). Armstrong (1996) classifies the business framework into five categories that are influential for personnel management. These are the external economic influences, the impact of social and political change (increasing participation of women in the workforce), the international dimension of business (maturation of global markets), technological change (new information technologies) and the demand for increasing shareholder value and for improved quality and better customer services (including improved sustainability; that is better consideration of social concerns and concerns for the environment by firms).

As these categories are often interlinked and virtually permanently changing, separate trends are difficult to establish: for example with regard to gender aspects and environmental management (Mawle 1996). This makes it very difficult for a company as a whole as well as for the different business functions to develop a strategic response to them. The personnel function and HR management especially are in the forefront of change in order to adapt to tomorrow's world. What processes this might imply in the future with regard to environmental management shall be considered in the following in more detail.

Historical development of HR

According to Armstrong (1996) personnel management is concerned with the management of people which implies at least two important duties: the first is to create a surrounding that makes it possible for management to 'recruit, train and motivate' the workforce the company is in need of for their future tasks. Second, the personnel function is responsible for assuring 'the continuous development of people's potential and the creation of a climate in which all are motivated to meet the objectives of the enterprise'. There is a broad discussion as to what makes the difference between personnel management and HR management. Torrington and Hall (1995) describe HR management as a general management activity which is rather distant from employees and workplaces and more concerned with planning, monitoring and control than with mediation, in turn giving line management a more proactive role and allocating the responsibility for managing the enterprise culture to top management.

Some involved in the debate argue that personnel management or HR management are synonyms since the practical differences between both concepts seem to be marginal. However, they might be distinguished from each other as they describe different stages in the evolution of personnel during the last 40 years.

Personnel management has evolved through a number of stages (Armstrong 1996). While the 1960s and 1970s saw the mature phase of personnel management, the 1980s and the post-entrepreneurial, post-modernist world of the 1990s have seen the emergence and development of the human resource management paradigm. The mature phase of personnel management can be characterised by systematic training and manpower planning programmes, more sophisticated selection patterns, salary administration and appraisal techniques, organisation development programmes, job enrichment and an increased amount of employment legislation (Inmaculada *et al.* 2008).

The following, first phase of the human resource management paradigm emerging during the 1980s in America was mainly caused by the increasing pressure to adjust to a tighter economy during the entrepreneurial 1980s with a proliferation of takeovers, mergers and acquisitions. These earned themselves an especially bad name since few showed much concern for the people working for the organisations (O'Reilly 1995). During this phase, human resource management was concerned with how personnel could make an impact on the bottom line and, consequently, the era saw a rise of performance-related pay and the development of performance management systems. Personnel management became more business- and management-orientated, a process reinforced by the declining power of trade unions. The second phase of human resource management during the 1990s has emphasised the importance of being strategic and has given birth to the concept of strategic human resource management. This period stresses the learning organisation and continuous development, the total quality concept and teamwork (i.e. quality teams), the necessity of benchmarking and business process re-engineering and to some extent increasing employee empowerment. The framework of these developments was a far-reaching and prolonged recession leading to major downsizing and re-engineering exercises with the purpose of creating leaner and more flexible organisations. This was at least to some extent enhanced by the emergence of powerful information technologies.

While in this historical perspective HR management was initially a type of conformist innovation and a stronger need for cost justification of personnel activities, it is stressed that the reality of HR management and the original conception often differ with the term acting as a euphemism for cost-cutting and downsizing measures (Sisson 1994). In addition, contradictions are pointed out within the original concept itself (Beer *et al.* 1984) (especially with respect to the role of stakeholders) and hence a necessity to address a differentiated group of stakeholders with very different concerns (shareholders, environmentalists, politicians, socially concerned people) which directly relates to the link between environmental management and HR.

The link between HR and environmental management

A good corporate image has been suggested to help attract staff with above-average qualifications and motivations (Linnanen 1995), in turn making corporate environmental policy a part of the firm's goal to achieve a status of preferred employer (Ramus and Steger 2000) and it has been argued that this can be best achieved by means of functional integration (Wagner 2007).

For example, Egri and Hornal (2002) find that integration of environmental aspects into HRM enhances perceptions of organisational performance. Also, ecocentric leadership styles and values of managers can improve the conditions for integration (Egri and Herman 2000). Maignan and Ralston (2002) find that at least the public acknowledgement of social and environmental responsibility of firms differs between countries, which may mean that managerial attitudes towards ecocentricity also vary. Such cross-cultural differences are, however, not found for other managerial attitudes (Egri *et al.* 2000). Also, changes of attitudes from one generation of managers to the next have been observed (Ralston *et al.* 1999).

The resulting diversity in managing people is an increasing challenge for HR managers to gain employee commitment. It should be stressed that building trust might become pivotal as enthusiastic involvement differs from acquiescence, employees are not solely a factor of production and corporate values must be translated into action in order to make a contribution to short- as well as long-term profits. In increasingly globalised business structures and highly competitive marketplaces this puts new requirements on, and gives new importance to, the people involved in HR management, and sustainability seems to be a particularly appropriate means to address the above challenges in this context.

In addition to these strategic considerations at the level of the corporate mission and vision, at the operational level, sustainability and embracing environmental management in the firm can also have substantial implications for HR management. For example, enabled through modern information technology, a significant increase in outworkers through networks and electronic communication can be observed. A recent study by the Eco-Institute of Freiburg in Germany suggests, however, that the eco-balance of teleworking might be negative as it will mean an initially enormous investment, in terms of both energy and material, in technical infrastructure. Also, increased teleworking requires changes in organisational structures to enable full efficiency gains, as is witnessed by the information technology paradox of increased corporate investment and simultaneously unchanged productivity (Brynjolfsson and Mendelson 1993; Bresnahan *et al.* 2002). Since in this sense teleworking, as well as the need to tighten the organisation to become more flexible, lean and responsive, necessitate business process re-engineering, they hold considerable scope for increasing corporate sustainability. Research suggests that business process re-engineering is more likely to succeed if the motives are positive, while most failures can be attributed to neglect of the human aspect. Therefore, a positive effect of environmental management on HR aspects would also be desirable from this perspective.

In summary, the literature suggests that, when firms invest in CSR strengths beyond the minimum level legally required, improving the corporate image or the ability to recruit excellent staff are often important motivations, even though ultimately the hope is that this would also translate into more tangible benefits such as increased innovativeness of firms and corporate entrepreneurship (Ramus and Steger 2000). Given that HR benefits have been suggested as a particularly important category of 'softer' benefits resulting from EMS implementation (Wehrmeyer 1995, 1996a), the question immediately arises of whether such benefits are then also drivers for EMS implementation? To answer this question an implicit experiment is staged in this chapter, which can also provide evidence on the existence of signalling effects and benefits from EMS implementation. This is done by formulating hypotheses based on the assumption that, if actual HR benefits exist and the acknowledgement of HR benefits from environmental management is consequentially not just socially desirable response behaviour, then the larger such benefits are, the more likely firms would be willing to invest in EMS implementation in order to realise them. That is, one would expect a positive association of specific HR benefit categories and the level of EMS implementation. Focusing on two frequently suggested categories, namely worker/employee satisfaction and staff retention/recruitment, three hypotheses can be formulated based on the above arguments and reasoning:

- **Hypothesis 1.** A positive association exists between employee satisfaction, retention and recruitment and the level of EMS implementation

- **Hypothesis 2.** EMS-related activities are less frequently linked to the personnel function than to other corporate functions

- **Hypothesis 3.** Firm characteristics account for part of the variation in whether or not EMS-related activities are linked to the personnel function

Testing these hypotheses with large-scale empirical data is the objective of the remainder of the chapter.

Data and method

Collection of data

To analyse the above research questions, two surveys among German manufacturing firms are involved. In these surveys, through a number of questions, responses were solicited from firms on their environmental management activities and the relevance of environmental management for different competitiveness dimensions, as well as various firm characteristics such as firm size and whether or not the firm has a quality management system (QMS). The first survey was carried out in 2001. Of the 2000 firms contacted, 342 returned a completed questionnaire, resulting in a response rate of 17.1%. The second survey was carried out in 2006. Of the 581 firms contacted, 169 responded, resulting in a response rate of 30%.

To assess the representativeness and response bias, the procedures suggested by Armstrong and Overton (1977) and by Homburg and Bucerius (2006) are adopted, as far as possible. Comparing the earliest and latest 10% of respondents in terms of their characteristics and response behaviour, no significant differences in the mean values of the responses of all variables used in the analysis were found other than the fact that late responding firms were significantly smaller. Additionally, as can be seen from Tables A1 and A2 there is large variation across the responses in both surveys indicating that firms less active in terms of environmental management also responded to the survey. While these findings indicate that response bias is unlikely in the data, two procedures were additionally employed to reduce any remaining bias.

First, some individual missing values for other variables were imputed to be included in the multivariate analysis reported in the following. This was done using the Missing Value Analysis tool available in SPSS® based on the expected maximisation (EM) algorithm. This is a general method applicable to any missing data problem (Schnell 1986). It 'treats the missing data as random variables to be removed from (i.e., integrated out of) the likelihood function as if they were never sampled' (Schafer and Graham 2002: 148). The EM algorithm is currently considered (under the assumption that data is missing at random) the most suitable and state-of-the-art method to substitute missing values in data sets with estimated values (Schafer and Graham 2002).

Second, comparing with base data from the Bundesanstalt für Arbeit, it becomes clear that larger firms with more than 500 employees are represented over-proportionally in the responses, whereas firms with 151 to 500 and less than 150 employees are under-represented in the data.[1] More specifically, in the 2001 survey, 33% of the responding firms had more than 500 employees and 36% had 50 to 150 employees, and in the 2006 survey, 15% of the responding firms had up to 50 employees, and

---

1   Written communication of the Bundesanstalt für Arbeit on the number of firms in the German manufacturing sector as of 31 December 1999 (data provided on 8 August 2000).

19% 150 to 500 employees. A size bias compared with the universe of German manufacturing firms needs to be acknowledged, which, however, becomes smaller from 2001 to 2006. This type of bias is a common finding not only in surveys on environmental management but also in surveys of companies more generally (Armstrong and Overton 1977; Baumast and Dyllick 2001) and hence to some degree has to be considered as a general problem.

In 2001, 57% of the responding firms were solely owned, and 43% owned by another company or in another way part of a larger firm, whereas in 2006, 53% of the responding firms were solely owned, and 47% not. Inspection of correlations and variance inflation factors in Tables A1 and A2 reveals that, judging from the variance inflation factors (VIF), multi-collinearity is not an issue for the analysis.

Variable definitions and econometric approach

To address the hypotheses formulated earlier in the chapter, careful definition, especially of the main variables of the analysis, is necessary. This particularly concerns the index of EMS implementation as the dependent variable. More specifically, whether the proposed relationship can be identified empirically seems to crucially depend on the way the level of EMS implementation is measured. For example, Rehfeld et al. (2007) and Ziegler and Rennings (2004) have measured EMS implementation based on dummy variables capturing whether or not firms have achieved certification or verification according to ISO 14001 or the EU Eco-Management and Auditing Scheme. This however seems problematic, because approaches rooted in institutional economics (Russo 2002) argue the existence of asymmetric information in the case of EMS certification and from this derive incentives for firms to behave opportunistically. Also, neo-institutional organisational theory (DiMaggio and Powell 1983) argues that certification could be a symbolic gesture motivated out of institutional isomorphism and mimicry behaviour that has little influence on actual implementation levels. Opposed to this, the resource-based view (Wernerfelt 1984) suggests that EMS implementation that enables the development of strategic resources and competitive advantages occurs by implementation of actual environmental management activities (regardless of certification), ultimately leading to increased innovativeness of firms and corporate entrepreneurship (Ramus and Steger 2000; Pichel, 2008).

From these considerations it becomes obvious that, for the purposes of addressing the above research questions, it would be desirable to measure the level of EMS implementation independent of certification. Therefore, to measure the EMS implementation, an index variable is defined as the sum of a number of individual environmental management activities out of a total of ten. The ten EMS elements are: a written environmental policy; procedure for identification and evaluation of legal requirements; an initial environmental review; the definition of measurable environmental goals; existence of a programme to attain measurable environmental goals; clearly defined responsibilities; an environmental training programme; environmental goals are part of a continuous improvement process; a separate environmental/health/safety report or environmental statement; and an audit system to check the environmental programme. The scale of the index hence ranges from zero (no activity is carried out) to ten (all activities listed above are carried out).

In addition to avoiding the ambiguity related to certification depending on the theoretical perspective taken, this approach has the additional advantage of avoiding discrimination against smaller firms, since these often implement activities without certifying an EMS because of the higher relative cost for this category of firm. Since (especially in 2006, but to a certain degree also in 2001) a considerable number of small firms responded to the survey, this is an area of concern for the analysis that is also addressed by defining an EMS index in the way described above.

As concerns the explanatory variables, the three most important ones are: recruitment/staff retention; worker satisfaction; and whether environmental management activities are carried out in the HR/personnel function. The former two are defined on a five-point scale from very negative to very positive (perceived effect of environmental management).

Other benefit categories included as controls in a variant of the model (namely, increased sales, market share, cost savings, productivity increases, improved insurance conditions and better access to bank loans) are rated in the same manner, essentially based on an approach introduced by Sharma (2001).

Whether environmental management activities are carried out in the HR/personnel function is measured by means of a binary variable. Next to the three main explanatory variables, there are a significant number of explanatory factors such as existence of a quality management system (QMS), firm size and firm status. The existence of a QMS (as a binary dummy variable, yes or no) was included since the data shows that a larger share of firms with a QMS pursue environmentally related product innovations (64% versus 54% for those not having a QMS) and that the same applies to environmentally related process innovation (68% versus 57%). Given that environmental management activities represent organisational innovations and that QMS and EMS are strategic complements, an analogous effect can be expected here.

Firm size is expected to positively correlate with the level of environmental activities and was included in the analysis as the logarithm of the number of employees. Firm status was included in the analysis in terms of a dummy variable (yes or no) if the firm is completely independent because, for example, family firms have been shown to have a longer-term orientation (Block 2010; Wagner 2010).

A further control variable included in the analysis was the development trend faced by the respondent firm in its main market (measured on a five-point scale ranging from 'market is considerably decreasing' to 'market is considerably increasing'). This is because of a potential 'market pull' effect that has a significant positive baseline effect on environmental management from favourable market conditions.

Finally, overall business performance (measured on a five-point scale ranging from 'revenues are well in excess of cost' to 'revenues are so low as to cause large losses') was included as a control variable in the model to account for effects of slack resources and benefits from complementary investments that make the implementation of environmental management activities more valuable (Waddock and Graves 1997; Christmann 2000; Surroca *et al.* 2010).

Since the ten activities identified above as the basis for calculating the EMS index used as the dependent variable in this analysis are generic in the sense that in all manufacturing industries surveyed they are considered a standard for environmental management, it was not necessary to introduce industry dummies in the analysis. All models are estimated using standard ordinary least squares cross-sectional regression with heteroskedasticity-corrected standard errors.

Results

Tables 5.1 and 5.2 show the results for the separate estimation of the models for the 2001 and 2006 data to test Hypothesis 1. As can be seen, all models are significant overall with good explanatory value as is reflected in the high R^2 figures. Also, the results remain basically unchanged regardless of whether other benefits that can be derived from environmental management in terms of improved market performance, reduced financial risk and increased operational efficiency are accounted for (right column with estimation results in Tables 5.1 and 5.2) or not (left column with estimation results in Tables 5.1 and 5.2).

Table 5.1 **Model estimation for 2001 data, dependent variable: EMS index**

Variables	Model 1	Model 2
Worker satisfaction	1.391 (0.539)**	1.159 (0.552)**
Recruitment and staff retention	0.929 (0.518)*	0.871 (0.533)*
Number of employees	2.131 (0.386)***	1.800 (0.403)***
Quality management system	1.663 (0.573)***	1.566 (0.579)***
Overall business performance	0.211 (0.288)	0.230 (0.291)
Market development trend	-0.115 (0.224)	-0.168 (0.227)
Firm completely independent	1.578 (0.418)***	1.459 (0.492)***
Increased sales	–	0.117 (0.748)
Market share	–	0.676 (0.845)
Cost savings	–	0.466 (0.337)
Productivity increases	–	0.325 (0.557)
Improved insurance conditions	–	0.450 (0.425)

→

Variables	Model 1	Model 2
Better access to bank loans	–	0.186 (0.687)
Constant	-9.256 (2.286)***	-14.351 (3.245)***
R²	0.366	0.402
No. of observations	175	175
F test	13.836***	8.237***

Notes: Significance levels: * $p < 0.1$; ** $p < 0.05$; *** $p < 0.01$; heteroskedasticity-robust standard errors in parentheses

As Table 5.1 shows, for the 2001 data, worker satisfaction and recruitment and staff retention are both significantly positively associated with the EMS index, in turn supporting hypotheses 1 and 2 above. Beyond this, the controls for firm size, QMS and firm status are also significantly associated with the dependent variable in the expected direction.

Table 5.2 **Model estimation for 2006 data, dependent variable: EMS index**

Variables	Model 1	Model 2
Worker satisfaction	1.132 (0.401)***	0.925 (0.399)**
Recruitment and staff retention	1.022 (0.476)**	0.729 (0.554)
Number of employees	0.438 (0.086)***	0.508 (0.094)***
Quality management system	0.789 (0.662)	0.199 (0.639)
Overall business performance	-0.029 (0.290)	0.136 (0.299)
Market development trend	-0.187 (0.227)	-0.194 (0.243)
Firm completely independent	0.178 (0.448)	0.183 (0.452)
Increased sales	–	0.206 (0.649)
Market share	–	0.802 (0.738)
Cost savings	–	-0.218 (0.297)
Productivity increases	–	-0.524 (0.481)
Improved insurance conditions	–	1.559 (0.467)**
Better access to bank loans	–	-0.283 (0.870)
Constant	-3.415 (1.857)*	-6.426 (3.006)**
R²	0.347	0.416
No. of observations	135	135
F test	13.430***	8.350***

Notes: Significance levels: * $p < 0.1$; ** $p < 0.05$; *** $p < 0.01$; heteroskedasticity-robust standard errors in parentheses

Turning to Table 5.2 and the results for the 2006 data, in the model without controlling for other benefits, again a significant positive association of both worker satisfaction and recruitment and staff retention with the EMS index is found that lends support to hypotheses 1 and 2. Also, as for 2001 a significant positive association of firm size with the dependent variable is found. However, in 2006 no significant effect can be recorded for QMS and firm status. In addition to that, when introducing controls for the other benefits that can be derived from environmental management in the right column of Table 5.2, the association found for recruitment and staff retention becomes insignificant. This suggests that, in 2006, the benefits from environmental management that relate to improved insurance conditions have become relatively more relevant.

Another explanation why in this last model no association was found for recruitment and staff retention could be that in 2006 environmental management activities benefiting retention/recruitment have increasingly become a hygiene factor in the sense of Herzberg *et al.* (1999); that is, implemented in most firms. While with the data at hand this cannot be tested directly, it is at least clear that in 2001 the departmental environmental management activities varied significantly. For example, in 2001 only 13% of the responding firms stated that they had implemented such activities in the HR function, as opposed to 84% having done this in the production function and 18% in the marketing function. Given the increasing awareness among HR managers and ecological exposure of the HR function (PwC 2010), the share of firms with activities in their HR departments has increased since then and, because of saturation in other functions, variation across different functions and differentiation potential within the HR function with regard to at least some aspects have decreased.

Comparing the coefficients between Tables 5.1 and 5.2 for the two most important explanatory variables relating to HR, it becomes clear that the effect of worker satisfaction is higher and more pronounced than that of recruitment/staff retention. Also, when moving from the model variant without controlling for other benefits of environmental management (left column with estimation results) to the one accounting for this (right column with estimation results), the explanatory power of the two main explanatory variables decreases.

Finally, the results reported in Tables 5.1 and 5.2 remain qualitatively stable if instead of including the individual item variables in the extended variant of the model (reported in the right column in the tables), factors emerging from a principal component analysis (PCA) are included as controls. This is not surprising, as for each factor identified, the two most important individual items emerging from PCA are included as controls, but it also confirms the robustness of the analysis. Also, using indices calculated as means across the item variables identified in the PCA as belonging to one factor does not, perhaps unsurprisingly, change qualitatively the results of the analysis.

To test hypotheses 2 and 3, only data for 2001 could be involved. With respect to Hypothesis 3, an initial univariate analysis in Table 5.3 shows the incidence of environmental management activities in the personnel function relative to other business functions.

Table 5.3 **Incidence of environmental management activities by business function (n=322)**

Business function	Percentage of respondents confirming activities	Standard deviation of percentage confirming (%)
Purchasing and supply	61	49
Research and development	42	49
Production	84	36
Marketing and sales	18	39
Logistics	39	49
Recycling	74	44
Accounting	6	23
Personnel	13	33

What can be seen from Table 5.3 is that purchasing, production and recycling are the business functions in which technical or organisational environmental management activities are pursued most frequently in 2001 (on average 73%). Compared with this, HRM together with accounting and marketing/sales makes up the group of business functions in which such activities were least likely to be pursued, on average 12%, with HRM being closest to this average. While no direct survey evidence is available for 2006, secondary research suggests that raising awareness among HR managers and ecological exposure of the personnel function has increased the share of firms with activities in the personnel function since 2001 (PwC 2010). Furthermore, because of the saturation in functions that already often had activities in 2001, variation across different functions has probably decreased and hence the gap between the personnel and other functions has likely narrowed. To confirm this and to gain a more in-depth understanding of the temporal dynamics, both the 2001 and 2006 surveys were analysed based on the same set of individual technical and organisational environmental activities (Wagner 2011). This can be linked to the analysis by business function in that specific activities are usually implemented across firms in the same function. For example analysing the relevance of training activities on environmental issues compared with other technical and organisational activities such as material usage also provides some indication about the degree to which activities are pursued in the HRM function. Similarly, activities such as product or packaging recycling can be linked to the recycling function. Nevertheless, some activities cannot be related to only one function, such as use of measurable environmental goals or adoption of environmental performance indicators, both of which can be applied at the level of the firm or to individual employees. Therefore, while there is no direct mapping of activities onto functions, associations exist that enable indirect inferences.

To clarify what structural features determine that environmental activities are linked to the personnel function and to test Hypothesis 3, results of the corresponding multivariate regression analysis are presented in Table 5.4.

Table 5.4 **Model estimation for 2001 data, dependent variable: Activities in the HRM, personnel function**

Variables	Raw estimate	Marginal effect
Number of employees	0.388 (0.176)**	0.062
QMS	0.511 (0.303)*	0.069
Profitability	0.016 (0.138)	0.002
Munificence	-0.026 (0.115)	-0.004
Firm completely independent	-0.467 (0.266)*	-0.078
R^2	0.144	
Log-likelihood	-67.753	
No. of observations	215	
Wald test	30.59**	

Notes: Significance levels: * $p < 0.1$; ** $p < 0.05$; *** $p < 0.01$; heteroskedasticity-robust standard errors; 20 industry dummy variables at 2-digit NACE level included in estimation

What can be seen from Table 5.4 is that, with regard to the personnel function for the 2001 data, HRM-related environmental activities occur more often in larger firms, firms not completely independent (e.g. subsidiaries) and firms with a certified QMS. These results remain qualitatively the same in terms of coefficient signs and significance levels when a larger EU-wide survey is involved which suggests a strong cross-national stability of the factors that structurally determine whether environmental management activities are carried out in the HR/personnel function (Wagner 2007, 2009).

Conclusions and discussion

This chapter set out to test three hypotheses derived from an often-cited argument about the link between HR and environmental management: namely that EMS implementation renders competitive benefits for HR management. While this notion fits with the recent trend of sustainability becoming a more central and strategic theme for firms and business practice (Ehnert 2009), large-scale evidence going beyond anecdotal support is still missing for this claim. Based on two surveys among German manufacturing firms carried out in 2001 and 2006, this chapter supports two hypotheses claiming a significant positive association between EMS implementation and worker/employee satisfaction and recruitment/staff retention, respectively. Given that the hypotheses are largely supported both times, this paper also shows the longitudinal stability of the hypothesised relationship. This contributes to and confirms the notion that the observed effects are in fact salient relationships and not mere temporal facts and therefore supports earlier pleas for putting sustainability at the centre of future paradigm development in HR management (Boudreau and Ramstad 2005) and to elevate sustainability (and as part of this also environmental management considerations) to a strategic level, as far as the personnel function is concerned (Mariappanadar 2003).

Even though in 2001 only a minority of firms (13%) reported that they pursued environmental activities in the personnel function, it seems that the HRM relevance to environmental management has not increased since then and has potentially increased more in other business functions. This could, however, also be interpreted as an indication that HRM still has to engage more fundamentally with notions of sustainability, as has been done quite extensively for other business functions, most notably marketing and accounting (Lamberton 2005; Belz and Peattie 2009).

For example, in 2001, of the responding firms that implemented EMS-related activities, 84% stated that they had done this in the production function and 18% in the marketing function. Because of saturation in other functions, variation across different functions and differentiation potential within the HR function with regard to at least some aspects have decreased.

References

Armstrong, J.S., and T.S. Overton (1977) 'Estimating Non-Response Bias in Mail Surveys', *Journal of Marketing Research* 14: 396-402.

Armstrong, M. (1996) *A Handbook of Personnel Management Practice* (London: Kogan Page).

Baumast, A., and T. Dyllick (2001) *Umweltmanagement-Barometer 2001* (St Gallen, Switzerland: Institute for Economy and the Environment at the University of St Gallen).

Beer, M., B. Spector, P.R. Lawrence, D. Quinn-Mills, R.E. Walston (1984) *Managing Human Assets* (New York: Free Press).

Belz, F., and K. Peattie (2009) *Sustainability Marketing* (New York: Wiley).

Block, J. (2010) 'Family Management, Family Ownership, and Downsizing: Evidence from S&P 500 Firms', *Family Business Review* 23: 109-30.

Boudreau, J.W., and P.M. Ramstad (2005) 'Talentship, Talent Segmentation, and Sustainability: A New HR Decision Science Paradigm for a New Strategy Definition', *Human Resource Management* 44.2: 129-36.

Bresnahan, T.F., E. Brynjolfsson and L.M. Hitt (2002) 'Information Technology, Workplace Organization, and the Demand for Skilled Labor: Firm-Level Evidence', *Quarterly Journal of Economics* 117: 339-76.

Brynjolfsson, E., and H. Mendelson (1993) 'Information Systems and the Organization of Modern Enterprise', *Journal of Organizational Computing* 3: 245-55.

Christmann, P. (2000) 'Effects of "Best Practices" of Environmental Management on Cost Advantage: The Role of Complementary Assets', *Academy of Management Journal* 43.4: 663-80.

DiMaggio, P., and W. Powell (1983) 'The Iron Cage Revisited: Institutional Isomorphism and Collective Rationality in Organizational Fields', *American Sociological Review* 48 (April 1983): 147-60.

Egri, C.P., and S. Herman (2000) 'Leadership in the North American Environmental Sector: Values, Leadership Styles, and Contexts to Environmental Leaders in their Organizations', *Academy of Management Journal* 43.4: 571-604.

Egri, C.P., and R.C. Hornal (2002) 'Strategic Environmental Human Resource Management and Perceived Organizational Performance: An Exploratory Study of the Canadian Manufacturing Sector', in S. Sharma and M. Starik (eds.), *Research in Corporate Sustainability: The Evolving Theory and Practice of Organizations in the Natural Environment* (Northampton, MA: Edward Elgar): 205-36.

Egri, C.P., D.A. Ralston, C.S. Murray and J.D. Nicholson (2000) 'Managers in the NAFTA Countries: A Cross-Cultural Comparison of Attitudes toward Upward Influence Strategies', *Journal of International Management* 9.2: 149-71.

Ehnert, I. (2009) 'Sustainability and Human Resource Management: Reasoning and Applications on Corporate Websites', *European Journal of International Management* 3.4: 419-38.

Emerson, T. (1996) 'Global Warming Should Make HR People Sweat', *People Management*, 21 March 1996: 21.

Hamschmidt, J., and T. Dyllick (2001) 'ISO 14001: Profitable? Yes! But is it eco-effective?' *Greener Management International* 34: 43-54.

Hertin, J., F. Berkhout, M. Wagner and D. Tyteca (2008) 'Are EMS Environmentally Effective? The Link between Environmental Management Systems and Environmental Performance in European Companies', *Journal of Environmental Planning and Management* 51.2: 255-80.

Herzberg, F., B. Mauser and B.B. Snyderman (1999) *The Motivation to Work* (New Brunswick, NJ: John Wiley).

Hollinshead, G., and M. Leat (1995) *Human Resource Management: An International and Comparative Perspective* (London: Pitman Publishing).

Homburg, C., and M. Bucerius (2006) 'Is Speed of Integration Really a Success Factor of Mergers and Acquisitions? An Analysis of the Role of Internal and External Relatedness', *Strategic Management Journal* 27.4: 347-68.

Inmaculada, M.-T., J.A. Aragón-Correa and R. Llamas-Sánchez (2008) 'The Relationship between High Performance Work Systems and Proactive Environmental Management', in S. Sharma, M. Starik, R. Wüstenhagen and J. Hamschmidt (eds.), *Advances on Research in Corporate Sustainability* (Boston, MA: Edward Elgar): 197-225.

Lamberton, G. (2005) 'Sustainability Accounting: A Brief History and Conceptual Framework', *Accounting Forum* 29.1, 7-26.

Linnanen, L. (1995) 'Market Dynamics and Sustainable Organisations: HRM Implications in the Pulp and Paper Industry's Management of Environmental Issues', *Greener Management International* 10: 85-124.

Maignan, I., and D.A. Ralston (2002) 'Corporate Social Responsibility in Europe and the US: Insights from Businesses' Self-presentations', *Journal of International Business Studies* 33: 497-514.

Mariappanadar, S. (2003) 'Sustainable Human Resource Strategy: The Sustainable and Unsustainable Dilemmas of Retrenchment', *International Journal of Social Economics* 30.8: 906-23.

Mawle, A. (1996) 'Women, Environmental Management and Human Resources Management', in W. Wehrmeyer (ed.), *Greening People: Human Resources and Environmental Management* (Sheffield, UK: Greenleaf Publishing): 199-212.

O'Reilly, N. (1995) 'Marriage Guidance', *Personnel Today*, 18 July 1995: 29-30.

Pichel, K. (2008) 'Enhancing Ecopreneurship through an Environmental Management System: A Longitudinal Analysis of Factors Leading to Proactive Employee Behavior', in S. Sharma, M. Starik, R. Wüstenhagen and J. Hamschmidt (eds.), *Advances on Research in Corporate Sustainability* (Boston, MA: Edward Elgar): 141-96.

PwC (2010) *Corporate Sustainability Barometer* (Frankfurt: PwC).

Ralston, D.A., C.P. Egri, S. Stewart, R.H. Terpstra and Y. Kaicheng (1999) 'Doing Business in the 21st Century with the New Generation of Chinese Managers: A Study of Generational Shifts in Work Values in China', *Journal of International Business Studies* 30: 415-28.

Ramus, C.A., and U. Steger (2000) 'The Roles of Supervisory Support Behaviors and Environmental Policy in Employee 'Ecoinitiatives' at Leading-Edge European Companies', *Academy of Management Journal* 43.4: 605-26.

Rehfeld, K.M., K. Rennings and A. Ziegler (2007) 'Integrated Product Policy and Environmental Product Innovations: An Empirical Analysis', *Ecological Economics* 61.1: 91-100.

Russo, M.V. (2002) 'Institutional Change and Theories of Organizational Strategy: ISO 14001 and Toxic Emissions in the Electronics Industry', paper presented at the *Annual Meeting of the Academy of Management*, Denver, CO, August 2002.

Schafer, J.L., and J.W. Graham (2002) 'Missing Data: Our View of the State of the Art', *Psychological Methods* 7: 147-77.

Schaltegger, S., and R.L. Burritt (2005) 'Corporate Sustainability', in H. Folmer and T. Tietenberg (eds.), *The International Yearbook of Environmental and Resource Economics 2005, 2006* (Cheltenham, UK: Edward Elgar): 185-222.

Schnell, R. (1986) *Missing-Data-Probleme in der empirischen Sozialforschung* (Bochum, Germany: Ruhr University).

Sharma, S. (2001) 'Different Strokes: Regulatory Styles and Environmental Strategy in the North-American Oil and Gas Industry', *Business Strategy and the Environment* 10: 344-64.

Sisson, K. (1994) *Personnel Management: A Comprehensive Guide to Theory and Practice* (Oxford, UK: Blackwell).

Surroca, J., J.A. Tribo and S. Waddock (2010) 'Intangibles, Corporate Responsibility and Financial Performance', *Strategic Management Journal* 31.5: 463-90.

Torrington, D., and L. Hall (1995) *Personnel Management: HRM in Action* (Hemel Hempstead, UK: Prentice Hall International).

Waddock, S.A., and S.B. Graves (1997) 'The Corporate Social Performance: Financial Performance Link', *Strategic Management Journal* 18: 303-19.

Wagner, M. (2007) 'Integration of Environmental Management with other Managerial Functions of the Firm: Empirical Effects on Drivers of Economic Performance', *Long Range Planning* 40.5: 611-28.

Wagner, M. (2009) 'Innovation and Competitive Advantages from the Integration of Strategic Aspects with Social and Environmental Management in European Firms', *Business Strategy and the Environment* 18.5: 291-306.

Wagner, M. (2010) 'Corporate Social Performance and Innovation with High Social Benefits', *Journal of Business Ethics* 94.4: 581-94.

Wagner, M. (2011) 'Environmental Management Activities and Sustainable HRM in German Manufacturing Firms: Incidence, Determinants, and Outcomes', *Zeitschrift für Personalforschung* 25.2: 157-77.

WCED (World Commission on Environment and Development) (1987) *Our Common Future* (Oxford, UK: Oxford University Press).

Wehrmeyer, W. (1995) 'Environmental Management Styles, Corporate Cultures and Change', *Greener Management International* 12: 81-94.

Wehrmeyer, W. (1996a) 'Green Policies Can Help to Bear Fruit', *People Management* 2: 38-40.

Wehrmeyer, W. (1996b) *Greening People: Human Resources and Environmental Management* (Sheffield, UK: Greenleaf Publishing).

Wehrmeyer, W., and K.T. Parker (1995) 'Identification, Analysis and Relevance of Environmental Corporate Cultures', *Business Strategy and the Environment* 4.3: 135-44.

Wernerfelt, B. (1984) 'A Resource-Based View of the Firm', *Strategic Management Journal* 5: 171-80.

Ziegler, A., and K. Rennings (2004) *Determinants of Environmental Innovations in Germany: Do Organizational Measures Matter?* (Mannheim, Germany: ZEW).

Appendix

Table A1 **Descriptive statistics, correlations and multi-collinearity diagnostics for 2001**

Variable	Min.	Max.	Mean	Std Dev.	(1)	(2)	(3)	(4)	(5)	(6)	(7)	(8)	VIF
Environmental management system index (1)	0	10	5.964	3.883	1								–
Worker satisfaction (2)	2	5	3.660	0.576	0.326***	1							1.599
Recruitment and staff retention (3)	1	5	3.400	0.563	0.277***	0.601***	1						1.572
Firm size (4)	0.240	12	6.133	2.557	0.436***	0.199***	0.175***	1					1.170
Quality management system, 2 = yes (5)	1	2	1.750	0.435	0.279***	0.144**	0.073	0.201***	1				1.078
Overall business performance (6)	1	5	2.939	0.486	0.056	0.075	0.059	0.178***	-0.048	1			1.057
Market development trend (7)	1	5	3.485	0.723	0.337***	0.131**	0.090	0.181***	0.126**	0.143**	1		1.095
Firm completely independent, 2 = yes (8)	1	2	1.572	0.573	-0.200***	-0.120**	0.094	0.092*	-0.191***	0.050	0.040	1	1.354

* $p < 0.10$; ** $p < 0.05$; *** $p < 0.01$

Table A2 **Descriptive statistics, correlations and multi-collinearity diagnostics for 2006**

Variable	Min.	Max.	Mean	Std Dev.	(1)	(2)	(3)	(4)	(5)	(6)	(7)	(8)	VIF
Environmental management system index (1)	0	10	7.183	3.091	1								-
Worker satisfaction (2)	1	5	3.618	0.626	0.418***	1							1.690
Recruitment and staff retention (3)	2	5	3.312	0.541	0.362***	0.528**	1						1.940
Firm size (4)	1	13	2.151	0.715	0.457***	0.159*	0.142	1					1.350
Quality management system (5)	1	2	1.834	0.373	0.145*	0.111	0.035	0.137*	1				1.190
Overall business performance (6)	1	5	1.957	0.853	-0.148*	-0.021	-0.122	-0.374*	-0.135	1			1.250
Market development trend (7)	1	5	3.373	1.007	0.018	0.079	0.010	0.071	0.184**	0.117	1		1.120
Firm completely independent (8)	1	2	1.531	0.497	0.060	0.123	0.145*	0.050	0.131*	0.007	-0.163	1	1.100

* p < 0.10; ** p < 0.05; *** p < 0.01

Section III
EIS in mature industries

6

The role of government in shifting firm innovation focus in the automobile industry[1]

Preeta M. Banerjee and Micaela Preskill
Brandeis University, USA

Innovation management literature has found that government policy can significantly affect, both directly and indirectly, the innovative activity of profit-maximising firms (Jaffe *et al.* 2002). This 'sixth force' of government policy affects the primary five forces of business strategy: threat of new entrants, threat of substitute products or services, bargaining power of suppliers, bargaining power of buyers, and rivalry among existing competitors (Porter 1979; Porter and van der Linde 1995). For example, Johnstone *et al.* (2008) found that different types of environmental policy instrument had a significant positive direct effect on patent counts for new sources of renewable energy. In another example, Finkelstein (2004) showed that policies designed to increase the usage of pre-existing vaccines induced a 2.5-fold increase in clinical trials for new vaccines.

Firms generally respond to government policy in ways that can promote innovation, resource productivity and competitiveness (Porter and van der Linde 1995). While government regulation has been found to directly and indirectly affect innovative activity of firms, there is a lack of understanding of the process whereby policy shifts impact a firm's innovation focus. Shift in innovation focus can be brought about by either changes in the incentives for the supplier (technology-push) or changes in the incentives for the buyer (demand-pull) (Walsh 1984). On the one hand, inventive and innovative activity can itself increase demand and 'push' technology to the market, owing to the multiplier and accelerator effects associated with the launching of innovations (Schmookler 1966). On the other hand, in the

1 The authors would like to thank Christin Lee for her work in putting this manuscript together.

end market, consumers usually 'pull' the goods or information they demand for their needs (Schmookler 1966). In other words, necessity is the mother of invention or, vice versa, invention can be the mother of necessity (Diamond 1999). In fact, 'technology-push' and 'demand-pull' effects might be conceived of as complementary forces rather than mutually exclusive (Mowery and Rosenberg 1979). Moreover, both effects operate in a complex landscape of social and cultural forces.

In this chapter, using qualitative methods (ten in-depth, open-ended interviews), we examine the role of the US federal government in the shift of innovation focus of Toyota and Lexus to hybrid cars: the Lexus RX 400h and the Toyota Prius. The paper is organised as follows. Using the two cases, we present our findings by moving through each of six stages in automobile product development. We ascertain the impact of two federal government initiatives: the Partnership for New Generation of Vehicles (PNGV) established by the Clinton Administration in 1993 to improve fuel economy and the Alternative Motor Vehicle Tax Credit enacted by the 2005 Energy Policy Act.

By investigating the effect, if any, of government policy on shifting innovation, we contribute to theoretical and managerial insight on the potential usefulness of particular environmentally sustainable policies in spurring innovation, especially in solving concerns about the environment. We find that in the automobile industry, while competitive factors perhaps play a significant and sustained role, the PNGV and the tax credit do have an impact in jump-starting innovation and increasing overall demand of hybrid vehicles, respectively.

Theory

Understanding demand-pull and technology-push

Innovation occurs in the context of knowledge, consumer demand and in some cases, government support. Pinpointing the forces that spur innovation has been a continuing topic of discussion. There are two presiding theories, 'demand-pull' and 'technology-push', which take origin in the work of Jacob Schmookler and Joseph Schumpeter. Schmookler is best known for believing that scientific developments depend decisively on demand whereas Schumpeter argues against a single factor cause of innovation. He credits economic development to innovative ability and the introduction of new production methods (Schmookler 1966; Antonelli and De Liso 1997). 'Demand-pull', which recognises consumer demand as the main stimulus for advances in technology, was consistently supported by empirical data in the late 1960s and early 1970s (Walsh 1984). In 1979, Mowery and Rosenberg critically reviewed and invalidated these studies, none of which was statistically significant. They argued that the real force behind innovation is a combination of both demand and supply side influences (Mowery and Rosenberg 1979). In fact, useful innovation theory incorporates the ideology of both Schmookler and Schumpeter.

According to Nelson and Winter (1977), a useful theory of innovation must take into account the need for innovation at both levels.

Furthermore, a firm's decisions, especially innovation decisions, cannot be properly understood without viewing a firm in the context of social and cultural forces (Peng *et al.* 2005). Peng and his co-authors sought to answer the question: 'What determines the scope of the firm?' They found that the scope of the firm is caused by the firm's institutional relatedness. Institutional relatedness is the extent to which a firm's activities are influenced by non-market institutional factors such as social, political and reputational capital. Political capital, in this context, is defined as political connections and support from government agencies. The triple helix model (Leydesdorff and Etzkowitz 1998; Leydesdorff 2000; Etzkowitz 2003) similarly recognises the importance of government involvement; it models innovation as an outcome of interaction among three important institutional factors: the government, the firm and the university. The synergy between the university, industry and government emerges from a laissez-faire situation, with industry, academia and government working both separately and interactively (Etzkowitz 2003). Industry is the driving force, the university is the provider of basic research and trained persons, and the government regulates and in some cases buys products for its own use. Each entity often takes on the role of the other while maintaining its distinct identity.

There is a need for continued research on government involvement in firm innovation, especially when such innovations have positive externalities. Though the Academy of Management was founded 45 years ago to serve the public interest, recent studies have found that scholarship that addresses a company's social performance is very rare (Walsh *et al.* 2003). As a result, it is increasingly important to combine discussion on firm technology innovation with social concerns for managerial success. For example, Jaffe *et al.* (2004) discuss how innovation and the diffusion of new technologies are associated with market failures because they do not fully take into account negative externalities, such as environmental pollution.

Given the importance of addressing social concerns for managerial success, and the role of government in innovation policy, it is imperative that we examine whether government can instigate a shift in innovation focus by corporations to environment-friendly, innovative versions of existing or new products.

Shifts in innovation focus: the role of the US Federal Government

Research acknowledges innovation as a situated process (Tyre and von Hippel 1997), whereby innovators are myopically focused on a solution given the context. Therefore, engineers and scientists involved in innovation need to change their given context in order to shift the firm's innovation focus. Can government create this change in context through policy?

Government is a potential 'sixth force' that affects the primary five forces of business strategy (Porter 1979; Porter and van der Linde 1995). This sixth force has been found to impact innovation both directly and indirectly. Yin (2008, 2009) found that the Orphan Drug Act (ODA), which was designed to spur development in the treatment of rare diseases, mostly encouraged innovation for ODA-qualifying subdivisions of non-rare diseases, which deviated from the primary goals of the legislation. Furthermore, Acemoglu and Finkelstein (2008) found that the Medicare Prospective Payment System (PPS) encouraged the adoption of a wide range of new medical technologies. Popp (2003) found that the Clean Air Act of 1990, which instituted a market for sulphur dioxide (SO_2) permits, enhanced the efficiency of 'scrubbers', or flue gas desulphurisation units. Jaffe and Palmer (1997) concluded that environmental compliance standards increased R&D spending at the firm level, but did not necessarily induce inventive output directly in the form of successful patent applications.

On the one hand, government policy might create incentives for inventive and innovative activity, which itself can increase demand ('technology-push'), owing to the multiplier and accelerator effects associated with the launching of innovations (Mowery and Rosenberg 1979). In this case, the shift in innovation starts with the technology and then is matched to needs. On the other hand, government policy might create incentives for the end market. In this case, consumers 'pull' the goods or information they demand for their needs (Schmookler 1966). The firm would be focused on consumer needs discovery, then would tailor research and development to matching a solution to meet the needs discovered. Looking at both economic forces simultaneously, government can pass policy that creates the necessity that is the mother of invention; and government can also pass policy that creates favourable circumstances so that invention is the mother of necessity. Moreover, both effects operate in a complex landscape of social and cultural forces.

Methodology

Sample

The automobile industry has been the subject of many studies of innovation, starting with Abernathy's (1978) seminal study of productivity roadblocks. More recently, Clark et al. (1987) study the introduction of new products to the marketplace and find the most important factors to international competitiveness are found in process innovations that reduce lead time and maximise productivity of engineering hours. In fact, as Rao (1994) determines, during 1895 to 1912, special-purpose product rating agencies were absent for the automobile industry, and reliability and speed contests served as credentialling devices. Thus, reliability and speed were product development drivers as opposed to other aspects of innovation, including environmental concerns. Automobile companies such as GM have more recently recognised that more innovative products are necessary to grow market share around the world. The ultimate goal of investing in R&D was to boost the percentage of truly innovative products from single-digit percentages in the 1990s to over 50% for 2000–2004 (Howell 2000). This phenomenon is interesting and important to understand as government might play a significant role in shifting innovation focus. Thus, similarly to Abernathy's study, we move through the life-cycle of automobile production to understand how a shift in innovation focus arose in the case of hybrid cars. Unlike Abernathy (1978), we focus on innovation enablers as opposed to roadblocks.

Data collection

The research method is based on grounded theory (Glaser and Strauss 1967; Glaser 1998) using interviews conducted through a snowball sampling method (see Table 6.1; Biernacki and Waldorf 1981). Each interview is treated as a 'case' (Eisenhardt 1989) where the process is inductive and emergent. Validity in its traditional sense is not an issue, which instead is judged by fit, relevance, workability and modifiability (Glaser and Strauss 1967; Glaser 1998). Interview data is triangulated using an in-depth literature review on the hybrid vehicle product development cycle and with popular press and marketing literature. Since there are multiple stages in technology development, especially in hybrid car development, we examine governmental interplay in each of six broad stages (roughly following the stage gate process developed by Cooper (1990) as shown in Fig. 6.1): idea generation (identifying a breakthrough in science or a user need); idea screening (research and selection of product concept); development (establishing product specifications and design); testing (effective prototyping and ensuring quality); commercialisation (manufacturing and bringing a product to market); and adoption and diffusion (product acceptance by the market).

Figure 6.1 **Stage gate process**

Source: based on Cooper 1990

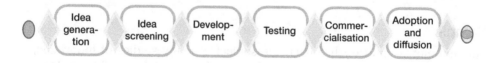

While the supply for hybrid vehicles is considerable and manufacturers have introduced several models, our findings focus on two hybrids in particular: the Toyota Prius and the Lexus RX 400h. These two cars were chosen because they provide glimpses into different aspects of the market for hybrid cars. Because the Prius was one of the first on the market, it had an established history before the tax credits came into effect. It also has been the most successful hybrid in the world and it was unclear whether tax credits had something to do with the car's success. We chose the Lexus RX 400h because it appeals to a different consumer base, the luxury consumer base. Lexus is the luxury vehicle division of Japanese automaker Toyota Motor Corporation. The development process for the vehicles did not occur simultaneously. The Prius idea generation stage began in the early 1990s, the car went on the market in Japan in 1997 and then in the US in 2000. The idea generation stage for the Lexus RX 400h began around 2000; the car went on the market in the US in late 2005. Both cars originated in the Japanese market, which provides interesting findings regarding the interplay of non-US government policies on products that ultimately find a large US consumer demand.

Table 6.1 **Interviews as chronologically conducted**

#	Name	Title	Location
1	Victoria	Manager of Clean Vehicle Program	DOE San Francisco
2	Larry	Sales manager	Longo Toyota Dealership, Los Angeles
3	Emily	Sales consultant	Lexus of Watertown Dealership
4	Bob	Alternative fuel vehicles adviser	Environmental Protection Agency
5	Nadia	Lexus public relations manager	Toyota Motor Sales Co.
6	Ellen	CPA	Gregory, Fillas & Associates LLP, Pasadena, CA
7	Jeff	Policy analyst	Sierra Club
8	Peter	Senior policy manager	Environmental Protection Agency
9	George	Toyota public relations manager	Toyota Motor Sales

Note: names are coded to protect anonymity

Findings

Idea generation

While hybrid vehicles have only been on the US market since 2000, environmental issues regarding automobile greenhouse gas emissions have been considered in determining government policy for decades. Understanding the political history leading up to the idea generation of the Prius and Lexus RX 400h is essential in understanding the political climate at the time. In the years before the Clinton administration (1993–2001), the United States government took the 'free market' approach in dealing with energy and environmental issues. It was believed, by the administration, that high oil prices would provide sufficient encouragement in the innovation and utilisation of alternative energy sources (Lazzari 2008). However, low oil prices between 1986 and 1999 encouraged gas consumption and led to the popularity of huge, gas-guzzling automobiles, such as SUVs.

In this context, California has consistently been a leader in enacting environmentally sustainable policy and, in the early 1990s, was an exception to the free market mentality that was dominant in Washington, DC. In 1990, California adopted the ZEV (zero emission vehicle) mandate, which aimed to make 10% of all vehicles marketed in California battery-electric vehicles by 2003. The initiative failed; Victoria at the San Francisco Department of Energy blamed the automakers. 'Automakers cry wolf every time you ask them to do anything', she said. 'Anytime there was any government mandate at any level they would claim it would increase car prices too much, and so every year the regulation was watered down'. The mandate was the first of its kind. It was one of the first government attempts in the United States to alter the types of vehicle on the road. Bob, adviser to the Environmental Protection Agency expressed the importance of keeping an eye on California: 'Whatever California does, other states do, and then often times it becomes federal policy'.

Even before fuel-efficient cars were on the market, there was public interest, at least in California. In 1992, a study by Southern California Edison found that nearly 67% of Californians would buy an electric vehicle that had a price comparable to a gas-powered vehicle (Anderson and Anderson 2005). Similarly, by 2000, Sierra Club had 550,000 members, a fair representation of how the environment was becoming an issue that people cared about (Mertig *et al.* 2000).

Toyota began the development of the Prius in the mid-1990s when both the US and Japanese governments were supporting the advance of vehicle technology and fuel economy. In the United States, the Clinton administration facilitated the development of American-brand diesel concept vehicles. The Partnership for New Generation of Vehicles (PNGV) was established in 1993 to create new vehicles with impressive fuel economy. It involved eight federal agencies, the national laboratories, universities and the US Council for Automotive Research. By 2000 the GM Precept, Ford Prodigy and the Chrysler ESX-3 were wheeled out onto the showroom floor; each vehicle achieved at least 72 mpg (Kolbert 2007). Japanese automakers, to their disappointment, were not included in the project and saw United States automobile companies as an emerging threat. Toyota Motor Corporation immediately felt pressure to jump-start internal R&D efforts.

Additionally, the California ZEV mandate prompted activity by the Japanese government. Japan saw this mandate as forecasting the United States' developing a position as a sustainability leader and felt a desire to remain on a similar track. Several Japanese environmental agencies were pushing for the development of environmentally sustainable vehicle technology, but support focused on battery-powered electric vehicles. MITI, Japan's Ministry of International Trade and Industry established a basic market expansion plan for battery-powered electric vehicles (BPEVs) as early as 1976. In 1991, the goal was to have 200,000 BPEVs on the road by the 2000 (Ahman 2006). MITI created an R&D consortium with only limited public funding. While the programme, which lasted 19 years, did not achieve the diffusion of BPEVs into the industry, it did foster automobile manufacturers' interest and R&D in the field of fuel-efficient vehicles.

For 20 years Toyota had considered placing a traditional gasoline motor alongside an electric one. Japanese government support provided encouragement for the project and the threat of the US leading the market stressed how important it was to jump-start this development. Toyota had been known as a 'fast follower' because it joined the auto industry around 30 years behind Ford and GM. In this case, Toyota felt pressure to follow in the footsteps left by PNGV (Taylor 2006).

In late 1993, the Toyota Motor Corporation Board started on the project that would lead to the development of the Prius. Initially, it was not a guarantee that the new vehicle would be a hybrid. Yoshiro Kimbara, then executive VP of R&D, wanted the new technology to improve efficiency by 150% over existing cars such as the Corolla (Morgan and Liker 2006). By the time a group of 1,000 employees were organised in 1997 to work on the project, management believed that the future of Toyota largely depended on the success of this particular project (Nonaka and Peltokorpi 2009). Takeshi Uchiyamada, the engineer assigned to the project, aimed not only to revolutionise fuel economy, but also to develop a new production method for Toyota vehicles (Taylor 2006).

The idea generation process of the Lexus occurred many years later. Lexus had quick success as a luxury brand for two reasons. First of all, Lexus prices were low relative to Mercedes and BMW. Second, the company used focus groups to make sure it was meeting the needs of its consumers (Avila and Isabel 2008). The Lexus RX series—the first luxury SUV—came to market in the 1990s and was the first of any Lexus vehicle to sell 100,000 cars (Dawson 2005). With the help of focus groups, Lexus found that consumers were looking for even more from the RX series—they wanted more power. In order to achieve more power, Lexus engineers embraced hybrid technology, but not for its environmental benefits. Lexus Public Relations Manager, Nadia, explains that 'luxury buyers saw hybrid technology as an opportunity for more power and Lexus engineers looked at our line-up and saw the 330 as an opportunity for reconfiguration'.

There was significant lag time between the development processes of the two vehicles because it took Lexus some time to integrate hybrid technology in their automobile line-up. According to Nadia, Lexus did not consider incorporating the hybrid technology until it became successful and well known, which occurred in 2004 when the second generation of the Prius was introduced. When the technology became popular, Lexus customers asked for it in Lexus vehicles, and this is what pushed Lexus to integrate the technology.

When the RX 400h was in its idea generation stage, George W. Bush had just been elected to office. From the very beginning, President Bush's policy encouraged increased production rather than reduced consumption. This was made especially evident by his choice of the former CEO of Halliburton to lead the newly formed Energy Policy Development Group (Hybrid Cars 2006). Thus, at this point it was not obvious that the Bush policy would support either environmentally sustainable policy or the facilitation of hybrid car development.

Idea screening

Idea screening is fundamental in vetting all production concepts prior to devoting resources to them. During this stage, Toyota and Lexus finalised technology choices and defined their target audience. Soon after Toyota generated the idea of the Prius, project managers set a new goal for the vehicle: 100% increase in fuel efficiency (Magnusson *et al.* 2003). In November 1994, it was decided the vehicle would be a hybrid, because the technology was already being developed by Toyota for use in another vehicle (Morgan and Liker 2006). Other technologies were available but none was thought to be practical. Battery electric vehicles could not compete commercially with the internal combustion engine (Chau and Wong 2002) and fuel cell technology required more R&D effort than was practical for a project under time constraint (Demirdoven and Deutch 2004).

An instrumental aspect of idea screening is making sure that a market exists for the new technology. Toyota predicted that there would be a strong market for the Prius. The vehicle not only saved on gas, but it also saved time at the pump and provided consumers with a role in addressing and taking a stand on environmental issues. However, as Larry, a sales manager, described: 'fuel efficient cars were not of interest to consumers until gas prices went up'. Studies have shown that Larry's insight was correct. A series of surveys recorded by Santini *et al.* (2000) found that the fraction of respondents who placed fuel economy as a priority dropped from 0.42 to 0.04 between 1980 and 1998—coinciding with a decrease in the price of gas. Santini *et al.* (2000) also found that nearly all consumers compromised performance for fuel economy when gas prices spiked between 1978 and 1981. Likewise, a 1999 survey found that consumers who drive SUVs do not consider fuel consumption to be important (Agras and Chapman 1999). It also found that households with incomes less than US$35,000 are almost twice as likely to prioritise fuel economy. Santini *et al.* (2000) concluded that integrating hybrid technology in a small car is advisable because those who purchased small cars are already price conscious and conscious of fuel economy.

While there were no substantial developments in environmentally sustainable policy during the Prius idea screening stage, there was discussion over the Corporate Average Fuel Economy (CAFE) standards. These standards, set in place as early as 1975, demonstrated the work of forward-looking policy thinkers. Like the ZEV mandate in California, however, auto manufacturers fought endlessly to lower the standards. As a further effort to stall any state or federal regulation, Ford, Chrysler and Toyota announced on 4 February 1998 that they would produce cars in model year 1999 with engine and catalytic converter technologies that would achieve lower emissions (Bamberger 2002).

It was expected that Lexus consumers would buy a hybrid for entirely different reasons from those of the average Prius customer. The fundamental difference between Toyota and Lexus consumers was that Lexus consumers were not as price-conscious. Emily, a sales consultant, mentioned:

> Someone looking at a Prius would not consider an RX 400h because it is an entirely different clientele. Someone who wants to roll around in a nice car and say 'I care about the environment' but who doesn't care about gas mileage is the type of person the RX 400h is aimed for.

Lexus was confident that the demand for a luxury SUV hybrid vehicle existed, because customer feedback had led them to believe that people were looking for a luxury SUV with more power.

During this time in the Lexus RX 400h production process, there was some activity in the Bush administration. In 2001, the CEO of US Chamber of Commerce, Tom Donohue (2001), advocated investing in energy infrastructure, but also articulated the importance of increased conservation and the development of 'feasible alternative and renewable sources of energy'. On 17 May 2001, Bush released an energy strategy for his administration. While it met outrage from environmental groups for many reasons, it did call for US$10 billion over 10 years for tax incentives including hybrid vehicle purchases (CNN 2001).

Development

Technology is perfected and finalised during the development stage of the production process. The Toyota Motor Corporation made the hybrid car a reality with the development of the Toyota Hybrid System. This technology is also used in the Lexus SUV hybrid. Even though the hybrid system appeared in a Lexus SUV many years later, the technology development for both vehicles occurred at the same time.

In order to develop the system, Toyota created various task forces formed around specific responsibilities. Vehicle prototypes were tested regularly in order to solve some of the biggest issues (Magnusson *et al.* 2003). The battery technology, for example, was a persistent obstacle. Toyota manufacturers partnered with Panasonic EV Energy Co. in order to develop the battery that would be used. It needed to have the electric potential of 200–300 volts, which led engineers to use NiMH (nickel magnesium hydride) cell batteries (Gutmann 1999). By the time the car was released on the showroom floor in the US the technology had been developed and perfected for nine years (Rego *et al.* 2007).

The rechargeable engine is the heart of the hybrid car technology. Prior to the Toyota Hybrid System, there were two ways to build a hybrid system. A series hybrid is a traditional vehicle with an electric engine alongside the internal combustion engine. A parallel hybrid system, as its name implies, allows both the electric motor and internal combustion engine to deliver power in parallel. The Prius uses a series-parallel hybrid system which incorporates features of both the series and parallel system. When the car is turned on, only the electric engine starts. During acceleration, the two sources of power work together. Then, during normal driving, the electric motor turns off and the engine takes over. During deceleration, the electric motor charges the battery via the power converter; it can continue to charge even when the vehicle is at a standstill (Chau and Wong 2002). The Toyota Hybrid System requires two electric motors so the front and rear wheel axles can be driven separately. The smaller motor starts and controls the spin rate of the internal combustion engine. The larger of the two is connected to wheels and thus has the capability to power the car (Davies 2001).

Even the internal combustion engine in the Toyota Hybrid System is adjusted to achieve the highest level of efficiency possible. The Prius's engine uses the Atkinson cycle, which increases efficiency but at the expense of power. It reduces pumping loss by shortening the compression stroke of the engine's piston relative to the power stroke, resulting in an engine that is 12–14% more efficient (Toyota USA Newsroom 2008). The electric motors make up for the less powerful internal combustion engine and achieve overall fuel efficiency.

The Lexus RX 400h uses the traditional Otto cycle engine which is not as fuel efficient. Unlike in the Prius, the RX 400h electric motor functions solely as a supplementary source of power. The Lexus RX 400h is therefore able to achieve 268 horsepower owing to the power of the supplementary electric motor (Strongman 2006). When hybrid technology was introduced to the Lexus SUV, Toyota began referring to the system as Hybrid Synergy Drive instead of the Toyota Hybrid System.

Additionally, before the 2000 Lexus RX model that was built to debut on the US market, Toyota made the battery pack much smaller. Before the third generation was released in 2003, the hybrid system was tweaked to increase its power output; control electronics were able to boost the system to create 500 watts of power (The Clean Green Car Company 2003). When the RX 400h was built in 2004 it was able to adopt the most advanced version of the Hybrid Synergy Drive.

There were advantages in incorporating hybrid technology into a popular SUV model. The shape of the SUV provided more space for the hybrid batteries. There were disadvantages to the design as well; even with hybrid technology, the car lacked impressive fuel efficiency. When asked if Lexus would do anything differently if it could start all over again with the RX 400h, public relations manager Nadia replied, 'We wouldn't do anything differently because we were responding to what the customers wanted at that time. Our customers told us to give them something more powerful. They didn't care about the cost of fuel'.

Testing

The Prius and RX 400h had to be tested extensively for fuel efficiency and safety (Graham 2001). In 1999, the US Department of Energy conducted testing of the Prius at Argonne National Laboratory and the National Renewable Energy Laboratory. It reported that the Prius has an acceleration time of 14.1 seconds and city fuel consumption of 43 mpg. In 2001, another report published by the Argonne National Laboratory reported on the Prius, comparing it with other concept vehicles, Honda Insight, Ford Prodigy, DC ESX3 and the GM Precept. Of the five vehicles, the Prius had the worst CAFE mpg, best 0–60 time, heaviest kerb weight and one of the largest engines. The Argonne National Laboratory evaluation disabled all hybrid features of the vehicles in order to pinpoint the origin of fuel economy gains. It was found that fuel economy gains for the Prius were divided into several categories: 9% was due to load reduction measures, such as the Prius's aerodynamic model which decreased air and tyre resistance; 18% of the vehicle's fuel economy gain was due to the use of the Atkinson cycle engine and CVT transmissions; and the remaining 19% was due to the vehicle's hybridisation (Graham 2001).

A similar analysis was carried out by the journal *Transportation Research* in which the Prius was compared with the Toyota Corolla. Relative to the baseline Corolla, the Prius achieved 80.6% increase in fuel economy in the city and 20.7% increase on the highway. The evaluation found that with gas prices at US$1.5/gallon, a Prius would save US$1,364 in fuel. But the Prius was priced at US$19,995, US$3,495 more than the Corolla (Lave and MacLean 2002).

The Prius went onto the market in Japan in 1997, three years earlier than it did in the United States. These years served as a testing period so that any necessary changes could be made before releasing the vehicle in the US; 3,000 cars were sold before the end of 1997 and almost 18,000 were sold in 1998 in Japan (Toyota USA Newsroom 2008). Before it debuted in the states in 2000, potential buyers in Orange County, California, were allowed to test drive model vehicles and give their opinion on the vehicle. Feedback was not good. People didn't like the feel of the brakes, thought the interior looked cheap, thought the arm rests were too low, and didn't like the fact that the rear seats couldn't fold down (Taylor 2006). This response, in addition to Toyota's already existing concern that the car would not be successful in the US, worried Toyota. The necessary changes were made; most notably, the battery pack was made smaller so the vehicle had enough space for the seats to fold down (The Clean Green Car Company 2003). Even with these changes in place, the car did not impress consumers right away. Larry saw the Prius before it was on the market because he worked at a Toyota Dealership. His first impression was that he 'didn't think it would do too well because it wasn't anything special to look at'.

Similarly, the Lexus RX 400h received critical attention even before it hit the showroom floor. The government rated the RX 400h at 31 mpg in city driving and 27 mpg on the highways (Job 2005). Some experts thought this was not enough for a hybrid, a car that was supposed to be marketed for conservation and improved fuel economy (Sabatini 2005).

Commercialisation

Prior to the 2005 Energy Policy Act

The Prius launched on 1 July 2000. In its first month on the market (with pre-orders), it sold 841,000 cars. Sales in the beginning of the Prius's career were actually higher than Toyota had hoped for (Taylor 2006). Over 5,500 cars were sold between July and September. In 2001, 15,556 cars were sold throughout the year. Sales steadily increased from year to year; in 2002, 20,119 were sold and in 2003, 53,009 were sold. George, a Toyota public relations manager, said, 'the initial powertrain appealed to early adopters of new technology—the kind of people who like to have the hottest new gadgets. And also those that were highly in tune with the environment'. Nadia said the early Lexus buyers were 'people who didn't want to compromise'.

High gas prices provided an incentive for consumers to buy fuel-efficient vehicles such as the Prius. This incentive did not exist when the Prius first came on the market because gas prices were low. In July 2000, gas prices fluctuated between 144 and 160 cents per gallon. Prices were consistent until the end of 2001 when the price of gas dropped to just slightly over 100 cents per gallon. In 2002, the weekly high occurred in October at 144.3 cents a gallon (Energy Information Administration 2009).

The first brochure the Department of Energy (2011) published was a 'Technology Snapshot featuring the Toyota Prius'. It outlined the Prius's innovative features including regenerative breaking, better fuel efficiency, lower emissions, and a sleek, aerodynamic streamlined exterior. It was most important for this brochure to emphasise that the 2001 Prius didn't sacrifice quality for fuel efficiency; it published some DOE testing results at the Argonne Laboratory which confirmed the Prius's 'picture-perfect performance'. Relative to the 2001 Camry and Corolla, the Prius shone in fuel economy, emissions and braking 60–0 mph distance. It had relatively comparable acceleration and passenger volume as reported by the Office of Energy Efficiency and Renewable Energy (Davis *et al.* 2010).

Soon after the commercialisation of the Prius, state governments began to encourage the technology. As of 2002, Arizona (started in 1999), Maryland and Oregon (expanded in the 1980s) adopted tax incentives that rewarded the purchase of energy-efficient vehicles (Brown *et al.* 2002). This contributed to a three-month back order of Prius models within Maryland. The promise of federal tax credits began during Prius commercialisation as Bush was just beginning his presidency at the time when the Prius first came onto the market. In May 2001, Bush proposed new tax incentives to encourage energy conservation, including assistance for people who buy fuel-efficient cars. He sought to distinguish between the traditional notions of conservation and urged the use of technology to make efficiency less of a compromise. While the White House did not specify the value of the tax credits, the President's words were incredibly promising (Dao 2001).

Meanwhile, the Lexus RX 400h came onto the market in mid-2005 and was immediately thought to be a success. Lexus reported more pre-launch orders for the 400h than any other vehicle in Lexus history (Llanos 2004). The *Los Angeles Daily News* reported that company officials predict 'most buyers to be women, with median age of buyers likely to be 45 to 55. Three-quarters will be married, and three-quarters will have a college education. Median household income is expected to be from $150,000 to $200,000' (Job 2005).

Post the 2005 Energy Policy Act

Serendipitously, in the same year as the Lexus RX 400h's release, the 2005 Energy Policy Act was passed—the first energy policy since 1992. According to Hymel (2006), the 2005 Energy Policy Act (summarised at GovTrack.us 2005) gave financial incentives for increased energy production, reduced the regulation of power companies and encouraged but did not require more conservation. Overall considered a Republican win, one Democratic proposal that did make it into the bill was a tax credit to subsidise the purchase of hybrid vehicles, the Alternative Motor Vehicle Credit.

The Lexus RX 400h was eligible for the Alternative Motor Vehicle Credit. When the Lexus came on the market, gas prices were starting to spike and the Prius was finally becoming popular. Hybrid became synonymous with being environmentally sustainable and fuel-efficient. Even though RX 400h didn't really fit this definition with fuel consumption at a maximum of 27 miles per gallon, consumers could still capitalise on the tax credit. Did tax incentives affect Lexus RX 400h sales?

Ellen, a tax accountant in Los Angeles, commented on the effectiveness of tax credits. 'Most of the time, they are [effective], except they are usually limited because higher income people can't get them. They have no benefit whatsoever for people who are in the alternative minimum tax'. Lexus customers generally have higher incomes and are likely to not be eligible for the tax credits. Ellen did add, however, that 'they can be effective in that people go out thinking they will get credit, but when they come in and hear they aren't eligible they get really upset'. At least at that point, they have already bought the car. Nadia affirmed this conclusion: 'Those tax breaks didn't affect a lot of luxury consumers because anyone who was paying AMT didn't qualify'. But Emily, a sales consultant at Lexus of Watertown said the credits helped 'people realise that if the government was willing to give you money to save the environment, then it must be something worthwhile to do'.

Lexus consumers could benefit from other incentives offered to hybrid car drivers at the state level, such as access to HOV (high-occupancy vehicle) lanes and parking privileges. Nadia added, 'If you have ever driven on an LA freeway, you understand the appeal of driving in the carpool lane'. This privilege was given to hybrid car drivers, regardless of the number of people in the car. In 2005, District of Columbia exempted owners of hybrids from excise tax. Slowly, more and more states joined the trend.

The Internal Revenue Service (2006), under the United States Department of Treasury, issued reports that outlined which vehicles were eligible for credits and the amount of the credit. Consumers of the Lexus RX 400h were eligible for credits until 30 September 2006 for the amount of US$2,200. While this occurred long after the Prius had been on the market, it was included as well. The phase out date was the same for the Toyota Prius because the two cars shared the same manufacturer, but the Prius was eligible for a higher credit of US$3,150. After 30 September, the credits decreased to US$2,575 for the Prius and US$1,100 for the Lexus RX 400h. After April 2007, credits were US$787.50 for the Prius and US$550 for the Lexus. The IRS published all these dates and numbers after the credits were first introduced.

Adoption and diffusion

In October 2003, the 2004-second generation Prius came onto the US market. At this point, 53,009 classic Prius had been sold since its launch in 2000. Between October and December, 13,694 2004 Prius were sold. By the end of 2005, 228,591

Prius were sold, putting the car well on its way to mainstream success. It was easy to get people to buy the new Prius, especially people who had already bought the older version. Motor Trend named the 2004 Prius the Car of the Year (Motor Trend 2003). Larry explained 'Prius customers are more loyal than the customers for any other Toyota vehicle'.

When the new Prius model came onto the market, perception of the hybrid car evolved, especially when Hollywood joined the craze. The list of Hollywood's hybrid car owners is extensive: Cameron Diaz, Leonardo DiCaprio, Carole King, Billy Joel, David Duchovny and Bill Maher. Larry David became a behind-the-scenes advocate; he bought three, including one he could drive on his HBO series, 'Curb Your Enthusiasm' (*Washington Post* 2002).

Also in 2004, gas prices increased significantly, reaching over US$2 per gallon for the first time in May, then again in March 2005. After March, prices remained over US$2, reaching US$3 per gallon in September. In 2006, prices never dropped below US$2.20 and remained close to US$3 a gallon for much of the year through the end of 2007. In June 2008, gas prices were above US$4 for the first time but dropped below US$2 by the end of the year (Energy Information Administration 2009).

In the case of the Lexus RX 400h, sales dropped as gas prices rose (Energy Information Administration 2009). As hybrid technology became more popular, consumers realised that the Lexus RX 400h didn't offer the same advantages of a more fuel-efficient hybrid. Its success suffered as a result. In April 2005, 2,345 vehicles were sold but November and October 2005 were the car's least successful months of the year, coinciding with the year's highest gas prices (MRV 2006; Energy Information Administration 2009). As 2007 closed, Lexus RX 400h sales continued to drop. At this time, gas prices were close to US$3 per gallon. Sales for the vehicle were higher at the end of 2006 when gas prices were consistently lower.

For all Toyota brand hybrid cars, the Alternative Motor Vehicle Tax Credit took effect on 1 January 2006. Prius sales in January 2006 reached 7, 654, more than 2,000 higher than the year before when Toyota sold 5,566 during the same month. The year before that, Toyota sold 2,925 Prius in the same month. Thus, while sales did increase with the onset of the tax credit, they did not increase any more than the car's upward trend in sales would have predicted. In March 2006, Toyota stopped releasing monthly sales data, but we do know that by the end of 2006, 109,000 Prius had been sold in all of North America. After 1 October 2007 consumers received no credit. Sales continued to increase even as the tax credits began to phase out. In 2007, 183,000 Prius were sold in North America (Toyota News Release 2008). In May 2008, Prius sales were up 23% relative to the same time the year before (Ohnsman 2008). The Alternative Motor Vehicle Tax Credits certainly inspired some people to get to the dealership and purchase a Prius. Larry at the Toyota dealership thinks the tax credits were the first part of the Prius's success. Of course it also coincided with a new model on the market and an increase in gas prices.

Because Prius sales didn't drop after the tax credits were phased out, it is hard to be certain of the effects the credits had on the success of the vehicle. George explained: 'the tax credits certainly enhanced sales, but to what degree is a good question. When you look at sales after the tax credits ran out you see that they weren't at all inhibited by the end of the credits'. Jeff, a policy analyst, agreed: 'tax credits help to make higher utility seem more acceptable. We at Sierra Club were trying to improve the image and profile of hybrids. Any kind of advantage you give to hybrids helps to increase the image of the vehicles'.

States all over the country began to adopt similar incentives. By 2009, 49 out of 50 states had some sort of policy, whether at the state or local level, that provided incentives for hybrid car consumption and ownership (Hybrid Cars 2009). As of December 2008, California authorised limited alternative fuel models to be eligible to apply for a sticker that would be valid until 2011 and allow single-occupant use of HOV lanes. Of the vehicles authorised, the Honda Insight, Honda Civic Hybrid and Toyota Prius were the only hybrids eligible.

In March 2009, Toyota and Lexus hybrids sold their one-millionth car in the US. Seventy-five per cent of all hybrid vehicle sales in the US have been the Toyota brand (The Auto Channel 2009). Toyota's hybrid car success developed after the 2004 Prius achieved mainstream attention, encouraging hybrid reconfiguration in existing vehicles. The Lexus RX 400h came out in April 2005, followed by the Toyota Highlander SUV, the Camry hybrid, Corolla hybrid and more. The one million mark for Toyota Motor Sales establishes that the market for hybrid vehicles had become an emerging force.

2010 marked an exciting year for Toyota hybrids. Both the Prius and Lexus RX 400h had new model versions coming to the market: the third generation Prius and the second generation RX 400h. In its physical appearance, there are subtle differences in the new 450h relative to the 400h. In response to customer need, the new Lexus will be built with fuel economy in mind unlike its original version. In fact, the Atkinson cycle gasoline engine, one of the reasons why the Prius runs so efficiently, will be integrated in the new Lexus, contributing to its superior fuel-efficiency. A *New York Times* article in June 2009 said the Lexus 450h is 'the first Lexus hybrid that lives up to the hype and puts up big numbers'. The numbers are indeed impressive for an SUV: 45 mpg in the city and 31 on the highway (Ulrich 2009).

In recent years, American automakers have received unprecedented support from the US government. In 2008, Obama campaigned on the issue of increasing fuel-economy standards. In doing this, he pledged to support domestic automakers, provide tax credits and loan guarantees for domestic auto plants and parts manufacturers and increase federal funding to help bring plug-in hybrids and other advanced vehicle technologies to American consumers. Finally, he campaigned to expand consumer tax incentives by lifting the 60,000-per-manufacturer cap on buyer tax credit (Obama 2008).

In January 2008, Toyota announced that it would offer a plug-in hybrid by 2010. Katsuaki Watanabe, then president of Toyota, announced that the company was working on developing a fleet of plug-in hybrids that run on lithium-ion batteries (just like the Chevy Volt), expected to achieve 230 mpg, and reach the market in 2011. The problem is, lithium-ion batteries are far more expensive than NiMH, the battery currently used in the Prius (Maynard 2008). In electric models, the

Prius achieves 99.9 mpg. With a plug-in, the car can run in electric mode for longer because the battery does not have to be constantly recharging with the help of the gas engine (Maynard 2008). When asked about what influenced Toyota to begin working on a plug-in hybrid, product communications manager, George replied,

> plug-in technology is the natural progression to the Prius. We wanted to see what customers thought about the concept of plug-in vehicles and they seemed interested. Customer feedback is the main driving force behind Toyota's interest in the new technology.

It is hard to imagine that Toyota's interest in the technology does not also stem from the United States already having its foot in the door.

Even more recently, the Obama administration instituted the Cash for Clunkers programme that has undoubtedly increased sales for fuel-efficient vehicles. The programme exchanges vouchers of up to US$4,500 for old gas-guzzling cars to replace them with fuel-efficient cars. Larry, sales manager at Longo Toyota in Los Angeles, said their dealership was open until 3a.m. on the first day of the programme because people were lined up to replace their cars not only with Prius but also with Camrys, Corollas and other cars that get good fuel economy. Inventories at Toyota and other manufacturer dealerships all over the nation are emptying out (Hedgepeth 2009). Arguably, this could be the first US federal government policy that has effectively impacted the sale of fuel-efficient cars.

Discussion

The purpose of this paper was to initiate thinking about how government policies can shift the focus of firm innovation, especially in light of concerns about the environment. From the technology-push side, a shift in innovation comes about by changing the context of innovation: by creating competitive pressures as happened with the creation of the PNGV and by changing product specifications as happened through the modification in EPA CAFE regulations. For the Prius, it appears that Toyota was forward-thinking about US policies and adopted a pre-emptive strategy by investing in hybrid vehicles.

From the pull side, government policies, such as tax credits, seem to work best if the customer is price sensitive to the product. This was perhaps not the case with all hybrid vehicles. Especially for the Lexus RX 400h, which is geared towards the luxury market, demand was predominantly price inelastic. For both the Lexus RX 400h and the Prius, initial demand appears to arise from innovators and early adopters, market segments that are not price sensitive and desire products for their novelty (Moore 1991). Later adopters will most likely be more price sensitive, especially for the Prius. As such, we see recent news about innovation of lower-priced Prius models.

We should keep in mind that when this analysis was done the American automobile lobby was very powerful so legislation that was passed was minimal; thus, the impact of government policy was limited. Also there are other external factors that seem to have contributed to the shift in innovation focus. The first was gas prices. Increased demand coincided with the rapid escalation of gas prices reaching above two dollars a gallon in 2004 (Energy Information Administration 2009). The second was consumer 'bandwagonning'—the need to jump onto a fad, particularly with regard to the sleek and stylish look of hybrid vehicles (Motor Trend 2003). The third was state and Japanese government's action which helped jump-start idea generation and encourage sales after commercialisation (though this can be included as government policy initiatives). For example, 49 out of 50 states provide incentives for hybrid vehicles in the US, such as HOV lanes, which hybrids were allowed to utilise even with one occupant (Hybrid Cars 2009). These state and local polices appear to have a more direct effect on Lexus sales than tax credits per se.

Conclusion

Environmentally sustainable policy for hybrid cars evolved throughout the production of the Lexus RX 400h and the Toyota Prius. It seems that the most effective policy that contributed to the shift in innovation was the PNGV, which created a competitive push for Toyota. On the demand-pull side, it appears that the Alternative Motor Vehicle Tax Credit had more of an impact on the Toyota Prius than the Lexus RX 400h. Other government policies (at state and local levels) appear to have had a significant impact on demand pull. In future policy determination, if the government can harness other external, competitive forces, hybrids and other fuel-efficient cars will have the best chance of succeeding in the market. This insight can have an impact on other environmentally sustainable initiatives that hope to promote sustainable, innovative versions of existing products.

Government does and will play a major role in the coming decades to transform the way firms innovate, as will the need for environmentally sustainable products and services. For academics and practitioners alike, these additional factors need to be integrated into the study and management of innovation. In the case of hybrid vehicles, we have seen the success of government intervention with federal- and state-level incentives. Programmes such as these need to continue, so firms persist in shifting innovation focus to environment-friendly and sustainable products. Above all, it is important for firms to avoid being myopic and keep their eyes open in order to anticipate policies that might promote a shift in innovative focus, as shown by the example of Toyota Motor Corporation.

References

Abernathy, W.J. (1978) *The Productivity Dilemma: Roadblock to Innovation in the Automobile Industry* (Baltimore, MD: Johns Hopkins University Press).

Acemoglu, D., and A. Finkelstein (2008) 'Input and Technology Choices in Regulated Industries: Evidence from the Health Care Sector', *Journal of Political Economy* 116.5 (May 2006): 837-80.

Agras, J., and D. Chapman (1999) 'The Kyoto Protocol, CAFE Standards, and Gasoline Taxes', *Contemporary Economy Policy* 17.3 (July 1999): 296-308.

Ahman, M. (2006) 'Government Policy and the Development of Electric Vehicles in Japan', *Energy Policy* 34.4 (March 2006): 433-43.

Anderson, C.D., and J. Anderson (2005) *Electric and Hybrid Cars: A History* (Boston, MA: McFarland & Company).

Antonelli, G., and N. De Liso (1997) *Economics of Structural and Technological Change* (London: Routledge).

Avila, M., and S. Isabel (2008) 'Lexus: A Premium Brand', *The Ritksumeikan Business Review* 47.2 (July 2008): 71-89.

Bamberger, R. (2002) 'Automobile and Light Truck Fuel Economy: The CAFE Standards', *Almanac of Policy Issues* (www.policyalmanac.org/environment/archive/crs_cafe_standards. shtml, accessed 9 July 2011).

Biernacki, P., and D. Waldorf (1981) 'Snowball Sampling: Problems and Techniques of Chain Referral Sampling', *Sociological Methods Research* 10.2 (November 1981): 141-63.

Brown, E., P. Quinlan, H. Sachs and D. Williams (2002) *Tax Credits for Energy Efficiency and Green Buildings: Opportunities for State Action* (Report Number E021; Washington, DC: American Council for an Energy-Efficient Economy).

Chau, K.T. and Y.S. Wong (2002) 'Overview of Power Management in Hybrid Electric Vehicles', *Energy Conversion and Management* 43.15 (October 2002): 1953-68.

Clark, K.B., W.B. Chew and T. Fujimoto (1987) 'Product Development in the World Auto Industry: Strategy, Organization and Performance', *Brookings Papers on Economic Activity* 3: 729-71.

CNN (2001) 'Bush Energy Plan Looks to Future', CNN, 18 May 2001, articles.cnn.com/2001-05-17/politics/bush.energy.plan_1_energy-strategy-gasoline-prices-bush-energy-plan/2?_s=PM:ALLPOLITICS, accessed 8 June 2011.

Cooper, R.G. (1990) 'State-Gate Systems: A New Tool for Managing New Products', *Business Horizons* 33.3 (May-June 1990): 44-54.

Dao, J. (2001) 'Bush Plans Incentives for Energy Conservation', *New York Times*, 13 May 2001, www.nytimes.com/2001/05/13/us/bush-plans-incentives-for-energy-conservation. html?scp=1&sq=James%20Dao%20%E2%80%98Bush%20Plans%20Incentives%20 for%20Energy%20Conservation%E2%80%99&st=cse, accessed 26 October 2011.

Davies, G. (2001) 'Understanding your Prius: The Power Split Device', Graham's Toyota Prius Topic Area, prius.ecrostech.com/original/Understanding/PowerSplitDevice.htm, accessed 9 July 2011.

Davis, S.C., S.W. Diegel and R.G. Boundy (2010) *Transportation Energy Data Book* (Oak Ridge, TN: Oak Ridge National Laboratory, 29th edn; www.scribd.com/doc/54732369/ Transportation-Energy-Data-Book-OrNL-6985).

Dawson, C. (2005) *The Secrets of Lexus' Success: How Toyota Motor Went from Zero to Sixty in the Luxury Car Market* (New York: Columbia Business School).

Demirdoven, N., and J. Deutch (2004) 'Hybrid Cars Now, Fuel Cell Cars Later', *Science* 13 305.5686 (August 2004): 974-76.

Department of Energy (2011) 'Technology Snapshot featuring the Toyota Prius', Argonne National Library, www.fueleconomy.gov/feg/tech/TechSnapPrius1_5_01b.pdf, accessed 19 May 2011.

Diamond, J.M. (1999) *Guns, Germs, and Steel: the Fates of Human Societies* (New York: W.W. Norton & Company).

Donohue, T. (2001) 'Bush Energy Plan Could Be the Best Economic Stimulus of All', US Chamber of Commerce, 29 May 2001, www.uschamber.com/press/opeds/2001/bush-energy-plan-could-be-best-economic-stimulus-all, accessed 18 September 2011.

Eisenhardt, K.M. (1989) 'Building Theories from Case Study Research', *Academy of Management Review* 14.4 (October1989): 532-50.

Energy Information Administration (2009) 'California Gasoline Price Study', 10 May 2005, www.eia.gov/pub/oil_gas/petroleum/presentations/2005/house050905/house050905.html, accessed 12 May 2011.

Etzkowitz, H. (2003) 'Innovation in Innovation: The Triple Helix of University–Industry–Government Relations', *Social Science Information* 42.3 (September 2003): 293-337.

Finkelstein, A. (2004) 'Static and Dynamic Effects of Health Policy: Evidence from the Vaccine Industry', *Quarterly Journal of Economics* 119.2 (January 2004): 527-64.

Glaser, B.G. (1998) *Doing Grounded Theory: Issues and Discussions* (Mill Valley, CA: Sociology Press).

Glaser, B.G., and A.L. Strauss (1967) *The Discovery of Grounded Theory: Strategies for Qualitative Research* (New York: Aldine de Gruyter).

GovTrack.us (2005) 'H.R. 6 Energy Policy Act of 2005: 109th Congress', GovTrack.us database of federal legislation, www.govtrack.us/congress/bill.xpd?tab=summary&bill=h109-6, accessed 10 July 2011.

Graham, R. (2001) 'Comparing the Benefits and Impacts of Hybrid Electric Vehicle Options', ourenergypolicy.org/docs/9/Comparing_Hybrid_Electric_Vehicle_Options.pdf, accessed 24 October 2001.

Gutmann, G. (1999) 'Hybrid Electric Vehicles and Electrochemical Storage Systems: A Technology Push-Pull Couple', *Journal of Power Sources* 84.2 (December 1999): 275-79.

Hedgepeth, D. (2009) 'Clunkers Program Clears Out Car Lots', *Washington Post*, 12 August 2009 (www.washingtonpost.com/wp-dyn/content/article/2009/08/11/AR2009081101474.html, accessed 24 October 2011).

Howell, L.J. (2000) 'Innovation in the Automobile Industry: A New Era', *Chemical Innovation* 30.11 (November 2000): 16-21.

Hybrid Cars (2006) 'Origins of Bush Administration Energy Policies', 2 March 2006, www.hybridcars.com/current-policies.html, accessed 9 July 2011).

Hybrid Cars (2009) 'Hybrid and Plug-in Incentives and Rebates: Region by Region', last modified 8 March 2010, www.hybridcars.com/local-incentives/region-by-region.html, accessed 7 July 2011.

Hymel, M.L. (2006) 'The United States' Experience with Energy-Based Tax Incentives: The Evidence Supporting Tax Incentives for Renewable Energy', Arizona Legal Studies Discussion Paper No. 06-21, *Loyola University Chicago Law Journal*: 43-80.

Internal Revenue Service (2006) 'Additional Toyota and Lexus Vehicles Certified for the Energy Tax Credit', 29 September 2006, www.irs.gov/newsroom/article/0,,id=163103,00.html, accessed 9 July 2011.

Jaffe, A.B. and K. Palmer (1997) 'Environmental Regulation and Innovation: A Panel Data Study', *Review of Economics and Statistics* 79.4 (November 1997): 610-19.

Jaffe, A.B., R.G. Newell and R.N. Stavins (2002) 'Environmental Policy and Technological Change', *Environmental and Resource Economics* 22.1 (April 2002): 41-69.

Jaffe, A.B., R.G. Newell and R.N. Stavins (2004) 'A Tale of Two Market Failures: Technology and Environmental Policy', *Ecological Economics* 54.2 (October 2004): 164-74.

Job, A.M. (2005) 'Lexus Introduces First Luxury Hybrid SUV', *Los Angeles Daily News*, 26 October 2005, www.dailynews.com/search/ci_3076458, accessed 24 October 2011.

Johnstone, N., I. Hascic and D. Popp (2008) 'Renewable Energy Policies and Technological Innovation: Evidence Based on Patent Counts', *NBER Working Paper Series No. 13760* (January 2008): 1-34.

Kolbert, E. (2007) 'Running on Fumes', *New Yorker*, 5 November 2007.

Lave, L.B., and H.L. MacLean (2002) 'An Environmental-Economic Evaluation of Hybrid Electric Vehicles: Toyota's Prius vs. its Conventional Internal Combustion Engine Corolla', *Transportation Research Part D: Transport and Environment* 7.2 (March 2002): 155-62.

Lazzari, S. (2008) 'Energy Tax Policy: History and Current Issues', CRS Report for Congress, 10 June 2008, www.fas.org/sgp/crs/misc/RL33578.pdf, accessed 8 July 2011.

Leydesdorff, L. (2000) 'The Triple Helix: An Evolutionary Model of Innovation', *Research Policy* 29.2 (February 2000): 243-55.

Leydesdorff, L., and H. Etzkowitz (1998) 'The Triple Helix as a Model for Innovation Studies', *Science and Public Policy* 25.3 (December 1998): 195-203.

Llanos, M. (2004) 'Lexus Hybrid SUV Orders Set Record', MSNBC, 14 September 2004, www. msnbc.msn.com/id/5941899/ns/us_news-environment/t/lexus-hybrid-suv-orders-set-record, accessed 18 September 2011.

Magnusson, T., L. Goran and C. Berggren (2003) 'Architectural or Modular Innovation? Managing Discontinuous Product Development in Response to Challenging Environmental Performance Targets', *International Journal of Innovation Management* 7.1: 1-26.

Maynard, M. (2008) 'Toyota Will Offer a Plug-in Hybrid by 2010', *New York Times*, 14 January 2008, www.nytimes.com/2008/01/14/business/14plug.html, accessed 24 October 2011.

Mertig, A.G., R.E. Dunlap and D.E. Morrison (2000) 'The Environmental Movement in the United States', in R.E. Dunlap and W. Michelson (eds.), *Handbook of Environmental Sociology* (Westport, CT: Greenwood Publishing): 448-81.

Moore, G.A. (1991) *Crossing the Chasm: Marketing and Selling Technology Products to Mainstream Customers* (New York: Harper Business).

Morgan, J.M., and J.K. Liker (2006) 'Prius: A New Chief Engineer and New Engineering Process for a Twenty-first Century Car', in J.M. Morgan and J. Liker (eds.), *The Toyota Product Development System: Integrating People, Process, and Technology* (New York: Productivity Press).

Motor Trend (2003) 'Motor Trend Announces 2004 Car of the Year: Toyota Prius', 20 November 2003, www.motortrend.com/roadtests/alternative/112_031120_coty_winner_2004_toyota_prius/index.html, accessed 7 July 2011.

Mowery, D., and N. Rosenberg (1979) 'The Influence of Market Demand upon Innovation: A Critical Review of Some Recent Empirical Studies', *Research Policy* 8.2 (April 1979): 102-53.

MRV (2006) 'Toyota/Lexus US hybrid unit sales history', priuschat.com/forums/prius-hybrid-news/17302-toyota-lexus-us-hybrid-unit-sales-history.html, accessed 24 October 2011.

Nelson, R.R., and S. Winter (1977) 'In Search of Useful Theory of Innovation', *Research Policy* 6.1 (January 1977): 36-76.

Nonaka, I., and V. Peltokorpi (2009) 'Knowledge-Based View of Radical Innovation: Toyota Prius Case', in J. Hage, T.H. Meeus and C. Edquist (eds.), *Innovation, Science, and Institutional Change* (New York: Oxford University Press).

Obama, B. (2008) 'Barack Obama's Plan to Make America a Global Energy Leader', Obama'08, 8 November 2008, obama.3cdn.net/4465b108758abf7a42_a3jmvyfa5.pdf, accessed 9 July 2011.

Ohnsman, A. (2008) 'Toyota Prius Supply Shrinks as Waiting Lists Grow', Bloomberg, 13 May 2008, www.bloomberg.com/apps/news?pid=newsarchive&sid=ahXAyNA7my1E, accessed 9 July 2011.

Peng, M.W., S.H. Lee and D.Y.L. Wang (2005) 'What Determines the Scope of the Firm Over Time? A Focus on Institutional Relatedness', *Academy of Management Review* 30.3: 622-33.

Popp, D. (2003) 'Pollution Control Innovations and the Clear Air Act of 1990', *Journal of Policy Analysis and Management* 22.4 (September 2003): 641-60.

Porter, M.E. (1979) 'How Competitive Forces Shape Strategy', *Harvard Business Review* 57.2 (March 1979): 137-45.

Porter, M.E., and C. van der Linde (1995) 'Toward a New Conception of the Environment-Competitiveness Relationship', *Journal of Economic Perspective* 9.4 (Fall 1995): 97-118.

Rao, H. (1994) 'The Social Construction of Reputation: Certification Contests, Legitimation, and the Survival of Organizations in the American Automobile Industry: 1895–1912', *Strategic Management Journal* 15 (Winter 1994): 29-44.

Rego, J., J. Stempel and R. Mintz (2007) 'The Prius Effect: Learning from Toyota', *Brand Neutral White Papers* (December 2007): 1-11.

Sabatini, J. (2005) '2006 Lexus RX 400h: The Hybrid Emperor's New Clothes', *New York Times*, 31 July 2005, www.nytimes.com/2005/07/31/automobiles/31AUTO.html?pagewanted=all, accessed 24 October 2011.

Santini, D.J., P.D. Patterson and A.D. Vyas (2000) 'The Importance of Vehicle Costs, Fuel Prices, and Fuel Efficiency in HEV Market Success', *The Transportation Research Board Issue* 1738: 11-19.

Schmookler, J. (1966) *Invention and Economic Growth* (Cambridge, MA: Harvard University Press).

Strongman, T. (2006) 'A Preview of the Lexus Hybrid SUV', Family Car Parts, 10 June 2006, www.familycar.com/RoadTests/LexusRX400h, accessed 8 July 2011.

Taylor, A. (2006) 'Toyota: The Birth of the Prius', *Fortune Magazine*, 21 February 2006, money.cnn.com/2006/02/17/news/companies/mostadmired_fortune_toyota/index.htm, accessed 8 July 2011.

The Auto Channel (2009) 'Toyota and Lexus Hybrids Top One Million Sales in the US', 11 March 2009, www.theautochannel.com/news/2009/03/11/453029.html, accessed 9 July 2011.

The Clean Green Car Company (2003) 'Toyota Prius Generation II Hybrid Information', www.cleangreencar.co.nz/info_toyota-priusII.asp, accessed 9 July 2011.

Toyota News Release (2008) 'Worldwide Prius Sales Top 1 Million Mark', 15 May 2008, www.toyota.co.jp/en/news/08/0515.html, accessed 8 July 2011.

Toyota USA Newsroom (2008) 'Atkinson Meets Otto: Why the Prius is So Efficient', 8 September 2008, pressroom.toyota.com/article_display.cfm?article_id=2722, accessed 9 July 2011.

Tyre, M.J., and E. von Hippel (1997) 'The Situated Nature of Adaptive Learning in Organizations', *Organization Science* 8.1 (January 1997): 71-83.

Ulrich, L. (2009) 'The Greening of the Hybrid Crossover', *New York Times*, 4 June 2009 (www.nytimes.com/2009/06/07/automobiles/autoreviews/07hybrid.html, accessed 24 October 2011).

Walsh, J.P., K. Weber and J.D. Margolis (2003) 'Social Issue and Management: Our Lost Cause Found', *Journal of Management* 29.6 (December 2003): 859-81.

Walsh, V. (1984) 'Invention and Innovation in the Chemical Industry: Demand-Pull or Discovery-Push?' *Research Policy* 13.4 (August 1984): 211-34.

Washington Post (2002) 'Half Gas, Half Electric, Total California Cool', *Washington Post*, 6 June 2002, www.washingtonpost.com/ac2/wp-dyn?pagename=article&node=&contentId=A2 587-2002Jun5, accessed 24 October 2011.

Yin, W. (2008) 'Market Incentives and Pharmaceutical Innovation', *Journal of Health Economics* 27.4 (July 2008): 1060-77.

Yin, W. (2009) 'R&D Policy, Agency Costs, and Innovation in Personalized Medicine', *Journal of Health Economics* 28.5 (September 2009): 950-62.

7

Drivers for sustainability-improving innovation

A qualitative analysis of renewable resources, industrial products and travel services

Patrick Llerena
BETA, Université de Strasbourg, France

Marcus Wagner
Julius-Maximilians-University of Würzburg, Germany

Sustainability-improving innovations are considered a core element of achieving the longer-term ecological, social and economic goals of the European Union (EC 2008). The theoretical approach of this chapter focuses on two streams of literature. First, using concepts from the strategic management literature, it is argued that special organisational capabilities or routines which improve responsiveness to sustainability challenges are needed, such as capabilities for stakeholder integration, higher-order learning and/or for continuous innovation as well as higher-order dynamic capabilities related to these (Aragón-Correa and Sharma 2003; Marcus and Anderson 2006). This view is related to the evolutionary perspective of the firm (Cohendet *et al.* 2000) which is based, among other things, on a dual theory of the firm (Cohendet and Llerena 2005). Reasoning based on this stream of literature leads to the question of whether leadership for sustainability is a new dynamic capability or an augmentation of established capabilities (Teece *et al.* 1997; e.g. Marcus and Anderson 2006) and whether stakeholder integration or innovation capabilities are novel and separate capabilities or established capabilities that are changing incrementally towards sustainability. Second, drawing on the literature on technology and innovation management, a focus is put on the role of individuals as 'promotors' (e.g. Witte 1973; Hauschildt and Gemünden 1998) and on the gatekeeper concept (Allen and Nochur 1992) to illuminate how the actual process of integrating sustainability aspects in innovation activities and corporate strategy works.

The chapter discusses preliminary results from an analysis of 13 firms for which case studies were carried out. The research finds that some leadership for environmentally and socially beneficial innovation is needed in terms of board responsibility and formal integration of sustainability aspects in processes and that the realisation of environmentally and socially beneficial innovation and the integration of sustainability aspects with corporate strategy is often a bottom-up activity, leading to new emergent strategies in the sense of Mintzberg and Quinn (1991).

The chapter is structured as follows: the next section outlines the concept of sustainability-improving innovation and the role of leadership, functional integration and regulation. The following section discusses how evolutionary perspectives of cooperation and, here in particular, open innovation processes and user innovation, especially in the context of lead markets, matter for sustainability-improving innovation. This is followed by the empirical analysis and a section presenting the results in terms of empirical insights into the role that leadership, integration, regulation and cooperation, open innovation and user innovation have for sustainability-improving innovation based on the case studies carried out. The final section discusses the findings and conclusions.

Conceptualising sustainability-improving innovation

Sustainable development is defined in the Brundtland Report, *Our Common Future*, as follows: 'Sustainable development is development that meets the needs of the present without compromising the ability of future generations to meet their own needs' (WCED 1987: 54). Immediately after this famous definition, the Brundtland Report states that in terms of needs, the focus should particularly be on those of the poor in developing countries, and in doing so provides an early link to the current bottom-of-the-pyramid (BOP) innovation debate (Prahalad and Hammond 2002; Prahalad 2005, 2006). In this sense, one can conceptualise sustainability as a bundle of public goods (intra- and inter-generational equity, improvement or preservation of environmental quality, protection of human health) and innovation is one key approach to preserve these public goods. For example, Fichter (2005: 84-87, 371-73) distinguishes five types of sustainability strategy and identifies among these the innovation-based strategy as the one which can contribute most to sustainable development. At the same time he argues that the innovation strategy enables private benefits to firms by creating new markets and market segments.

Because of this conceptual prominence for sustainable development, sustainability aspects in innovation processes have received increased attention by policy-makers. For example, in October 2006, Germany's then Federal Secretary of State for the Environment, Sigmar Gabriel, proposed at a Ministry of Environment Innovation Conference that 'Germany should establish itself as a responsible energy efficiency and environmental technologist in the global division of labour between nations' (Gabriel 2006, translated from German by the authors). He made this statement while pointing out the high relevance to the ministry of the link between innovation and the environment, particularly stressing the role of industrialised countries as lead users and lead markets in areas such as sustainable energy technologies, products based on bio-materials or nanotechnology and recycling processes.

In order to enable a more specific analysis, the term sustainability-improving innovation shall be defined more precisely. From the literature, one can derive that sustainability-improving innovations are characterised by highly inventive steps, since in their case the environmental and social effects are intended; that is, they represent additional demands.

Based on this reasoning a very valid question is whether sustainability-improving innovation is a special type of innovation in a qualitative sense, or just 'better managed innovation'; that is, innovation where more target criteria are integrated and made mutually compatible. Such innovation would in this sense only be a quantitative extension of the above performance categories of innovation success, rather than a qualitatively new form of innovation.

Given that earlier Ogburn (1933) defines innovation as the solving of societal problems, it seems difficult to identify the added benefit of defining a 'sustainability innovation' (based on the definition of an 'environmental innovation') beyond additional environmental benefits in a similar manner as for 'environmental innovation'. However, one way of defining 'sustainability innovation' (Fichter 2005) could be to divide it into 'environmental innovation' (Rennings 2000) and social innovation in terms of bottom-of-the-pyramid (BOP) innovation (Prahalad 2005, 2006). The latter seems to be an important future form of sustainability-improving innovation because it addresses directly some of the foci mentioned directly after the definition of sustainable development in WCED (1987). Whereas for environmental innovation, for example as defined by Rennings (2000: 322), reduced environmental burdens (i.e. reduced external effects) are an essential and quantifiable criterion to delineate them from other innovation activities, it seems that the benefit of a 'social' innovation is hard to discern from the generally positive social welfare effects ascribed to innovations in general. Even for environmental burdens, the actual effect can often only be established *ex post* and an analogous transfer to the social effects of an innovation (such as e-learning) seems not to be trivial. In summary, these considerations raise doubts about the feasibility of a definition of 'sustainability innovation' which (as a consistency criterion) would also include all environmental innovations and only those as a subset. This, together with the doubt over whether there are qualitative differences between innovations, leads us to the use of the term sustainability-improving innovation in the remainder of this chapter.

In a more detailed analysis, it seems to be relevant to whom the social benefits (i.e. the positive social welfare effects/reduced negative external effects) accrue: for example, do they run completely in parallel with private benefits? For instance, if an oil company introduces biofuels this may significantly cannibalise existing sales (in the case of a largely stagnant market or in case the company cannot introduce this fast enough in rapidly growing markets such as China). More generally, one can distinguish, based on these examples, first, sustainability-improving innovations in which (partly incremental) product or process modifications lead to reductions in energy or material consumption or emission reductions at the implementing firm or the customers of its products, who consequently should have a positive willingness to pay (at least in the order of the material or energy or waste/emission disposal cost saved by the firm or its customers). Examples of this type of innovation are cars with lower petrol consumption, more energy-efficient industrial processes or water recycling, and even though both the social and the private benefits stem from the same reduction of a negative external effect, they are additive (because for a firm under perfect competition a cost reduction would transfer into a price reduction that would enable customers to increase their utility by freeing part of their budget for additional consumption of goods). Second, there are sustainability-improving innovations where such cost savings are not the case and in this case the innovator would not be able to appropriate private benefits, but would exclusively increase social welfare by reducing negative external effects (which does not imply that this positive externality is higher than in the case of the first type of innovation, nor that the increase in social welfare is higher than for the first type of innovation, but that an innovator will not be able to gain additional private benefit from carrying out the innovation). However, the innovators may demand compensation from society for carrying out the innovation and may make this a precondition for actually innovating, for example by adding a mark-up to the price of their products which obviously partly depends on their market power and on the regulatory situation.

Distinguishing the two types of sustainability-improving innovation reveals a more general issue of the crowding out of sustainability-improving innovations. Assume that social benefits S1 and S2 and private benefits P1 and P2 (including the appropriable private benefit relating to the reduction of a negative external effect) exist for two innovations 1 and 2, then crowding out of the innovation with higher S (innovation 1 in this case without affecting the generality of the argument) occurs if $S1 + P1 > S2 + P2$ and $P2 > P1$ (i.e. $S1 \gg S2$). In this case a firm would have the incentive to pursue innovation 2 despite the fact that innovation 1 would result in a bigger increase of social welfare, representing a case of market failure. Arguably, different solutions exist to rectify market failure. For example, a subsidy ($P2 - P1$) could be provided to the firm, compensating it for the forgone private benefit if realising the socially more desirable innovation. Of course in this case, the net social benefit of that innovation would be only (S1 – S2 – P2 + P1) and this does not have to be positive in all situations.

The above reasoning counters the argument that innovations with a private benefit will be carried out anyway by firms (and explains the anomalies observed in firm behaviour with regard to energy efficiency investments). Hence the sustainability-related innovation would only be pursued autonomously by a firm if the private benefit is also higher (i.e. if P1 > P2).

Finally, Figure 7.1 illustrates that the higher level of economic 'radicality' (as defined in Arrow 1962) of an innovation (i.e. the cost reduction the innovation brings about for e.g. producing a good while keeping the benefit of that good constant) is relevant for sustainability-related innovation, too. This is because the higher the economic radicality, the higher the potential of an innovation to compensate for negative social effects of that innovation (e.g. because it implies a high level of resource consumption). Assume the grey and dashed-grey area in Figure 7.1 (i.e. the full circle) is the set of all possible innovations. If social benefits and economic radicality are monetarised in such a way that both axes of Figure 7.1 have the same scale, then conceptually, all innovations below the dashed line running from the upper left to the bottom right are not sustainable in that either they have both negative social effects and no economic radicality, or their compensation potential due to the (lacking) economic radicality of the innovation is so low that it cannot compensate fully for the increased resource use. This can be termed the 'Playstation World' based on the notion that such innovations neither provide positive social effects, nor do they meet consumer demands at a cost so much lower that the consumer could at least in principle compensate society with his or her savings for the negative social effect. The areas denoted (1) and (2) in Figure 7.1 represent innovations that are: (1) sufficiently economically radical to compensate for negative social effects; or (2) where the positive social effect would justify society accepting a lower level of economic radicality (i.e. reduced consumer surplus) because the total cost/benefit (i.e. the increase of consumer surplus through price reductions plus the monetarised positive social benefit) to society would remain unchanged. Innovations in areas (1) and (2) could thus be termed compensatory sustainability-improving innovations. Finally, those innovations in area (3) of Figure 7.1 (represented by the dashed-grey quarter of the circle) are those that are Pareto-superior; that is, if technologies or innovation opportunities exist in areas (1) and (3) with the same level of economic radicality then the latter are to be preferred from a societal point of view. Innovations in areas (2) and (3) of Figure 7.1 are what are traditionally understood as sustainability-improving innovations (or, more specifically, if the positive direct social effect refers to a reduced environmental externality, an environmental innovation). In an ideal world where negative externalities are fully internalised via the price mechanism, society would be indifferent to any negative social effect such as a negative environmental externality and thus would have no preference towards innovations in areas (2) and (3) of Figure 7.1. However, in a material world where absolute physical limits exist with regard to non-renewable resources as well as concerns about the stability of the climate system and the carrying capacity of global ecosystems, increasing the economic radicality of an innovation without reducing negative social effects is insufficient. In other words, next to the rate of technological change (and its acceleration), the direction of such change needs to be taken into account by society to ensure that limits are reached as late as possible and this requires innovation that has positive social effects.

Figure 7.1 **Link between economic radicality and direct social benefit of an innovation**

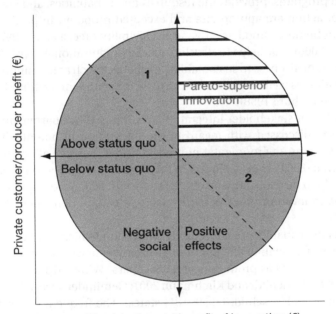

Direct (net) social benefit of innovation (€)

Note: Direct social benefits refer essentially to the reduction of negative externalities which exist under the current regulatory regime.

Theory development and research questions

Induced innovation has been much framed by the debate about the Porter hypothesis, positing private benefits of firms from stringent (but economically efficient) environmental or social regulation by means of 'innovation offsets' (Porter 1991; Porter and van der Linde 1995). Case studies of firms are again very suitable to analyse the incidence of such innovation offsets, their determinants and their relevance relative to other factors, for example R&D subsidies. Regulation can create lead markets (see Beise-Zee and Rennings 2005 for a conceptual definition) which seems to be particularly relevant for sustainability innovation in business-to-business (B2B) markets.

Concerning leadership in firms versus regulatory pressure (i.e. proactive versus reactive action) as drivers for firms' activities towards sustainability-improving innovation, important interactions exist between regulation and leadership for sustainability, especially as concerns governance systems (Tidd *et al.* 2005) in that a co-evolutionary process can be proposed for the development of relevant capabilities within firms. According to Rainey (2006: 348), leadership 'determines the plans and programs, provides the resources and capabilities, and ensures that the courses of action are appropriate and executed properly'. In particular, such leadership can be understood as a dynamic capability (Teece *et al.* 1997; Marcus and Anderson 2006) that helps to develop special organisational capabilities that improve the responsiveness to sustainability challenges such as learning and stakeholder integration as well as continuous improvement and innovation (Hart 1995; Sharma and Vredenburg 1998).

The capability for stakeholder integration, as proposed by Sharma and Vredenburg (1998) and discussed with regard to the integration of potentially adverse stakeholders such as environmental non-governmental organisations (NGOs) by Hart and Sharma (2004), is also relevant in this context for innovation cooperation, since it can help to develop early-on cooperation with stakeholder groups that are crucial for the innovation process, partly also to create option value (Adner and Levinthal 2004).

As concerns the capability of continuous innovation (which can be understood as a special case of a capability for continuous improvement), the role of individual employees or managers as promotors or gatekeepers (Witte 1973; Hauschildt and Gemünden 1998; Hauschildt and Kirchmann 2001; Gemünden *et al.* 2006) is of particular relevance. As Hauschildt (1999: 181) states: 'The frequent observation [is] that champions or promotors occur "spontaneously" and that their emergence is not amenable to organisational intervention'. Related to this, as concerns the gatekeeper concept, Allen and Nochur (1992: 267) point out: 'Empirical studies . . . find that an effective gatekeeper role cannot be filled by simply identifying and assigning a member of staff to this position'. Also, as in the case of stakeholder integration, it should be clarified to which degree capabilities are truly novel or an incremental extension of existing capabilities.

Finally, establishing the firm-level implications of evolutionary concepts and models such as system failures or lock-in (David 1985), sociotechnical regimes (Smith *et al.* 2005), strategic niche management and transition management (Kemp *et al.* 1998), and windows of opportunity (Zundel and Sartorius 2005) can inform questions for empirical research. How these different perspectives matter for sustainability-improving innovation should be addressed in an empirical analysis based on the case studies below. Based on the considerations in this section with regard to the interplay of regulation and leadership and the resulting capabilities, a number of important research questions can be asked:

- Do lead markets exist, where the company preferably introduces innovations that contribute much to sustainability, and what role does regulation take?

- What role does the integration of the objectives of different corporate functions have for sustainability-improving innovation?

- How does leadership assist in the process of integration and the formulation of sustainability-improving innovation strategies?

- Are stakeholder integration or innovation capabilities novel and separate capabilities or are they essentially established capabilities that are incrementally incorporating sustainability aspects?

- Are there specific competences related to environmental/sustainability aspects that trigger sustainability-improving innovation?

- Who in the company is pivotal for including environmental or sustainability aspects into innovation processes?

- Is leadership for sustainability a new dynamic capability or an augmentation of established capabilities?

Empirical analysis

Exploratory interview data was collected during 13 in-depth case studies in American, French, German and Swiss firms which were matched for size and industry. Of the firms, three each were in the chemicals (all medium-sized) and electronics industries, two each in the automotive (of which one was a small firm) and machinery and equipment industries (of which one was medium-sized) and one in the printing industry (small firm). Two firms were in the travel services industry (of which one was a small firm). Overall, 7 of the 13 firms are SMEs within their industry, of which three are small firms. Hence across industries, countries and firm size, the sample has considerable variation which is advocated for case study research (Ellinger *et al.* 2005; Ruola 2005; Eisenhardt and Graebner 2007).

The case studies focus on renewable resources for mobility and communication applications as well as industrial (i.e. mechanical, chemical and electronics) products and travel services and draw on interviews with one or several members in each organisation at senior management level with responsibility for sustainability, strategy or innovation aspects. The interviews were based on a standardised qualitative guideline and the responses were triangulated with third-party sources such as content analysis of electronic and printed documents to support the interview information in order to increase the reliability of the analysis. The guideline was adapted to account for additional themes that emerged as the interviews progressed.

Table 7.1 **Key parameters and company characteristics (names disguised for confidentiality)**

Firm	Size (number of interviews)	Industry	Board level sustainability responsibility	Main sustainability-related innovation	Country
D1	S (1, common[a])	Printing	Yes	Printing process	Switzerland
M1	M (1, common)	Machinery	Uncertain	Uncertain	Switzerland
M2	L (3)	Machinery	No	Engines	Germany
A1	L (1)	Automotive		Various	France
A2	S (1, common)	Automotive	No	Electric vehicles	Canada
C1	M (2)	Chemicals	No[b]	Process efficiency	France
C2	M (2)	Chemicals	No[a]	New chemicals	Germany
C3	M (1)	Chemicals	No, but council	New chemicals	United States
E1	L (3)	Electronics	No, but council[d]	Energy-efficient products	France
E2	L (1)	Electronics	No, but council	Remanufacturing process	United States
E3	L (5)	Electronics	No[e]	Energy-efficient products	Germany
T1	S (1, common)	Travel services	Yes	Sustainable/low carbon/carbon-free tourism	Switzerland
T2	L (1)	Travel services	Uncertain	Uncertain	Switzerland

a   denotes that the person interviewed has sustainability and innovation responsibilities

b   At group vice president level one person is tasked solely with sustainable development

c   Sustainability aspects are discussed in the firm's technology council, a public relations function at manager level in the corporate communications department and a vice president for chemical services exists

d   Ethics committee; the company also has a corporate responsibility officer one level below the board level

e   A function for corporate responsibility exists at manager/vice president level; the firm's corporate technology council discusses and decides strategic aspects of sustainability as far as they relate to innovation and technology aspects

The data collection process was halted when new perspectives on the issues under study were no longer recorded, indicating that theoretical saturation was reached (Glaser and Strauss 1967; Miles and Huberman 1994; Lamnek 2005). While inclusion of additional cases in the analysis may have resulted in some additional insights, Glaser and Strauss (1967) argue that when theoretical saturation is reached, data collection should stop in favour of a comparative cross-case analysis.

Data collection was carried out in the second half of 2006 and all through 2007 yielding over 30 hours of structured interviews with 23 senior and middle managers (e.g. managing directors, vice presidents, senior managers, senior principal engineers, managers, directors, research scientists) in the 13 case firms. Interviews were recorded and subsequently transcribed in the majority of cases. If recording was not possible, detailed handwritten notes were taken. It was attempted to interview in each firm a senior environmental representative and a senior innovation manager to avoid common source bias. To triangulate perceptions within the company, it was also attempted to interview more than one person in an environmental and/or innovation function within the company, to reduce hindsight and related perception biases.

In smaller firms, where the environment and innovation functions were sometimes combined into one position, fewer interviews were carried out. Table 7.1 summarises the key parameters of the case firms. Firms are reported anonymously for reasons of confidentiality. The results from the case studies relate mainly to the research questions above which can be grouped into three overarching themes: markets/regulation, leadership/integration and capabilities/promotors. These are discussed one by one below.

Results

Markets and regulation

Market demand is identified in the case studies as a pivotal factor in B2B contexts that justifies sustainability as a strategic topic. This has been mentioned more than once in the case studies, and was put by one interviewee as follows: 'If the customer does not want this, then you can develop as much as you want' (C2; translated from German). Related to this, a risk of leadership in the B2B context was pointed out in that customers do not immediately introduce an improvement on a large scale, even though they may be very vocal in demanding the improvement in the first place. Often the need is for an external event to push adoption by customers and the interviews revealed that frequently this can be novel regulation. Regulation has also been identified in the interviews as a driver for public–private alliances that can ultimately result in the emergence of lead markets fostered by regulation (E3). Finally, cost issues have been identified as an obstacle to leadership for sustainability-improving innovation and it was pointed out that, for example, in the chemical industry, there is usually no payback for an early change to a cleaner process technology, as customers would not accept higher prices for a product produced in such a way (C1).

Leadership and integration

From the case study interviews it emerges that leadership for sustainability-improving innovation exists in terms of organisational structure as well as the integration of sustainability considerations in processes. In terms of organisational structure, two aspects stand out. First, a board member with responsibility for sustainability can act as a power promoter for sustainability-improving innovation. This view is reflected by the following statement: 'In large, hierarchical organisations clear leadership from the board is critical. The role of middle management is less important' (E3; translated from German).

The role of middle or senior management below board level seems to be assessed differently by the interviewees in different companies (e.g. one interviewee in A1 subscribes to the view above, whereas one in M2 pointed out that middle management often initiates innovation activities) and it was pointed out that, regardless of the management hierarchy, the personality of the leader has to reveal competence as well provide credibility to any statements with regard to sustainability or sustainability-improving innovation. However, while board leadership provides a context for sustainability-related innovation, it was also pointed out in the interviews that this has only limited influence if the board as a whole does not embrace a holistic approach to sustainability and that this also limits the possibilities for middle managers.

As an alternative to assigning board-level responsibility for sustainability, most of the larger companies interviewed usually have technology or sustainability councils at the corporate level (e.g. A1 or C2), which discuss and decide on sustainability topics and as part of this on sustainability-improving innovation. Related to this, interviewees in one company felt that leadership for sustainability-improving innovation and the resulting integration of sustainability into innovation processes was also brought about through a corporate longer-term focus on mega-trends, which themselves relate to sustainability issues, such as mobile communication, energy or water supply, or healthcare (E3; E1).

Second, integration is achieved through formal consideration of sustainability topics with regard to innovation in pre-development and stage-gate processes and related guidelines. This approach to achieving integration has become increasingly relevant as is witnessed by the following quote: 'They [environmental criteria] are covered in a systematic way . . . I would say: 5 years ago this was only piecemeal . . . it is now structured in a way that we [environmental department] do not have to do much any more' (M2; translated from German). Next to such formal integration, informal integration into processes and guidelines is additionally achieved by means of clear statements of direction by senior managers, voluntary support offers to business units by central environmental units and by means of bottom-up activities of individual employees. From the interviews it emerged that if strong leadership exists in terms of, for example, board responsibility or clear statements of direction, then systematic integration of, for instance, environmental aspects in innovation processes is often substituted by more informal mechanisms such as voluntary support offers to business units or bottom-up activity with regard to sustainability-improving innovation. The insights born out by interviews are also consistent with findings in the literature that a charismatic leader is important but needs to be supported by processes and structures (e.g. in terms of guidelines, operating procedures or routines) which can be linked to the evolutionary view in terms of learning and improving routines (Nadler and Tushman 1990).

Capabilities and promotors

The finding of the previous section that sustainability-improving innovation is often a bottom-up activity links to the questions about capabilities and promotors in that it indicates an emergent strategy (Mintzberg and Quinn 1991). One important aspect of this is that sustainability issues according to several interviewees (e.g. in A1) are more accepted among middle management and researchers now than they were in the past (though it was pointed out that this depends on department and corporate function considered). One interviewee stated:

> In the '70s, '80s maybe also there was a generation . . . for which environmental protection was only cost . . . But today we pursue integrated environmental protection . . . That is a completely different type of environmental protection . . . This generation conflict does not exist anymore in the company today (C2; translated from German).

Concerned and aware employees often act as technological promotors for sustainability-improving innovation activities, as was pointed out in the interviews. However, such bottom-up activity where individual employees that are very concerned about sustainability act as promotors needs subsequent board-level support, as is illustrated by the following statement:

> The pattern is more that there are people. There were people then who said: let's pursue this . . . Let's push this. We cannot enforce it, but we have to see if this is relevant . . . And then the board discovered it and said: Wow, this could be very important (M2; translated from German).

This finding shows that senior management essentially functions as a gatekeeper for the bottom-up activity of individual employees that work on sustainability-improving innovation; that is, senior managers were identified as power promotors who help to increase the acceptance of a sustainability-improving innovation and who break organisational resistance resulting from the firm being only a partly rational social system.

Concerning the question of whether sustainability-improving innovation capabilities are novel or established capabilities incrementally incorporating sustainability aspects, the interviews provide evidence for both interpretations. One interviewee stated that a chain starting from the attempt to improve the corporate image via the corporate culture/climate and from individual employee motivation results in a process of continuous improvement (D1). It was also pointed out, however, that the continuous improvement process that resulted in innovation was fuelled out of the company's environmental management system and that, next to this, another key driver for innovation was a corporate culture in the company that was allowing mistakes and hence experimentation; this culture was largely promoted by management, but was not related to environmental or sustainability issues.

On the other hand, some interviewees identify specific competences related to sustainability aspects that support sustainability-improving innovations. This is illustrated in the following quotes relating to life-cycle analysis which has been identified in more than one interview as an important sustainability-improving capability:

> ... e.g. what we call the life-cycle analysis: This is clearly an input or decision that I support, that I've launched because I felt that we need to. But from another side, we have somebody who is a responsible care director. So, to define who is at the origin is very difficult, it's mixed, I would say (C1).

However, concerns were also voiced in the interviews as in the following statement:

> All of this has exploded in the market place ... I am right now going out and making presentations getting people to think about life cycle perspectives ... I am a little weary about that. We are using life cycle analysis and higher level life cycle type tools ... I think I get very nervous about the trade-off ... I'd rather have them thinking about things that are pretty simple ... I don't want to get them tied up in complex analysis ... that they get paralyzed ... I try to get them to understand that life cycle analysis is just one element in the toolbox (E2).

Concerning stakeholder integration and the question of whether it is a novel and separate capability or an established capability that is incrementally incorporating sustainability aspects, there is evidence for both interpretations. In one of the large electronics companies interviewed, it was pointed out that a significant amount of stakeholder integration is achieved through the function of a corporate responsibility officer. However, it was also noted that this function was more oriented towards public relations and that it had only existed for less than two years, hence making an assessment of its effect difficult.

Conclusions

The analysis reported here was aimed at developing a better understanding of the way environmental and social considerations are integrated into business strategy and how this influences sustainability-improving innovation aspects. The case studies in this respect should help to develop a more detailed picture of exactly how sustainability is integrated in corporate and business strategy in a way that fosters innovation. The aim was to derive from the case studies a better understanding of the joint role of institutional factors (such as regulation and markets) and firm-internal factors for the pursuance of sustainability-improving innovation in firms.

The analysis in this respect finds that market demand is a pivotal factor that limits or pushes suppliers in B2B contexts towards leadership for sustainability and that regulation is frequently an enabler of increased diffusion and adoption. Also it reveals that sustainability-improving innovation is fostered by board responsibility and formal as well as informal integration of sustainability aspects in processes and that sustainability-improving innovation is often a bottom-up activity. These insights improve the knowledge base for EU policy-making with regard to sustainability and industrial innovation. In particular, they reveal that capabilities are path dependent and depend on historic irreversibility. For example, in the case of one of the American firms, the most important sustainability-improving innovation in their judgement of recent years related to a new approach to micro-biocides for wood preservation that allows for controlled release, maintaining the intended effect without being based on substances such as chromated copper arsenate while minimising the potential for skin irritation in users. It is based on a predecessor technology for marine use biocides that reduces the impact on marine life and that is designed for degradation. That technology again was initially developed for agricultural applications many years ago where it was long in use. This provides an interesting perspective on how firms can innovate strategically for sustainability, as is often proposed or at least desired by policy-makers. As the example and similar ones in other firms show, a more sustainable product is often based on long-existing competences of the company that are transferred from one application field to another rather than a firm developing a technologically radical new product or process design. The development of the underlying knowledge base in the company is a historical and evolutionary process which may involve irreversible decisions about technologies, market foci or other parameters and in this sense is path-dependent.[1] Frequently, it seems, these decisions are taken when there is large uncertainty about future sustainability challenges; therefore, whether firms are today in a position to address commercially and successfully novel or tightened

---

1 An important example of a historic market focus that has become an issue is the current debate of the European Commission with European car manufacturers over fleet emission targets for carbon dioxide; Italian and French car manufacturers are in a less entrenched position than some German car manufacturers because of their historically evolved market focus on smaller cars (*The Economist* 2007).

environmental or socially related regulation seems to depend in this respect on a rather haphazard historical process that may or may not have equipped them with suitable capabilities, routines or competences to address that regulation. An important implication of this for policy-making seems to be that innovating for sustainability is maybe not as strategically feasible as is demanded by policy-makers, meaning that the timelines required for addressing current sustainability challenges are even more demanding given that firms possibly need considerable time to develop relevant knowledge if this is not by (historical) chance already well developed in their organisation. This of course makes strong incentives to do so even more crucial, but also means that policy-makers cannot simply assume that the relevant knowledge is available but should ideally take an active role in the creation and quick diffusion of such knowledge to firms.[2] The situation can also be understood as a co-evolving system of regulatory demands and knowledge needed to meet these demands in which both aspects need to be in balance for the system to function. Concerning the question of whether leadership for sustainability is a new dynamic capability or merely the augmentation of established dynamic capabilities (or in the terminology of evolutionary theorising higher-order routines, see Nelson and Winter 2002), the fact that regulatory demands and knowledge are co-evolving indicates that a combination of new and existing dynamic capabilities applies, which is in line with the finding of Marcus and Anderson (2006) that it is not one general dynamic capability, but different ones for business and social responsibility objectives that are at work in the US food industry.[3]

In this respect, while an empirical analysis of the interaction of corporate and business strategies with innovation activities should be able to elucidate resulting changes in firms' economic, social and environmental performance, the results from the case studies show, however, that often it is actually the expectation of improved economic performance that leads firms to ultimately pursue sustainability-improving innovation (i.e. such innovations are not treated differently from any other innovation). This is particularly the case in the larger firms analysed, implying that established dynamic capabilities matter more here for changes in organisational routines. Here, improved environmental performance is frequently a prerequisite to pursue sustainability-improving innovation. An environmental management system which has been described in some of the case firms as one source for sustainability-improving innovation can be interpreted in this regard as a dynamic capability (Avadikyan et al. 2001) that, however, mainly relates to social responsibility objectives.[4] It can be interpreted as a novel dynamic capability, while

2 Grubb (1997) points to the relevance of this time lag, e.g. in the context of climate change.

3 While the empirical evidence for one generic dynamic capability affecting both business and social responsibility objectives seems limited, such a capability has been proposed frequently in the conceptual literature, e.g. by Hart (1995) who suggested that the capability of establishing a shared vision could be one such generic dynamic capability.

4 Avadikyan et al. (2001) argue that environmental management capacities result from the adaptation of three types of mechanism within companies: namely incentive,

the dynamic capabilities that react to regulation and market forces in terms of incorporating sustainability-improving demands (e.g. in innovation processes or strategy making) seem to be mainly existing dynamic capabilities. In the case of the smaller firms analysed, sustainability entrepreneurship as discussed above seems to be at least partly based on new dynamic capabilities relating to leadership for sustainability. In small firms this seems to lead to more comprehensive sustainability-improving innovation which may ultimately result in technologically more radical innovation or a more comprehensive incorporation of sustainability aspects into operations. For example, in one case firm, even the service truck was converted to run on biofuel (which in a large firm would correspond to essentially their full fleet being converted). To some degree this seems to indicate that the co-evolution of industry structure and technology artefacts, understanding and practice (Nelson and Winter 2002) seems to be faster and more comprehensive in smaller firms and the consequences of this for institutions and innovation systems should be analysed further. Another aspect that emerged as an interesting area for future research is the parallel development in large firms of increased attention towards sustainability-improving innovation and a much more strategic approach to communicating about sustainability. This could mean that firms attempt to make up for their lack of capabilities with more elaborate communication, which would be less desirable.

In line with this argument it seems that large firms attempting sustainability-improving innovation are more constrained in their freedom of action, which may drive them more towards incremental and thus potentially sub-optimal solutions (one example being the slow and incremental efforts of oil companies to integrate biofuels and hydrogen into their product portfolio, which are not close to what would be needed in a hydrogen economy). Also this could imply that large incumbents would be guided in cooperative activities more by their current and short-term interests which essentially may pose an obstacle to more radical, system-wide, sustainability-improving innovation. This dilemma, which seems to be much more pronounced in large (especially multinational) incumbents should be further analysed in future research.

---

coordination and cognitive mechanisms. The environmental management process means according to them a process through which organisations change structures and corporate cultures resulting from a combined effect of individual learning and organisational transformation.

References

Adner, R., and D. Levinthal (2004) 'What is Not a Real Option', *Academy of Management Review* 29.1: 74-85.

Allen, T.J., and K.S. Nochur (1992) 'Do Nominated Boundary Spanners Become Effective Technological Gatekeepers?' *IEEE Transactions on Engineering Management* 39.3: 265-69.

Aragón-Correa, J.A., and S. Sharma (2003) 'A Contingent Resource-Based View of Proactive Corporate Environmental Strategy', *Academy of Management Review* 28.1: 71-88.

Arrow, K. (1962) 'Economic Welfare and the Allocation of Resources for Invention', in R. Nelson (ed.), *The Rate and Direction of Inventive Activity* (Princeton, NJ: Princeton University Press): 609-25.

Avadikyan, A., D. Llerena and K. Ostertag (2001) 'Organisational Mechanisms in Environmental Management: An Evolutionary Analysis Confronted with Empirical Facts', *International Journal of Environmental Technology and Management* 1.1/2: 45-60.

Beise-Zee, M., and K. Rennings (2005) 'Lead Markets and Regulation: A Framework for Analyzing the International Diffusion of Environmental Innovation', *Ecological Economics* 52.1: 5-17.

Cohendet, P., and P. Llerena (2005) 'A Dual Theory of the Firm between Transactions and Competences: Conceptual Analysis and Empirical Considerations', *Revue d'Économie Industrielle* 110 (2éme trimestre): 175-98.

Cohendet, P., P. Llerena and L. Marengo (2000) 'Is There a Pilot in the Evolutionary Firm?' in N. Foss and V. Mahnke (eds.), *New Directions in Economic Strategy Research* (Oxford, UK: Oxford University Press): 95-115.

David, P. (1985) 'Clio and the Economics of QWERTY', *American Economic Review* 75.2: 332-37.

EC (2008) *Progress on EU Sustainable Development Strategy (Final Report)* (Brussels: European Commission).

Eisenhardt, K.M., and M.E. Graebner (2007) 'Theory Building from Cases: Opportunities and Challenges', *Academy of Management Journal* 50.1: 25-32.

Ellinger, A.D., K.E. Watkins and V.J. Marsick (2005) 'Case Study Research Methods', in A. Swanson and E.F. Holton (eds.), *Research in Organizations: Foundations and Methods of Inquiry* (San Francisco: Berrett-Koehler Publishers): 327-50.

Fichter, K. (2005) *Interpreneurship: Nachhaltigkeitsinnovationen in interaktiven Perspektiven eines vernetzten Unternehmertums* (Marburg, Germany: Metropolis).

Gabriel, S. (2006) 'Innovativ für Wirtschaft und Umwelt: Leitmärkte der Zukunft ökologisch erobern', keynote speech at the *BMU – Innovationskonferenz*, dbb Forum, Berlin, 30 October 2006.

Gemünden, H.G., K. Hölzle and C. Lettl (2006) 'Formale und informale Determinanten des Innovationserfolges: Eine kritische Analyse des Zusammenspiels der Kräfte am Beispiel der Innovatorenrollen', *Zeitschrift für betriebswirtschaftliche Forschung* 58: 110-32.

Glaser, B., and A. Strauss (1967) *The Discovery of Grounded Theory: Strategies in Qualitative Research* (London: Weidenfeld & Nicolson).

Grubb, M. (1997) 'Technologies, Energy Systems and the Timing of CO2 Emission Abatement: An Overview of Economic Issues', *Energy Policy* 25.2: 159-72.

Hart, S.L. (1995) 'A Natural-Resource-Based View of the Firm', *Academy of Management Review* 20.4: 986-1014.

Hart, S.L., and S. Sharma (2004) 'Engaging Fringe Stakeholders for Competitive Imagination', *Academy of Management Executive* 18.1: 23-33.

Hauschildt, J. (1999) 'Opposition to Innovations: Destructive or Constructive?' in K. Brockhoff, A. Chakrabarti and J. Hauschildt (eds.), *The Dynamics of Innovation* (Berlin: Springer): 217-40.

Hauschildt, J., and H.G. Gemünden (1998) *Promotoren: Champions der Innovation* (Wiesbaden, Germany: Gabler).

Hauschildt, J., and E. Kirchmann (2001) 'Teamwork for Innovation: The 'Troika' of Promoters', *R&D Management* 31.1: 41-49.

Kemp R., J. Schot and R. Hoogma (1998) 'Regime Shifts to Sustainability through Processes of Niche Formation: The Approach of Strategic Niche Management', *Technology Analysis and Strategic Management* 10.2: 175-95.

Lamnek, S. (2005) *Qualitative Sozialforschung* (Weinheim Basel, Germany: Beltz Verlag).

Marcus, A.A., and M.H. Anderson (2006) 'A General Dynamic Capability: Does it Propagate Business and Social Competencies in the Retail Food Industry?' *Journal of Management Studies* 43.1: 19-46.

Miles, M.B., and A.M. Huberman (1994) *Qualitative Data Analysis: An Expanded Sourcebook* (Thousand Oaks, CA: Sage).

Mintzberg, H., and J.B. Quinn (1991) *The Strategy Process: Contexts, Concepts, Cases* (London: Prentice-Hall, 2nd edn).

Nadler, D.A., and M.L. Tushman (1990) 'Beyond the Charismatic Leader: Leadership and Organizational Change', *California Law Review* 32.2: 77-97.

Nelson, R.R., and S. Winter (2002) 'Evolutionary Theorizing in Economics', *Journal of Economic Perspectives* 16.2: 23-46.

Ogburn, W. (1933) 'The Influence of Invention and Discovery', in H. Hoover (ed.), *Recent Social Trends in the United States. Report of the President's Research Committee on Social Trends* (New York: McGraw Hill): 122-66.

Porter, M. (1991) 'America's Green Strategy', *Scientific American* 264.4: 96.

Porter, M., and C. van der Linde (1995) 'Toward a New Conception of the Environment-Competitiveness Relationship', *Journal of Economic Perspectives* 9.4: 97-118.

Prahalad, C.K. (2005) *The Fortune at the Bottom of the Pyramid: Eradicating Poverty Through Profits* (Upper Saddle River, NJ: Wharton School Publishing).

Prahalad, C.K. (2006) 'The Innovation Sandbox', *Strategy & Business* 44: 1-10.

Prahalad, C.K., and A. Hammond (2002) 'Serving the World's Poor Profitably', *Harvard Business Review* 80.9: 48-57.

Rainey, D. (2006) *Sustainable Business Development* (Cambridge, UK: Cambridge University Press).

Rennings, K. (2000) 'Redefining Innovation: Eco-Innovation Research and the Contribution from Ecological Economics', *Ecological Economics* 32: 319-32.

Ruola, E.W. (2005) 'Analyzing Qualitative Data', in A. Swanson and E.F. Holton (eds.), *Research in Organizations: Foundations and Methods of Inquiry* (San Francisco: Berrett-Koehler): 233-63.

Sharma, S., and H. Vredenburg (1998) 'Proactive Corporate Environmental Strategy and the Development of Competitively Valuable Organizational Capabilities', *Strategic Management Journal* 19.8: 729-53.

Smith, A., A. Stirling and F. Berkhout (2005) 'The Governance of Sustainable Socio-Technical Transitions', *Research Policy* 34: 1491-510.

Teece, D., G. Pisano and A. Schuen (1997) 'Dynamic Capabilities and Strategic Management', *Strategic Management Journal* 18: 509-33.

The Economist (2007) 'The European Car Industry: Collusion Course', *The Economist*, 22 December 2007: 103-104.

Tidd, J., J. Bessant and K. Pavitt (2005) *Managing Innovation* (Chichester, UK: Wiley, 3rd edn).

WCED (World Commission on Environment and Development) (1987) *Our Common Future* (Oxford, UK: Oxford University Press).

Witte, E. (1973) *Organisation für Innovationsentscheidungen – Das Promotoren-Modell* (Göttingen, Germany: Schwartz & Co.).

Zundel, S., and C. Sartorius (2005) *Time Strategies for Innovation Policy towards Sustainability* (Cheltenham, UK: Edward Elgar).

Section IV
EIS in developing countries

8

Obstacles to innovation and entrepreneurship in Ghana
An analysis of opportunities for sustainable development

Christopher Mensah-Bonsu and Florian Jell
Technical University Munich, Germany

> The 21st century will be shaped by what happens not just in Rome or Moscow or Washington, but by what happens in Accra, as well.

This is what US President Barack Obama forecast in his speech to the Ghanaian parliament during his 2009 visit to Ghana (US State Department 2009). There is no doubt that worldwide sustainable development is impossible without countries from the developing world catching up with the more powerful economies from the Western world and Asia. Few would argue that innovation is not an engine for improving the outlook for the developing world, but many say that the obstacles along the way are too great for innovation to set foot. In this chapter we analyse such obstacles for Ghana, which is representative of many African countries. Specifically, we focus on obstacles that hinder entrepreneurship, which is one of the major drivers of innovation and the basis for sustainable development in many fields.

New companies create employment, which would ultimately enhance fair allocation of wealth in Ghanaian society. As a result, more Ghanaians could, for example, afford access to education, which is an important driver of **social sustainability**. Further, entrepreneurship fosters the growth of new industries. New industries are the only way to transform the Ghanaian economy from being dependent on the exploitation of natural resources, to value creation through innovative products. This would be an important step to make Ghana an environmental-friendly nation and foster **ecological sustainability**. Other African and developing nations could learn from the Ghanaian example. This way, entrepreneurship in Ghana could be a trigger for worldwide sustainable development.

To analyse this field, we conducted 11 interviews with entrepreneurs from Ghana and with experts on the Ghanaian economic situation.

Our case studies of failed ventures confirm that a wide range of obstacles is relevant in the context of Ghana. Many of them have been discussed in the extant literature (e.g. Sørensen 2003). Among them are lacking infrastructure, corruption, inflation, limited access to financing, suffocating and unstable public policy, loose regulation, lacking standards and failure of enforcement, limited human capital, miniscule private research and development efforts, misguided education, an overzealous adoration for the educated elite and lack of trust. We contribute to this literature by analysing a phenomenon that has been less intensively discussed in this context: low quality imitation of innovative ideas. In general, imitation leading to increased competition and lower prices would be beneficial to customers. Yet, we find that in conjunction with the low quality of the imitations and the lack of *ex ante* observability—comparable to the market for lemons problem stated by Akerlof (1970)—imitation leads to market failure, and ultimately to a breakdown of the newly emerging market. The ineffectiveness of protection mechanisms, such as patents or trademarks, and the weak appropriability regime in Ghana aggravate the problem (Teece 1986; Ceccagnoli and Rothaermel 2008). Our results even indicate that entrepreneurs anticipating this kind of market failure have not founded businesses that they would have founded under a stronger appropriability regime.

The remainder of the chapter is structured as follows. We commence with a brief overview of Ghana and its economy. Then we will look to the problems: the common themes hindering innovation and entrepreneurship discussed in literature. In-depth interviews with entrepreneurs currently conducting business in Ghana, and past entrepreneurs, will illustrate how these problems manifest themselves.

Background

Ghana's economy

Known as the Gold Coast while under British colonial rule until 1957 because of its rich mineral reserves, Ghana is a sub-Saharan democracy located in West Africa. The country has a population of just over 24.3 million people living in area of 238,533 km^2 consisting of ten administrative regions subdivided into a total of 138 districts. Close to 70% of the population is Christian, followed by approximately 15% who are Muslim. The country's capital is the city of Accra. The judicial system is based on British common law, a remnant from colonial times. The same is true for the official language, English; although a large number of indigenous languages and dialects are used to communicate in everyday life by the locals, especially in rural areas where few speak English. The nation's current president, John Atta Mills of the National Democratic Congress, was democratically elected in 2008 and democratic elections have been the norm since 1992 (CIA 2011). Ghana had a gross domestic product (GDP) of US$38.24 billion in 2010. Imports consisting of capital equipment, petroleum and foodstuffs, exceeded exports consisting of gold, cocoa, timber, tuna, bauxite, aluminium, manganese ore, diamonds and horticulture by close to US$3 billion (CIA 2011). Ghana, being one of the largest gold producers in the world, is currently benefiting from high world market prices for gold and cocoa. It generates more than a third of its total export earnings from gold (BMZ 2010). Oil is to play another major role as an export in the near future, as large reserves of at least 2 billion barrels were discovered in Ghana's Jubilee field and are to be exploited starting in 2011 (Smith 2011b). The majority of the labour force (56%) is active in agriculture. The service sector employed 29% of the labour force and only 15% was active in industry in 2005 (CIA 2011). Although agriculture employs more than half the working population, productivity remains very low (BMZ 2010). In 2010, Ghana's currency, the cedi (GHC), on average traded at 1.4 cedis per US dollar. The average Ghanaian earns just over US$1 per day and 11% of the population is unemployed. In 2007, 28.5% of the population was living beneath the poverty line.

Why focus on Ghana?

The unfortunate truth is that there are many developing countries, especially on the African continent; so why focus on Ghana? Ghana broke free from its British colonial rule and gained its independence in 1957; the first African nation to do so. Ghana benefits from a stable and robust democracy (BMZ 2010; Harvey 2010). A stable political environment allows for a more accurate portrayal and analysis of innovation and entrepreneurship by taking civil wars and absolute destitution, still common all over the African continent, out of the equation. The World Bank ranks Ghana as number 67 of 183 nations with regard to the ease with which business is conducted. Criteria include 'starting a business' and 'registering property', among others. In comparison, the United Kingdom is ranked fourth and Germany 22nd, losing ground mainly because of its bureaucracy and non-transparent tax structure. The Ivory Cost, Ghana's neighbour to the west, ranking at 169 and Togo to the east, at 160, are nearly at the bottom of the list, suggesting that Ghana is progressing in the right direction (World Bank 2010a, b, c, d, e). It appears more beneficial, in the name of progress, to focus on the obstacles specific to an advanced nation such as Ghana that seem to be hindering the move out of the developing world, rather than on the problems that less advanced countries like its neighbours face. If a nation like Ghana is successful in shedding its developing world status, other African nations can benefit through the knowledge that a path exists and that it has been taken once before.

Entrepreneurship and imitation

An entrepreneur is an individual doing something different or new, and should not be confused with anyone starting a small business (Drucker 2007). Closely related to this kind of innovative activity is imitation. Sørensen (2003) refers to the Ghanaians' desire to imitate and copy, a phenomenon which he coined 'more-of-the-same'. He says that Ghanaians are more likely to imitate than innovate. 'When an entrepreneur has successfully established a production of an item, others will copy him or her'. He believes that certain sectors in Ghana are overpopulated and that imitation and too many 'band wagon-entrepreneurs' are threats to markets. Much competition means individual businesses cannot accumulate enough capital for investment in further innovations owing to intensive price competition. On the other hand, he argues that imitation is an inherent part of a market economy and is therefore essential for creating competitive conditions. This can lead to a more highly skilled labour force in the sector and eventually the creation of dynamic clusters 'where price competition is replaced by innovation competition' (Sørensen 2003: 293-98). Baumol (1986) refers to imitative entrepreneurship as a positive force for growth through competition and further innovation. Yet, in conversations with Ghanaians about business in Ghana, the subject of imitation and copying came up again and again, and it became apparent that products and processes were not only imitated and copied but copied badly. If customers *ex ante* cannot observe the bad quality of the imitations, market failure can result (Akerlof 1970). In the course of this chapter, we will explore whether such mechanisms are slowing down entrepreneurship in Ghana.

Methods

We interviewed 11 individuals, either in person or via telephone. Nine of them were or are conducting business in or with Ghana personally. Their activities all have or had an innovative aspect. The remaining two can be considered experts. They have spent the majority of their lives in Ghana but have had the benefit of post-secondary Western education and have worked not only in Ghana but also the in the West. They are educated, knowledgeable and well travelled. A list of our interviewees is provided in Table 8.1. All interviewees, as well as a few points of interest regarding each, have been listed in the table. All interviews were recorded and partially transcribed. In addition, written protocols were prepared.

Table 8.1 **List of interviewees**

Name (anonymised)	Currently residing in	Industry	Innovative activity	Active when
Mr R. A.	Accra, Ghana	Microfinance	Supplies small loans to local trades people	2008–present
Mr D. E.	Accra, Ghana	Recording	One of Ghana's first record producers	1959–present
Mr S. K.	Cologne, Germany	Pharmaceuticals/ Pharmacy	Offered German-produced medications in his pharmacy in Accra	2004–present
Mr B. K.	Hamburg, Germany	Production and export of shea butter	Production and export of Ghana's indigenous shea butter	1990–2000, currently reviving business
Mr F. L.	Cologne, Germany	Communication centre	Opened one of Accra's first communication centres	1996–2003
Dr V. M.	Accra, Ghana	Production and export of handicrafts	Combined production from local artisans to meet export demand	1994–present
Mr K. M.	Houston, USA	Import of commodities with focus on rice	Imported and distributed high-quality rice milled at his US facility	1997–2003
Dr M. M.	Ottawa, Canada	Import of auto parts	Imported high-quality used tyres using efficient packaging methods	1989–1995
Mr Y. T.	Hamburg, Germany	Import of auto parts	Imports sought-after automobiles and auto parts	2005–present
Mr S. O.	Accra, Ghana	Holds a degree in civil engineering from the Technical University in Munich, Germany	Grew up in Ghana and worked there as a civil engineer after completing his undergraduate degree before coming to Germany in 2005. Returned to Accra at the beginning of 2011	1982
Mr G. O.	Unna, Germany	Holds degrees in agriculture and tropical engineering from the universities of Kassel and Cologne, Germany	Grew up in Ghana and came to Germany in 1969 to study. Farmed indigenous plants in Ghana from 1982 to 1989. Has been working as a traditional health professional in Germany and Ghana since 1989	1945

General obstacles to entrepreneurship in Ghana

The main goal of this chapter is to explore obstacles to entrepreneurship in Ghana, with a special focus on imitation of entrepreneurial activities. We start with the presentation of our findings on general obstacles. When appropriate, we directly juxtapose our results to findings from the extant literature. A detailed analysis of imitation as an obstacle to entrepreneurship follows in the next section.

Access to finance and the banks

A common theme surfacing all throughout the discussion on innovation and entrepreneurship in Ghana, sub-Saharan Africa and the developing world as a whole is access to finance; more specifically, the lack of access to finance. Seventeen banks operate in Ghana. They can be further categorised into commercial banks[1] of which there are nine, five merchant banks[2] and another three development banks.[3] The Ghana Commercial Bank (GCB), which is state-owned, holds approximately 25% of total assets and 20% of deposits (Buchs and Mathiesen 2008). We need only to begin by looking at the number and location of bank branches, to realise that banking as such, at least by Western standards, is not the norm. Thirty-five per cent of all bank branches are located in the greater Accra area which only accounts for 13% of the population. All in all, formal banks only reach 5% of Ghana's inhabitants (Buchs and Mathiesen 2008). Only 3.4% of Ghanaians held loans from commercial banks in 2009. In comparison, 28.7% of Malaysians, who achieved independence in the same year as Ghana, 1957, hold loans from commercial banks (IMF 2010).

Ghanaian banks are quite hesitant when it comes to handing over funds in the form of loans. Our interviews confirm that access to finance, especially for young entrepreneurs, is an immense obstacle, but also that the banks are right to be concerned. It is not just that the banks do not want to give out money, but that their risks are extremely high, and lending criteria are therefore extremely stringent. Traceability of individuals was mentioned as a big problem. Addresses are far less specific and it is very easy for individuals to disappear. Public credit bureaux are non-existent and private credit bureaux only carry information on 10.3% of the adult population (World Bank 2010a).

Not only are banks hesitant when it comes to lending, but interest rates are exorbitant by Western standards and not because of risks alone. 'High real interest rates driven by excessive local borrowing by government have long hindered private enterprise access to affordable financing' (African Development Fund 2005: 5). The

---

1 'Commercial banks engage in traditional banking business, with a focus on universal retail services' (Buchs and Mathiesen 2008: 173).
2 'Merchant banks are fee-based banking institutions, mostly engaging in corporate banking services' (Buchs and Mathiesen 2008: 173).
3 'Development banks specialise in the provision of medium- and long-term finance' (Buchs and Mathiesen 2008: 173).

private sector is crowded-out, as most of the banks' resources are absorbed by the public sector. This could be in the form of either loans to state-owned enterprises or holdings of government securities (Buchs and Mathiesen 2008). Interest on a loan was specified to be 33% by one interviewee: 'Nobody makes this much profit'. It is therefore extremely difficult to finance any capital-intensive venture. Even the interbank interest rate posted by the bank of Ghana on 17 January 2011 was 11.63% (Bank of Ghana 2011). Table 8.2 provides a comparison of banking system indicators of Ghana, Germany, Malaysia and the United States.

Table 8.2 **Access to finance country comparison**

Source: Bank of Ghana 2011; Bank Negara Malaysia 2011; Federal Reserve 2011; Deutsche Bundesbank 2011; IMF 2010; World Bank 2010a, c, h, i

	Indicator		
Country	**Share of population for which private credit bureau information is available (2010) (%)**	**Share of population holding loans from commercial banks (2009) (%)**	**Interbank interest rate (2011) (%)**
Ghana	10.3	3.4	11.63
Germany	98.4	24.6	0.12
Malaysia	100.00	28.7	2.74
United States	100.00	42.3	0.16

For many entrepreneurs, there only remains the informal sector. The chances of approval are better, although lenders are becoming more stringent as well. One interviewee was working at an informal credit office that supplied small loans to 35 local merchants. He also mentioned that repayment was a big problem. They were looking into ways to secure their loans, such as requiring their borrowers to leave collateral, such as a car. The current process is that in order to receive a loan of 500 cedis for a period of six months, you must first make an initial deposit of 100 cedis; but if the interest rates of the formal sector seemed too high and kept you from borrowing, then the informal sector with interest rates of 40% or more would not be a viable option for you and your business either.

Another interviewee pointed to a further problem with respect to banking. He says that from his experience, the biggest problem, particularly when you are operating a large business, is that it is not possible to get your revenue out of the country. The interviewee was exporting large quantities of rice from the United States to Ghana between 1996 and 2003. He says small entrepreneurs often use the black market to exchange the local currency from their proceeds into US dollars to pay suppliers overseas; but when dealing with amounts in the millions, banks are the only option. He recalls waiting up to six months for his revenues to be exchanged and transferred to his bank in the United States. The Ghanaian bank recorded the cedi value at the time of the deposit but by the time the transfer had taken place, inflation and the currency differential had eaten up to 20% of the value. He says the banks use the funds as long as possible but another reason for them to delay is that they simply do not have such large quantities of US dollars available to them.

Infrastructure

In Ghana, the main problem areas in the realm of public capital seem to be electricity and transport. An interviewee recalls using generators to keep his communication centre in Accra operational during the frequently occurring blackouts. He remembers the irregular availability of electricity as a serious problem, especially for somebody operating high-tech equipment which is also sensitive to power fluctuations. Valco (the Volta Aluminum Company) is an aluminium processing plant which started operation in the 1950s, processing alumina imported from Jamaica. Ghana has been mining bauxite, the raw material required for aluminium, for quite some time, but Valco remains dormant, with none of its potlines[4] working because of the shortage of power. 'Until now the problem has been that there is not enough energy for our domestic needs, let alone Valco' (Smith 2011a: 12).

Another interviewee talks about the problems he had transporting his merchandise. The journey from the north where the shea trees—carrying the nuts made into shea butter—grow, to the south where the harbours are located, is painstaking. The roads are bad, causing long delays and putting extra stresses on already battered vehicles. Another interviewee agrees, indicating that transportation was also a major concern of his. He says the north, where most of the artisans producing his handicrafts resided, is so badly connected that the journey to the port on the coast in the south adds another 15% to his costs.

Transparency, regulation and standards

Transparency, or better, a lack of transparency is another hurdle to innovation and entrepreneurship in Ghana (Johnson and Lundvall 2003; Agyeman-Duah 2008). An excellent example to illustrate this lack of transparency and how it presents itself as an obstacle can be seen by looking at land ownership in Ghana. The World Bank commented on the land issue in April 2010 by saying that 'Ghana's economic growth and development has faced severe challenges that include difficulty accessing land, insecurity of land tenure and mismanagement of the nation's land resources' (World Bank 2010f).

The problem has a historical perspective. Traditionally Ghana has no private land ownership. Land is public domain and administered by the local chiefs. Even today the chiefs and their authority play a significant role (Berry 2009). The specifics of these customs have spawned a variety of literature as well as a number of reform initiatives. But the importance in the realm of this chapter lies in the implications. 'Legal and judicial recognition of customary claims to land and community

---

4 A row of smelting cells used in aluminium production.

membership tend to reproduce layered claims to land and recurring disputes over custom and historical precedent' (Berry 2009: 1351). When speaking to one of our interviewees, the issue of rental customs and land ownership came up immediately when discussing the obstacles to entrepreneurship. He says that landlords often demand a so-called 'goodwill'; this means that the tenant is required to pay the rent up to two years in advance, which is extremely difficult, especially for entrepreneurs starting out. Land ownership is problematic as it is not properly regulated. There is a lot of risk involved as the property might be sold to more than one individual at the same time.

For an entrepreneur to invest in a manufacturing operation requiring machinery and the construction of facilities on ground with uncertain claims is unarguably a risky proposition. Adding to this already less than favourable situation, the World Bank's *Doing Business Analysis 2011* ranks Ghana 151st out of 183 countries when it comes to ease of dealing with construction permits (World Bank 2010a).

The lack of standards, regulatory measures and enforcement of existing measures can be seen in the following simple but nonetheless striking example. A study conducted of the safety of street foods[5] in Ghana's Ga district in 1998, serving traditional Ghanaian cuisine, paints a clear but unsettling picture. Out of 160 establishments, only three met all the requirements for basic hygiene. More than 65% of the establishments did not obtain their meat from an approved source (King *et al.* 2000).

Lacking regulation, which creates a variety of unknowns, appears to be the pattern. An interviewee says that a serious concern of his is never knowing exactly how much he will end up paying in tariffs and duties for his imported merchandise: 'There is a bit of luck involved every time'.

Another interviewee sees the inefficient patent system as a major problem and therefore a hindrance to innovation. Although progress has been made since its inception, operating a fully fledged patent system is not easy, especially for a developing country. The resources required for the proper examination of applications are immense (Mills 1995). An article written by C.A. Cofie, President of Ghana's Employers Association, in June 2010 notes that:

> counterfeiting and piracy undermine innovation which is key to economic growth. More importantly, a nation where counterfeiting is rampant, quickly gains a reputation as a safe haven for people who wish to engage in economic crimes, shattering any hard won positive reputation we may have built over time (Cofie 2009).

5 'Street food refers to food and beverages prepared and sold by vendors in streets and other public places for immediate consumption' (King *et al.* 2000: 39).

Corruption

Even if we assume that regulation and standards have been efficiently drawn up, enforcement is a big issue in Ghana. An interviewee says that even with regulation and standards in place, enforcement would still pose a problem because police officers, for example, are paid so little that they look for bribes to supplement their incomes whenever possible. Such problems also seem to be present at higher levels. Killick (2008) adds corruption as another reason why funding for private enterprise is lacking. He suggests financial repression and the politicisation of credit decisions are a result of officials needing to be able to offer cheap loans to supporters. In the case of Ghana, he speaks of a protected crony capitalism based on privileged access to public resources, rather than on entrepreneurial talent and genuine risk-taking. A survey conducted in 2000 showed that 75% of Ghanaians saw corruption as a major problem in Ghana (Fosu and Aryeetey 2008). Anokhin and Schulze (2008: 467) argue that the control of corruption would motivate increased levels of innovative and entrepreneurial activity.

Many of the entrepreneurs interviewed spoke of 'connections' as a prerequisite for successfully conducting business in Ghana. One of them operates a pharmacy in Accra. He says that corruption is still rampant in all areas. 'If you don't know the criminals, you will not be successful, neither in politics nor in business.' He says it is unfortunate but he considers his connections his most valuable asset. Another interviewee, an importer of auto parts, pointed to an uncertainty with regard to the amount of tariffs and duties that have to be paid on the parts which he brings into the country. The customs officials exploit weak regulation. The amount to be paid greatly depends on the official, the broker and his relationship with them. Yet, it has to be mentioned that not all interviewees agreed. One interviewee, who was active in the production of shea butter in Ghana, paints a rather positive picture. He says he did not experience any problems with corrupt officials, nor the local people in terms of corruption, but in the end he did agree that long-winded bureaucratic processes could be expedited by paying tribute to the right individuals. A summary of the problem was provided by an interviewed entrepreneur: 'I have a little money, capital to start up a business but I'll end up using all of it to pay bribes.' A positive trend in Ghana's development has to be mentioned in this context. The World Bank ranks countries by governance, specifically the criteria 'control of corruption'. Ghana has moved up from the 48th percentile in 1998 to the 60th percentile in 2009 (Kaufmann *et al.* 2010).

Human capital, education and trust

'Education is one of the most powerful instruments for reducing poverty and inequality and lays a foundation for sustained economic growth' (World Bank 2010g). Oyelaran-Oyeyinka and Barclay (2003) recognise human capital formation as a key factor for the success of Southeast Asian latecomer economies. In Ghana, 31% of the adult population has never been to school. That being said, school attendance among Ghana's youth is quite high: 97% of Ghanaian males between the ages of 6 and 25, and 95.5% of females in the same age group in Accra, Ghana's capital, attend school. Numbers are lower in rural areas, but school attendance averages at 86.1% for the entire country (GSS 2008). The current educational structure in Africa, however, has been argued to be 'unsuitable for industrialisation' (Lall cited in Oyelaran-Oyeyinka and Barclay 2003: 96). Explanations include a curriculum inherited from colonial times focusing on producing an academic elite, argued to be irrelevant to Africa's development needs. The majority of university graduates hold degrees in the arts and humanities, leaving demand for science and engineering graduates unfulfilled (Oyelaran-Oyeyinka and Barclay 2003). One of our interviewees added that there is also a cultural fixation on classical professions such as medicine or law. People are not encouraged to take the entrepreneurial route. Education in the traditional avenues is equated to success by society. He says a lot of private universities are emerging, but their focus is still on traditional disciplines. Enterprise does not seem to be doing its part either when it comes to the development of its human capital. The training of employees is widely neglected and there appears to be an absence of formal technological activity by enterprise. Industry operates with inappropriate and even obsolete technologies which are rarely improved. Public institutions, not private enterprise, conduct the majority of research and development work (Lall *et al.* 1994).

Education is undoubtedly a key factor for creating an environment that spawns innovation and entrepreneurship. It is quite peculiar that in Ghana education is regarded so highly that it in itself may get in the way of development. Sørensen (2003: 291) explains that, because of entrepreneurs' usually high level of formal education, they are regarded as 'born to lead' and are trusted to have an understanding of all aspects of an operation, administrative or technical, which is of course not necessarily the case. This same line of thought leads to innovative ideas being overlooked. An interviewee recalls the story of an uneducated local man who built entire automobiles from scrap. People did not take the time to judge his work objectively based on merit, because he held no degree and lacked formal training. They simply assumed that a man not formally educated could build nothing of value.

A further problem seems to be trust: trust, not in institutions as discussed above, but between individuals. 'Ghanaian businessmen do not trust each other to any large extent' (Sørensen 2003: 292). This distrust is not limited to dealings between businessmen. It also affects the employee/employer relationship, with the implication that companies will tend to be small, as the owner is likely to want to oversee all activities personally (Sørensen 2003). One interviewee, supported by others, adds that if you conduct a business that requires employees, reliability and trustworthiness become a major factor. From his days as a farm operator in Ghana, he recalls that hand tools went missing rather quickly. The only measure that worked as a deterrent was to make examples of some of the employees suspected of stealing by involving the police and pressing charges. He says dismissal alone simply was no deterrent: 'they did not care . . . You constantly have to be watching every aspect of your operation yourself in order to ensure that you are not being robbed'.

Trust was also a factor that became apparent during the interview process. Several interview attempts failed; interviewees, especially those residing in Ghana, were sceptical about our intentions, even when introductions had been previously established through third parties.

Imitation as a reason for market failures in Ghana

This section provides a more detailed discussion of imitation as a major obstacle to entrepreneurship in Ghana. It starts with the story of an entrepreneur, Mike, who ran a business importing tyres from Western countries to Ghana, and also invented technological equipment to facilitate the transport. His business and invention were rendered worthless after low quality imitators entered the market. That market is now on the verge of breaking down. Mike's story is followed by a series of smaller case studies that exhibit a similar pattern.

Mike's story: import of used tyres

In 1989, a former classmate from Ghana came to visit Mike in Cologne, Germany, where he had been living for almost 20 years. This old friend had already been established in the tyre business in Ghana for 10 years. He had just received a shipment of tyres of inferior quality from his supplier in Germany, and did not get very far in the negotiations himself, so he enlisted Mike's help. As this was not the first time he had received inferior goods or had problems with suppliers, he needed somebody he could trust and proposed a partnership where Mike would procure the tyres in Germany, and he would sell them in Ghana. They purchased a van and rented a warehouse where the tyres could be sorted and stored until shipment.

It is important to mention here, that these were not new but used tyres. Due to stringent regulations regarding tread depth and an overall emphasis on tyre safety in the Western world, especially Germany, tyres which were replaced and considered worn out were still in great demand in Ghana, as new tyres were out of the reach of most Ghanaians. Mike went around to garages and car dealerships collecting the tyres. They were happy to see them go, as this reduced their own disposal activities and costs. Tyres that appeared 'good' on first inspection but showed defects during more careful inspection back at the warehouse, were sorted out and then collected by another company that only required the rubber for the production of cement. Mike was able to dispose of his 'refuse' at no cost and the other company saved time and effort by not having to travel from garage to garage collecting the tyres themselves.

Mike says the activity was innovative—using one country's refuse to profit in another—but he was not the originator. He does, however, see the improvement of the process as innovative, which was also reflected in the product. Mike differentiated himself by only supplying the best quality tyres. His partner in Ghana, dealing with the distribution side of the business, was facing increasing competition. Quantities needed to be raised, and shipping costs, the biggest expense in the venture, needed to be brought down. The only way to accomplish this was by fitting more tyres into the same size container; but how? Mike received a call from his partner who said they had come across somebody in Ghana who had managed to insert one tyre into another. Shortly after, he received a video documenting this process, and another two weeks later he had managed to duplicate the process. This was a manual process requiring hard labour, which needed to be done thousands of times per container to achieve the desired cost-saving effect. A 40-foot container accommodates approximately 1,500 tyres in assorted sizes and just under 3,000 when inserting one into the other. Mike came up with a design for a machine which he contracted to have built, that automated most of the process. He was able to fit up to nine tyres into one but for the purposes of keeping the tyres intact and ease of extraction, he kept the number of tyres at four in one (see Fig. 8.1).

Figure 8.1 **Mike's press for inserting four tyres into each other**

The market for tyres in Ghana became more and more saturated as more and more entrepreneurs in Ghana started importing tyres from the West. Tyres of lesser quality were thoroughly cleaned and painted with black rubber paint in order to make them appear to be of better quality. In the midst of the increasing competition and a short but costly stint in politics, the partner in Ghana lost the financial means to continue his activities. When Mike set out to take over the distribution side of the operation as well several years later, he soon realised that without the proper connections, intricate knowledge of the market and no trustworthy partners, it was extremely difficult. He says information is outdated so quickly that, by the time the container arrives, the goods are no longer wanted. One has to have time to stay and wait until the demand returns, but since he had to manage both sides of the operation he did not have this time. He could not compete on his own. The Ghanaian government has recently been debating a ban on the import of used tyres altogether because of the overall lack in quality.

> The Motor Transport and Traffic Unit (MTTU) of the Ghana Police Service, the Ministry of Transport, and the Customs, Excise and Preventive Services are currently discussing what to do with the continued importation of the used or inappropriate tyres, said to be a major contributor to road accidents (Myjoyonline.com 2009).

Such a ban would fully destroy the newly emerged market. Mike's invention, the Bonsu Press, has now stood unused for almost a decade now, in a storage facility in Canada.

Case studies on imitation and market failure

Pharmaceuticals

The import of low-quality drugs is a big problem (Cockburn *et al.* 2005). It implies the risk of a breakdown of the market for high-quality drugs, which finally leads to severe health risks for the Ghanaian people from poor-quality drugs. One interviewee has been operating a pharmacy in Accra since 2004. He began by importing high-quality drugs manufactured in Germany. He had noticed a lack of premium-grade medications for serious illnesses such as epilepsy. His competitors started offering products imported from China and India at significantly lower prices but with low, often insufficient doses. A problem arises since the general public is often not aware of the differences. They simply seek the lower price not knowing that the cheaper products are often inferior. This, in turn, brought these lower grade products into direct competition with his premium pharmaceuticals. Another avenue of competition is the counterfeiters whose concoctions produced in illegal, makeshift laboratories or imported from overseas pose serious health risks. Once again, lacking consumer awareness allows the counterfeit medications to directly compete against premium products. In addition to this, they make the consumers wary of pharmaceutical distributors as a whole, as it is difficult for them to correctly allocate blame for their negative experiences to specific products. Our interviewee has moved away from premium German products and now also imports medicines from China and India.

Herbal beverages

One interviewee mentions a revival of herbal alcoholic beverages by a company that reverted to traditional recipes for their production. People were familiar with the names of the beverages through stories they had heard from their elders. Some of the drinks were actually known to have medicinal characteristics. After a short time, competitors began to surface, but the majority did not adhere to traditional recipes, and health claims for their products ranged from the subtle to the outrageous. Consumers became wary of the claims and the ingredients, which led to their avoidance of this niche product all together. Consequently, the originator's business suffered despite using quality and authentic ingredients.

Sachet water

Another example is the case of sachet drinking water. Sachet drinking water is sold in plastic bags or sachets. A study published in 2008 reveals that less than half of Accra's residents (43.3%) felt comfortable drinking water from the tap (Lundéhn 2008). A 500 ml bottle of water costs approximately 50 pesewa[6] and is therefore extremely expensive by Ghanaian standards. Sachets on the other hand cost only one-tenth of that price at 5 pesewa, for the same quantity (Frempong 2010). One of our interviewees talked about the origins of this product. According to his account, it was a woman who came up with the idea to sell water in sachets, which she had previously purified, chilled and sold to drivers stuck in Accra's numerous traffic jams. She employed mostly young, out of work women as sales people and called her product 'pure water'. It did not take long for others to come along and sell water under a variety of names in plastic sachets as well. The major issue was that their water was often not purified. It was regular tap water, or even worse, river water. The sachet water has been linked to many cases of illness. In 2007, the Ghana Medical Association published a study with the objective to assess the safety of sachet drinking water. The researchers tested 500 ml sachets of 27 different brands selected at random and purchased from various vendors in Accra between January and May 2005. 'Seventy-seven per cent of the samples contained infective stages of pathogenic parasitic organisms' (Kwakye-Nuako *et al.* 2007: 62). The interviewee says that there are so many distributors of sachet water (approximately 45,000 producers according to Frempong 2010), and prices have fallen so low through the intense competition, that he finds it hard to believe that the sale of truly purified, safe sachet water remains a profitable business. The result was a breakdown of the market for high-quality sachet water.

·

6 100 pesewa = 1 cedi

Discussion and conclusions

Five out of the 11 interviewees mentioned the theme of imitation without being specifically prompted when discussing obstacles to innovation and entrepreneurship in Ghana. Five of the nine entrepreneurs had personal experiences related to the theme in their business activities. All interviewees were familiar with the phenomenon. In addition to the five entrepreneurs that had personally experienced unfair competition in their business activities, another four interviewees were able to recall specific examples where it occurred. The problems in the country create an environment where imitation flourishes.

Summing up, one of our interviewees draws a very pessimistic picture of Ghana's situation: 'There is no creativity there. If you have an idea people will copy it. We in Ghana are not educated to be creative but this is not a problem specific to Ghana or even Africa.'

The ease of imitation is enhanced by a set of structural deficits. There is a lack of access to well-established capital markets and only a few individuals have educations in engineering, or similar professions. As a result, entrepreneurs are unable to invest in unique assets (physical or intellectual), which are hard to copy and thus protect against imitation.

Ghanaians have been said to not be directing their educational efforts towards innovation and entrepreneurship. In a climate where not enough young people are steered towards the applied sciences, and entrepreneurial activity is not something that is strived for but is more or less a last resort,[7] ideas and solutions to conquer the hurdles in the path of true, complex, value-added businesses will not be spawned. Lack of access to finance explains why activities are uncomplicated, easily copied and mainly involve the simple buying and selling of goods. There is no funding available for entrepreneurs at reasonable rates to invest in a real business requiring significant know-how. Weak infrastructure has a similar effect as a financial obstacle. It forces people without means into simple, low-tech, low know-how, 'buying and selling' activities, which in turn are easily imitated.

In addition, institutional problems lead to the under-provision of effective protection for the already easily imitable ideas. Market entry barriers are lowered by lack of standards and regulation, unequal access to finance, politics and corruption. Entrepreneurs in Ghana are not operating in an environment where fair competition is encouraged. Corruption nurtures an environment of imitation and unfair competition by fuelling the lack of transparency. The ability to push substandard merchandise through weak regulatory controls by bribing the right individuals lowers market entry barriers significantly.

An interviewee shows his disappointment: 'It seems to be the nature of the people; everybody is looking for the quick buck'. Many Ghanaians seem to think that the 'quick buck' is most easily reached by doing what is already being done.

---

7 For more detailed analysis of such 'necessity entrepreneurship' refer to Block and Sandner 2009 and Block and Wagner 2010.

However, there are also promising examples. One is the company 'Blue Skies' which exports prepacked fruit salads and juices from Ghana, Brazil, Egypt and South America to Europe (Ross 2009). Fresh fruit is cut and prepackaged in the country of origin and shipped directly to retailers (Cooper 2007). Through the reliance on airfreight, Blue Skies successfully circumvents most of the hurdles of road traffic when supplying its customers in Europe. Anthony Pile, a British national, established Blue Skies in 1998. He set up his first operation in the north of Accra, employing approximately 1,000 workers in 2009. In 2008, sales from the Ghanaian operation totalled close to €15 million (Ross 2009). The venture was financed by friends, private investors and a mortgage on Pile's house (Cooper 2007). The example shows that once entrepreneurs have successfully secured financing, relatively low amounts of capital can suffice to start a fast-growing business with significant impact. Since wages and asset prices are low, more can be done with less. One interviewee adds that for somebody who has lived and studied abroad and is considering returning to Ghana as an entrepreneur, there always remains the possibility of pursuing financing through that nation's development bank, or through capital acquired elsewhere in Western countries.

Ghana is rich with resources that would allow sustainable development of the country if structural problems could be overcome. Shea butter is just one example. The shea tree is indigenous to Africa and grows in the north of Ghana. The tree is wild and cannot be farmed, as it is impossible to predict which seeds will germinate and it takes decades before it bears fruit. According to one of the interviewed entrepreneurs, shea butter is best used in its pure form as an all-natural moisturiser. When asked if he considers his activities innovative, he said: 'I did not consider myself innovative, the product has been used for thousands of years by our people, it has just been forgotten'. He credits shea butter in part for the Ghanaians' lack of wrinkles.

Renewable energy technology could be a further avenue for sustainable economic development in Ghana. Not only would solar energy create a new branch of business, it could also solve many of the problems that other businesses face as a result of the shortage of electricity. One interviewee commented:

> It is hard to believe to this day, that a country that has sunshine almost 365 days a year has a shortage of electricity. Maybe Ghanaian entrepreneurs should look up and not down, when trying to find solutions to the power requirements of their operations.

For businesses that only cater to the Ghanaian customer, other avenues have to be explored. One interviewee says that people in Ghana do appreciate quality. There does seem to be a market for quality products in Ghana under the right circumstances. The interviewee adds that branding of products is a key, because being recognisable in a sea of imitators gives you a fighting chance. A strengthening of the effectiveness and affordability of legal protection mechanisms could provide a solution.

Despite the obstacles, it has been shown that the problems can be tackled or at least circumvented until a better, more suitable environment develops, which most commentators seem confident will emerge. Even most of the entrepreneurs and experts, although cautious, believe Ghana has a promising future. The most recent edition of *The Africa Report*, calls Ghana the 'Black star rising' (*The Africa Report* 2011, cover page).

References

African Development Fund (2005) *Country Strategy Paper 2005–2009* (Ghana: Country Department, West Region).

Agyeman-Duah, I. (2008) *An Economic History of Ghana: Reflections on a Half-Century of Challenges and Progress* (Banbury, UK: Ayebia Clarke Publishing Limited).

Akerlof, G.A. (1970) 'The Market for "Lemons"', *Quarterly Journal of Economics* 84: 488-500.

Anokhin, S., and W.-S. Schulze (2008) 'Entrepreneurship, Innovation, and Corruption', *Journal of Business Venturing* 24: 465-76.

Bank Negara Malaysia (2011) 'Conventional Interbank Rates', Central Bank of Malaysia, Kuala Lumpur, www.bnm.gov.my/index.php?ch=12&pg=622&eId=box1, accessed 17 January 2011.

Bank of Ghana (2011) 'Interbank Interest Rate', The Bank of Ghana, Accra, www.bog.gov.gh, accessed 17 January 2011.

Baumol, W. (1986) 'Entrepreneurship and a Century of Growth', *Journal of Business Venturing* 1: 141-45.

Berry, S. (2009) 'Building for the Future? Investment, Land Reform and the Contingencies of Ownership in Contemporary Ghana', *World Development* 37.8: 1,370-78.

Block, J., and P. Sandner (2009) 'Necessity and Opportunity Entrepreneurs and their Duration in Self-Employment: Evidence from German Micro Data', *Journal of Industry, Competition and Trade* 9.2: 117-37.

Block, J., and M. Wagner (2010) 'Necessity and Opportunity Entrepreneurs in Germany: Characteristics and Earnings Differentials', *Schmalenbach Business Review* 62.2: 154-74.

BMZ (Bundesministerium für wirtschaftliche Zusammenarbeit und Entwicklung) (2010) 'Ghana', Federal Ministry for Economic Cooperation and Development, www.bmz.de/en/what_we_do/countries_regions/subsahara/ghana/index.html, accessed 17 June 2011.

Buchs, T., and J. Mathiesen (2008) 'Banking Competition and Efficiency in Ghana', in E. Aryeetey and R. Kanbur (eds.), *The Economy of Ghana: Analytical Perspectives on Stability, Growth and Poverty* (Accra: Woeli Publishing Services): 173-94.

Ceccagnoli, M., and F.T. Rothaermel (2008) 'Appropriating the Returns from Innovation', in G. Libecap (ed.), *Advances in the Study of Entrepreneurship, Innovation & Economic Growth* (Bingley, UK: Emerald): 11-34.

CIA (Central Intelligence Agency) (2011) *The World Factbook: Ghana* (Washington, DC: CIA, version of 15 January 2011).

Cockburn, R., P.-N. Newton, E.-K. Agyarko, D. Akunyili and N.-J. White (2005) 'The Global Threat of Counterfeit Drugs: Why Industry and Governments Must Communicate the Dangers', *PLoS Medicine* 2.4: e100.

Cofie, C.-A. (2009) 'The Impact of Illicit Trade and Counterfeit Goods on National Development', Multimedia Group Limited, Accra, business.myjoyonline.com/pages/news/200906/31043.php, accessed 29 October 2011.

Cooper, B. (2007) 'The just-food interview: Anthony Pile, Blue Skies', just-food, www.just-food.com/interview/the-just-food-interview-anthony-pile-blue-skies_id100213.aspx, accessed 21 September 2011.

Deutsche Bundesbank (2011) 'Base Rate', Deutsche Bundesbank, Frankfurt, www.bundesbank.de/index.en.php, accessed 17 January 2011.

Drucker, P.-F. (2007) *Innovation and Entrepreneurship: The Classic Drucker Collection Edition* (Oxford, UK: Elsevier).

Federal Reserve Bank of New York (2011) 'Fed funds', Federal Reserve Bank of New York, www.newyorkfed.org/index.html, accessed 17 January 2011.

Fosu, A.-K., and E. Aryeetey (2008) 'Ghana's Post-Independence Economic Growth: 1960–2000', in E. Aryeetey and R. Kanbur (eds.), *The Economy of Ghana: Analytical Perspectives on Stability, Growth & Poverty* (Accra: Woeli Publishing Services): 36-75.

Frempong, B. (2010) 'New Prices for Sachet and Bottled Water to Take Effect in Feb', Citi FM, Accra, *Online Business News*, 2 February 2010.

GSS (2008) *Ghana Living Standards Survey: Report of the Fifth Round (GLSS 5)* (Accra: Ghana Statistical Service).

Harvey, R. (2010) *Will Oil Build or Break the Back of Ghana's Democracy?* (Policy Briefing 14, Governance of Africa's Resources Programme; Johannesburg: South African Institute of International Affairs, SAIIA).

IMF (2010) 'Financial Access Survey 2009', fas.imf.org/Home.aspx, accessed 17 June 2011.

Johnson, B., and B.-A. Lundvall (2003) 'National Systems of Innovation and Economic Development', in M. Muchie: Gammeltoft and B.-A. Lundvall (eds.), *Putting Africa First: The Making of African Innovation Systems* (Aalborg, Denmark: Aalborg University Press): 13-28.

Kaufmann, D., A. Kraay and M. Mastruzzi (2010) *The Worldwide Governance Indicators: Methodology and Analytical Issues* (Policy Research Working Paper 5430; Washington, DC: The World Bank Development Research Group Macroeconomics and Growth Team).

Killick, T. (2008) 'What Drives Change in Ghana? A Political-Economy View of Economic Prospects', in E. Aryeetey and R. Kanbur (eds.), *The Economy of Ghana: Analytical Perspectives on Stability, Growth & Poverty* (Accra: Woeli Publishing Services): 20-35.

King, L.-K., B. Awumbila, E.-A. Canacoo and S. Ofosu-Amaah (2000) 'An Assessment of the Safety of Street Foods in the Ga District, of Ghana: Implications for the Spread of Zoonoses', *Acta Tropica* 76: 39-43.

Kwakye-Nuako, G.:B. Borketey, I. Mensah-Attipoe, R.-H. Asmah and P.-F. Ayeh-Kumi (2007) 'Sachet Drinking Water in Accra: The Potential Threats of Transmission of Enteric Pathogenic Protozoan Organisms', *Ghana Medical Journal* 41.2: 62-67.

Lall, S., G.-B. Navaretti, S. Teitel and G. Wignaraja (1994) *Technology and Enterprise Development: Ghana under Structural Adjustment* (New York: St Martin's Press).

Lundéhn, C. (2008) *Consumer Trust in Drinking Water Supply: Assessing the Interface between the Supplier and the Consumer* (PhD thesis; Gothenburg, Sweden: Department of Civil and Environmental Engineering, Water Environment Technology, Chalmers University of Technology).

Mills, D.-M. (1995) 'Some Observations on the New Patent Law of Ghana', *World Patent Information* 17.4: 234-40.

Myjoyonline.com (2009) 'Used-Tyres Imports Face Ban', 9 March 2009, news.myjoyonline.com/news/200903/27290.asp, accessed 17 June 2011.

Oyelaran-Oyeyinka, B., and L.-A. Barclay (2003) 'Human Capital and Systems of Innovation in African Development', in M. Muchie: Gammeltoft and B.-A. Lundvall (eds.), *Putting Africa First: The Making of African Innovation Systems* (Aalborg, Denmark: Aalborg University Press): 93-107.

Ross, W. (2009) 'Ghana's Juicy Economic Lesson', BBC News Ghana, 13 March 2009, news.bbc.co.uk/2/hi/africa/7939221.stm, accessed 29 October 2011.

Smith: (2011a) 'After a Long March, a Great Leap Forward', *The Africa Report: Investing in Ghana* 26: 12-13.

Smith: (2011b) 'Banking on Barrels', *The Africa Report: Investing in Ghana* 26: 16-17.

Sørensen, O.-J. (2003) 'Barriers to and Opportunities for Innovation in Developing Countries: The Case of Ghana', in M. Muchie: Gammeltoft and B.-A. Lundvall (eds.), *Putting Africa First: The Making of African Innovation Systems* (Aalborg, Denmark: Aalborg University Press): 287-303.

Teece, D. J. (1986) 'Profiting from Technological Innovation: Implications for Integration, Collaboration, Licensing and Public Policy', *Research Policy* 15.6: 285-305.

The Africa Report (2011) Cover page, *The Africa Report: Investing in Ghana*, 26: cover.

US State Department (2009) 'Remarks by the President to the Ghanaian Parliament', 7 November 2009, www.whitehouse.gov/the-press-office/remarks-president-ghanaian-parliament, accessed 29 October 2011.

World Bank (2010a) *Doing Business 2011: Ghana* (Washington, DC: The World Bank Group).

World Bank (2010b) *Doing Business 2011: United Kingdom* (Washington, DC: The World Bank Group).

World Bank (2010c) *Doing Business 2011: Germany* (Washington, DC: The World Bank Group).

World Bank (2010d) *Doing Business 2011: Côte d'Ivoire* (Washington, DC: The World Bank Group).

World Bank (2010e) *Doing Business 2011: Togo* (Washington, DC: The World Bank Group).

World Bank (2010f) 'Ghana Land Administration Project Improves Ease of Land Registration', News & Events Accra, World Bank Group, 29 April 2010, web.worldbank.org/WBSITE/EXTERNAL/COUNTRIES/AFRICAEXT/GHANAEXTN/0,,contentMDK:22562684~pagePK:141137~piPK:141127~theSitePK:351952,00.html, accessed 29 October 2011.

World Bank (2010g) 'Education', The World Bank Group, data.worldbank.org/topic/education, accessed 17 June 2011.

World Bank (2010h) *Doing Business 2011: Malaysia* (Washington, DC: The World Bank Group).

World Bank (2010i) *Doing Business 2011: United States* (Washington, DC: The World Bank Group).

9

The social sustainability of entrepreneurship

An ethnographic study of entrepreneurial balancing of plural logics[1]

Toke Bjerregaard and Jakob Lauring

University of Aarhus, Denmark

Sustainable entrepreneurship is attracting increasing attention in the entrepreneurship literature. This is reflected in, for instance, the proliferation of concepts of sustainable entrepreneurs such as 'ecopreneurs' (Hockerts 2006; Harbi *et al.* 2010) and social entrepreneurs (Robinson *et al.* 2008). Hence, entrepreneurial action may be seen as central to the creation of sustainability. Social sustainable entrepreneurship is often conceived as entrepreneurial action that leads to social value creation. In the present chapter we illuminate how small business entrepreneurs engage in activities of importance for social sustainability and development as they undertake entrepreneurial ventures.

Moreover, social entrepreneurship has become central to the issue of social sustainable development. Social entrepreneurship can be understood as 'a process involving the innovative use and combination of resources to pursue opportunities to catalyze social change and/or address social needs' (Mair and Martí 2006). Social

1 We wish to thank Inge Pasgaard without whom this chapter would not have been possible.

entrepreneurship, like other entrepreneurial activities, is shaped by the broader institutional contexts and logics in which it is embedded (Polanyi 1944; Marquis and Lounsbury 2007). Development actors, as one type of social entrepreneur, work with building the institutions that support poor people's market participation (Mair and Martí 2009). Hence, for such entrepreneurial actors the aim is sustainable development (Mair and Martí 2009). Poor people's participation in markets is, however, in many development countries restricted by 'institutional voids' (Mair and Martí 2009). In contexts characterised by institutional voids, institutions that support markets are absent or malfunction (Khanna and Palepu 1997). Extant research primarily differentiates between three types of institutional void: namely, voids that restrict market creation, obstruct market functioning and impede market participation (Mair and Martí 2009). Voids that impede market creation may comprise weak or absent governance structures, property rights and the rule of law (Mair et al. 2007). Developing countries characterised by institutional voids often lack formal institutions that support market functioning. However, lack of formal rules and institutions does not imply an absence of informal, social or cultural-cognitive institutions and norms (Bohannan and Dalton 1965; Moore 1978). Developing countries may be characterised by formal institutional voids but are rich on informal institutions, traditions, customary practices and beliefs which are believed to often impede social and economic development by restricting people from access to the market (Mair and Martí 2009).

Extant research has focused on how social entrepreneurs such as NGOs exert institutional work (Lawrence and Suddaby 2006) by changing the informal institutions, traditions, customary norms and practices that are believed to prevent poor people from market participation in developing countries (Martí and Mair 2009; Mair and Martí 2009). Hence, social entrepreneurs such as NGOs recombine available resources and institutions to fill institutional gaps that impede market participation and activity (Mair et al. 2007). Relatively little, however, has been done to elucidate the work of the poor people in developing countries as they, through entrepreneurial ventures, cope and work with the institutional environments that supposedly restrict them from market participation.

In this chapter we aim to bridge parts of this gap. Our argument is illustrated by an ethnographic field study that examines the strategies used by small entrepreneurs in an area of extreme resource scarcity to navigate coexisting and potentially contradictory social and market logics. The entrepreneurs cope with and exploit institutional contradictions through their sphere-straddling ventures to maintain enterprise sustainability during institutional change from an economy based on traditional exchange relationships to a situation with an emerging market economy. We examine the strategies through which the entrepreneurs navigate and work with the multiple institutional logics of the different spheres in which they operate in order to facilitate entrepreneurial venturing and, in turn, contribute to both sustaining and changing societal structures. Informal institutional structures and logics were believed by local NGOs to impede economic and social development by demotivating poor people from market participation. However, by examining the actual perceptions and strategies of the local poor people and their entrepreneurial ventures, we illuminate how customary norms, beliefs and institutions not merely imposed institutional constraints on economic practice, but were used by entrepreneurs to create opportunities for individual value generation.

This chapter proposes an alternative conceptualisation of institutional entrepreneurship to the predominant one. Traditionally, institutional entrepreneurship has been conceived as actors' activities with changing social structures to realise opportunities (DiMaggio 1988): that is, changes that deviate from the established institutions in a field of activity (Battilana *et al.* 2009). The present study illustrates that institutional entrepreneurship in pluralistic contexts is as much about the activities of actors in maintaining or sustaining societal structures, as about changing them. Hence, entrepreneurs bridging pluralistic institutions devise strategies to strike a balance between the logics on which their ventures are based to support enterprise sustainability and thereby work simultaneously with sustaining and changing social structures. Issues of pertinence to social sustainability are in this perspective an imminent aspect of the entrepreneurial process (Barth 1967b).

Conceptual background: social sustainability in entrepreneurship

Economic activities are embedded in broader institutional spheres and logics which impose constraints and opportunities on entrepreneurial ventures and market activity (Malinowski 1922; Polanyi 1944; Parry and Bloch 1989). Various formal or informal institutions and sanctions enable and constrain exchange across spheres of value circulation and activity within them (Bohannan and Dalton 1965; Barth 1967b).

Institutional theory is based on a notion of institutions as durable, taken-for-granted social structures (Hughes 1942; Jepperson 1991). Hence, according to institutional theory, it requires an effort to change an institution or social structure (Battilana *et al.* 2009). Institutional entrepreneurship is then about how actors change institutions to realise valued opportunities (Eisenstadt 1980; DiMaggio 1988; Battilana *et al.* 2009). Hence, research on social entrepreneurship has elucidated how microcredit organisations recombine available institutions and resources to create new institutions or change existing societal norms to facilitate social and economic development (Martí and Mair 2009).

In this present chapter we suggest a conceptualisation of institutional entrepreneurship by drawing inspiration from practice theory represented in models such as Barth's theory of entrepreneurship (Barth 1967a, b, 1981). In this perspective societal and cultural-cognitive structures or institutions are in a process of emergence. In such a perspective it is likely to require an effort to maintain or sustain societal structures as well as changing them. Conceptualising entrepreneurship in a process perspective conceives of entrepreneurial praxis in pluralistic contexts as an ongoing activity with balancing the maintenance of existing institutions and integration of new institutional structures. Efforts aimed at ensuring social sustainability are thus an inherent aspect of entrepreneurial processes which are bound up with multiple spheres and logics. Actors operating amid institutional contradictions must simultaneously undertake activities to maintain existing institutions and integrate new ones. Hence, rather than being restricted to a few actors, institutional agency is potentially present in all social or economic activities that are bound up with multiple spheres and logics. To account for how entrepreneurship capitalises on and influences institutional change and stability, the present research draws inspirations from the notions of: (1) institutional logics; (2) structural overlaps between spheres; and (3) institutional entrepreneurs (Thornton *et al.* 2005).

A burgeoning stream of institutional literature addresses the ways in which individuals, organisations and field-level actors deal with situations characterised by multiple, often opposing institutional logics (Lounsbury 2007; Reay and Hinings 2009; Battilana and Dorado 2011). Institutional logics can be considered as 'toolkits' (Swidler 1986) available for actors to elaborate on (Friedland and Alford 1991; Thornton and Ocasio 2008) and thus both constrain and enable social action. Institutional entrepreneurs construct opportunities by identifying cultural discontinuities in the meaning of institutional logics across spheres (Thornton *et al.* 2005). Structural overlaps between spheres expose actors to multiple logics, which they, in turn, may use to initiate change (Thornton *et al.* 2005). Hence, when actors are exposed to the logics of multiple sectors, they have the opportunity to hybridise institutions (Thornton *et al.* 2005). Extant research has examined how institutional entrepreneurs make use of institutional logics to promote change within a field by transposing institutional elements or logics between fields. Comparatively less research has illuminated those actors that operate in different spheres simultaneously where they, according to Martí and Mair (2009), at the same time have to juggle and navigate multiple and often contradictory logics. Research shows how organisations may become sustainable by striking a balance between the institutional logics they bind together (Battilana and Dorado 2011). However, there is a need for more research on the challenges faced and skills needed by actors operating across societal spheres and logics (Martí and Mair 2009: 112). This is often a characteristic of entrepreneurship, which in the words of Barth,

> frequently involves the relationship of persons and institutions in one society with those of an other . . . and the entrepreneur becomes an essential 'broker' in this situation of culture contact. But in the most general sense, one might argue that in the activities of the entrepreneur we may recognise processes which are fundamental to questions of social stability and change, and that their analysis is therefore crucial to anyone who wishes to pursue a dynamic study of society (Barth 1967b: 3).

According to practice-based theories, social continuity and change is the product of an articulation process occurring at the level of macro structures as well as the level of actors' transformative praxis (Comaroff 1985). Novel institutional orders and logics come into being through a process of reorganisation (Comaroff 1985). Social continuity and reorganisation takes place through a dialectical articulation process of institutional structure and action which may create a syncretistic institutional bricolage (Comaroff 1985; Lévi-Strauss 1966). Such a bricolage includes both a reproduction of existing institutions and a change with the introduction of new elements: that is, a joining together of distinct systems—themselves dynamic orders of practice and meaning. By using and recombining the institutional logics and resources at hand, brokers in this articulation process partake in the construction of new orders of legitimate social and economic action. Hence, in a practice perspective, the focus is not merely on whether economic action breaks or conforms with a social norm (cf. Holy and Stuchlik 1983). Rather, the focus is on which institutional logics and norms are invoked in taking particular actions, whether actors under- or over-perform given norms in their actual interactions and, in turn, reproduce or transform those norms and logics of legitimate action (cf. Holy and Stuchlik 1983). This dialectic of institutional system and practice continuously reproduces or transforms institutional spheres of value circulation and channels of conversion and thereby shapes the strategic agency of the entrepreneur (Barth 1967b).

The approach outlined is grounded on a concern to decipher social patterns-in-the-making and connecting different levels of analysis (Gluckman 1955; Barth 1981; Comaroff and Comaroff 1999; Powell and Colyvas 2008). In the following sections we illustrate the value of this perspective by use of an ethnographic field study of how small business entrepreneurs cope with and exploit the institutional contradictions forming the basis for social and economic changes in the wider societal context. This is done by illuminating the entrepreneurs' strategies of balancing coexisting social and market logics on which their ventures are dependent during a societal transition phase.

Methodology

Barth (1967a) suggests that an analytical and methodological framework for research on entrepreneurship should account for the ways in which relations of exchange and value circulation are produced and reproduced, by addressing the entrepreneurial process as it unfolds. Hence, an analytical and methodological approach to entrepreneurship research should be founded on the assumption that the unfolding of interactions and transactions between individuals cannot be deduced from established institutional structures and logics. According to Barth (1967b), an analysis based on assumptions of linear causality and predictability will most likely fail to provide insight into the social dynamics and dialectics of the entrepreneurial process. Hence, an ethnographic methodology is appropriate as it allows us to portray entrepreneurial actions not merely as illustrative of identified structures, but as constitutive of such patterns (Barth 1967b; Velsen 1967; Evens and Handelman 2006).

Data collection

Using a full-scale, five-month ethnographic fieldwork of small-scale central Malawi entrepreneurs, conducted by an associate researcher (Pasgaard 2005), we have outlined a short case illustrating our theoretical argumentation.

This fieldwork used an exploratory qualitative approach to data collection, which in a prospective way continuously introduced new information and questions to the research cycle (Spradley 1980; Bernard 1995). This methodological approach was applied to reach an understanding of issues which the informants might take for granted (e.g. Bourdieu 1977; Agar 1986). The ideal, generally, was to generate questions as well as answers in close proximity to the research setting.

In keeping with the ethnographic approach, data collection relied heavily on participant observation. When using participant observation, the aim is for the researcher to gain the ability to recognise and understand the social organisation of interaction. This provides an opportunity to register processes producing and reproducing social categories applied at the scene (Brubaker 2002).

Villagers were told that the researcher was interested in the entrepreneurial activities. However, the researchers tried generally to keep as low a profile as possible and not to ask questions or perform actions that would create social behaviour in others that would not have occurred ordinarily and thereby bias observations. Through observation and participation, research questions were developed, changed or focused on, in mutual interaction with the daily activities of the informants (Spradley 1980).

To supplement observations, informal interviews were conducted with most families of the village and with individual key informants (Bernard 1995). All in all, more than 100 individuals contributed to the data material. Physically, the interviews took place in open spaces or in villagers' houses and lasted between one and two hours. To minimise the effects of the setting, elite bias was avoided by interviewing individuals from different levels of the small society.

Early results were continuously discussed and cross-checked with different key informants. Two interpreters were used to assist during the interviews. Through their social contacts and local knowledge, they had a substantial influence on the final results. The interpreters' statements and explanations, however, were continuously cross-checked. The ethnographic approach is particularly valuable in the study of implicit or sensitive issues, elucidating the nature of social relations, occult forces and value accumulation during societal transformations and ruptures.

Data analysis

Analysis of the data was guided by the notion that it is the connection with empirical reality that permits the development of a relevant and valid theory (Van Maanen 1988). Hence, the aim was to tell a story based on the analysis of central themes. The theme analysis followed the steps described by Spradley (1980) and involved detailed close reading and coding of field notes, interview transcripts and documents, which led to the development of relatively rich descriptions of the research site. These descriptions helped to identify key aspect of entrepreneurial practices. By use of the qualitative analysis-program Nvivo, the data was sorted. The coded data provides relatively rich examples of how entrepreneurs cope and work with institutional contradictions. In the analysis, the researcher relied on triangulation of data wherever it was possible to check the validity of statements obtained from interviews, observations and secondary sources. The reporting includes only data substantiated over multiple information sources.

Research site and socioeconomic context

The ethnography was conducted in 2002 under the ongoing efforts to implement liberal democracy in Malawi, which were initiated in 1995, and hence during a fragile institutional transition process. This transition comprises attempts to build stronger pillars for democratic governance such as the development of a market economy. From 1891, Malawi came under the British Empire. In 1964, Malawi had its first election whereafter it became independent. Hastings Kamuzu Banda was absolute president and dictator from 1964. However, under the famine in 1992, the church and many Malawis increasingly criticised the system. In 1994, the first free election was carried out, and in 1995 Malawi got a new constitution which ensured multi-party democracy (Larney 2001: 69). Ninety per cent of Malawi's population lives in rural areas (Larney 2001: 115). Malawi is, like many other developing countries, rich on informal institutions, but less so on formal institutions that support a modern market economy (Mair and Martí 2009). Malawi's democratisation project is characterised by institutional fragility. The country has practically come under the administration of international actors who influence the formulation of national policies and programmes, and the international development industry is strongly present in the country.

The village of Mitengo was chosen because there was existing knowledge about the social and political situation and the local language, Chichewa. Previously, work for a nearby poverty alleviation organisation operating microcredit programmes showed that the organisation believed that local, customary practices and myths impeded economic and social development by, for instance, restricting women from participation in value-generating activities outside the house. From the perspective of the NGO, economic practice was impeded by institutional voids expressed in occult forces which functioned as a leveraging sanction. Coming back to the area a few years later to carry out the ethnographic study, it was deliberately chosen not to gain access to the field through this NGO in order to be able to break with its representations of the local economic practices and institutional systems. This was decided in order to get closer to the actual perceptions and strategies of the poor informing their economic practice. Moreover, being associated with an NGO could limit the access to certain kinds of information among the poor. According to several informants, access to startup capital and hence market participation is hampered by a long history of Western intervention comprising 50 years of British colonial administration, Western support to the dictator under the cold war and the international development industry, which is currently strongly present in Malawi, leading to a lack of belief in local resources and abilities. The field worker stayed with a family in Mitengo for some of the time. However, owing to a situation of extreme resource scarcity and a death per week, it was decided to stay with a comparatively wealthier family in the outskirts of Mitengo as well.

Out of the 500 inhabitants in the village of Mitengo, the majority belonged to the Chewa tribe. However, migrations from other parts of the country and from Zimbabwe or Mozambique led to an increasing number of outsiders settling down in the area. Traditionally, the distribution of land has been guided by societal structures of inherited status and following social obligations as levelling mechanisms—wealthy inhabitants were obliged to assist relatives, friends and neighbours. Through his power to distribute land, the chief traditionally was the top administrator of the exchange of value. This position has, in recent years, increasingly been replaced by market forces. More land is now available on the financial market, and government institutions are continuously taking over larger parts of authority previously held by the chief. In addition, villagers are feeling less obliged to follow the tradition of economically supporting less fortunate households and relatives in the immediate surroundings.

The primary income of the villagers comes from maize production but, because of the scarcity of land, additional sources of income are necessary for most inhabitants. First, this can be seasonal farming labour, often paid by provisions such as maize. Second, it can be trade of handiwork or prostitution in the city, for example. Third, it can be the production of goods such as bricks or beer. There are, however, certain types of trade and production that are especially nurturing entrepreneurial ventures in Mitengo, such as the trade of meat, wood, hardware, foreign medicine or credit, and the production of tobacco, furniture and textiles. These types of business generate a relatively larger surplus compared with the conventional small-scale businesses, but also assume a more substantial startup capital and a higher risk.

Findings

The market logic has been gaining in strength and is increasingly replacing the established social logic of rights and obligations. Hence, money is achieving a steadily more central position in Mitengo's system of value circulation. This is both conditioned by and results in changes in the local power and distribution structure as the market is being distanced from local power institutions. As explained by a local person:

> Nowadays, I tell you, there is no one who doesn't like money. Everybody is working to have money. Everyone is looking for money. I tell you . . . And people kill each other for money, I tell you. Not only by magic. Even killing, reality killing.

In order to create a space for exchange in the system of value circulation, the entrepreneur must act as a broker between the opposing logics in the articulation process, which serves as a basis for the changing position of money and market in the system. The question is how occult forces affect the entrepreneurs' role as institutional brokers in this process. Societal institutions impose constraints and social sanctions on entrepreneurial activity in Malawi by, for instance, restricting women from undertaking value-generating activities. They are thus subject to a variety of social sanctions, such as witchcraft accusations. Witchcraft is a sanction that is activated by the observation of a practice of exchange that challenges the social and cultural norms of the conventional distribution structure. In other words, the risk of jealousy is particularly high when individuals accumulate power and material resources that are in opposition to the established logic of social rights and obligations. However, the entrepreneurs' activities are not only affected by institutional changes, but sustain and transform societal structures. Entrepreneurship in Mitengo is thus conditioned by the entrepreneurs being able to base their ventures on existing institutional structures and at the same time building bridges to new, upcoming institutions. The entrepreneurs, in different terms, develop strategies to bridge the institutional contradictions that form the basis for changes in the societal context. Through the ongoing interaction between macro-institutional structures and entrepreneurial practice, different spheres of value circulation are sustained and changed. Questions of importance to social sustainability and development are thus highly reflected in the entrepreneurial process.

The socially responsible entrepreneur

Mr Mguoto is the only farmer making a living from growing tobacco. This is the reason why people in the village call him 'Tobacco Man'. He is Chewa, born in Mitengo and in accordance to traditions he has inherited his land from his mother's brother. The Tobacco Man is retired from a job at a large commercial tobacco plantation, which provided him with the knowledge on growing tobacco, which is uncommon in Mitengo.

Being a local farmer, the Tobacco Man attracts capital to the village and distributes it through social obligation and a demand for labour. In addition, Mr Mguoto is very active in the local community. He is a member of the Catholic Church, the government party UDF, connected to the chiefdom as a substitute for his brother and the founder and an important financial contributor to the Mitengo school. The Tobacco Man is the only person in Mitengo who is a member of all authoritative institutions, and he has achieved these positions mainly through strategic financial investments in important social relations.

By growing tobacco, Mr Mguoto is bridging the present divide between commercial large-scale plantation farming and the common local subsistence farming. Consequently, he is able to save money in the bank, which is rather unusual in the local area. In Mitengo, private land is usually only used for growing maize and other food crops, but after changes due to the democratisation and privatisation process after 1994, he is able to utilise the openings between the authority of the chiefdoms and the new, emerging market economy. Hence, the Tobacco Man is one of the few villagers not complaining about the expanding role of the money economy and the centrality taken by the institutional logic of the market in the system of value circulation.

Though his specialised production is based on his education and experience from previous employment as well as the changing economic conditions on a national level, the Tobacco Man is bridging different institutional domains in Barth's (1967a) terms, since he utilises the new opportunity of exchanging money for positions in the powerful institutions. Thereby the Tobacco Man is trying to integrate market forces into the traditional hierarchy—and building a bridge between the traditional, social logic of rights and obligations and the new logic of market exchange. Based on the new rules of privatisation he is now able to grow tobacco, generating profit that can be invested to acquire power in relation to the traditional hierarchy, the church and the government party.

The Tobacco Man, according to himself, is not being an entrepreneur to generate wealth solely to make life easy for him. On the contrary, he is sharing his economic surplus with family and the different social institutions. Mr Mguoto has all of his relatives living in Mitengo and highly prioritises his financial obligations to them. And during interviews none of his relatives expressed any negative emotions towards him, which was rather uncommon when speaking of wealthy family members. Thereby he is still subordinating himself to a traditional normative pattern of rights and obligations to add legitimacy to economic action.

The economic entrepreneur

As a member of the Ngoni tribe in Zimbabwe, Mossa was an outsider to Mitengo. In the 1980s he left his home country and most of his relatives in search of new opportunities in Malawi. In Mitengo he asked the chief for a piece of land that he secretly paid for. This transaction was possible only because Mossa was a newcomer and because he disguised the transaction with the chief. By using concealment along with money to acquire a resource traditionally only available through the local hierarchy of inheritance and social obligations, Mossa was bridging different normative spheres.

Mossa is solely supporting his own children, his mother-in-law and his wife's brother, and he does not engage in social obligations outside this close family. Accordingly, as an outsider, he is able to put priority on new investments at the expense of financial obligations to his kinsmen. Mossa thus has a different approach to this practice compared with the Tobacco Man. As a consequence of his entrepreneurial activities he is the wealthiest inhabitant of Mitengo. He has much land, a car, a motorcycle and a large house with a fence and an iron gate, and he owns several apartment houses in the village and in the nearby town.

Mossa generates the main part of his surplus from credit business and from rental housing. This is unique to the area, since it is highly unusual to generate profit from relations to people with fewer resources than oneself. Traditionally, the system of social obligations is directing the flow of money the other way around. Mossa, however, is not interpreting the norm of social obligation the way it has usually been conceived in Mitengo. When people ask him for money he, instead, offers them a loan and thereby actively utilises the tradition of social obligation to expand his business area. According to him, he is doing this through a social obligation not to discourage hardworking individuals, thus promoting entrepreneurial activities throughout the village. In this way Mossa is integrating the existing logic of rights and obligations into the new market economy and thereby brokering between two oppositional, institutional structures of value distribution.

Mossa is a newcomer. This facilitates his strategy, which is made possible because he actively distances himself from social relations in the area. He does not give in to people's 'begging', and he opens the large iron gate only for very few of his fellow villagers. Each day he goes to town on his motorbike and this is where he has his friends.

The two entrepreneurs are bridging social and economic spheres in the sense that they operate across the embedded contradiction of the social and economic change processes. They base their ventures on the 'bricolage' of the meeting between an existing social structure and a new structure in progress (Lévi-Strauss 1963). The experiences (from an earlier job and a foreign background) of the entrepreneurs are the basis of a knowledge differentiation and an understanding of new logics of value and exchange. This knowledge is used in the exploration of the already initiated changes of the value circulation in Mitengo. Linked to opportunities and financial surplus, however, is also the risk of envy and social sanctions.

The role of witchcraft in sustaining social structure

Witchcraft is an example of how established institutional structures may affect the entrepreneurial process, making it a dialectical rather than a linear process including broader societal structures.

Confronted with the notion of witchcraft, all informants to begin with deny its existence, but after being assured that the researchers do not find it ridiculous or un-Christian to acknowledge the powers of the supernatural, all informants can describe situations where friends or relatives have used or been affected by witch-craft. As one argues, witchcraft or occult forces are real:

> Magic is science. Because if we talk of magic, we talk of something that is there. But for one to understand it, he has to use all his wisdom and all his intelligence to understand it or to discover it . . . Africans have their own science, the azungus (white people) have their own science, the azungus have their own magic.

Behaviour associated with the accumulation of wealth and power is deemed anti-social according the established social logic of rights and obligations, and increases the risk of being exposed to witchcraft as a result of jealousy. Witchcraft is thus a sanction that is activated by the observation of a practice of exchange that breaks with the institutional logic of the conventional distribution structure. Witchcraft has a levelling character in relation to the power and resource distribution. In other words: the risk of jealousy is particularly high when individuals accumulate power and material resources that are in opposition to established normative spheres of rights and obligations. If a man owns a car in an area where people are starving, it is seen as a proof that he is not facing his social obligations. Instead, he should share his property with relatives and others in need.

Mankwala can be described as a witchcraft prophylaxis that can protect against all risks. The access to *mankwala* protection, however, is dependent on finance and relations to a trustworthy *singanga* or witch doctor. Apart from protection through counter-witchcraft, altruistic behaviour is also believed to provide protection.

Entrepreneurs obviously are highly exposed to witchcraft as a result of jealousy and need strong protection. Mossa's norm-breaking venture is conditioned by and maintains a need for social relations outside the local area. He consciously excludes himself from interaction with the other villagers by building iron railings around his house. He explains that because many villagers cannot pay back what they owe him they might try to harm him through witchcraft. To Mossa, *mankwala* is the most important protection from witchcraft, even though it is expensive because he has much property to protect. The protective devices that Mossa is using against witchcraft (*mankwala*, secrecy and social distance) all need access to money. With money he can buy himself *mankwala* and free himself of social relations in Mitengo while nursing his friendship with more wealthy friends and business con-tacts in town. Mossa himself is also frequently suspected of using witchcraft in his prosperous venture.

The Tobacco Man, to a much greater extent, follows a strategy of attending to his social obligations in accordance with the established institutional logic of legiti-mate value circulation. He is socially active in the local community. He shares his wealth with relatives, supports the school and has no walls around his house. To face his social obligations he needs money, which is why, according to him, he produces tobacco. But that alone does not totally free him from jealousy. He is making a fine surplus on his tobacco production and people have started to wonder why he cannot afford a car. A number of informants even mention that they suspect he is spending his money on witchcraft. As one informant expresses it: 'He had a job and he could easily have bought a vehicle, but instead he bought *ndondoches* [zombies to work for him]'.

The Tobacco Man and Mossa constantly legitimise their interest in individual profit by a concern for social relations and by basing their ventures on the established logic of social rights and obligations. Mossa justifies his lack of assistance to the villagers by arguing that they need to learn how to take care of themselves. The Tobacco Man, in contrast, legitimises his motive for generating profit by an urge to support his relatives, the school and other relations in Mitengo. The entrepreneurs, however, do not achieve full social acceptance of their ventures in the local area, and because of these legitimacy cracks they face suspicion or envy in their social surroundings. In consequence, they are accused of being concerned with individual material needs at the expense of the responsibility for social relations in accordance with the established logic of the system of rights and obligations. Furthermore, they are accused of using witchcraft to reach their needs.

The two local entrepreneurs mention jealousy as an explanation for the resistance they face in the local community. To them jealousy indicates traditionalism, ignorance and inactivity. A substantial difference, however, is the way entrepreneurs and non-entrepreneurs interpret the role of witchcraft. To the entrepreneurs witchcraft is a way to explain the resistance they meet in the village. Jealousy is the foundation for social exclusion and is a reason to direct evil witchcraft against those who know how to integrate institutional changes in their economical and social practice. The villagers, on the other hand, use the term witchcraft to explain the entrepreneurs' ability to create profit.

The relation between entrepreneurship, the established logic of social obligations, the upcoming logic of market exchange and witchcraft is dialectical and dynamic. The two cases show how the entrepreneurs, through their alternative profit-oriented practice, contribute to integrating new institutional structures of exchange with regard to social rights and obligations into the existing system of value circulation. Thereby, the traditional informal system of social levelling and sanctions is slowly changed. Hence, entrepreneurship in Mitengo is conditioned by the entrepreneurs being able to base their ventures on existing institutional structures and logics and at the same time building bridges to upcoming institutions. The entrepreneur, in other words, has to bridge the paradoxes that form the basis for institutional changes in the context—also in relation to the perception of witchcraft that is integrated in such a process.

Constraints and opportunities in the entrepreneurial process are bound up with the shifting relations between broader societal logics and the changing policies of national and international actors attempting to establish new venues for economic and social development under Malawi's fragile democratisation project. In summary, the findings illustrate how institutional changes are not only driven by macro forces and institutional actors at the national or community level, but are also built up from ongoing micro-social interactions with the entrepreneurial process as the nexus. The individual entrepreneurs' ventures sustain established societal structures and integrate new upcoming institutions. As the entrepreneurial ventures are based on contradictory institutions, the entrepreneurs must strike a balance between the social and market logics. Hence, the entrepreneurs working amid institutional contradictions must maintain a balance between the opposing logics on which they are dependent. Imbalances between logics result in witchcraft accusations.

Discussion

This chapter has examined the strategies employed by small-scale entrepreneurs in balancing coexisting, potentially conflicting social and market logics on which their ventures are based during institutional changes in order to become socially sustainable. By illuminating the efforts of the two entrepreneurs in influencing and exploiting institutional changes in their entrepreneurial ventures, this study has addressed calls for more research on how entrepreneurs interact with the broader institutional environments and logics with which they are bound up and thereby research on the intersections of the institutional and entrepreneurship literature (Hwang and Powell 2005; Tillmar 2006; Marquis and Lounsbury 2007; Sarasvathy 2007; Phillips and Tracey 2007; Garud *et al.* 2007; Devereaux Jennings *et al.* 2009). The findings furthermore shed light on entrepreneurial processes that are not purely restricted to business, but pertain to social issues: that is, how the entrepreneurs both sustain social order to acquire legitimacy and introduce changes (Steyaert and Katz 2004; Steyaert and Hjorth 2006). Moreover, the study elucidates the relatively under-researched role of individuals in institutional change and continuity (Battilana 2006; Battilana *et al.* 2009).

The entrepreneurs are brokers in the articulation of the oppositions forming the basis for the changes in the context. Rather than merely impeding economic action, entrepreneurs used established institutional structures for individual value generation. As shown in the case, the relation between entrepreneurship, social obligations and cultural institutions—in this case witchcraft—is dialectical. The two entrepreneurs, through their alternative profit-oriented practices, contribute to the integration of new structures of exchange with regard to social rights and obligations into the existing system of value circulation. Thereby, the traditional system of social levelling and sanctions is changing. In consequence, entrepreneurship in Mitengo is conditioned by the entrepreneurs being able to base their ventures on existing social structures and at the same time building bridges to new upcoming structures. The entrepreneur, in other words, has to bridge the institutional contradictions that form the basis for changes in the context, also in relation to the perceptions of witchcraft that are integrated in such a process. The entrepreneurial ventures are conditioned by operating in the current institutional spheres of exchange (logics of social relations and networks) as well as in upcoming spheres (logics of independent market forces). They maintain enterprise sustainability by striking a balance between the institutional logics their ventures bind together (Battilana and Dorado 2011). Thereby, the entrepreneur is actively using and transforming the social structures in the surroundings. Institutional changes are driven by macro forces as well as being built up from ongoing micro-social interactions with the entrepreneurial process as the nexus.

Thus, on the one hand, the field study indicates that the two entrepreneurs are faced with inertia and frictions in the institutional setting in which they operate. On the other hand, the two entrepreneurs do not take inertia and barriers in the institutional setting for granted. They actively use contradictory logics, separating different social and economic spheres to create new channels of exchange. They convert barriers of exchange to channels of exchange through their bridging of institutional contradictions. Hence, the two entrepreneurs make their wealthy livelihoods by overcoming or using constraints institutionalised in their local society. In order to sustain their business, both of them have been entrepreneurial in overcoming levelling mechanisms in society and escaping traditional exchange modes. Their endurance and success has depended on their achievements as institutional entrepreneurs.

Hence, the stories of the two entrepreneurs illustrate the need to include the societal context as an active element in the analyses of entrepreneurial processes, since micro and macro processes of institutional change and economic practice interact in highly dynamic ways. From Barth we learn that entrepreneurship is a process of bridging between existing institutional structures and upcoming structures. His focus on the dialectical movement between structure and agency provides an account for the entrepreneurial process including both individual entrepreneurial actors and collective social structures in a dynamic and dialectic fashion. The contribution of Barth's practice-based theory of entrepreneurship is thus the conception of entrepreneurship as an ongoing social bridging between spheres.

The local microcredit organisation held beliefs that customary practices and myths impede economic development, and occult forces, such as witchcraft, maintain an egalitarian social structure through social control. However, the study illustrates how customary practices and beliefs not only functioned as constraints, but also held a capacity for individual value generation. Hence, the study illustrates that norms and beliefs associated with witchcraft are not merely traditionalistic and retrospective resistance to change, but multiple, dynamic and part of modern developments (Geschiere 1997). While the emergence of occult forces in economic practice, highlighting social sustainability concerns, may partly express key transitional moments and social ruptures (Geschiere 1997; Comaroff and Comaroff 1999), this, however, does not necessitate their discontinuity with 'past' or 'traditional' practices (Kapferer 2003). Social sustainability in entrepreneurship could then refer to upholding certain societal structures by an equal supporting resource distribution among community members.

References

Agar, M.H. (1986) *Speaking of Ethnography* (Newbury Park, CA: Sage).

Barth, F. (1967a) 'Economic Spheres in Darfur', in R. Firth (ed.), *Themes in Economic Anthropology* (London: Tavistock Publications): 149-74.

Barth, F. (1967b) *The Role of the Entrepreneur in Social Change in Northern Norway* (Bergen, Norway: Universitetsforlaget).

Barth, F. (1981) *Process and Form in Social Life* (London: Routledge).

Battilana, J. (2006) 'Agency and Institutions: The Enabling Role of Individuals' Social Position', *Organization* 13.5: 653-76.

Battilana, J., and S. Dorado (2011) 'Building Sustainable Hybrid Organizations: The Case of Commercial Microfinance Organizations', *Academy of Management Journal* 53.6: 1,419-40.

Battilana, J., B. Leca and E. Boxenbaum (2009) 'How Actors Change Institutions: Towards a Theory of Institutional Entrepreneurship', *Academy of Management Annals* 3.1: 65-107.

Bernard, R.H. (1995) *Research Methods in Anthropology: Qualitative and Quantitative Approaches* (Thousand Oaks, CA: Sage).

Bohannan, P., and G. Dalton (1965) 'Introduction', in P. Bohannan and G. Dalton (eds.), *Markets in Africa* (Garden City, NY: The American Museum of Natural History).

Bourdieu, P. (1977) *Outline of a Theory of Practice* (Cambridge, UK: Cambridge University Press).

Brubaker, R. (2002) 'Ethnicity without Groups', *European Journal of Sociology* 43.2: 163-89.

Comaroff, J. (1985) *Body of Power, Spirit of Resistance: The Culture and History of a South African People* (Chicago: University of Chicago Press).

Comaroff, J., and J.L. Comaroff (1999) 'Occult Economies and the Violence of Abstraction: Notes from the South African Postcolony', *American Ethnologist* 26.2: 279-303.

Devereaux Jennings, P., R. Greenwood, M. Lounsbury and R. Suddaby (2009) 'Call for Papers: Institutions, Entrepreneurs, and Communities', *Journal of Business Venturing* 24.

Dimaggio, P.J. (1988) 'Interest and Agency in Institutional Theory', in L.G. Zucker (ed.), *Institutional Patterns and Organizations: Culture and Environment* (Cambridge, MA: Ballinger): 3-22.

Eisenstadt, S.N. (1980) 'Cultural Orientations, Institutional Entrepreneurs, and Social Change : Comparative Analyses of Traditional Civilisations', *American Journal of Sociology* 85: 840-69.

Evens, T.M.S., and D. Handelman (2006) *The Manchester School: Practice and Ethnographic Praxis in Anthropology* (New York: Berghahn Books).

Friedland, R., and R.R. Alford (1991) 'Bringing Society Back In: Symbols, Practices, and Institutional Contradictions', in W.W. Powell and P.J. Dimaggio (eds.), *The New Institutionalism in Organizational Analysis* (Chicago: University of Chicago Press): 232-63.

Garud, R., C. Hardy and S. Maguire (2007) 'Institutional Entrepreneurship as Embedded Agency: An Introduction to the Special Issue', *Organization Studies* 28: 957-69.

Geschiere, P. (1997) *The Modernity of Witchcraft* (Charlottesville, VA: University Press of Virginia).

Gluckman, M. (1955) *Custom and Conflict in Africa* (Oxford, UK: Blackwell).

Harbi, S.E., A.R. Anderson and S.H. Ammar (2010) 'Entrepreneurs and the Environment: Towards a Typology of Tunisian Ecopreneurs', *International Journal of Entrepreneurship and Small business* 10.2: 181-204.

Hockerts, K. (2006) 'Ecopreneurship: Unique Research Field or Just "More of the Same"', in J. Mair, J. Robinson and K. Hockerts (eds.), *Social Entrepreneurship* (New York: Palgrave Macmillan): 209-14.

Holy, L., and M. Stuchlik (1983) *Actions, Norms and Representations. Foundations of Anthropological Inquiry* (Cambridge, UK: Cambridge University Press).

Hughes, E.C. (1942) 'The Study of Institutions', *Social Forces* 20.3: 307-10.

Hwang, H., and W.W. Powell (2005) 'Institutions and Entrepreneurship', in S.A. Alvarez, R. Agarwal and O. Sorenson (eds.), *Handbook of Entrepreneurship Research: Disciplinary Perspectives* (New York: Kluwer Publishers): 179-210.

Jepperson, R.L. (1991) 'Institutions, Institutional Effects, and Institutionalization', in W.W. Powell and P.J. Dimaggio (eds.), *The New Institutionalism in Organizational Analysis* (Chicago: University of Chicago Press).

Kapferer, B. (2003) 'Sorcery and the Shapes of Globalization Disjunctions and Discontinuities: The Case of Sri Lanka', in J. Friedman (ed.), *Globalization, the State, and Violence* (Walnut Creek, CA: AltaMira Press): 1-34.

Khanna, T., and K. Palepu (1997) 'Why Focused Strategies May Be Wrong for Emerging Markets', *Harvard Business Review*, July-August 1997.

Larney, K.T. (2001) *Malawi. En Politisk Og Økonomisk Oversigt* (Copenhagen: Udenrigsministeriet).

Lawrence, T.B., and R. Suddaby (2006) 'Institutions and Institutional Work', in S. Clegg, C. Hardy, T. Lawrence and W.R. Nord (eds.), *Handbook of Organization Studies* (London: Sage Publications): 215-54.

Lévi-Strauss, C. (1963) *Structural Anthropology* (New York: Basic Books).

Lévi-Strauss, C. (1966) *The Savage Mind* (Chicago: The University of Chicago Press).

Lounsbury, M. (2007) 'A Tale of Two Cities: Competing Logics and Practice Variation in the Professionalization of Mutual Funds', *Academy of Management Journal* 5: 289-307.

Mair, J., and I. Martí (2006) 'Social Entrepreneurship Research: A Source of Explanation, Prediction, and Delight', *Journal of World Business* 41: 36-44.

Mair, J., and I. Martí (2009) 'Entrepreneurship in and around Institutional Voids', *Journal of Business Venturing* 24: 419-35.

Mair, J., I. Martí and K. Ganly (2007) 'Institutional Voids as Spaces of Opportunity', *European Business Forum* 31: 34-39.

Malinowski, B. (1922) *Argonauts of the Western Pacific* (London: Routledge).

Marquis, C., and M. Lounsbury (2007) 'Vive La Résistance: Competing Logics and the Consolidation of U.S. Community Banking', *Academy of Management Journal* 50.4: 799-820.

Martí, I., and J. Mair (2009) 'Bringing Change into the Lives of the Poor: Entrepreneurship Outside Traditional Boundaries', in T. Lawrence, R. Suddaby and B. Leca (eds.), *Institutional Work* (Cambridge, UK: Cambridge University Press): 92-119.

Moore, S.F. (1978) *Law as Process: An Anthropological Approach* (London: Routledge).

Parry, J., and M. Bloch (1989) *Money and the Morality of Exchange* (Cambridge, UK: Cambridge University Press).

Pasgaard, I. (2005) *Antropologi & Entrepreneurship* (Aarhus, Denmark: University of Aarhus, Department of Anthropology).

Phillips, N., and P. Tracey (2007) 'Opportunity Recognition, Entrepreneurial Capabilities and Bricolage: Connecting Institutional Theory and Entrepreneurship in Strategic Organization', *Strategic Organization* 5.3: 313-20.

Polanyi, K. (1944) *Great Transformation: The Political and Economic Origins of Our Time* (Boston, MA: Beacon Press).

Powell, W.W., and J.A. Colyvas (2008) 'Microfoundations of Institutional Theory', in R. Greenwood, C. Oliver, K. Sahlin and R. Suddaby (eds.), *Handbook of Organizational Institutionalism* (London: Sage Publishers): 276-98.

Reay, T., and C.R. Hinings (2009) 'Managing the Rivalry of Competing Institutional Logics', *Organization Studies* 30.6: 629-52.

Robinson, J., J. Mair and K. Hockerts (2008) *International Perspectives on Social Entrepreneurship* (New York: Palgrave Macmillan).

Sarasvathy, S.D. (2007) *Effectuation: Elements of Entrepreneurial Expertise* (Northampton, MA: Edward Elgar).

Spradley, J.P. (1980) *Participant Observation* (New York: Holt Rinehart and Winston).

Steyaert, C., and D. Hjorth (2006) *Entrepreneurship as Social Change* (Cheltenham, UK: Edward Elgar).

Steyaert, C., and J. Katz (2004) 'Reclaiming the Space of Entrepreneurship in Society: Geographical, Discursive and Social Dimensions', *Entrepreneurship & Regional Development* 16: 179-96.

Swidler, A. (1986) 'Culture in Action: Symbols and Strategies', *American Sociological Review* 51: 273-86.

Thornton, P.H., and W. Ocasio (2008) 'Institutional Logics', in R. Greenwood, C. Oliver, R. Suddaby and K.-S. Anderson (eds.), *The Sage Handbook of Organizational Institutionalism* (London: Sage): 99-129.

Thornton, P.H., C. Jones and K. Kury (2005) 'Institutional Logics and Institutional Change in Organizations: Transformation in Accounting, Architecture, and Publishing', *Research in the Sociology of Organizations* 23: 125-70.

Tillmar, M. (2006) 'Swedish Tribalism and Tanzanian Entrepreneurship: Preconditions for Trust Formation', *Entrepreneurship & Regional Development: An International Journal* 18.2: 91-107.

Van Maanen, J. (1988) *Tales of the Field: On Writing Ethnography* (Chicago: University of Chicago Press).

Velsen, J.V. (1967) 'The Extended-Case Method and Situational Analysis', in A.L. Epstein (ed.), *The Craft of Social Anthropology* (London: Tavistock Publications): 129-52.

10

Business, but not as usual

Entrepreneurship and sustainable development in low-income economies

Boukje Vastbinder, Otto Kroesen, Esther Blom and Roland Ortt
Delft University of Technology, Netherlands

This chapter will explore how an entrepreneurial approach can help to create sustainable development in low-income economies by focusing on small-scale entrepreneurial initiatives. We will not look at governmental aid (government to government) or existing big companies. The chapter focuses on the following question: **How can an entrepreneurial approach help low-income economies develop sustainably?** In this problem statement three terms play a central role: sustainable development, entrepreneurship and low-income economies. These terms will be defined below.

At first sight, sustainable development means development that can be sustained over time. But we will refer to sustainable development when development is *financially, socially* and *ecologically responsible and therefore can be sustained over time* (WCED 1987). Activities that contribute to sustainable development should be financially, socially and ecologically sustainable. Financially responsible means that the total income of an endeavour minimally covers the total costs. Socially responsible means that the profits from the activity are shared equally among the involved stakeholders, but also includes equity, participation and human rights for these stakeholders. Ecologically responsible means that the activity also preserves the world's ecosystem in the long term.

Many different definitions of entrepreneurship can be found. We will refer to entrepreneurship when three elements are combined: (1) something new is created (an innovation); (2) customers are identified for the new product or service (a market); and (3) an entrepreneur creates value by producing and selling something new to the customers (a business model).

One of the indicators used by the World Bank to distinguish between economies is the percentage of people living on less than US$995 a year. When we mention low-income economies, we also include the lower middle income group with an income of US$996–3,945 a year (lower middle income). So in this chapter, by using the term low-income economies, we refer to countries, or parts of countries where the majority of people lives on less than US$3,945 a year. High-income economies are those with a gross national income per capita of more than US$12,196 or more (World Bank 2011).

To answer the main question (How can an entrepreneurial approach help low-income economies develop sustainably?) we formulated four research questions:

1. Which types of economic relationship between high- and low-income economies already exist?

2. How did these economic relationships contribute to sustainable development in low-income economies?

3. Why is entrepreneurship so important for sustainable development in low-income economies?

4. How can we apply entrepreneurship to attain sustainable development in low-income economies?

In the next section we will first describe what we call the colonial model for framing relationships between high- and low-income economies and then attend to the development aid model as a second way of framing those relationships. Next, we introduce sustainable entrepreneurship as a new and promising approach. Then we will proceed to give a full description of what this approach entails and give examples and a provisional evaluation of how it can be applied.

Different ways of framing relationships between high- and low-income economies

There is an ongoing discussion about the best approach for high-income countries to support the low-income economies of the world. In this section we will roughly distinguish two existing approaches to collaborate with these low-income economies. Each of these two types of relationship fosters its own kind of entrepreneurial behaviour and has its own consequences for sustainability. These two types of relationship are: colonialism and developmental aid.

Within the colonial relationship, high-income economies exploit the natural or human resources from low-income economies because they are available at low cost. This relationship creates a great deal of financial profit and economic development for these high-income economies. In the development aid relationship, which emerged as a reaction to the exploitative colonial relationship, both governments and individuals of high-income economies donate money, products and services to help develop low-income economies. This approach creates a reverse flow of finances compared with the colonial relationship and leads to the low-income economies depending strongly on donors. Each of the two types of relationship will be discussed in more detail below and will be assessed by looking at their contribution to sustainable development in low-income economies.

Type 1: Colonialism

The combination of entrepreneurship and low-income economies is usually associated with a low-cost resource model such as in the old colonial relationship. In the colonial relationship, entrepreneurs from high-income economies exploit resources from low-income economies, sometimes by using military force (so no payment is required at all). Nowadays, a more civilised form of the colonial relationship can be witnessed, in which entrepreneurs from high-income economies extract raw materials and cheap human resources from low-income economies and refine these materials in their own country. In this relationship, development is framed in purely economic and 'efficient' technical terms (Gasper 2004). These entrepreneurs contribute to society by making a financial profit, which supports employment, wages, purchases, investments and taxes. As economist Adam Smith stated in 1776, as markets grow, entrepreneurship would lead to innovation, which would lead to an increasing division of labour and increased productivity, in the end causing economic growth (Smith 1776).

These often large firms behave like self-contained entities, and ecological, social or community issues usually fall outside their scope (Friedman 1970; Samli 2009). A number of large projects even involved consciously sacrificing the well-being of certain groups: for example, indigenous peoples whose land and resources were taken for the sake of 'progress'. The colonial relationship helped create many multinationals owned by entrepreneurs from high-income economies that mainly fulfilled the needs of their own economy. The low-income economy only receives a modest profit for the raw material and the labour (if at all). The value chains of these firms inevitably affect, and are affected by, numerous societal issues, such as the use of natural resources, health and safety, education, working conditions and equal treatment in the workplace. The products based on the raw materials, the higher level jobs and the majority of the profits are for high-income economies, while the workforce in low-income economies is exposed to hazardous chemicals and receives barely enough wages to stay alive, let alone send their children to school. The colonial economic relationship has not resulted in equality in development of the high- and low-income economies.

An assessment of the contribution of colonial development to sustainable development reveals that the approach has mixed results. The colonial relationship was durable: it lasted for many decades. However, as mentioned before, sustainability involves more than durability. Sustainability refers to *financially, socially* and *ecologically* responsible activities. The main reason for the durability of the colonial system can be found by looking at the financial aspects and the power distance generated by high-income economies. The powerful actors, the high-income economies, profited a great deal by exploiting the low-income economies. The main problems in this type of relationship are the lack of involvement, responsibility, growth, development and profit for the low-income economy. These firms are externalising the social and ecological cost created by them and are using human and natural resources faster than they can be replenished, often supported by a narrow definition of economic value (Daly and Cobb 1989). As a result, governments are forced to impose taxes, regulations and penalties so that firms 'internalise' these externalities. Firms have taken the broader context in which they do business as given and resist regulatory standards as invariably contrary to their interests (Porter and Kramer 2011). Solving social problems has been ceded to governments and to NGOs. The colonial relationship actually blocked sustainable development by ignoring the social responsibility that went together with its activities. In his work, Jeffrey Sachs mentions this lack of development and refers to it as a self-maintaining vicious circle also referred to as a poverty trap (Sachs 2005). The trap should be removed, in his opinion, by a big leap forward in terms of investment, knowledge and technology transfer. Paul Collier adds several more traps, especially in relation to Africa. Not all of these traps are directly caused by the colonial relationship, but nevertheless these traps interacted with, or reinforced, the results of that approach (Collier 2007). In conclusion, the colonial relationship has shown to be durable over time, but is nowadays considered unsustainable in terms of social and ecological aspects. Furthermore, the financial beneficiaries of this system are usually only the high-income economies, which in an ever globalising world, can no longer be sustainable.

Type 2: Development aid

The development aid relationship came into existence as a reaction to the exploitative nature of the colonial relationship (Easterly 2006). Within this development aid relationship both governments and individuals of high-income economies donate money, products and services to low-income economies. Development aid focuses on the type of development that is neglected in the colonial relationship and involves rural development, education, services and health at the grass-roots level. This approach was helpful, especially regarding healthcare and education, but in retrospect it did not contribute sufficiently to the general development of these countries. The question in our time that bothers the main actors in the development aid approach (such as NGOs, donors, governments and civil society agents) is: *Why did six decades of development aid do so little good* (Moyo 2009)? It even appears that the countries that received little development aid, such as China and India, are doing economically much better than the big development aid consumers such as Bangladesh and many African countries (Easterly 2006). The donating organisations, mostly NGOs, in the high-income economies cannot remain responsible for the development of the low-income economies in the long term. Often when these main actors stop their donations, the development activity ends because the actors in the low-income economy are neither owners of, nor responsible for, the activity (Schouten and Moriarty 2003). Governments and NGOs could be more effective if they would think in terms of value, considering benefits relative to costs, and focus on the results achieved rather than funds and effort expended. The main actors in this relationship have tended to approach social improvement from a strong ideological perspective, as if social benefits should be pursued at any cost. Governments and NGOs often assume that trade-offs between economic and social benefits are inevitable, exacerbating these trade-offs through their approaches.

An assessment of the development aid relationship reveals that this type of relationship has many negative results. High-income economies and their inhabitants tend to give what they perceive as needed (Easterly 2006), and that does not necessarily coincide with what is actually needed by the population of low-income economies. And when aid provided by donor countries was needed, it sometimes was not received by the population that needed it (most). On top of this, development aid did not contribute to the economic growth of the low-income economies. Local entrepreneurs cannot compete with the donated products and services that are often offered for free. As a result the development aid relationship even seems to have reduced the number of entrepreneurs in low-income economies and caused a lack of appreciation of the value of products or services, which draw from valuable ecological and social resources. In addition, this continues to be a relationship of dependence, which is not based on collaboration. From a financial perspective, the development aid relationship lacked entrepreneurial aspects, or more specifically, the use of viable business models that enabled initiatives to generate sustainable impact (Samli 2009). In a way, development aid was created as a socially responsible way to develop countries, but turned out to have almost the opposite effect.

Conclusions regarding the different types of relationship

In this section, we focused on two research questions: (1) Which types of economic relationship between high-income and low-income economies exist? (2) How did these types of economic relationship contribute to sustainable development in low-income economies? We distinguished two types of relationship, referred to as colonialism and development aid. In short, we conclude that the colonial approach was durable; it lasted for decades because of the financial benefits for the high-income economies that exploited resources from low-income economies. However, it was not sustainable as it lacked the ability to include externalised costs and strive for the creation of social or ecological value. In contrast, the development aid approach was socially and/or ecologically responsible, but lacked the financial incentives to last over time.

It is in reaction to the failure of development aid to level out the exploitative nature of colonialism that a third approach came to the fore. This third, new type of economic relationship, referred to as sustainable entrepreneurship, strives to combine the strengths of the colonial and the developmental aid relationship: that is, aiming to create social and/or ecological value besides financial value and internalising all costs (financial, social and ecological). Sustainable entrepreneurship, aimed at low-income economies, combines business strategy and poverty alleviation, which normally were considered in isolation (Prahalad and Hammond 2002). Eventually, sustainable entrepreneurship should become a viable substitute for the colonial and development aid approach, integrating the strengths of both, again in one economic system. The result is a more holistic approach to development aiming at an economy in which (existing) entrepreneurs will become more sustainable, and NGOs or governmental aid programmes become more entrepreneurial, blurring the line between for-profit and non-profit organisations. From society's perspective, it does not matter which types of organisation created the value. What matters is that benefits delivered by those organisations are positioned to achieve the most impact for society for the least cost.

An assessment of the sustainable entrepreneurship approach, in terms of its contribution to sustainable development, is hard to make as yet. More research and experimentation needs to be done to find out what the exact nature of the role of entrepreneurs will be in sustainable development (Hall *et al.* 2010). Although many initiatives have contributed to some of the aspects within the sustainable entrepreneurship system as described above, such as internalising the cost of pollution, examples of initiatives that strive to incorporate all external and internal costs and values are rare. We think that, rather than giving a full assessment of this approach now, it makes more sense to explain what this approach could mean in practice. Therefore we will first describe this approach conceptually and then proceed to its application.

Sustainable entrepreneurship

In the preceding section, it was stated that entrepreneurship can contribute to sustainable development in low-income economies. The colonial relationship focused on financial goals, the development aid relationship focused on social and/or ecological goals. Sustainable entrepreneurship tries to combine the strengths of both the colonial and the development aid relationship, aiming to balance financial, social and ecological goals, therewith creating a viable alternative for both. In this section, we will first discuss why an entrepreneurial perspective might help in attaining developmental goals. We will subsequently describe what is required for this entrepreneurial approach.

Why entrepreneurship?

Entrepreneurship can help create sustainable development in low-income economies for many reasons. By working out a feasible business model which includes all the costs and possible revenues, an enterprise can be organised in such a way that long-lasting positive impact can be achieved more readily than in the colonial or development aid approach and without using human and natural resources faster than they can be replenished. J. Austin even claims that sustainable entrepreneurship should be defined as an entrepreneurial activity with an embedded sustainable purpose, therefore even adding a positive effect to the definition (Austin *et al.* 2006).

Initiatives need to take responsibility for their complete societal impact by internalising the costs that are externalised in the old systems, and start aiming at creating social, ecological and financial value—also referred to as mutual value creation. The better the enterprise meets the needs of its customers, suppliers and partners, the greater the likelihood of long-term viability (London *et al.* 2010). Addressing societal harms and constraints does not necessarily raise more costs, because the (new) enterprises can innovate by using new technologies, service systems and management approaches and as a result achieve better productivity and an expansion of their markets. The societal benefits of providing appropriate products to lower-income and disadvantaged consumers can be profound, while the financial profits for these sustainable enterprises can be substantial (Prahalad and Hart 2002). And the growth of those new sustainable enterprises has a multiplier effect, as jobs are created in supporting industries, new companies are seeded and demand for ancillary services rises, in the end causing economic growth (Porter and Kramer 2011). As capitalism begins to work in low-income economies, which seems inevitable, sustainable entrepreneurs could unlock new opportunities for economic development and social progress within these economies.

One of the other reasons why using sustainable entrepreneurship could help low-income economies develop is that entrepreneurship can create independence and reappraise self-esteem; in a way countering the negative results of development aid. Entrepreneurship facilitates a fast learning process. Individual entrepreneurs quickly adapt their strategy and learn quickly, because the market results of their efforts provide direct feedback in terms of profits or losses. The possibility for the new entrepreneurs to even make financial profit provides the entrepreneur with another drive to start an entrepreneurial initiative and decreases the dependence on donors from high-income economies. This lack of financial dependence on high-income economies contributes to the self-esteem and financial stability of the low-income economies.

Furthermore, entrepreneurship creates equality in communication between the different stakeholders. The target group of an initiative is not approached as 'those in need', but as customers or partners with their own requirements and restrictions. This means that the customers within the business model are in a position to set requirements for the product offered to them. This yields a much better feedback loop and makes the interaction between actors of high- and low-income economies a great deal less exploitative in nature than previously in the colonial or development aid approach. If the target group does not feel that the offered product or service will fulfil a need, they will not purchase it.

The final reason why entrepreneurship could play an important role in developing the low-income economies is the fact that high-income economies are already very familiar with entrepreneurship. Much research has already been done on entrepreneurship in general and currently researchers are expanding the domain of the study of entrepreneurship towards the field of sustainability. For example, new business opportunities derive from seeing the market failure of existing social and environmental systems as market opportunities (Cohen and Winn 2007). In this context Samli argues that the global giants cannot function in small, remote and scattered markets of poor economies and that an innovative entrepreneurial bottom-up globalisation is required by means of many small initiatives (Samli 2009).

How to incorporate entrepreneurship?

How will this work in practice? More and more organisations in high-income economies help create sustainable entrepreneurial activities in low-income economies. We will illustrate that this can be done with almost the same methods and entrepreneurial spirit as 'general' entrepreneurs, although a difference in including societal costs and benefits should be kept in mind.

The adoption of an entrepreneurial approach yields a holistic approach by combining different aspects that are usually undervalued in development aid initiatives. Examples of aspects incorporated in an entrepreneurial approach are marketing, financial models, stakeholder analyses, intellectual property and so on. Even though these aspects may sound very commercial and financially driven, they also contribute to the success of initiatives aiming at mainly social and ecological value creation. By paying attention to marketing aspects for instance, the initiator is 'forced' to develop a strategy on how to approach the intended target group. Even social and ecological initiatives have to be sold. Why should the target group make use of the product or services offered by the initiator? How should the initiator inform the target group and how can the target group be convinced to make use of the product or service offered by the initiator? By working out a holistic and feasible business model, the entrepreneur is forced to look at the project from all angles.

To illustrate how sustainable entrepreneurship aiming at development works in practice we will describe how a specific business model methodology, developed for entrepreneurs, can be used in analysing and starting up sustainable enterprises that strive to contribute to the development of a region. A business model describes the rationale of how an organisation creates, delivers and captures value and in the

Figure 10.1 **Extended business model canvas derived from Osterwalder's model**

Source: adapted Business Model Canvas from: www.businessmodelgeneration.com

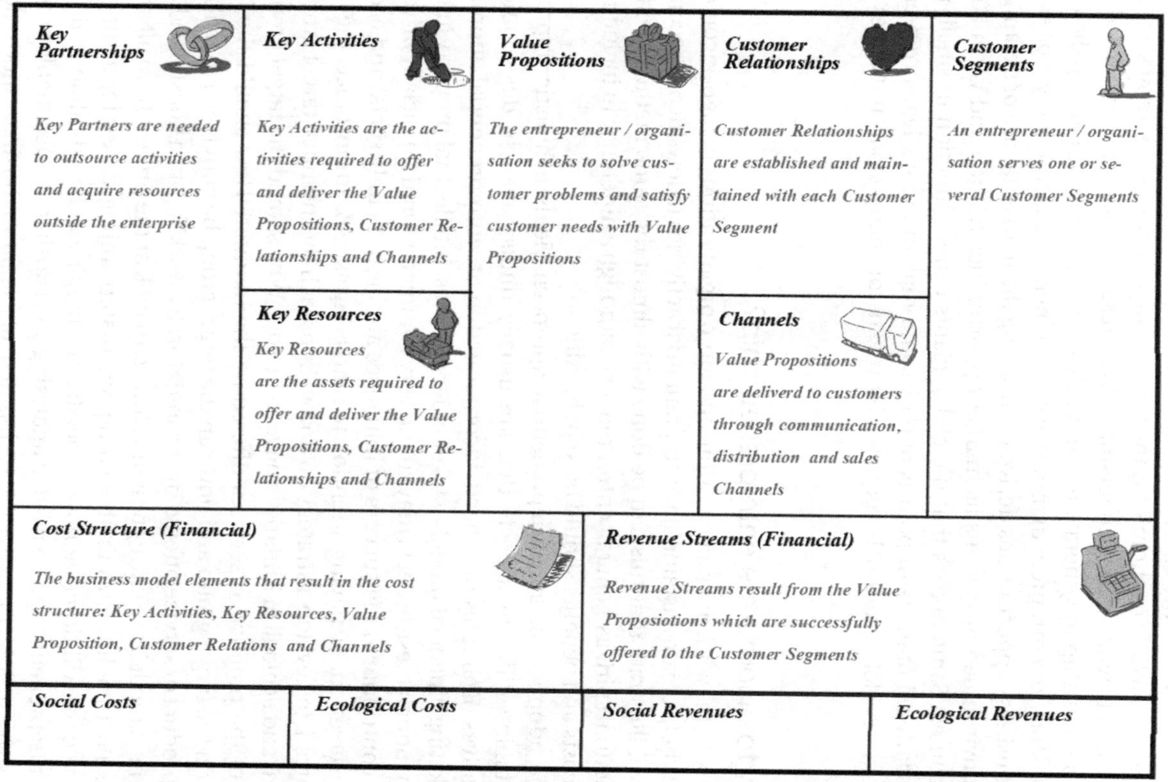

Key Partnerships	Key Activities	Value Propositions	Customer Relationships	Customer Segments
Key Partners are needed to outsource activities and acquire resources outside the enterprise	*Key Activities are the activities required to offer and deliver the Value Propositions, Customer Relationships and Channels*	*The entrepreneur / organisation seeks to solve customer problems and satisfy customer needs with Value Propositions*	*Customer Relationships are established and maintained with each Customer Segment*	*An entrepreneur / organisation serves one or several Customer Segments*
	Key Resources		Channels	
	Key Resources are the assets required to offer and deliver the Value Propositions, Customer Relationships and Channels		*Value Propositions are delivered to customers through communication, distribution and sales Channels*	

Cost Structure (Financial)		Revenue Streams (Financial)	
The business model elements that result in the cost structure: Key Activities, Key Resources, Value Proposition, Customer Relations and Channels		*Revenue Streams result from the Value Propositions which are successfully offered to the Customer Segments*	

Social Costs	Ecological Costs	Social Revenues	Ecological Revenues

case of sustainable entrepreneurship this aims not only at financial value but also social and/or ecological value. We will use a business model methodology developed by Alexander Osterwalder and Yves Pigneur called the 'Business Model Canvas' (Osterwalder and Pigneur 2010).

The Business Model Canvas (see Fig. 10.1) is a tool used to describe, analyse and design business models. The canvas consists of nine building blocks that show how a company or organisation delivers a product or service to the customers or target group. The nine building blocks within the template represent nine elements that are essential for a successful enterprise. The nine blocks are: customer segments, value proposition, customer relationships, channels, key activities, key partnerships, key resources, revenue streams and cost structure. The upper part of the canvas describes the way the organisation is set up. The lower part shows (on the left) the costs of the blocks of the upper part, as well as (on the right) the revenues of the initiative. More explanation on every block can be found in Figure 10.1. Filling in the blocks forces the initiator to carefully think through the different aspects that could influence the final success of an initiative.

Even though the Business Model Canvas of Osterwalder was initially designed to provide more insight into enterprises that have primarily financial goals, the model can also be applied to initiatives that deliberately include social or ecological goals. An adaptation to the canvas in order to make this possible, suggested by us, is to add social costs and revenues as well as ecological costs and revenues in order to reflect the extra goals that have to be met for sustainable entrepreneurship. By doing this, the number of blocks is increased from 9 to 13 as can be seen in Figure 10.1.

We adopt an entrepreneurial perspective and use the Business Model Canvas to make a distinction between the colonial, the development aid and the sustainable entrepreneurship approach. We can also use the canvas in order to show the difference in focus between the different relationships and how we try to combine and integrate this in the third relationship: sustainable entrepreneurship.

Figure 10.2 visualises the three different relationships using the extended Business Model Canvas as shown in Figure 10.1. The first canvas shows how the business models of resource-based entrepreneurs in the colonial relationship generate financial revenues by not paying for (and therefore destroying) the social and natural resources. The second canvas shows how the costs of the business models within the development aid approach, which aims at social and environmental benefits, are covered by an endless stream of funding from high-income economies. And finally, the third canvas shows how business models used by sustainable entrepreneurs integrate the first two approaches and strive to reach an optimum between the costs and revenues for financial, social and ecological aspects.

After describing this difference in the lower part of the canvas, which is very straightforward, describing the differences in the upper part of the canvas, which shows how the organisation is set up, is slightly more complicated. Still there are some striking differences in outcome and application between a sustainable entrepreneurship business model and colonial or development aid business models that are worth mentioning.

Figure 10.2 Canvas 1: resource-based entrepreneurship within the colonial relationship; canvas 2: charity within the development aid relationship; canvas 3: sustainable entrepreneurship

Source: adapted Business Model Canvas from: www.businessmodelgeneration.com

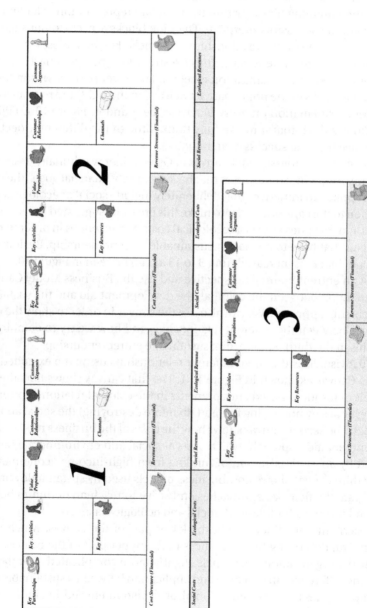

A sustainable entrepreneur needs to analyse all the costs and revenues for all major stakeholders (customers and key partners), consequently internalising the costs to society and environment that were almost always externalised within the colonial approach. The Business Model Canvas methodology is developed from the perspective of one entrepreneur with mainly financial goals and responsibilities and thus focuses on assessing the costs and revenues for this entrepreneur. In a sustainable entrepreneurship approach, meant to meet societal goals, the costs and revenues of multiple stakeholders have to be taken into account in order to see whether there is a fair balance in the revenues and costs for each group of stakeholders. This is reflected in the top seven blocks of the Business Model Canvas starting with the value proposition.

The value proposition from a sustainable entrepreneur describes the product or service that delivers value to the customer and differs from a 'traditional' value proposition because the described value within a sustainable enterprise always (also) contributes to societal development.

This difference in value proposition then influences the other blocks in the top half of the canvas. For example, the employees and (part of) the community could be considered as additional customer segments because they are affected by the mutual value delivered by the enterprise. The value proposition as offered to the employees can then be described as employment and additionally as education, healthcare and/or housing. Therefore, in initiatives that aim at employment besides the design, production and/or delivery of products or services, a twofold value proposition will emerge as well as a second group or sometimes even a third group of customers.

Conclusions regarding the use of the extended Business Model Canvas

The above section focused on two research questions: (3) Why is entrepreneurship so important for sustainable development in low-income economies? (4) How do we apply entrepreneurship in order to attain sustainable development in low-income economies? Entrepreneurship is important because it has shown to be a durable approach in the past. Its financial orientation and the use of proven business methods increase the durability of the approach. Furthermore, entrepreneurship is an approach that provides quick feedback loops and consequently stimulates a quick learning process of all involved stakeholders in high-income and low-income economies. This quick learning process and the option for the entrepreneurs to create financial profits for themselves, imply that these entrepreneurs can become independent from development aid or from investors from the Western world and have a strong incentive to continue with the enterprise even when these donations or investments end. The quick feedback loop mentioned earlier should improve the chances that these sustainable value propositions really fulfil the most important needs of the low-income economies, because products that are not needed will not be bought, and by communicating with the target group as customers and not as 'those in need', equality in communication is restored. Sustainable entrepreneurship could contribute to the development of low-income economies by balancing the goals of all stakeholders involved rather than just the most powerful ones.

The fourth research question (How to apply entrepreneurship?) is addressed by using the Business Model Canvas, a standard tool to make and analyse business models. Using the canvas, we showed how the focus of the colonial relationship and the development aid relationship was different and how the sustainable entrepreneurship approach combines the insights from these two types of relationship.

Two differences in the use of the model for sustainable entrepreneurs in contrast to resource-based entrepreneurs in the colonial approach have been elaborated. First, the canvas should include social and ecological costs and revenues, besides the financial costs and revenues for the entrepreneur alone. We implemented this modification by adding four additional building blocks to the canvas. In practice, all types of cost and revenue have to be assessed for different stakeholders to see whether costs and revenues are shared in a fair way. This will prevent exploitation of one group by another group. Second, the canvas needs to be applied in an entirely different societal context from the Western one for which it was designed. The consequences of this adaptation will be explored in the next section where the canvas is applied in a real-world case.

Sustainable entrepreneurship aimed at sustainable development in low-income economies

Now that we have described how an entrepreneurial relationship can be more sustainable, we want to illustrate how this may work in practice. In the preceding section we explained a tool to analyse entrepreneurial activities: the Business Model Canvas. We also extended the tool, in order to make it more applicable for sustainable entrepreneurship cases. In this section we will illustrate how sustainable entrepreneurship can contribute to development by using this tool to analyse the sustainability of a real-world case project in South Africa.

This section mainly deals with a sustainable enterprise named The Ubuntu Company in Durban, South Africa. This enterprise aims to generate social, environmental and financial revenues by increasing local employment opportunities (social goal), decreasing garbage/pollution (ecological goal) and generating sufficient income to be independent of donors from high-income economies (financial goal). We take this as a base to make digressions to other cases; projects our students at the Delft University of Technology have been involved in, in order to ensure that the findings from The Ubuntu Company can be generalised to other cases. By researching such practical cases, we hope to gain more insight into the 'how', 'what' and 'who' of the business models for sustainable entrepreneurship in low-income economies represented by the top seven building blocks in the canvas. Finally, we will draw conclusions on whether this entrepreneurial approach does really contribute to sustainable development. Also, we will elaborate on the strong and weak points of this entrepreneurial approach and crystallise lessons for the future.

The Ubuntu Company, better known as the Plakkies factory, was recently founded by Delft University of Technology students near the Durban townships in South Africa. The Plakkies factory produces so-called Plakkies, which is Afrikaans for flip-flops. These fashionable flip-flops were launched on the Dutch market in May 2009 and became the Dutch summer hype of that year. Two students of the Delft University of Technology, Arnoud Rozendaal (aerospace engineering) and Michel Boerrigter (industrial design) together with Robert Baruch, board member of the Dutch non-profit organisation, KidsRights, were the founding fathers of this unique and socially responsible factory.

Most of the (female) workers of The Ubuntu Company are HIV infected and they receive medical treatment from The Ubuntu Company during working hours. Inspired by the local community which makes sandals out of worn tyres, the sole of the Plakkies is also made from old car tyres. Thanks to the Plakkies factory these tyres are collected and re-used. The financial profits made by The Ubuntu Company are donated to local AIDS orphan projects supervised by KidsRights.

What started as an ambitious idea on paper grew into a modern factory in Durban, South Africa, in just one year. In February 2009, production started with an output of less than ten Plakkies a day. Within only four months this factory evolved to the production of 800 pairs a day and employed 70 underprivileged inhabitants from the Durban townships. After many years of unemployment this job brings back the dignity of these inhabitants and gives them a chance to work towards a better future. With their salary every employee can take care of him or herself and about ten others, making approximately 700 people profit directly from this factory!

The extended Business Model Canvas for The Ubuntu Company

The value proposition of the Ubuntu Company is fourfold: 1) creating, producing and selling a socially sound flip-flop for the Western market which fits current Western fashion trends; 2) training their local, often underprivileged and HIV-infected, employees to prepare them for local ownership; 3) providing healthcare to the female workforce, many of whom are HIV-infected; and 4) donating the remaining profit to KidsRights, an organisation that supports orphaned children in the same community. This example shows that a value proposition can fulfil several consumer needs, creating mutual value but also reducing societal costs.

In this regard we can give many other examples that combine several of these aspects, such as a business that provides spare parts for water pumps to water committees in Kenya, or a business plan to provide electricity to an off-grid village in India. Another example is the Trashy Bag Company in Ghana. This company uses plastic waste as a resource and its value proposition not only entails a profitable re-use of these wastes, but also creates awareness in customers in Ghana as well as in the West (Troost and Twillert 2011). The value proposition of the Trashy Bags Company actually has four different aspects: (1) creating, producing and selling ecologically friendly bags to local and Western customers; (2) at the same time cleaning the streets of Ghana; (3) creating jobs and educating their employees; and (4) raising awareness of environmental problems.

The value proposition of The Ubuntu Company almost automatically leads to three different categories of key activity which support the value proposition: the production process, the management process and the training process. We will now look into those.

The production is mainly done using sewing machines, which means that the labour force available is predominantly female. The personnel are trained to work on different stations, doing different activities. This is not only done in order to make the employees more flexible, but also to promote and stimulate cooperation and bonds of trust between different tribal factions. The existence of tribal factions is an important element in the context for sustainable entrepreneurial activities in many African countries (Wiarda 2003; OSSREA 2009). Tribal factions can hamper business when goods are primarily supplied to people of the same tribe or when jobs are divided among people from the same tribe. A sense of belonging among employees, outside tribe membership, is provided by wearing the same overall.

Another important element that had to be dealt with by The Ubuntu Company was the lack of a disciplined workforce. Training of the personnel is a prerequisite for reaching sustained production. Most of the workforce comes from slum areas and disciplined work on a daily routine is new to them. It takes some authority on the part of the local manager to teach the workforce to adapt to the new circumstances, but the management of The Ubuntu Company tries to avoid merely bossing workers around. The management style consists of a mixture of strictly maintaining the rules and at the same time being open to exceptions and to the special circumstances of each individual. The workers are provided with insight into productivity in that on a daily basis the required level of production is indicated and if the production surpasses that target the personnel will receive a bonus. By providing healthcare to the employees a sincere interest is displayed by the management which in the long term creates loyalty. At the same time, not only is loyalty stimulated, but also individual and independent judgement on matters which affect cooperation and the quality of the working environment. This way, an increase in skills, capacities and judgement of the workers is stimulated. In short, in this company there is an explicit management strategy aiming at a cultural transition, which is greatly needed, but rarely witnessed in development projects and businesses (Samli 2009; Kroesen and Rozendaal 2010).

In other cases that we were involved in, such an explicit management strategy was often lacking. Some business cases for entrepreneurial activities in low-income economies simply assume a disciplined local organisation and then conclude that the activity can be profitable. In the same water pump project in Kenya as mentioned above, for example, the business plan designed by students from the Delft University of Technology envisaged a strict and disciplined system for the storage and selling of spare parts to the water committees in a large area. Only if this works can the business function profitably, because its competitive advantage is based on the fact that only transports of a large number of spare parts are necessary from Nairobi to the far-off area where the business is meant to function (Oltheten *et al.* 2011). But actually this can only work if the people on the job are properly trained in very accurate stock-keeping and planning, and if the different water committees are willing to join their efforts towards one common goal.

The key resources of The Ubuntu Company can also be divided into three categories. The first category consists of the resources required to produce the Plakkies: the materials for the production of the flip-flop and the intellectual property needed to exploit the brand name. The Ubuntu Company tries to use as many local resources as possible. The leather is originally African, as well as the soles, which are made from old car tyres. The foot beds are imported from Portugal, but in the near future these will also be replaced by African ones. It is estimated that The Ubuntu Company provides approximately 700 jobs in total, if its supplying companies are included. The second category is the resources required for managerial activities. These are knowledge of the local culture as well as management and communication skills and the resources needed to provide healthcare to the workforce. This we discussed in the paragraph above. The third category refers to the resources needed for training and educating the employees. The resources required for this activity are the same as those for managerial activities. The managerial quality of the company in addition to the quality of communication and cooperation of the employees forms the so-called cultural capital of the company. The employees need to embrace certain values and have to show commitment to make all these activities possible.

In many other business cases in low-income economies, the training, education and communication activities with employees are often lacking. In a multicultural setting these activities are absolutely required. In the case of The Ubuntu Company these activities were an integral part of the company; in other cases these activities are forgotten. An example of this is the design of a business plan for an off-grid solar panel company in an Indian village (Wouters *et al.* 2011). Students came up with a technically sound design. But a critical issue, communication between castes, was ignored within the approach they suggested. In the village two different castes were represented. To create the necessary scale of operation, cooperation between stakeholders from the entire village was required. But cooperation between different castes is difficult in the Indian culture (Gupta 2007) and the business idea therefore may even be unfeasible.

The Ubuntu Company is at the moment only feasible because of many key partnerships with reputable (Dutch) companies and organisations. The relationship between the founders of the company (Arnoud Rozendaal and Michel Boerrigter) was probably the most important partnership of the company. These two students and the initial partners they involved in the project fed the company with their knowledge, enthusiasm and persistence and spent a lot of time voluntarily thinking up ideas, management and acquiring funding for the company. Right from the start they found a partner in the (Dutch) non-profit KidsRights organisation. This organisation opened doors in South Africa which would otherwise have remained closed. The profit made by The Ubuntu Company will be reinvested by KidsRights into children's projects in the same community. This is made very visible in the design of the flip-flops, as the children were asked to draw the patterns that are now used for the leather insole of the flip-flop. Besides these important partnerships, Arnoud and Michel approached the famous Dutch shoe designer, Jan Jansen, for the design of the Plakkies, and an advertising agency for a large advertisement campaign in the Netherlands. This is actually a very strong point of The Ubuntu Company. Instead of doing everything themselves, they immediately searched for strong partnerships with existing companies and organisations which created support and (media) attention for the Plakkies. However, this relationship with the international market is also a point of concern. Enterprises like The Ubuntu Company need outside suppliers for key resources which entails the risk that a monopolist may sell them too expensively. They are also very dependent on the amount of customers willing to pay sufficiently for their product, which makes it necessary for the company to spend a good deal of time and money on advertising the product and looking for new market options. This dependence on partnerships derives from the entrepreneurial approach, and is an issue that we encountered in many cases of entrepreneurial activities in low-income economies. Initiatives that derive from development aid and that adapted entrepreneurial principles later on have particular trouble adjusting to this market principle.

An open question is to what extent these sustainable enterprises need to be kept alive by the efforts of volunteers. Within The Ubuntu Company committed volunteers, donors and governmental subsidies have played a major role in maintaining customer relationships and advertising at an adequate level. For example, the retailers in the Netherlands that currently sell the Plakkies were asked to lower their profit margin on the flip-flops as part of their CSR, and a big advertising agency was asked to develop the advertisement campaign for free. During their startup phase, The Ubuntu Company tried to be very careful that these voluntary contributions did not unfairly compete with local businesses, but were only deployed when there were no other, similar, local alternatives. The startup phase has ended and The Ubuntu Company is now working on engaging more small, local businesses to fill the positions that were previously taken by these mainly Dutch volunteers.

As mentioned above, The Ubuntu Company supplies to different customer segments. The first customer group consists of the different types of customer and reseller of the flip-flop in the Netherlands. The flip-flop is sold in several Dutch stores and each of these stores again attracts different segments. There is the young (aged 20–30), fashionable man or woman who likes the design of the flip-flop and there is the customer who is, in some way, involved in sustainable development and who likes the underlying idea of Plakkies (and the design). This type of customer is much harder to describe in terms of age, sex or income. We already pointed out that, although these customers are easily attracted to a new product, it is difficult to keep interest alive in the long run. This entrepreneurial principle could be difficult to cope with for projects aiming primarily at social or ecological goals such as The Ubuntu Company. We see that many projects, especially those such as The Ubuntu Company or the Trashy Bag Company that produce consumer products for the high-income economies, are very vulnerable to changes in consumer preferences, much more than initiatives with similar goals in the development aid approach.

A second group of customers consists of the employees of The Ubuntu Company. They receive training, a job, proper healthcare and of course a wage. Concerning the latter, there is even a deliberate effort to show the personnel whether the weekly target has been reached and from that point a bonus system for all the personnel starts functioning. Both the employees of The Ubuntu Company and the buyers of the flip-flop are considered customers and both benefit from the equality in communication between the different stakeholders as mentioned above. The target groups of this initiative are not approached as 'those in need', but as customers or partners, having their own requirements and limits. This means that the customers within the business model are in a position to set requirements for the product offered to them, but also have their own responsibilities (self-empowerment).

The relationship of The Ubuntu Company with its customers is therefore also twofold. The employees of The Ubuntu Company receive training and thus increase their knowledge. This relationship is one of dedicated personal assistance and co-creation. On the other hand, there is a distant and impersonal relationship with the Western customer. The customer buys the flip-flops in a Dutch shop and maybe even feels more related with the shop than with The Ubuntu Company itself. Many projects aim to sell their products in markets in high-income economies, because consumers in their own country lack the resources to buy these products. As a result, the producer–consumer relationship is indirect and feedback from these consumers takes a while. In these cases it is more difficult for entrepreneurs in low-income economies to adapt their market offer to (changing) consumer preferences.

We can observe that the company uses different channels to advertise its products. Because the relationship with the employees is a dedicated one on a personal basis, the company does not need complex channels to get its products to the employees. That is part of the daily management (described above). Training is delivered face-to-face. For communication with the Western customer, various marketing strategies have been developed. One of these is an innovative website and the creation of 'Terrence', a virtual Plakkies salesperson. These channels, along with key partners to keep the channels open, are also a point of concern. By means of a successful advertising campaign, supported by committed partners in the West, The Ubuntu Company has become very successful. The problem is to keep the attention of the public alive, as we pointed out above. Besides the communication channels there are physical channels required to bring the product to its customer, such as the trucks and aeroplanes that transport the Plakkies to the Western shops. This unfortunately creates ecological costs such as CO_2 emissions.

The financial cost structure of Plakkies is mainly determined by three dominant costs: namely, investments in the local factory, the buying of raw materials and the wages of the employees. It seems that, after its initial startup phase over the last two years, The Ubuntu Company is making profit. But the equilibrium between cost and return stays fragile. If some big resellers, currently willing to pay a high price, lose interest, the pressure for a more cost-efficient production will increase. Attracting interest from new retailers and improving the cost-efficiency of production are important for survival in the long run. Because The Ubuntu Company is an enterprise that has to compete with other enterprises in similar value chains, the company will always need to invest time and money in innovation and marketing.

The employees have a double role in the cost structure. In order to operate effectively, there are not only financial costs, but also social costs involved with the employment of the current workforce. Social costs include, for example, the fact that participation in the production process requires a change of lifestyle for the employees from the townships. As has happened so many times before, they both lose and gain. They can now support their families and they learn and enlarge their horizons. But their new life can create tensions in their social environment.

Finally, there are also costs for the environment: the smaller or larger ecological footprint. Since local waste products are used in the production process, an overly large footprint on the planet is prevented. This in turn is part of the attractiveness of the product for Western customers. But there is still an ecological footprint created by the production, distribution and disposal of the product and its packaging.

By tradition and often because of the focus on survival, there is no long-term orientation and planning in many African countries, both in business and in personal relationships (Hofstede 1997). That does not mean, however, that long-term business initiatives are impossible. On the contrary, what those problems teach us is that they need to be dealt with, for example, by including training and education in the business model.

Finally, the return on investment or revenue streams is not only framed in financial terms. Of course, a business needs to be financially sound in order to be competitive. But that does not preclude other costs as well as returns, as we pointed out earlier. There is also revenue, in the case of The Ubuntu Company, in terms of the education of the employees, the investments in the health of the employees, the recycling of tyres, the various projects of KidsRights and the multiplier effect which affects many businesses and people around the business model.

Other case examples show that revenues can be even further increased if revenues from one entrepreneurial project are fed into another project. For example, in an Indian village families can have an electrical lamp recharged for a commercial rate of 2 rupees per day (Ghosh *et al.* 2010). In addition, the family needs to pay off the lamp which they bought with the help of a small subsidy. At the same time a collaborating project teaches the women to weave cloth during the longer hours of light, made possible by the lamp. This cloth can be sold at the price of 50 rupees per metre (one evening's work), which enables them to pay for the electrical lamp.

Source: adapted Business Model Canvas from: www.businessmodelgeneration.com

Key Partnerships	Key Activities	Value Propositions	Customer Relationships	Customer Segments
Funders: A. Rozendaal & M. Boerrigter (students) KidsRights Organization Delft University of Technology Retailers in the Netherlands	**Key Activities** Product Activities Managerial Activities Training Activities	Creating, producing and selling *a socially and ecologically sound flip-flop for the western market which fits into current western fashion trends and at the same time training their local, often underprivileged and HIV-infected, employees to prepare them for local ownership*	Distant non-personal relationship with the user of the flip-flop by means of a more personal relationship with the different retailers Dedicated personal assistance and co-creation between employees and management	**Customer Segments** Users: young (20-30) fashion-minded western customers who like the design of the flip-flop A second segment of users consists of Western customers of all ages who like the socially sound idea of the flip-flop Employees: Inhabitants of the Durban townships, often female, underprivileged and HIV-infected
Supliers of different key resources like the old tyres and the cork Volunteers: consisting of individuals, companies and other organisations that support the project in kind or through governmental subsidies, such as the Rabobank, KLM, Cordaid, Accenture, Bijenkorf, Wilde Ganzen, etc.	**Key Resources** Raw materials such as cork, rubber and leather & intellectual property of the design and the brand Knowledge of local culture, management and communication skills Cultural capital		**Channels**  Marketing strategy which involves an innovative website and poster campaign Distribution of the product to the retailers Face-to-face transfer of knowledge	

Cost Structure (Financial)		Revenue Streams (Financial)	
Investments in factory Buying of raw material Wages of employees Intellectual property	HIV medication, etc. Training Transportation Marketing (website and posters)	Return on investment consists of the financial revenues generated by paying customers of the flip-flop in the Netherlands Contribution to the economic development of South Africa	

Social Costs	Ecological Costs	Social Revenues	Ecological Revenues
High impact on the lifestyle of local employees (dependence)	Ecological footprint of production and disposal of flip-flop and packaging (Among other things: CO_2 emissions during transport of both the product and the raw materials)	Awareness in the Netherlands of sustainability, waste recycling, HIV and the development of the region Education, healthcare and empowerment of the employees & the profit made by the company will be invested in projects of KidsRights	Recycling of tyres

Figure 10.3 shows the extended Business Model Canvas as applied to The Ubuntu Company, giving an overview of all the aspects mentioned above.

Summarising the value creation of The Ubuntu Company

Does The Ubuntu Company contribute to the sustainable development of Durban in South Africa? We tried to answer this question by looking at the extent to which the project has succeeded in creating financial, social and ecological value using the extended Business Model Canvas as can be seen in Figure 10.3.

We can conclude that The Ubuntu Company is currently no longer dependent on donors or volunteers for its daily functioning and even makes financial profit, which can be reinvested into KidsRights. This makes the company financially independent, creates a clear incentive for the employees to continue with the business even when collaboration with the Western initiators stops. The company also generates enough work for a large number of suppliers in and outside South Africa, creating a multiplier effect in the region. The Ubuntu Company offers its employees fair wages, training and HIV medication, which stimulates their self-empowerment. The Ubuntu Company locally also creates ecological value by recycling old car tyres, which otherwise would have become a safety or health hazard. The business model canvas shows that there are also some local ecological costs created by the production, packaging, transportation and disposal of the product. Whether these ecological costs exceed the ecological revenue is hard to determine. The Ubuntu Company is aware of this imperfection within its current business model and strives to lower the ecological costs in the future for example by using locally produced cork instead of importing cork from Portugal. By marketing the company and brand in the Netherlands with these social and ecological objectives, awareness of all these issues is created in the Netherlands, again creating social value. In summary, The Ubuntu Company seems to really contribute to the sustainable development of the regional economy by creating mutual value.

Conclusions, discussion and future research

Our initial question was: how can an entrepreneurial approach help low-income economies develop sustainably? Is it possible to use the same methodologies such as business modelling as for entrepreneurs in general? In order to answer this question we first distinguished three different ways of framing relationships between high-income and low-income economies: the colonial relationship, the development aid relationship and sustainable entrepreneurship. The colonial relationship was not sustainable but was durable, because it was profitable for high-income economies. However, it lacked social and ecological responsibility. In contrast, the development aid relationship was socially responsible but its lack of focus on financial sustainability caused too much dependency and lack of initiative from relevant stakeholders in low-income economies. Sustainable entrepreneurship combines the positive features of both, in that businesses in low-income economies are expected to be independent, profitable and socially sustainable at the same time.

We illustrated by means of our case study that the use of entrepreneurship is important for five reasons. First, an entrepreneurial approach is sustainable in time because it makes individuals in low-income economies responsible for their own situation and helps them to improve their daily life by granting them the opportunity to start a business. It is also more sustainable from the perspective of a high-income economy: rather than merely being a donor and having to face more and more resistance against development aid, the actors in the high-income economy now become investors. Initiatives will be less vulnerable to donors that stop their funding, because the entrepreneurs become financially independent. Second, adoption of an entrepreneurship approach creates a holistic approach by incorporating relevant aspects that are usually undervalued in development initiatives (aspects such as marketing, financial models, stakeholder analyses, intellectual property and so on) and thereby increases the chances of success. Third, the approach creates equality in communication between the customers and the entrepreneurs (instead of the poor and the donors). Fourth, the approach stimulates learning of entrepreneurs because their income will serve as a feedback mechanism on their way of working. Additional coaching or formal learning activities may become more desirable if starting a business reveals a need for specific competences. Finally, the social and ecological sustainability can be stimulated by the investors, for example by selecting projects that qualify in terms of social and ecological sustainability. Because entrepreneurship creates more equality in communication between different actors it also stimulates more socially sustainable activities. Entrepreneurship creates a basis for a dialogue in which the initiative for development is gradually taken over by actors in the low-income economy.

We showed that the extended Business Model Canvas can be very helpful to check relevant stakeholders and activities involved in entrepreneurship and to combine and analyse them in a consistent way. The extended canvas succeeds in being a holistic tool for describing, analysing and designing individual business models and can be used to analyse business models in low-income economies with an embedded sustainable purpose if the model is modified by adding social and ecological costs and revenues besides the financial costs and revenues.

The application of the extended Business Model Canvas in the context of a developing, low-income society was explored in a real-world case: The Ubuntu Company. This case shows how this context influences the company and how it can affect entrepreneurial activity in general. It also clearly showed differences in approach from traditional entrepreneurship; for example, the employees are now also considered customers of the business model, as one of the embedded purposes of the project was creating employment for a target group which is normally hard to employ.

Several issues appear which require additional research and experimentation in order to apply the extended business model canvas on a larger scale, better informed and more effective. We mention five of them:

1. The internal management model of an enterprise requires proper attention. Starting a business in the context of low-income economies that are not used to large-scale cooperation and disciplined labour, requires effort in terms of training and education of the workforce. In other words, the technical innovation introduced also requires a social innovation. This social innovation entails a cultural transition in which traditional collectivist and agrarian values should be complemented with modern, effective, interventionist and often individualistic codes of behaviour. Such management models require conscious reflection and explicit solutions in a business plan for low-income economies. The canvas makes it possible to integrate such activities in the business, but cannot by itself prescribe what they should be. Entrepreneurship as such is a value which may need to be introduced from the outside in collectivist and risk-avoiding contexts (Samli 2009)

2. The social and institutional context of a local entrepreneurial initiative need to be taken into account. Entrepreneurship for developing economies implies that a business context which can be relied on as a common base of resources in terms of knowledge, materials and people is not available. There is no such thing as a business hub which generates its own momentum (Collier 2007). Ideas from outside are necessary, the market is outside and often investments, too, come from distant sources. Usually, the problem is not the distance itself, the problem is that everything is more complicated and needs an extra effort in translating and transferring (including adaptation) to the other context. If such a transfer of knowledge, technology, policies and also capacities and skills is not part of the business strategy, new initiatives may fail and old initiatives die (de Jong *et al.* 2003)

3. The case that was analysed in this chapter was The Ubuntu Company, a sustainable enterprise from day one. When we look at similar initiatives we can also see NGOs becoming more entrepreneurial or 'traditional' enterprises becoming more sustainable. What are the differences? Which of these will generate the most impact?

4. The role of external support and efforts from volunteers within the business model requires more attention. In sustainable entrepreneurship and business development, social idealism and financial realism dovetail into each other. Government agencies, NGOs or students do help small companies get started. Changes are initiated by idealism, but they should be followed up by sober realism in order to make them sustainable. More

additional research and experimentation is necessary in order to explore how this transition can best be brought about

5. Assessing mutual value creation remains problematic for many sustainable enterprises. While enterprises in the colonial system have metrics to evaluate their economic performance, assessing social or ecological performances in the development aid or sustainable entrepreneurship relationship systematically seems more difficult (Ekins and Max-Neef 1992). Which current options are there? And which of these would be suitable to use in combination with the extended Business Model Canvas?

Future research and experimentation should deal with those issues that concern the individual sustainable enterprises. In addition, future research should also explore the bigger picture of the social environment (infrastructures) in which these businesses are meant to function. Sustainable entrepreneurship needs a set of institutional conditions, such as a society with the rule of law, checks and balances, and law enforcement so that business disputes can be solved in a fair way, unreliable companies can be pushed out of the market and so on (Fukuyama 2011). It also requires an open civil society which is characterised by free association of individuals, universal rules and neutral roles; anonymous trust instead of clientelistic or patrimonial systems and tribal factions manipulating the government bureaucracy. Finally, it needs a sound information and transport infrastructure (Collier 2007). However, small steps made by individual enterprises could also lead to a solution for these infrastructural and institutional problems. Or, to put it more precisely, a change of culture, institutions and regulations needs to reinforce, but also be reinforced by, many small-scale, bottom-up initiatives such as The Ubuntu Company and the other examples we mentioned. Future research should therefore also include the ways in which individual companies by their business strategies can contribute to such larger-scale solutions. By showing that and how it can be done, in theory (the Business Model Canvas) and in practice (The Ubuntu Company and other examples), we have demarcated the way forward in order to contribute to sustainable development and social innovation by means of a holistic sustainable business approach.

References

Austin, J., H. Stevenson and J. Wei-Skillern (2006) 'Social and Commercial Entrepreneurship: Same, Different, or Both?' *Entrepreneurship: Theory and Practice* 30.1: 1-22.

Cohen, B., and M.I. Winn (2007) 'Market Imperfections, Opportunity and Sustainable Entrepreneurship', *Journal of Business Venturing* 22: 29-49.

Collier, P. (2007) *The Bottom Billion: Why the Poorest Countries are Failing and What Can Be Done about It* (New York: Oxford University Press).

Daly, H.E., and J.B. Cobb Jr (1989) *For the Common Good, Redirecting the Economy to towards Community, the Environment and to a Sustainable Future* (London: The Merlin Press).

Easterly, W. (2006) *The White Man's Burden: Why the West's Efforts to Aid the Rest Have Done So Much Ill and So Little Good* (New York: Penguin).

Ekins, P., and M. Max-Neef (ed.) (1992) *Real-Life Economics, Understanding Wealth Creation* (New York: Routledge).

Friedman, M. (1970) 'The Social Responsibility of Business is to Increase its Profits', *New York Times Magazine*, 13 September 1970.

Fukuyama, F. (2011) *The Origins of Political Order from Pre-Human Times to the French Revolution* (London: Exmouth House).

Gasper, D.R. (2004) *The Ethics of Development* (Edinburgh: Edinburgh University Press).

Ghosh, A., N. Bose, J.O. Kroesen, J. Bruining, V.K. Bawane and P.K. Chaubey (2010) 'Water Management in a Developing Country: A Case Study of a Watershed Development Program in the State of Bihar, India', paper presented at *ERSCP*, Delft, 25–28 October 2010.

Gupta, D. (2007) *Mistaken Modernity, India between Worlds* (New Delhi: HarperCollins).

Hall, J.K., G.A. Daneke and M.J. Lenox (2010) 'Sustainable Development and Entrepreneurship: Past Contributions and Future Directions', *Journal of Business Venturing* 25: 439-48.

Hofstede, G. (1997) *Cultures and Organizations; Software of the Mind* (New York: McGraw Hill).

De Jong, M., K. Lalenis and V.D. Mamadouh (eds.) (2003) 'The Theory and Practice of Institutional Transplantation Experiences with the Transfer of Policy Institutions', *GeoJournal Library* 74.

Kroesen, O., and A. Rozendaal (2010) 'A Cross-Cultural Management System: The Ubuntu Company as Paradigm', *International Journal of Technology, Policy and Management* 10.3: 284-98.

London, T., R. Anupindi and S. Sheth (2010) 'Creating Mutual Value: Lessons Learned from Ventures Serving Base of the Pyramid Producers', *Journal of Business Research* 63: 582-94.

Moyo, D. (2009) *Dead Aid: Why Aid is Not Working and How There is another Way for Africa* (London: Penguin).

Oltheten, M., T. Kroese and B. Tap (2011) *Repairing Water Pumps: Working for the Water of Our Future* (student's internship report; Delft, Netherlands: TU Delft).

OSSREA (Organization for Social Science Research in Eastern and Southern Africa) (2009) *Good Governance and Civil Society Participation in Africa* (Addis Ababa, Ethiopia: OSSREA).

Osterwalder, A., and Y. Pigneur (eds.) (2010) *Business Model Generation* (Toronto: self-published).

Porter M.E., and M.R. Kramer (2011) 'Creating Shared Value', *Harvard Business Review*, January/February 2011: 62-77.

Prahalad, C.K., and A. Hammond (2002) 'Serving the World's Poor, Profitably', *Harvard Business Review* 80.9: 48-57.

Prahalad, C.K., and S.K. Hart (2002) *The Fortune at the Bottom of the Pyramid* (Upper Saddle River, NJ: Pearson Press).

Sachs, J.D. (2005) *The End of Poverty* (New York: Penguin Press).

Samli, A.C. (2009) *International Entrepreneurship: Innovative Solutions for a Fragile Planet* (New York: Springer).

Schouten, T., and P. Moriarty (2003) *Community Water, Community Management: From System to Service in Rural Areas* (London: IRC).

Smith, A. (1776) *An Inquiry into the Nature and Causes of the Wealth of Nations* (London: W. Strahan and T. Cadell).

Troost, A.P., and E. Twillert (2011) *Trashy Bags* (student's internship report; Delft, Netherlands: TU Delft).

WCED (World Commission on Environment & Development) (1987) *Our Common Future* (Oxford, UK: Oxford University Press).

Wiarda, H.J. (2003) *Civil Society: The American Model and Third World Development* (Boulder, CO: Westview Press).

World Bank (2011) 'World Development Indicators', data.worldbank.org/data-catalog/world-development-indicators, accessed 23 September 2011.

Wouters, M., J. Huijts and W. De Wit (2011) *Implementing Solar Power in our Rural Village in Bihar, India* (student's internship report; Delft, Netherlands: TU Delft).

Section V
EIS in small firms

11

Corporate social responsibility in the relationships between large retailers and Italian small and medium food suppliers

Fabio Musso
University of Urbino, Italy

Mario Risso
University of Rome, Italy

Global economic development has increased firms' opportunities to achieve their economic goals and, at the same time, has facilitated the consciousness of consumers in expressing their need for more transparency in production processes and supply chain operations. This issue has been investigated in many studies (Dagnoli 1991; Shaw and Clarke 1999; Shaw and Shiu 2003; Caselli 2003; Maignan and Ferrel 2004; Sciarelli 2007).

Today, aware and educated consumers are not only interested in new products, but they also require more information about manufacturers, labour conditions and how production systems impact the environment and the economic growth of the local communities along the entire supply chain (Strong 1996; Shaw and Clarke 1998, Harrison *et al.* 2005).

As consumers are becoming more responsive to ethical behaviours, they are also more aware of product evaluations (Macchiette and Roy 1994; Hemingway and Maclagan 2004) and their motivations are increasingly related to the need for personal and social benefits (Freestone and McGoldrick 2008).

Consequently, companies are becoming more ethical and socially responsible, by developing methodologies and tools linked to corporate social responsibility (CSR) initiatives.

Recently, the importance of CSR has increased in all economic sectors, including retailing. In this sector, large international retailers are investing relevant resources to cope with consumers' ethical needs (Whysall 2000; Pepe 2003; Jones *et al.* 2005). They have begun to consolidate their approach to CSR offering ethical products which incorporate the principles related to sustainable development, fairness and a balanced distribution of value among all actors within the supply chain.

Consumers seem to be less critical of retailers than they are of large manufacturers. In many cases, they perceive retailers as only partially responsible for the activities along the supply chain of products and tend to reserve more trust towards retailers' behaviours. Nevertheless, some retailers are becoming known as socially irresponsible companies, such as Wal-Mart (De Man 2005; Wilson 2005) and Benetton, with the latter being accused of child exploitation in Turkey in 1998 (Boyd *et al.* 2005). At the same time, the level of public awareness of CSR initiatives has illustrated the challenge that companies face in building a positive reputation. Companies that identify themselves as CSR leaders will enhance their reputation (Cooper *et al.* 1997; Maignan *et al.* 2002, Boyd *et al.* 2005; De Man 2005; Pepe 2007; Schlegelmilch and Öberseder 2007; Amaeshi *et al.* 2008; Majumdar and Nishant 2008; Salam 2009).

Retailers are often channel leaders and can control various activities in the supply chain. As a result, they appear more capable of adopting active roles in sustaining and leading international supply chains following a CSR approach. The most advanced retailers have capitalised on this opportunity and have managed their retail assortments and marketing policies by considering the extra-economic values in all the activities of supply chain partners (Schaltegger 2002; Risso 2007; Andersen and Larsen 2009).

This chapter explores the influence of CSR policies of large retailers on small- and medium-sized enterprises (SMEs) that are part of their supply chain. Three areas of theoretical analysis were considered.

The first referred to CSR in large, retailer-led channel relationships (Baily 1987; Davidson *et al.* 1988; Shuch 1988; Packard *et al.* 1996; Musso 1999). Afterwards, literature on main strategies and policies adopted by retailers in managing CSR issues was considered, and finally literature on issues related to CSR for SMEs was analysed.

Second, the results of empirical quantitative research are reported. The research was focused on Italian small and medium manufacturers in the agro-food sector involved in international supply chains led by large retailers. The aim of the research was to analyse the grade of diffusion of CSR practices among large retailers' small suppliers and the main factors influencing the relationships within a retailer's CSR approach. The choice of the food sector was due to the increased sensitivity of consumers to ethical issues in this field, which requires retailers to give priority to the adoption of CSR practices within this sector.

CSR, retailers and SME suppliers

CSR has recently become a new corporate buzzword, as well as an emerging field of competition among companies. CSR is an enlarged concept of responsibility, according to a general evolution of 'values' linked to the relationship between a business organisation and its environment. For companies, this means responsibility to consumers and shareholders, with the latter linked to the maximisation of profit and assets.

In the literature, several studies have been concerned with corporate ethics and corporate responsibilities. Most of them investigated the importance of ethics in the purchasing and selling activities of industrial companies (Redelius and Bucholz 1979; Dubinsky and Gwinn 1981; Trawick et al. 1988; Wood 1995). However, few studies have explored the importance of ethics in the buyer–seller relationships of retail companies (Dickerson and Dalecki 1991; Arbuthnot 1997; Musso 1999).

More recently, the boundaries of the classic concept of business ethics have enlarged, entering the wider realm of CSR and sustainable development. Indeed, the expression 'sustainable development' synthesises the three dimensions of the problem: the safeguarding of the environment, the respect for human rights and the fairness in the redistribution of value among all actors of the supply chain.

The supply chain perspective for CSR and large retailers' role

Many authors have focused on CSR within supply chains, mainly in relation to industrial, multinational corporations. Many of them are leaders of wide and complex supply chains (Carter 2000; Park and Stoel 2005; Mamic 2005; Maloni and Brown 2006; Amaeshi et al. 2008; Gonzalez-Padron et al. 2008), but leadership within supply chains is also exerted by large retailers, both at national and international level (Nicholls 2002; Pepe 2003; Jones et al. 2005; Risso 2007).

Indeed, the supply chain represents a focal point to adopt strategies related to the concept of responsibility, and to evaluate them. It is significant to understand the specific role of each player and the general action conducted by all the supply chain members. In the case of retailers, their role becomes relevant when their capability to influence consumer choices brings it to a position of channel leader. Retailers have the ability to better understand final demands and to activate marketing tools based on economic values, as well as extra-economic values and needs. Thus, they are the first to face consumers' requests for more ethical and responsible approaches to production and distribution of goods. At the same time, they are able to play an active role in influencing consumers' behaviours towards ethical and social issues (Pepe 2003).

Given this condition, large retailers can play a predominant role in controlling the sustainability of both production and distribution processes. They frequently become guarantors of the entire value chains, particularly those of their own brand products, which directly reflect their corporate image.

The increasing consumer sensitivity to sustainability has encouraged several major retailers, particularly those from advanced countries within Europe, to adopt a CSR for managing their retail assortments (Freestone and McGoldrick 2008). Their involvement in ethical issues began in the 1990s, with the distribution of organic products and fair-trade food products. The same principles were then applied to beauty, personal care, handmade and clothing products (Balabanis *et al.* 1998; Harrison *et al.* 2005).

By the adoption of CSR in managing retail assortments and related supply chains, retailers can more quickly and effectively achieve the following goals:

- Reduced reputational risks/product warranty risks (Kytle and Ruggie 2005)

- Market differentiation (Piacentini *et al.* 2000)

- Enhanced word-of-mouth and reduction of expensive marketing investments (Pepe 2007)

- Increased customer and worker loyalty (Pepe 2003)

- Eligibility for inclusion in a stock market index that includes only those companies deemed to be socially responsible (Collison *et al.* 2009)

- Being ahead of regulation

Large retailers' attitude towards CSR

The retailers' approach to CSR mainly focuses on relationships with suppliers. Many of the retailers have adopted CSR reports and they have settled behaviour codes regarding labour safety and the environment (even the social environment), in which they and their suppliers (including those from the South) operate (Roberts 2003; Logsdon and Wood 2005).

The more active retailers promote activities in cooperation with non-governmental organisations (NGOs), philanthropic organisations and East Asian countries' local authorities (Musso and Risso 2006). Several retailers are also promoting joint activities to stimulate homogeneous criteria for social and environmental sustainability. In this case, a special role was played by CIES (Comité International d'Entreprises à Succursales, International Committee of Food Retail Chains), an independent network that brings together the CEOs and senior management of approximately 400 retailers and manufacturers in the food sector across 150 countries.[1]

1 The mission of the CIES is to provide a platform for knowledge exchange, thought leadership and networking, and to facilitate the development of common tools regarding key strategic and practical issues that affect the supply chains. In 2007, CIES began the Global Social Compliance Programme (GSCP), designed to harmonise companies' efforts to deliver a shared, consistent and global approach for the improvement of working conditions in global supply chains. GSCP offers a global platform to promote knowledge

Many retailers are actually responding to consumers' emerging awareness on social and environmental values by listing in their offer an increasing number of products coming from alternative trade systems, such as fair-trade organisations (FTOs). In some cases it is the retailer that directly organises 'fair' supply chains, that are accepted and certified by FTOs (Becchetti and Paganetto 2003; Pepe 2007).

In most cases, for the development of fair-trade product lines, retailers build a proper unit inside their organisation, with a CSR manager. Among the tasks of the CSR manager there are those aimed at maintaining contacts with the NGOs and other institutions involved, as well as with auditing companies that ensure control to the suppliers. The same organisational structure can also be involved in promoting CSR principles inside the retailer's internal organisation.

Specific organisational structures are also necessary for managing own brand fair-trade products. Two types of solution are typically adopted by retailers: in the case of products with an economic role (that is, with the objective of increasing sales or profitability) there is a direct responsibility of the category manager. In the case of products with a more 'ethical' role (to provide consumers with a message of high social responsibility, but also with lower prices and lower profits) there is a staff structure that supports buying, merchandising and communication activities related to the ethical sub-brand. In the case of new products coming directly from fair-trade supply chains, a specific team can be devised to manage supply relationships (Musso and Risso 2006).

CSR, traceability and SME suppliers

Managing CSR issues and ethical and fair-trade products can enable retailers to modify their existing relationships with their smaller suppliers, mostly at the international level: shorter supply chains can be organised compared with traditional ones, in which international trade organisations have a relevant role.

According to this approach, retailers promote traceability for food products, which becomes an important control tool. Traceability is linked to a legal framework and is a way of facing potential risks that can arise in the food production and logistic processes. In addition, traceability permits targeted withdrawals and the provision of accurate information to the public, thereby controlling each partner in the products supply chain. Traceability systems are not only a technical tool to monitor each step of the supply chain, but also a managerial system to reduce costs, as well as an intervention system in cases of non-compliance (Per Engelseth 2009).

---

exchange and best practices to build comparability and transparency between existing systems, whether they are individual or collaborative. Major retailers, such as Wal-Mart, Carrefour, Tesco, Migros and Metro, and branded manufacturers, such as Dole, Chiquita, Hasbro and HP, have joined the GSCP (Musso and Risso 2006; www.gscpnet.com, accessed 14 October 2011).

Traceability is more critical in international supply chains and in the relationships with SME suppliers, for reasons related to: the need for warranties on products coming from countries with different legal frameworks; labour conditions that apply to employees in less-developed countries; the fair distribution of value among suppliers; and the environmental impact of the production processes.

In regard to SME suppliers, there are some critical aspects to be considered (Spence 1999; Jenkins 2004). In particular, it is difficult for SMEs to respect CSR policies, because (Grayson and Dodd 2007):

- The application of codes of conduct can be perceived as too onerous

- SMEs may have less of a direct advantage in CSR policies

- SMEs have less time and fewer resources to invest in CSR processes, with more immediate business priorities

- Knowledge of CSR practices is limited among SMEs and they have problems in human resources training

- External supports to firms are inadequate

Recent studies argued that CSR is more difficult for SMEs because entrepreneurs do not have the experience to evaluate and manage CSR key factors (Murillo and Lozano 2006a, b; Lepoutre and Heene 2006; Williamson *et al*. 2006). Despite these difficulties, SME suppliers are trying to meet large retailers' requirements, by increasing their standards of safety, security, environmental sustainability and working conditions in the supply chains (Musso 1999; Grayson and Dodd 2007; Pepe 2007; Pepe *et al*. 2008).

Empirical research and methodology

To investigate the CSR approach of the SME suppliers within retailer-led supply chains, quantitative research was conducted.

The study focused on the food sector, as a sector in which traceability, supplier coordination and control over suppliers are critical to ensure an efficient supply chain. The research was addressed to Italian food SME manufacturers operating as suppliers of international large retailers. The aim was to understand the influence of CSR initiatives undertaken by large retailers on SME suppliers. Data were collected through telephone interviews to a sample of 59 manufacturers which have been identified through the Italian Association of Small and Medium Food Enterprises, by random extraction from a list of companies which supply large retailers (Table 11.1). Interviews were conducted with entrepreneurs and sales/marketing managers.

Table 11.1 **Food SME manufacturers sample description**

	Number of firms interviewed
No. of firms	59
Exporters	52
Suppliers of large retailers	59
• Italian retailers only	28
• International retailer only	3
• Both national and international retailer	28
Geographic area:	
• Northern Italy	23
• Central Italy	16
• Southern Italy	20
Size (no. of employees)	
• less than 30 employees	34
• from 30 to 50 employees	8
• from 51 to 100	8
• over 100 employees	9
Annual turnover (euros)	
• less than 5 million	24
• from 5 to 10 million	12
• from 10 to 20 million	7
• from 20 to 40 million	6
• from 40 to 60 million	4
• over 60 million	6
Annual export turnover (euros)	
• less than 5 million	34
• from 5 to 10 million	4
• from 10 to 20 million	6
• from 20 to 40 million	3
• from 40 to 60 million	4
• over 60 million	–

The questionnaire was focused on general issues related to supply relationships and specific issues related to CSR. The general issues have been divided into three main categories: market dynamics, export strategies and relationships with large retailers. The CSR issues related to the awareness of CSR, CSR implications in business processes, and CSR tools and instruments. The questionnaire was planned on the basis of three research questions that emerged from the literature review.

The first research question referred to the importance of CSR for the functional areas of the firm in the relationships with large retailers.

> RQ 1: What is the grade of diffusion of the CSR practices among SME manufacturers in the food sector?

The second research question was related to the aims of the CSR activities. It included: factors that stimulate firms to adopt CSR activities, requirements to manufacturers from large retailers, expected characteristics of CSR systems and guidelines for CSR activities.

> RQ 2: What are the main reasons for adopting or joining CSR initiatives and what topics/needs do they cover?

The third research question focused on the systems used to manage CSR activities (e.g. quality control and traceability of products, environmental rules, security and ethical codes). In particular, it was directed to verify whether CSR activities were developed through formal practices or through an informal approach.

> RQ 3: How formal/informal is the approach to CSR practices?

The results of the questionnaire have been analysed with the following linked variables: firm size, weight of sales to large retailers on turnover, degree of internationalisation (based on weight of export on turnover) and age of the firm. The questionnaire was semi-structured with items referring to the previously mentioned research questions. A five-point Likert scale was used for the evaluation of single items (1 = low importance to 5 = high importance). Responses to open-ended questions were classified and a dichotomous scale of 0/1 (0 not relevant, 1 totally relevant) was used for each item. The measurement instrument was developed using a combination of existing scales. Data analysis was conducted by a SPSS statistical tool. The following results were obtained through the description of frequencies and cluster and principal components analysis (PCA).

Results

The frequencies analysis showed a prevalence of inhomogeneous behaviours among firms. In order to have a better understanding of such behaviours a cluster analysis has been carried out. K-Mean methodology was applied, allowing for a minimised inertia within single groups and among clusters. Three clusters have been singled out on the basis of a series of tests which revealed the value of returns with the clearest differences.

The variables used to divide the sample into more homogeneous groups included: overall turnover, export turnover, importance of national large retailers as customers (as a % of turnover), and importance of international large retailers as customers (as a % of turnover). Table 11.2 illustrates the variables that contributed to defining the clusters within the sample. F-test revealed that turnover, the importance of national retailers in turnover, and the importance of international retailers in turnover were the more significant variables.

Differences in the means between clusters are due to the variance in responses and to the different consistencies of the single clusters (Table 11.3).

Table 11.2 **ANOVA (analysis of variance) with different significance levels**

	Cluster		Error		F	Sig.
	mean square	Df	mean square	Df		
Turnover	14.45	2.00	2.53	56.00	5.70	0.01
Export turnover	4.49	2.00	1.64	49.00	2.74	0.07
Importance of national large retailers	18337.21	2.00	214.78	51.00	85.38	0.00
Importance of international large retailers	6285.68	2.00	73.22	45.00	85.85	0.00

F-tests should only be used for descriptive purposes here, because the clusters were chosen to maximise the differences between the cases in the different clusters. The observed significance levels were not corrected for this, and thus, cannot be interpreted as tests of the hypothesis that the cluster means are equal.

Table 11.3 **Number of units per cluster**

Cluster	Number of firms
1 Big national suppliers	16
2 Small national suppliers	29
3 Big international suppliers	14
Total interviews	59

Cluster 2 resulted as the most numerous, with 29 firms that answered the questionnaire. Cluster 1 had 16 units, while Cluster 3 had 14 units. Data on the importance of large retailers in turnover was not available from all the manufacturers.

Considering their insignificant number, missing values have been treated with the option 'exclude cases pairwise' that permits the assignment of single cases based on the distances from the variables without missing values.

In Cluster 1, turnovers revealed an average value between €10 and 20 million, export turnover had an average value between €5 and 10 million, sales to national large retailers had an average weight of 77.53% on total sales (Table 11.4), and sales to internationally large retailers had an average weight of 5.33% on total sales.

In Cluster 2, average turnover was between €5 and 10 million, the same as export turnover; sales to national large retailers had an average weight of 16.51%, and sales to internationally large retailers had an average weight of 5.62%.

Cluster 3 showed an average turnover between €21 and 40 million, an export turnover between €5 and 10 million, sales to national large retailers had an average weight of 27.25%, and sales to international large retailers had a weight of 47%.

The three clusters differentiated from each other mainly by overall turnover and weight of large retailers (both national and international level). Cluster 1 had a distinctively higher weight of national large retailers on turnover and a lower weight of international retailers. As firms in Cluster 1 had an overall turnover mainly between €10 and 20 million, they can be named 'Big national suppliers'. Cluster 2 is characterised by fewer sales to large retailers and a smaller size of firms than Cluster 1 (mean of €5 to 10 million turnover). Its firms can be named 'Small national suppliers'. In Cluster 3, firm size is higher (mean of €20 to 40 million turnover) and large retailers are more important to turnover, particularly international retailers (47% on total turnover), than Italian retailers (27.25%). Firms of Cluster 3 can be named 'Big international suppliers'.

Table 11.4 **Weight of large retailers on turnover by cluster**

Cluster	Weight national retailers %	Weight international retailers %
1 Big national suppliers	77.53	5.33
2 Small national suppliers	16.87	5.62
3 Big international suppliers	27.25	47.00

As far as RQ 1 was concerned (which is the grade of diffusion of CSR practices among SME manufacturers in the food sector), Table 11.5 illustrates the importance attributed to distinct firm areas. Evaluation on importance of CSR practices was sought on a Likert scale from 1 (low importance) to 5 (high importance). A principal components analysis was conducted to identify a concise method for evaluation of CSR orientation and practices of the sample. PCA is a method that reduces data dimensionality by performing a covariance analysis between factors (Jolliffe 2002). It is suitable for data sets in multiple dimensions. PCA on CSR orientation and practices provides a way to identify predominant criteria expression patterns. When applied on conditions, PCA will explore correlations between samples or conditions. The goal of PCA is to 'summarise' the data, it is not considered a clustering tool. PCA does not attempt to group firms by user-specified criteria as does the clustering methods.

Table 11.5 **Total variance explained in PCA for manufacturers' evaluation on CSR practices**

Component	Initial Eigenvalues			Rotation sums of squared loadings		
	Total	% of variance	Cumulative %	Total	% of variance	Cumulative %
1	3.435	42.941	42.941	2.097	26.212	26.212
2	1.318	16.470	59.410	2.007	25.089	51.301
3	1.257	15.707	75.117	1.905	23.816	75.117
4	0.608	7.605	82.723			
5	0.509	6.359	89.082			
6	0.418	5.223	94.305			
7	0.274	3.429	97.733			
8	0.181	2.267	100.000			

Extraction method: principal component analysis

The overall assessment from Table 11.5 is that the three main components explain 75.117% of variance. Therefore, we used a PCA rotated matrix which allows us to enhance the more significant correlations among the three components (see Table 11.6).

The first component includes regular and complete information on product, anti-corruption practices, and support to local community development. It is strictly related to the legal and local aspects of SME supplier responsibilities. Therefore, the first component was named 'legal responsibility'. The second component contains the criteria which explain labour conditions, product quality and traceability, and environmental impact of production. This component was named 'operational responsibility'. The third component mainly identifies ethical standards and communication to consumers and, hence, it was named 'marketing responsibility'.

The three principal components explained the critical aspects of the evaluation of firms on the importance of CSR practices. Analysing the components with some simple characteristics of firms (i.e. size, export turnover, location), some general trends emerged. In particular, we found a positive correlation between size and operational responsibility, and between size and marketing responsibility. The correlation is negative between size and legal responsibility.

In general, all enterprises considered 'operational' and 'marketing' responsibilities as fundamental issues. Less importance was given to supporting the local community and to the development of anti-corruption practices (legal responsibility).

Table 11.6 **Rotated component matrix**

	Component		
	1	2	3
Product quality and traceability	0.085	0.749	0.309
Labour conditions	0.112	0.820	-0.143
Environmental impact of production	0.242	0.689	0.421
Ethical standards	0.147	0.022	0.867
Communication (bi-directional) to consumers	0.141	0.205	0.859
Anti-corruption practices	0.785	0.401	-0.051
Support to local community development	0.768	0.285	0.285
Regular and complete information on products	0.878	-0.0118	0.197

Note: Rotation converged in five iterations
Extraction method: principal component analysis; rotation method: varimax with Kaiser normalisation

Comparing evaluations on the importance of CSR within clusters, and the initiatives conducted, a consistent approach to CSR emerged with regard to all internal and external fields considered (Table 11.7 and Figure 11.1). Results from Cluster 3 revealed a more active support to the local community and to anti-corruption activities, compared with the other clusters. However, these two factors were considered less important than others.

Table 11.7 **Principal components of manufacturers' evaluation of CSR practices by clusters**

Clusters		Legal responsibility	Operational responsibility	Marketing responsibility
1	Mean	-0.3327714	-0.4561017	0.2905456
	Std deviation	1.27005640	1.23534494	0.68342412
2	Mean	-0.2418355	0.0422882	-0.3292372
	Std deviation	1.12778604	1.40903392	1.49268203
3	Mean	0.8812552	0.4336622	0.3499393
	Std deviation	1.03220173	0.51925220	0.97659500

Figure 11.1 **Initiatives conducted for CSR development by clusters of business activities and relationships**

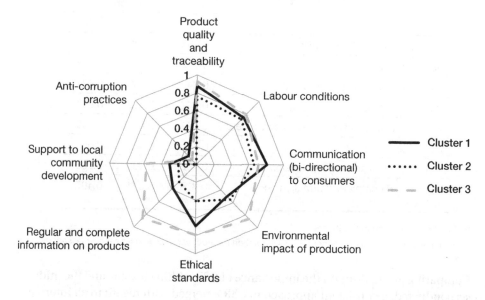

With regard to RQ 2 (main reasons for adopting or joining CSR initiatives and what topics/needs do they cover), results showed that firms seek to protect themselves from potentially negative effects such as reputational damage. As can be seen from Figure 11.2 (rates were given on a dichotomic scale 0/1, 0 no influence, 1 influence), CSR is developed by firms after requests from large retailers and consumers. In this way, product ranges can be perceived as more valuable. Less importance in terms of influencing factors is attributed to relationships with supply chain partners and to internal relationships.

As evidenced by Cluster 3, regarding larger-sized firms, more importance is given to reasons related to brand image construction and protection, as well as to the need to respond to consumers' requirements. In contrast, the response to large retailer requirements is not indicated as a primary reason because relationships with large retailers are in most cases well developed by firms. Hence, they don't need to increase CSR involvement as a tool to develop better relationships with large retailers.

This is further confirmed in Figure 11.3, where firms' awareness regarding large retailers' requirements is analysed. Large retailers tend to require, at first, high levels of reliability from suppliers (total mean rate 4.59), as well as conformity to hygiene and security standards (4.57), and high quality levels of products and services offered (4.46). Price/value comes after such factors, with a rate of 4.31.

Figure 11.4 synthesises the main points that should characterise a CSR system, according to the perspective of the firms. In a dichotomic scale 0/1 (0 not relevant to the presence in a CSR system, 1 necessary to a CSR system), all respondents

Figure 11.2 **Reasons that stimulate firms to adopt or join CSR initiatives and activities**

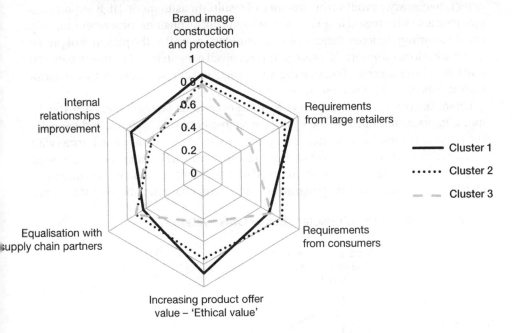

Figure 11.3 **Requirements to manufacturers from large retailers**

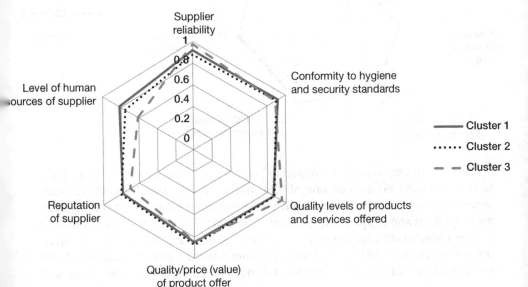

indicated the presence of measures for continuous improvement of environment sustainability as necessary. Most of them (mean 0.98) indicate that voluntary character is necessary, as well as the presence of results measurement. High importance emerged also with regard to quality and reliability of all business processes (not only manufacturing), independence from stakeholders, as well as the presence of public and institutional support. All these points received a mean indication between 0.90 and 0.69. The character of cost saving was recognised as not necessary by almost all the manufacturers (mean rate 0.36).

Larger firms and those more related to international large retailers (Cluster 3), ascribed major relevance to the voluntary character of CSR systems, and consider the presence of results measurement systems to be less necessary. Such firms, with a more advanced approach to management and control of business processes, tend to consider such points as regular parts of management criteria. At the same time, all of them consider voluntary nature as a necessary characteristic of CSR systems.

Figure 11.4 **Expected characteristics of CSR systems**

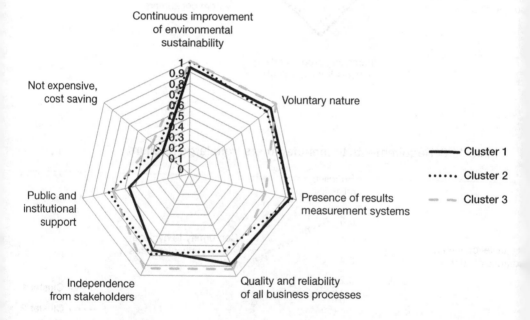

CSR activities are mainly addressed to consumers and large retailers (Fig. 11.5). Consumers received a mean rate of 0.94, while retailers 0.88. In addition, other stakeholders are frequently considered as addressees of CSR activities. Among them are employees and suppliers (respectively 0.83 and 0.76), stockholders (0.74), local communities (0.68) and institutional subjects (0.68). Less important were trade unions (0.57). Firms of Cluster 3 revealed more attention placed on all stakeholders, including trade unions. Small local firms and firms whose relationships with international large retailers are developed (Clusters 2 and 3) pay more attention to local communities.

Figure 11.5 **Addressees of CSR activities**

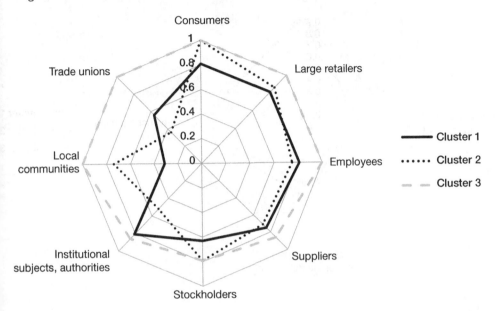

Items regarding RQ 3 (how formal/informal is the approach to CSR practices) emphasise a general orientation towards the reduced formalisation of processes related to CSR (Fig. 11.6). In particular, formal models are widely adopted for quality and traceability management and for safety inside manufacturing plants. In the first case, orientation to control quality and technical efficiency prevailed. In the second case, the choice was less voluntary: formal rules were mainly adopted according to laws on safety and health.

With regard to social, ecological and ethical values, less involvement in the formalisation of processes emerged, and the smaller the size of the firm, the more informal the approach.

All the surveyed firms, except for some smaller ones that were part of Cluster 2, adopt quality control and traceability certification systems (Fig. 11.7) that are typical in the food sector. Less use of standards emerges for environmental impact controls and for safety control systems inside manufacturing plants, with a mean indication of adoption on a dichotomic scale 0/1 of 0.68 and 0.43, respectively. Less use of certification standards is observed with regard to social and ethical values management (mean 0.31), even if several firms with significant sales to large retailers, both national and international (Clusters 1 and 3), tend to adopt them more frequently.

Figure 11.6 **Formalisation of processes for CSR improvement**

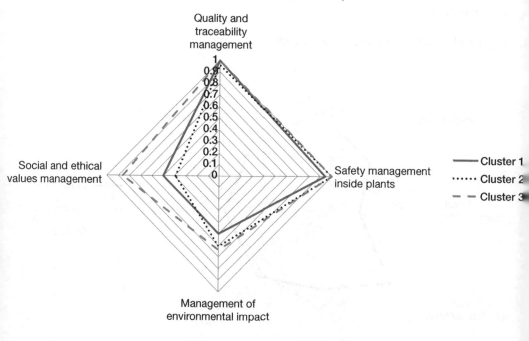

Figure 11.7 **Certification systems adopted in CSR areas**

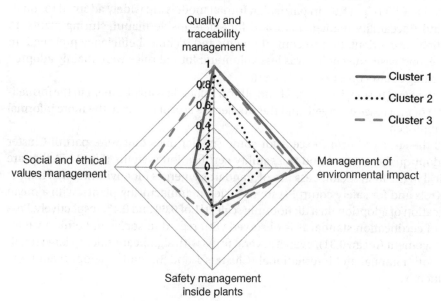

Discussion

The application of CSR practices by large retailers considerably affects supply chain relations. The entire structure of the buying network is influenced, as well as the quality of the relationships among partners and their behaviours.

For smaller suppliers, the level of cooperation is increasingly important as it contributes to long-term relationships. Large retailers' power is more often used, not to obtain better economic conditions (lower prices, longer payment terms), but more frequently to address smaller suppliers in improving their efficiency, innovation capability and organisational structure. What's more, a cultural change is stimulated and a systemic approach tends to be followed more frequently. This also happens at the international level with the involvement of a variety of actors that contribute their competences (in terms of logistics, finance and certification) to increase the level of integration among supply chain partners, and local and international institutions. Non-economic actors were more frequently involved in supporting the introduction of socially responsible principles in international sourcing.

Facing this approach of retailers, a wide awareness of CSR among SME manufacturers was observed. All CSR-related activities were more frequently adopted by smaller firms, wherein larger retailers accounted for a significant weight in their sales and when the retailer acted as a channel leader. In this case, retailers' requirements for the adoption of CSR were a primary stimulus for structuring CSR activities and adopting specific standards.

In cases where large retailers were less relevant as customers, or where large retailers were less advanced (such is the case of national retailers for Italian manufacturers), CSR-related activities began to be adopted as well, but more informally and with less use of standards, formalised processes and certification systems (excluding those related to quality control and traceability, which are widely used in the food sector). For other manufacturers and those less involved in relationships with large retailers, CSR was not seen as necessary, even if it was considered a possible field for the differentiation of market positioning.

As a general result of the influence of large retailers on CSR-related issues for SMEs, the analysis showed the importance given to cooperative issues (stimulated or, in most cases, necessarily required by larger retailers), supported by the commitment to share knowledge, capabilities, information and innovation. At the same time, there was noted an attenuation of the hierarchical/conflictual perspective in buyer–seller relationships and a reduction of margin-compression effects for smaller suppliers as a consequence of power imbalances.

Retailers provided support to SME suppliers to evolve towards more efficiency and higher quality levels. This allowed more flexibility for shortening supply chains, more direct manufacturer–retailer relationships, and consequently more effectiveness within the network, cost savings, quicker adjustments in the product offer by suppliers and in retailer assortments.

The relationships between retailers and suppliers are characterised by socially respectful principles in all activities, including communication, logistics and service management. Additional opportunities were created to pursue a relationship development model in which all the involved actors can benefit, including smaller partners within the supply chains.

As a consequence, large retailers can facilitate positive spillover effects in their relationship with suppliers that build more sustainable international supply chains, in particular where SME manufacturers are involved.

Conclusions and implications for future research

The increasing diffusion of CSR principles among large retailers, particularly in the food sector, is stimulating a progressive change along entire supply chains and their members, including smaller manufacturers and intermediaries.

Consumer perceptions allow retailers to assume a central role as a guarantor for control over safety, equality and ethically correct practices along the supply chain. The more consumers are aware of ethical and sustainability issues, the more retailers can play a coordinating role to ensure a transparent supply chain in which the value produced is equally distributed among all participating actors.

International retailers are quickly responding to this change, promoting initiatives and tools as a result of increasing public demand for more sustainability in economic processes. Small Italian manufacturers in the food sector are adapting to the requirements of retailers. As the study emphasised, those more involved in relationships with large retailers have reached a higher level of consciousness in CSR relevance and, above all, are more capable of managing CSR activities by adopting standards and certification systems. Those with a lighter weight of large retailers in sales (that are also smaller) revealed a delay in adopting more advanced criteria for CSR management.

The analysis has pointed to some areas of research that can be further developed.

A limited diffusion of systematic and structured approaches to CSR emerged among those manufacturers that did not develop significant relationships with large retailers. Since the retailers' role is critical to stimulate a diffusion of CSR practices and culture among the supply chain members, it is important to analyse these firms in more depth. Further research should deepen the motivations for retailers to develop CSR systems and to extend them to smaller suppliers in the supply chain, focusing on the expected advantages and disadvantages.

This study highlights some trends in CSR policies of SME manufacturers considering also their perceptions of large retailers' CSR requirements. Thus, a complementary analysis focused on the large retailers' perspective could be useful.

Moreover, a comparative analysis should be conducted with the manufacturers of other European countries to verify similarities and differences, and also to consider the specific characteristics of the industrial structure of each country.

References

Amaeshi, K.M., O.K. Osuji and P. Nnodim (2008), 'Corporate Social Responsibility in Supply Chains of Global Brands: A Boundaryless Responsibility?', *Journal of Business Ethics* 81: 223-34.

Andersen, M., and T. Skjoett-Larsen (2009) 'Corporate Social Responsibility in Global Supply Chains', *Supply Chain Management: An International Journal* 14.2: 75-86.

Arbuthnot, J.J. (1997) 'Identifying Ethical Problems Confronting Small Retail Buyers During the Merchandise Buying Processes', *Journal of Business Ethics* 16: 745-55.

Baily, J.B. (1987) *Purchasing and Supply Management* (London: Chapman & Hall).

Balabanis, G., H. Phillips and J. Lyall (1998) 'Corporate Social Responsibility and Economic Performance in Top British Companies: Are They Linked?' *European Business Review* 98.1: 25-44.

Becchetti, L., and L. Paganetto (2003) *Finanza etica. Commercio equo e solidale* (Roma: Donzelli).

Boyd, D.E., R. Spekman and P.H. Werhane (2005) 'Corporate Social Responsibility and Global Supply Chain Management: A Normative Perspective', *Darden Business School Working Paper* 4/5.

Carter, C.R. (2000) 'Ethical Issues in International Buyer–Supplier Relationships: A Dyadic Examination', *Journal of Operation Management* 18: 191-208.

Caselli, L. (2003) 'La ri-legittimazione sociale dell'impresa', *Sinergie* 61/62: 117-31.

Collison, D., G. Cobb, D. Power and L. Stevenson (2009) 'FTSE4Good: Exploring its Implications for Corporate Conduct', *Accounting, Auditing & Accountability Journal* 22.1: 35-58.

Cooper, R.W., G.L. Frank and R.A. Kemp (1997) 'Ethical Issues, Helps and Challenges: Perceptions of Members of the Chartered Institute of Purchasing and Supply', *European Journal of Purchasing and Supply Management* 3.4: 189-98.

Dagnoli, J. (1991) 'Consciously Green', *Advertising Age* 14: 41.

Davidson, W.R., P.J. Sweeney and R.W. Stampfl (1988) *Retail Management* (New York: Wiley).

De Man, F. (2005) 'Corporate Social Responsibility and its Impact on Corporate Reputation', *Brand Strategy* 195: 40–41.

Dickerson, K.G., and M. Dalecki (1991) 'Apparel Manufacturers' Perceptions of Supplier-Retailer Relationships', *Clothing and Textiles Research Journal* 9.3: 7-14.

Dubinsky, A.J., and J.M. Gwinn (1981) 'Business Ethics: Buyer and Seller', *Journal of Purchasing and Materials Management* 17.4: 9-16.

Freestone, O.M., and P.J. McGoldrick (2008) 'Motivations of the Ethical Consumer', *Journal of Business Ethics* 79: 445-67.

Gonzalez-Padron, T., G.T.M. Hult and R. Calantone (2008) 'Exploiting Innovative Opportunities in Global Purchasing: An Assessment of Ethical Climate and Relationship Performance', *Industrial Marketing Management* 37: 69-82.

Grayson, D., and T. Dodd (2007) *Small is Sustainable (and Beautiful!). Encouraging European Smaller Enterprises to be Sustainable* (Occasional Paper; Cranfield, UK: Doughty Centre for Corporate Responsibility, Cranfield School of Management).

Harrison, R., T. Newholm and D. Shaw (2005) *The Ethical Consumer* (London: Sage).

Hemingway, C.A., and P.W. Maclagan (2004) 'Managers' Personal Values as Drivers of Corporate Social Responsibility', *Journal of Business Ethics* 50.1: 33-44.

Jenkins, H. (2004) 'A Critique of Conventional CSR Theory: An SME Perspective. How can small and medium enterprises embrace corporate social responsibility?' *Journal of General Management* 29.4: 37–57.

Jolliffe, I.T. (2002) *Principal Component Analysis* (New York: Springer-Verlag).

Jones, P., D. Comfort and I. Eastwood (2005) 'Retailers and Sustainable Development in the UK', *International Journal of Retail & Distribution Management* 33.3: 207-14.

Kytle, B., and J. Ruggie (2005) 'Corporate Social Responsibility and Risk Management: A Model for Multinationals', in *Corporate Social Initiative* (Working Paper no. 10; Cambridge, MA: John F. Kennedy School of Government, Harvard University).

Lepoutre, J., and A. Heene (2006) 'Investigating the Impact of Firm Size on Small Business Social Responsibility: A Critical Review', *Journal of Business Ethics* 67: 257-73.

Logsdon, J.M., and D.J. Wood (2005) 'Global Business Citizenship and Voluntary Codes of Ethical Conduct', *Journal of Business Ethics* 59.1-2: 55-67.

Macchiette, B., and A. Roy (1994) 'Sensitive Groups and Social Issues: Are You Marketing Correct?' *Journal of Consumer Marketing* 11.4: 55-64.

Maignan, I., and O.C. Ferrel (2004) 'Corporate Social Responsibility and Marketing: An Integrative Framework', *Journal of the Academy of Marketing Science* 32.1: 3-19.

Maignan, I., B. Hillebrand and D. McAlister (2002) 'Managing Socially Responsible Buying: How to Integrate Non-economic Criteria into the Purchasing Process', *European Management Journal* 20.6: 641-48.

Majumdar, S., and R. Nishant (2008) 'Sustainable Entrepreneurial Support (in Supply Chain) as Corporate Social Responsibility Initiative of Large Organisations: A Conceptual Framework', *The Icfai University Journal of Entrepreneurship Development* 5.3: 6-22.

Maloni, M.J., and M.E. Brown (2006) 'Corporate Social Responsibility in the Supply Chain: An Application in the Food Industry', *Journal of Business Ethics* 68.1: 35-52.

Mamic, I. (2005) 'Managing Global Supply Chain: The Sports Footwear, Apparel and Retail Sectors', *Journal of Business Ethics* 59: 81-100.

Murillo, D., and J. Lozano (2006a) 'SMEs and CSR: An Approach to CSR in their Own Words', *Journal of Business Ethics* 67: 227-40.

Murillo, D., and J. Lozano (2006b) 'CSR and SMEs: Perceptions on the Relation of CSR and Competitiveness', Draft Paper for the *EABIS 5th Annual Colloquium* (www.eabis.org/csrplatform/colloquium/2006/2006proceedings/2006workshop5, accessed 26 November 2007).

Musso, F. (1999) *Relazioni di canale e strategie di acquisto delle imprese commerciali* (Trieste, Italy: Edizioni Lint).

Musso, F., and M. Risso (2006) 'CSR within Large Retailers International Supply Chains', *Symphonya: Emerging Issues in Management* 1 (www.unimib.it/symphonya).

Nicholls, A. (2002) 'Strategic Options in Fair Trade Retailing', *International Journal of Retail & Distribution Management* 30.1: 6-17.

Packard, S., A. Winters and N. Axelrod (1996) *Fashion Buying and Merchandising* (New York: Fairchild Publications).

Park, H., and L. Stoel (2005) 'A Model of Social Responsible Buying/Sourcing Decision-making Processes', *International Journal of Retail & Distribution Management* 33.4: 235-48.

Pepe, C. (2003) 'Grande distribuzione, globalizzazione e responsabilità aziendale', *SYMPHONYA: Emerging Issues in Management* 1 (www.unimib.it/symphonya).

Pepe, C. (2007) 'Filiere tradizionali e filiere alternative nel commercio dei prodotti dal Sud del mondo', in C. Pepe (ed.), *Prodotti dal Sud del mondo e mercati avanzati. Potenzialità e contaminazioni tra commercio equo e solidale e commercio internazionale* (Milano: FrancoAngeli).

Pepe, C., F. Musso and M. Risso (2008) 'SME Food Suppliers versus Large Retailers: Perspectives in the International Supply Chains', *Proceedings of the 15th International Conference on Retailing and Services Science*, European Institute of Retailing and Services Studies (EIRASS), Zagreb, 14–17 July 2008.

Per Engelseth (2009) 'Food Product Traceability and Supply Network Integration', *Journal of Business & Industrial Marketing* 24.5–6: 421-30.

Piacentini, M., L. MacFadyen and D. Eadie (2000) 'Corporate Social Responsibility in Food Retailing', *International Journal of Retail & Distribution Management* 28.11: 459-69.

Redelius, W., and R.A. Bucholz (1979) 'What Industrial Purchasers See as Key Ethical Dilemmas', *Journal of Purchasing and Materials Management* 15.4: 2-10.

Risso, M. (2007) 'Il ruolo del distributore nell'offerta dei prodotti a carattere etico-sociale', in C. Pepe (ed.), *Prodotti dal Sud del mondo e mercati avanzati* (Milano: FrancoAngeli).

Roberts, S. (2003) 'Supply Chain Specific? Understanding the Patchy Success of Ethical Sourcing Initiatives', *Journal of Business Ethics* 44.2–3: 159-70.

Salam, M.A. (2009) 'Corporate Social Responsibility in Purchasing and Supply Chain', *Journal of Business Ethics* 85: 355-70.

Schaltegger, S. (2002) 'A Framework for Ecopreneurship. Leading Bioneers and Environmental Managers to Ecopreneurship', *Greener Management International* 38: 45-58.

Schlegelmilch, B.B., and M. Öberseder (2007) 'Ethical Issues in Global Supply Chains', *SYMPHONYA Emerging Issues in Management* 2 (www.unimib.it/symphonya).

Sciarelli, S. (2007) *Etica e responsabilità sociale nell'impresa* (Milano: Giuffrè Editore).

Shaw, D., and I. Clarke (1998) 'Culture, Consumption and Choice: Towards a Conceptual Relationship' *Journal of Consumer Studies and Home Economics* 22.3: 163-68.

Shaw, D., and I. Clarke (1999) 'Belief Formation in Ethical Consumer Groups: An Exploratory Study', *Marketing Intelligence and Planning* 17.2–3: 109-19.

Shaw, D., and E. Shiu (2003) 'Ethics in Consumer Choice: A Multivariate Modelling Approach', *European Journal of Marketing* 37.10: 1,485-98.

Shuch, M. (1988) *Retail Buying and Merchandising* (Hemel Hempstead, UK: Prentice Hall).

Spence, L. (1999) 'Does Size Matter? The State of the Art in Small Business Ethics', *Business Ethics: A European Review* 8.3: 163-74.

Strong, C. (1996) 'Features Contributing to the Growth of Ethical Consumerism: A Preliminary Investigation', *Marketing Intelligence and Planning* 14.5: 5-13.

Trawick, F., J.E. Swan and D.R. Rink (1988) 'Back-door Selling: Violation of Cultural versus Professional Ethics by Salespeople and Purchasers Choice of the Supplier', *Journal of Business Research* 17: 299-309.

Whysall, P. (2000) 'Addressing Ethical Issues in Retailing: A Stakeholder Perspective', *International Review of Retail Distribution and Consumer Research* 10.3: 305-18.

Williamson, D., G. Lynch-Wood and J. Ramsay (2006) 'Drivers of Environmental Behaviour in Manufacturing SMEs and Implications for CSR', *Journal of Business Ethics* 67: 317-30.

Wilson, M. (2005) 'Doing Good is More than a Feel Good Option', *Chain Store Age* 81.10: 77-78.

Wood, G. (1995) 'Ethics at the Purchasing/Sales Interface: An International Perspective', *International Marketing Review* 12.4: 7-19.

12

Market demand, eco-products and entrepreneurship in the 'natural cosmetics sector' in Greece

Ioannis N. Katsikis

Athens University of Economics and Business, Greece

The increasing public requests for better, greener, environmentally efficient and healthy approaches to conducting business and producing products has raised both academic and business world interest in the development of related topics. Today, it is also widely acknowledged that the co-evolution of demand characteristics and industry structure is a crucial process affecting not only innovation and the growth of firms, but also the transformation of industries, thus influencing the dynamics of the overall economic system. At the same time, today, the borders between sectors, such as the pharmaceutical and cosmetics industries, have become increasingly blurred concurrent with the development of 'radically innovative' new products within the health and wellness market.

In this chapter, we study the role of demand and the way in which this affects business activities, drives entrepreneurial processes and leads to the creation of new firms, products, services and even sectors. Our analysis is focused on the examination of the dynamics of the cosmetics industry in Greece and the movement from 'conventional' practices to environmentally healthy and 'natural' products leading to the formulation of the 'natural cosmetics sector'.

The chapter unfolds as follows: in the first section of the theoretical part, we review the literature based on the tradition of evolutionary economics and we discuss the hermeneutical value of market process theories and of the resource- and competence-based research. In the second section of the theoretical part, we discuss the market demand characteristics for natural and environmental products and the consequent move from 'conventional' to 'natural' products. This stands as a significant movement, which defines the dynamics of the natural cosmetics sector and determines its growth as an independent cluster of companies. In the empirical part of this work, we shall analytically examine the case of Apivita SA, a firm operating in the natural cosmetics sector in Greece, by presenting a short, firm-level case study developed using a qualitative research protocol.

The demand for natural and environmental products

The role of demand on new sector formation

The role of demand has been emphasised in the process of new products, services and sector formation (Cohen and Winn 2007). Gersch and Goeke (2007) highlight that recent research under the umbrella of **market process theories** (e.g. von Mises 1949; Kirzner 1973; van Hayek 1978; Vaughn 1994) and resource and competence research (e. g. Hamel and Prahalad 1994; Sanchez *et al.* 1996; Sanchez and Heene 2004; Foss and Ishikawa 2006) facilitates an evolutionary interpretation of observable transformation processes. Applying these theoretical lenses, change processes can be analysed in an integrated way, taking into consideration: (1) the level of acting single players (firms); (2) market-levels; and (3) the whole industry value chain. Within such a framework, according to market process theory's basic rationale, entrepreneurial action is viewed as 'the premium mobile of any kind of change process'. In this regard, business can play two different roles: (1) they can actively create and drive the transformation process on higher levels of aggregation, such as markets or industries; and (2) they can also be forced and driven by it.

Under this view, the postulations of many strategic management scholars for 'co-evolutionary development', 'strategic fit' or 'coherence' (Venkatraman 1989; Zajac *et al.* 2000; Morgan and Hunt 2002; Volberda and Lewin 2003) can now be consistently implemented on a theoretical basis. This is why a targeted integrated framework for multiple levels of analysis is deemed essential in order to finally provide a useful support for strategic management practice but, as Gersch and Goeke (2007) find, such an integrated and theoretically consistent framework does not exist in extant literature. Thus, the interaction between individuals, market- and industry-level is finally highlighted exemplarily by exploring the question of why firms tend to collaborate in changing environments.

This chapter aims at analysing the determinants of the co-evolution between demand and industry structure by investigating the joint dynamics of 'users' and consumers' competences and behaviour, product characteristics and industry structure. In the following section we shall focus our analysis on the demand and sectoral characteristics of the cosmetics sector in Greece and the dynamics contributing to the formation of the 'natural cosmetics' sector.

Market demand characteristics in the cosmetics industry

In the following paragraphs we will examine to what extent and through what processes market demand and changing consumer characteristics drive the environmental dimension applied to a specific sectoral context leading to the creation of a distinctive sector, as our case of the 'natural cosmetics' in Greece exhibits.

Growth of cosmetics and toiletries products containing natural ingredients is reviving in maturing cosmetics markets (Euromonitor International 2008). Over the past five years, developed markets, such as the United States, have been facing stagnating cosmetics and toiletries sales and slowing growth. In an effort to improve sales, manufacturers have capitalised on growing consumer interest in health and wellness and have started to invest in new products containing natural ingredients. This investment looks to be paying off; according to certain industry sources, the natural/organic skin care, hair care and colour cosmetics markets have grown by an impressive average of 9% a year between 2003 and 2008. This growth was expected to provide a boost to the total cosmetics and toiletries sector, which Euromonitor International (2008) expected to grow by only 1% a year.

Although there is no widely accepted definition of natural cosmetics, these can be regarded as a natural final product containing raw materials or materials of botanical origin such as mineral oils, essences, salts and water and not containing a large number of chemical raw materials, such as parabens, petrochemicals and silicones, thus rendering the final product more friendly to both the consumer and the environment. In terms of product characteristics, the natural cosmetics sector can be analysed in three different sub-sectors according to the definition of 'natural' and the degree to which this is embedded in products produced and which is relevant to the degree of the inclusion of natural ingredients, the removal of artificial ingredients and the adoption of ethical business practices.

One of the major drivers of growth in natural cosmetics has been the consumer trend towards healthier lifestyles. Consumer demand for natural ingredients and the increased desire for healthy lifestyles are directly affecting the market in sectors such as personal care, packaged foods and the cosmetics industry. Rightly or wrongly, good health is often associated in consumers' minds with all things 'natural' or 'traditional', while chemicals are considered by some to be the root of all evil. Consequently, these perceptions have given rise to demand for natural additives and ingredients used in cosmetics. Additionally, natural and organic products are being seen and appreciated as safe, efficacious, earth-friendly beauty solutions that are better for one's well-being. Euromonitor International analysis (2008) exhibits that consumers are drawn to cosmetics containing natural ingredients not just because of their perceived health benefits, but also because many believe these products have higher standards of quality. This fact has enabled cosmetics manufacturers to charge higher prices for natural products, thereby injecting value into the market. Major manufacturers have also used this perception of quality to drive packaging developments, which convey fresher, more upscale appearances for natural products. 'Origins' and 'Aveda', for example, have achieved success by emphasising the quality of their products, which in turn have prompted smaller producers to introduce competing products and rejuvenate their packaging. Also benefiting manufacturers of natural cosmetic products is their widening availability. Upscale department stores such as Nordstrom in the US are taking advantage of the growing interest in natural personal care products and are expanding their selections accordingly. 'Natural supermarket' chains and health food stores, such as Whole Foods Market in the US, are also educating consumers on the benefits of natural personal care products and some now devote considerable space to natural personal care products, including moisturisers, lip glosses and toothpaste. Finally, in some cases, the concept of 'traditional' or 'local' is used in parallel with natural or organic in order to provide a distinctive image for products. This is extremely helpful since the specific term is closely connected with the idea of pure nature.

Over the next five years, Euromonitor International (2008) predicts that natural cosmetics and toiletries will grow strongly, but will remain inferior to mainstream products in terms of overall sales. The largest potential for growth in the natural cosmetics and toiletries market seems to lie in the natural cosmetics sector. It is expected that, in the future, manufacturers are likely to increase the amount of natural ingredients used in their products in order to satisfy consumers, without completely abolishing chemicals that they deem necessary to increase the shelf life or effectiveness of their products. At the same time, the major players are likely to dedicate huge marketing budgets to promoting the 'natural' aspects of their products. A potential hindrance to the industry, however, might be the forthcoming regulations in the EU and US that will force manufacturers to disclose ingredients that are known to cause allergic reactions. Since many synthetic ingredients are actually found to be safer than natural ingredients, this could potentially damage the natural market for some natural cosmetics and toiletries products that use simple formulas or low technologies during their manufacturing processes.

The dynamics of the natural cosmetics sector in the Hellenic cosmetics industry

Contemporary lifestyles and modern role models are key factors that set in motion the market and determine growth rates. Demand for convenience and luxury, along with the desire to maintain a youthful appearance, represent sizeable drivers for the cosmetics and toiletries market in Greece, and seem to underpin every trend in every niche. Greeks augmented their total demand in 2007, leading to overall market growth of 4% in current value terms. The categories and products that have actually benefited are those which correspond to the need for comfort and lav-ishness, and/or those which can make a person look younger and more confident (Euromonitor 2008).

Faced with a continuous stream of health alerts and growing fears regarding the environment, consumers are seeking reassurance from their cosmetics and toilet-ries as much as from their food and drink products. Greek consumers are increas-ingly looking for purified and natural products, and are becoming very selective regarding what they trust to apply to their bodies and faces. Feelings for reassurance are manifesting themselves in the desire for products and brands that offer greater reliance on their ingredients. Traffic through chemists/pharmacies increased in 2007 as consumers increased demand for cosmeceuticals and more pseudo-medi-cal brands. Leading pharmacy brands Vichy and RoC further enhanced their value share in 2007, as did all-natural pharmacy brand Apivita. Developments indicate that pharmacy brands are to increase their growth rate even more in the near future and expand to less ordinary categories such as colour cosmetics or bath and shower products.

As far as the logistics are concerned, supermarkets/hypermarkets continued to lose ground to perfumeries and pharmacies in terms of value share, despite their growing share in volume terms. Consumers have been increasing their visits to supermarkets and grocery retailers when in need of convenience. However, they have started to shift towards pharmacies and perfumeries when looking for qual-ity or assistance in buying. Premium products cannot be found in grocery stores, while at the same time mass products are usually over-priced in pharmacies, and that naturally benefits perfumeries, which have increased their range of both mass and premium offerings.

Greek consumers are not traditionally known for their environmental concerns. However, the catastrophic fires that swept the country during the summer of 2007 seem to have awakened some concerns. This could drive manufacturers into repo-sitioning their brands in order to attract new ethical consumers. Environmental claims on cosmetics and toiletries remain very constrained, yet brand owners may be forced to adopt a more 'green' image in future. Consumers are expected to respond positively to recycling packaging, environmentally friendly materials and 'natural' products. Consumers increasingly care about the origins of their products, providing manufacturers with an additional dimension with which to distinguish themselves. Environmental awareness is becoming more and more important to people. In the sector of cosmetology, environmental awareness results in increas-ing demand and use of natural and organic ingredients in cosmetic formulations.

Research methodology

Case study approach

The empirical part of this chapter is dedicated to the examination of the way in which market demand can lead on the creation of a new firms and products, based on the case study method. More analytically, the research consisted of a qualitative case study approach. This method was employed given that little research has been undertaken into the effect of entrepreneurial activities on the creation of a new sector, as well as the fact that case study research 'is an empirical inquiry (that allows for) a contemporary phenomenon to be investigated within its real-life context, especially when the boundaries between phenomenon and context are not clearly evident' (Yin 2003: 13). Also, given that the research questions focused on 'how and why', it is congruent with Yin's (2003) recommendation that such research, when requiring no control over behavioural events, should be carried out with case studies.

The selection of the case study followed the criterion sample strategy developed by Miles and Huberman (1994) and analysed and exemplified by Eisenhardt (1989) and Eisenhardt and Graebner (2007). This ensured that out of various ventures evolving along the lines of green entrepreneurship, the selected case study fulfilled a certain number of criteria, identified from related literature. This enabled us to, first, control for contingency factors which are critical for defining the limits of the study (criteria one and two, below) and, second, replicate and extend the emerging findings with respect to the conceptual criteria to the greatest possible completeness or until theoretical saturation, in the language of qualitative methodology (Yin 2003), was obtained (criterion three, below). These criteria were:

1. Be representative of the sector of fast-growing entrepreneurial ventures in Greece with a sustained growth and profitability over recent years—controlling for variation in terms of economic value created

2. Be representative of the leading for-profit organisations in Greece in terms of engagement in environmental product innovations, controlling for variation in terms of the potential for creating social and environmental value

3. Consider simultaneous and strategic concerns for creating economic, social and/or environmental value as the fundamental reason (teleology) for being of the venture. This controls for the selected organisation enabling a replication and extension logic of the successively collected data

Data collection and analysis

Data were collected through interviews, documentary analysis and review of firm internal and external information sources, such as company documentation,

Internet sources and publicly available sectoral and firm studies and reports. A detailed research protocol, including interview guides reflecting the areas of investigation, underpinned the study. A number of study visits were conducted and besides the CEO, the general manager and shop managers were interviewed.

Our methodology was enriched by a collection of both primary and secondary resources for the other firms. As far as the primary resources are concerned, information was collected through the use of a semi-structured questionnaire. Additionally, during the past six years, a process of non-participatory business observation of the development of the specific organisation was in progress. This process helped us collect valuable information through the media and other secondary resources concerning the evolution of organisations' strategies and dynamics. Strategic issues behind the entrepreneurial activities undertaken were explored, such that the environment and general conditions leading to those activities could be understood in detail.

In the following section, we shall develop a descriptive case study of Apivita SA, a firm operating in the natural cosmetics industry which experienced significant growth through the adoption of environmentally friendly practices. Apivita managed to develop green entrepreneurial activities, as indicative examples of the different green approaches to entrepreneurship, which further aim at clarifying the teleological notions described above.

Entrepreneurship and eco-product innovation: the case of Apivita SA

Data collection and analysis

'Apivita' is a Greek company based in Athens that operates in the field of natural cosmetics. Originally established as a family-owned pharmacy in 1979, by two pharmacists, Niki and Nikos Koutsianas, who were inspired greatly by nature and Greek philosophy, it was the first Greek company to use natural ingredients such as bee products (honey, beeswax, propolis, pollen, royal jelly), herbs (thyme, calendula, rosemary, etc.), vegetable products (Kozani saffron, Chios mastic, etc.) and essential oils in the production of cosmetics. The rich biodiversity of the Greek flora and the mild Mediterranean climate are responsible for the highly beneficial properties of Apivita's plant extracts. Some plants such as Chios mastic and dittany of Crete are unique to Greece. Apivita is one of the few companies in Greece that possesses the know-how to produce premium quality extracts. The quality, safety and efficacy of the products are due to the expertise and scientific knowledge of its innovative R&D department.

The development of the concept

These Greek floras and the firm's faith in their value and in the beneficial effects of herbal cosmetic products were envisioned in order to create a different pharmacy, a pharmacy that goes beyond the conventional standards of that era, namely, to buy and sell drugs. So, Niki and Nikos turned to the use of plants and bee products to create cosmetics and tried to upgrade the role of the laboratory in the pharmacy by using scientific knowledge from the field of pharmacy for the creation of cosmetics.

In 1987 the company 'Bee Products Ltd' was established under the name Apivita (derived from the Latin words 'apis' = bee and 'vita' = life). Under this name, they created their first soaps and shampoos using propolis and herbal extracts from Greek habitats. The main idea behind the operation of Apivita was to promote high-quality, natural living and produce innovative natural products that provide safe and effective care and protection with respect to nature. The company developed its current facilities, while Nikos Koutsianas took the decision to stop operating the pharmacy and dedicate himself solely to the company.

During the same period the company became very active in the development of technology in the extraction plant. This activity was important since it helped to develop a platform technology and an opportunity to gradually develop a cutting-edge expertise as an important indicator of differentiation from competition. In 1991 the corporation was established under its current form under the name 'Apivita Cosmetic Medicine Dietary SA' which absorbed the activity of the previous company. During the same year, it introduced, for the first time in Greece, a full range of aromatherapy products, including products for face and body based on vegetable and essential oils. Apivita undertook the sale of specific products in line with its strategy in the pharmacy, thus attempting to position its products in more pharmacies and strengthen its distribution network. At this point the sales network expanded and in early 1991 it comprised more than 5,000 outlets.

Now, the majority of cosmetics on the market are a combination of natural ingredients and chemical substances and preparations called cosmetics complex. The ingredients contained do fulfil the EU requirements (quality and technical) and are all developed and prepared in accordance with the European Union's Good Manufacturing Practices (GMP) for cosmetics, with strictly selected natural ingredients whose proven effectiveness and safety have been supported by laboratory and clinical studies. Apart from the complex cosmetics on the market there are also green or herbal cosmetics made from natural and biodegradable substances. Apivita's production process is based on the effort to minimise waste to the environment. No chemical propellants are used in spray or environmentally damaging ingredients. The packaging of natural cosmetics is ecologically based, and consists of recyclable materials. Also, none of these products has been tested on animals, thus avoiding a practice that is largely followed by the conventional cosmetics industry (ICAP 2003).

The success story

Today, Apivita develops plant extracts from more than 60 different plants and is one of the few European companies to have been certified with ISO 9001 for this purpose. The herbal extracts are developed, produced and controlled by the firm itself. The plants are collected, dried and stored in a specific area. These are then cut and a suitable solvent is used for the extraction of their active ingredients. Then, they are pressurised and filtered, the plant is removed and the solvent is extracted, which contains the active ingredients of the plant. After quality control, the extract is used as feedstock for the manufacture of herbal cosmetics.

Initially, the exports made by Apivita were not based on the idea of building an international trademark (brand). At that time, the target was to respond to the demand without any organised export strategy. Thus, the products were exported mainly to countries of the Middle East and the Balkans. In 1999 Apivita adopted a coherent export strategy and decided to expand its export activities in Western Europe and the US. To implement its export targets it became necessary to redesign the packaging of all products with the logic of an international brand. Thus a multilingual packaging was created to emphasise the identity of each product line, to show the philosophy of the company and to diversify the range of any competing products. The company spent more than €3 million on the redesign of the product packaging and then Nikos Koutsianas, the CEO, undertook the task to promote them to the best stores abroad, himself. The response of the international market to the products was impressive and quite encouraging and thus by the end of 2002, Apivita had entered all the developed markets. Today, Apivita's products can be found in many luxury (high prestige) stores, such as Harrods in London, Parfumerie Générale in Paris and the Printemps department stores, at El Corte Inglés department stores in Spain and a constantly growing network of pharmacies (800) in the US, in chains PureBeauty (60 points of sale) and Bath & Body Works (70 points) and 200 luxury stores in the US (Fred Segal, Nordstrom, etc.).

During the last six years Apivita has expanded its activities by producing more than 235 products which are now distributed to more than 5,000 pharmacies throughout Greece. The average annual growth rate increased to 30% and the total turnover in 2010 was over €29 million. Today, its products are sold in chains in Western Europe, the USA, Japan, Taiwan, Philippines and other countries. Particular penetration took place in the markets of South-East Asia. In China, there is a strong presence in Hong Kong, three stores in Taiwan with three shops exclusively selling the firm's products and more than 20 stores in Japan, such as Sony Plaza. Products also appear in more than 100 outlets in Sweden, Belgium, Netherlands, Ireland, Bulgaria, Dubai and the Philippines.

The determinants of success

According to the general manager of the company, the great market response to Apivita's products in chains of luxury stores and the high export performance can be attributed to four product characteristics that are difficult to replicate:

- **Use of local resources**. Greece has a very rich flora which includes many medicinal plants. For example, the local ecosystem includes about 5,500 plants, a large number of which are endemic and very rare (e.g. dittany), while in other European countries this ranges from 2,500 to 3,000 plants. Because of the favourable local conditions (excellent weather, sunshine and less polluted air, in contrast to other parts of the world), Greek plants have much better biosynthetic properties and are highly bioactive (i.e. in terms of substances that affect the human body)

- **Living tradition**. Apivita takes into account the entire Greek tradition associated with the use of plants. From the times of Hippocrates to the present day, the use of plants has been studied and scientifically documented. In Greece, a country with excellent biodiversity, humans have lived for thousands of years by developing culture and accumulated knowledge for the use of the local resources. The firm uses this knowledge to establish and to provide the original form of natural products, so offering the Greek lifestyle as an alternative to the global one

- **Quality and control**. The integrated production process adopted by the firm, from the collection of the plant to production of the product (e.g. documentation of the active substances of the extracts) provides high-quality final products

- **Aesthetics**. The aesthetics of the final product and packaging contribute significantly to the creation of a distinctive image. Their aesthetic value is evidenced by the many international prizes received for their packaging

Of the above four advantages, the general manager argues that what is of most importance, when a company tries to sell to luxury stores in the global market, is the myth, or the story that the company has to tell. Apivita SA adopts virtual marketing in order to introduce the myth or dream (dream marketing) aiming not only to connect to the products themselves, but also to highlight their connection to the Greek way of living, not just as a unique experience but an alternative philosophy of living and therefore something more permanent.

Discussion and conclusions

In this work, we aimed to examine the way in which firms recognise emerging market trends and demand and adopt new business practices, develop innovative products or new entrepreneurial processes that lead to the creation of new products, services and even sectors. Our analysis was focused on the determinants of the co-evolution between demand and new product creation. In the theoretical part we focused on the demand and sectoral characteristics of the cosmetics sector in Greece and the dynamics contributing to the formation of the 'natural cosmetics' sector. At the empirical level, we employed a case study research approach, presenting a descriptive case study as an example of green entrepreneurial activities of a Hellenic company, Apivita SA, in order to demonstrate its relevance to the above theoretical concepts.

In Figure 12.1 we present an illustration of the process of the firm's repositioning that led to the formation of the new 'natural cosmetics' sector in Greece. Initially, the firm examined here was established as a pharmacy which gradually started offering its own products in order to face the particular demand of their customers. As the success of its products developed, and in response to market dynamics and demand, it moved up the scale of production and thus reorganised as a production firm moving away from the pharmacies sector and entering the cosmetic sector. Thus, the company changed sector and industry by moving from the service sector to product manufacturing. Following that, it developed a large number of products that it now offers mainly through pharmacies as this is distribution network that it still understands the best.

Figure 12.1 **Process of firm entry in the natural cosmetics sector**

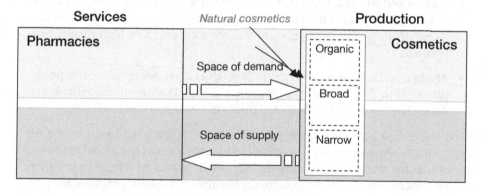

Apivita demonstrates a case of corporate entrepreneurial practices leading to important corporate success. With the use of local resources (based on the very rich flora of Greece) they manage to use this knowledge in order to establish and to provide the original form of natural products, so offering an alternative lifestyle to the global one. At the production level, the integrated process adopted by the firm, from the collection of the plant to production of the product (e.g. documentation of the active substances of the extracts), provided high-quality final products. Finally, the aesthetics of the final product and packaging have contributed significantly to the creation of a distinctive brand image.

This research contributes to the advancement of theory and practice on ways in which entrepreneurial processes unfold towards the attainment of a greener world by introducing eco-products or developing eco-sectors. In particular, it contributes to the literature in four distinctive ways. First, this study is one of few efforts to map the intersection of two currently disparate fields, that of ecological products and that of entrepreneurship. The two fields have for many years been considered as contradictory and sometimes even conflicting. Second, since 'eco-entrepre-neurship' is only a recent phenomenon that emerges in the management studies literature both as a theoretical notion and as an empirical approach, our chapter contributes to its enhancement, by showing how the response to market demand and strategic positioning of those firms was taken, leading to the formation of a new industry sector and to corporate success. Our research shows that this success was largely based on the abilities of the firms to adapt to the public demand for a greener way of being by developing products that encompass the natural, environmental and traditional elements. Third, we provide an explanatory case study as supporting evidence and an empirical example of the way in which each of the three green approaches of entrepreneurship materialised through the activities of a small or medium-sized enterprise from Greece.

At the same time, the case study employed offers some important empirical contributions to the field of entrepreneurial activities. First, it demonstrates the way in which the dimensions of green entrepreneurship are interconnected (nature, tradition, etc). Second, it reveals the presence of large-scale entrepreneurial opportunities grounded in problems of lack of proper supply, since the firms studied developed innovative products in order to respond to a specific niche of the market. Third, this work may help to answer Venkataraman's (1997: 122) question on 'where opportunities to create goods and services in the future come from'. Fourth, as Dean and McMullen (2007) highlight, such cases aid us in understanding the role that developmental, economic and environmental problems play in creating opportunities, and bring us closer to a theory of sustainable entrepreneurship that more broadly addresses the role that entrepreneurs can play in creating a more socially and environmentally sustainable economy.

As far as future research directions are concerned, the challenge facing scholars studying alternative forms of entrepreneurship, such as green entrepreneurship, is to differentiate between concepts and ideas that are common to entrepreneurship of all kinds and those that are particularly associated to/oriented towards a specific teleology. Ideas that apply to entrepreneurship broadly defined are likely to have significant value in understanding its other forms as well. Various streams of literature have addressed the issues of how and why co-evolution plays an important role in linking innovation and industrial dynamics. One strand focuses on how R&D activity and knowledge generate innovative opportunities. Other strands look at the role of economic incentives and focus on strategising by firms as well as on the role played by changing users' tastes. Some stress the specificity of industries whereas others stress the idiosyncratic role of competences of specific firms and organisations. As a result, existing contributions reach different conclusions about why demand, technology and industry structure co-evolve. However, in many ways these different conclusions have not been linked. Further theoretical as well as empirical evidence on the existence as well as on the nature of these linkages is needed. It seems that there is evidence to show that, under the condition that production meets market demands, environmental and economic growth objectives are compatible and indeed they co-evolve.

References

Cohen, B., and M. Winn (2007) 'Market Imperfections, Opportunity and Sustainable Entrepreneurship', *Journal of Business Venturing* 22: 29-49.

Dean, T., and J. McMullen (2007) 'Towards a Theory of Sustainable Entrepreneurship: Reducing Environmental Degradation through Entrepreneurial Action', *Journal of Business Venturing* 22: 50-76.

Eisenhardt, K.M. (1989) 'Building Theories from Case Study Research', *Academy of Management Review* 14.4: 532-50.

Eisenhardt, K.M., and M.E. Graebner (2007) 'Theory Building from Cases: Opportunities and Challenges', *Academy of Management Journal* 50.1: 25-32.

Euromonitor International (2008) *The Growth of Natural Ingredients* (London: Euromonitor International).

Foss, N.J., and I. Ishikawa (2006) 'Towards a Dynamic Resource-Based View: Insights from Austrian Capital and Entrepreneurship Theory', Danish Research Unit for Industrial Dynamics, Working Paper 06–16, www.druid.dk/uploads/tx_picturedb/wp06-16.pdf, accessed 14 October 2011.

Gersch, M., and C. Goeke (2007) 'Industry Transformation: Conceptual Considerations from an Evolutionary Perspective', *Journal of Business Management* 1.2: 151-81.

Hamel, G., and C.K. Prahalad (1994) *Competing for the Future* (Boston, MA: Harvard Business School Press).

ICAP (2003) *Sectoral Study on Cosmetology* (Athens: ICAP).

Kirzner, I.M. (1973) *Competition and Entrepreneurship* (Chicago: Chicago University Press).

Miles, M.B., and A.M. Huberman (1994) *Qualitative Data Analyses: An Expanded Sourcebook* (Thousand Oaks, CA: Sage Publications).

Morgan, R.E., and S.D. Hunt (2002) 'Determining Marketing Strategy: A Cybernetic Systems Approach to Scenario Planning', *European Journal of Marketing* 36.4: 450-78.

Sanchez, R., and A. Heene (2004) *The New Strategic Management* (New York: Wiley).

Sanchez, R., A. Heene and H. Thomas (1996) 'Introduction: Towards the Theory and Practice of Competence Based Competition', in R. Sanchez, A. Heene and H. Thomas (eds.), *Dynamics of Competence-based Competition: Theory and Practice in the New Strategic Management* (Oxford, UK: Pergamon): 1-35.

Van Hayek, F.A. (1978) *New Studies in Philosophy, Politics, Economics and the History of Ideas* (Chicago: University of Chicago Press).

Vaughn, K.I. (1994) *Austrian Economics in America: The Migration of a Tradition* (Cambridge, UK: Cambridge University Press).

Venkataraman, S. (1997) 'The Distinctive Domain of Entrepreneurial Research: An Editor's Perspective', in J. Katz and J. Brockhaus (eds.), *Advances in Entrepreneurship, Firm Emergence and Growth* (Greenwich, CT: JAI Press).

Venkatraman, N. (1989) 'The Concept of Fit in Strategy Research: Toward Verbal and Statistical Correspondence', *Academy of Management Review* 14: 423-44.

Volberda, H.W., and A.Y. Lewin (2003) 'Guest Editors' Introduction: Co-evolutionary Dynamics within and between Firms: From Evolution to Co-evolution', *Journal of Management Studies* 40.8: 2111-36.

Von Mises, L. (1949) *Human Action: A Treatise on Economics, The Foundation for Economic Education* (Irvington-on-Hudson, New York: Foundation for Economic Education).

Yin, R.S. (2003) *Case Study Research: Design and Methods* (London: Sage Publications, 3rd edn).

Zajac, E.J., M.S. Kraatz and R.K.F. Bresser (2000) 'Modeling the Dynamics of Strategic Fit: A Normative Approach to Strategic Change', *Strategic Management Journal* 21: 429-53.

13

Publicly mediated inter-organisational networks

A solution for sustainability-oriented innovation in SMEs?

Erik G. Hansen and Johanna Klewitz
Leuphana University Lüneburg, Germany

Corporate sustainability has become an important imperative on the way towards sustainable development (Sharma 2002; Schaltegger and Burritt 2005; Wagner 2009a). One major means to address corporate sustainability in corporations is sustainability-oriented innovation (SOI), which is broadly conceptualised as leading to improved environmental and social characteristics of products (and services), processes or organisational mechanisms in comparison with a prior or other version (Paech 2005; Wagner and Llerena 2008; Hansen *et al.* 2009). While most research has focused on SOI management in large firms, the role of small and medium-sized enterprises (SMEs)—which as a group play a major role economically—has only recently become a focus of interest (e.g. Bos-Brouwers 2009). SOI in SMEs is particularly challenging, as SMEs are often said to be constrained in such resources as time, personnel and financial capital; that is, they are subject to SME peculiarities (Del Brio and Junquera 2003). This makes it difficult for an SME to allocate any of its limited resources to SOIs, which can be much riskier than conventional innovations, and this for two reasons (a more thorough explanation is given in the first section). First, SOI can result in products and services which are more expensive than those of its competitors and thus the market risk associated with innovation is increased. Second, managing SOI is more resource intensive because of the directional risk connected with the uncertainty of the ultimate environmental and social impacts of SOI (Paech 2005; Hansen *et al.* 2009). In consideration of this extended risk of SOI, it can be expected that, apart from a few proactive, innovative companies or 'ecopreneurs' (Schaltegger 2002; Schaltegger and Wagner 2011), the larger part of SMEs will usually maintain their rather reactive stance which is focused on complying with current regulations.

However, as SMEs are both generally owner managed and tend to have less formalised structures and processes, they may well be confronted with less bureaucracy and enjoy greater flexibility (Jenkins 2004), which can in turn promote SOI in SMEs. Furthermore, research on learning and action networks shows that SMEs, when collaborating, can overcome some of their constraining peculiarities (Clarke and Roome 1999; Cooke and Wills 1999; Lawrence *et al.* 2006; Bos-Brouwers 2009). SME networks can become an important mechanism for SOI through various activities, such as: fostering a critical mass of companies to advance certain topics and set the agenda; transferring knowledge between partners; and distributing costs for capability building and innovation activities across a larger number of actors. While SMEs that engage more proactively in sustainability may initiate and coordinate such networks themselves, for more reactive SMEs, which we will focus on in this chapter, such networks are usually initiated and/or maintained by a third-party actor or intermediary (Howells 2006). Intermediaries in this context are understood as third parties that act as bridge builders and thereby initiate and maintain network ties, diffuse innovation and aid technology and knowledge transfer (Howells 2006). As for potential actors, these are public or non-profit organisations, such as governments, universities and non-governmental organisations (NGOs) as well as 'semi-private' actors such as chambers of commerce, or, on the other hand, private organisations, such as consultancies or companies themselves.

Because of the high risk of SOI, public intermediaries are especially important as an external stimulus for SOI in companies as they may offer their intermediation service for free or for considerably lower costs than, for example, a private consultancy and because participation in public or non-profit initiatives is often directly related to gains in publicity and reputation (Klewitz and Zeyen 2010). Such direct benefits in the absence of high (initial) costs can be an important success factor in overcoming an SME's reactive posture, which is rooted in the high risk associated with SOI. In this contribution, we are therefore most interested in public–private partnerships or cross-sectoral partnerships and, more specifically, in publicly mediated SME networks. Moreover, we focus on bipartite cross-sectoral networks; networks where beyond the participating companies only the intermediary belongs to another sector. There are also network approaches that span more than two sectors (tripartite partnerships, multi-stakeholder initiatives), but these differ significantly from bipartite partnerships in the diversity of their actors and more complex governance structures (Warhurst 2001; Vellejo and Hauselmann 2004; Hansen and Spitzeck 2010).

We, therefore, aim to apply knowledge about collaborative inter-organisational networks to the enhancement of SOI in SMEs. Our research question is: what role can publicly mediated inter-organisational networks play in the promotion of SOI in SMEs? From this follow some more specific questions:

1. In what ways can SME peculiarities influence SOI?

2. What are the governance structures of inter-organisational networks and their potential effects on SOI in SMEs?

3. Who are likely public intermediaries, and what role can they play in inter-organisational networks?

The remainder of this contribution is structured as follows: the first section gives a detailed account of SOIs and focuses on inherent directional and market risks. This lays the ground for the second section, which reviews the role and characteristics of SMEs for SOI. This is followed by a discussion of the governance structures and benefits of inter-organisational networks for SOI. To broach the role of *public intermediaries*, we offer an overview of intermediaries in the innovation literature in general, and then explore specific implications for SOI development in SMEs. This section also mentions two concrete modes of collaborative relationships with public intermediaries: *public–private partnerships* and *university–industry relationships* for SOI development in an SME context. In the final section, we summarise these implications in an integrated framework, before mentioning in our conclusion a few topics for future research.

Sustainability-oriented innovation

In this section, we give a more detailed discussion of SOI and the risks associated with such innovation.

Sustainability-oriented innovation

Corporate sustainability can be referred to the triple bottom line developed by Elkington (1998), which broaches the economic, environmental and social dimensions (or capitals). More specifically, it covers the relationships between each of these capitals, of which the most important is the relationship between economic and environmental (eco-efficiency and eco-effectiveness) and economic and social (socio-efficiency and socio-effectiveness) capitals (Schaltegger and Burritt 2005; Schaltegger *et al.* 2007). Another relationship often neglected is the one between social and environmental capitals. Dyllick and Hockerts (2002) argue that this relationship is characterised both by *sufficiency*, in that societal actors choose to consume less, and by *ecological equity*, in that natural capital needs to be consumed in a socially just way (in both intra- and inter-generational terms). It is widely accepted that corporate innovation activities can address efficiency (e.g. less energy consumption) and effectiveness (e.g. closed-loop production systems), and it is also now increasingly understood that companies can—at least partly—address sufficiency (e.g. develop more service-intensive goods or even become a solution provider) and ecological equity (e.g. produce sustainable value chain designs for biofuels which do not interfere with food production). Improving one or more of these aspects within companies is a central theme in innovation literature.

Innovation in the context of sustainability has received broad attention from a multitude of researchers and a myriad of competing terms has emerged, including—among others—*sustainability innovation* (Hockerts 2003; Schaltegger and Wagner 2008), *sustainable innovation* (cf. Wüstenhagen *et al.* 2008), *CSR-driven innovation* (Hockerts 2009) and *sustainability-related innovation* (Wagner and Llerena 2008; Wagner 2010). Another group of researchers proposed the German term, *Nachhaltigkeitsorientierte innovation* (sustainability-oriented innovation), which highlights the fact that sustainability can only be the management of a 'direction' (i.e. products or services are more sustainable than earlier versions) rather than the arrival at a final destination (i.e. a truly sustainable product) (Fichter and Paech 2004; Paech 2005; cf. Hansen *et al.* 2009, who adapt this term). Most of these terms have influenced one another and thus strongly overlap. Based on this research, we consider a relative improvement of products, processes or services towards sustainability as most important; that is we speak of innovation as a process or direction towards the goal of sustainability. Consequently, we find the term sustainability-oriented innovation (SOI) most suitable and now define it as:

> an improvement of an existing (and/or introduction of a new) product, technology, service, process, management technique, or business model which, in comparison to a prior version and based on a rigorous and traceable (comparative) analysis, has a positive net effect on the overall capital stock (economic, environmental and social). A limited substitution between the types of capital is possible, but should only be pursued if the reduction of any one type of capital is compensated by a sufficiently high increase in the other.

With consideration to both weak and strong sustainability, SOI intends to improve the triple bottom line (cf. Schaltegger and Burritt 2005). As SOI considers the whole physical life-cycle of products and services, both product and process innovation are relevant (Hansen *et al.* 2009; Wagner 2009b). Moreover, SOI deals not only with incremental innovation, but also with more radical innovations such as product-service systems (Mont 2002) and entirely new business models (Hansen *et al.* 2009). While innovation literature has traditionally focused on issues directly related to products and processes, innovation can also occur at the broader organisational level, in which case it is also termed *management innovation* (Birkinshaw *et al.* 2008). An example of such sustainability-oriented management innovation is furnished by the introduction of a sustainability balanced scorecard with the goal to integrate environmental or other sustainability aspects into top-management decisions (e.g. Figge *et al.* 2002; Hansen *et al.* 2010b).

The environmental and social dimensions of SOI need to be specified further. From an *environmental* perspective, innovation either addresses efficiency (e.g. lower energy consumption), consistency (e.g. replacement of toxic materials) or sufficiency (e.g. replacement of products with services, or of products through the integration of functions). From a *social* perspective, innovation may address a betterment of stakeholder integration in the value chain (e.g. social standards in the supply chain) or may aim to ease the provision of (customised) products and services to otherwise neglected groups (e.g. the base of the pyramid markets). SOI offers vast business opportunities, for example through potential cost reductions in the case of eco-efficiency innovation and product differentiation (e.g. by using eco- and social product labels), as well as the possibility of unlocking new markets through radical new product concepts, product-service systems and business models (Hansen *et al.* 2009). While these are indeed potential opportunities, the prerequisites presented earlier and the goals inherent in SOI are manifold as well as complex and are thus also related to high risks, to which we will turn next.

Risks associated with SOI

The development of SOIs first needs to control two important risks: directional and market risks. The *directional risk* (Fichter and Paech 2004: 100; Paech 2005) is related to the actual sustainability performance of SOIs. Even though it may be possible to estimate the immediate effects of SOIs (i.e. from a short-term perspective), the estimation of long-term environmental and social effects, including the consideration of potential rebound effects, is nevertheless a challenging undertaking (Kemp *et al.* 1998; Fichter and Paech 2004). For instance, an *ex post* evaluation of innovations stemming from a conventional innovation process may sometimes turn out to be an (unintended) SOI (Fichter *et al.* 2007). However, to go beyond such accidentally derived SOI, the innovation process needs to take complexities into account and deliberately steer product and service development towards SOI. For example, users and other stakeholders could help companies to detect sustainably superior product and service ideas through practices of open innovation in the ideation phase (Hansen *et al.* 2010a, 2011). Eco-action practices could be applied in the early stages of the innovation process (Lang-Koetz *et al.* 2009) and sustainability checkpoints could be integrated into a company's overall stage gate innovation process (Blomquist and Sandström 2004). All of the latter practices are to a certain extent dependent on intra- and inter-organisational collaboration, as the complexity inherent in multi-dimensional sustainability evaluation often requires different types and sources of knowledge (Clarke and Roome 1999; Schaltegger and Burritt 2005; Wagner and Llerena 2008). Overall, developing SOIs is a complex matter and rather than being an entirely *different* type of innovation, they might be characterised as 'better managed innovations' (Wagner and Llerena 2008). Despite considerable efforts, however, it is extremely difficult to make a sound *ex ante* evaluation of environmental and social effects in the early phases of the innovation process.

The second risk, the *market risk*, needs further elaboration as its implications are considerably different for SOIs from the case of conventional innovations. Market risk refers to the risk that innovations, especially new product developments, will not meet customer demands and therefore fail in the market (which is indeed quite often the case; cf. Cooper 2001). Obviously, SOIs also need to succeed in the market (Schaltegger and Wagner 2011), as mere inventions locked in corporate R&D archives or in pilot projects will not develop the intended social or environmental effects, nor will they meet economic goals. But SOI may also hamper the positioning of companies in competitive markets: as these companies internalise external costs (e.g. less pollution) they often need to incorporate a price premium in the related product or service, which makes the products more expensive than products or services from competitors that do not internalise external costs, a problem which has been recognised as part of the 'double externality problem' (Rennings 2000). This problem describes a situation in which it is often difficult to compete with competitors offering less sustainable products and services, as these do not have to internalise societal costs (e.g. pollution) into product prices. It is also because of this circumstance that governments and public policy instruments can claim increasing relevance in nurturing SOI (Rennings 2000; Hockerts and Wüstenhagen 2010).

In principle, SOI may present a means of differentiation in the market and customers might be willing to pay a premium price. However, more generally speaking, the market risk for SOIs can be significantly higher than for conventional innovations in view of the double externality problem (Rennings 2000), as just described.

In addressing both risks (directional and market), we highlighted the riskier nature of SOI as compared with conventional innovation. This higher risk, in turn, calls for an innovation process that is managed accordingly and requires a whole range of resources. This also goes a long way towards explaining why research into SOI tends to target resource-rich corporations while neglecting resource-constrained SMEs.

The role and characteristics of SMEs for SOI

As we mentioned at the end of the last section, research on SOI often focuses on large-scale, multinational corporations (Simon *et al.* 2000; Blomquist and Sandström 2004; Hansen *et al.* 2009). This research has significantly developed our understanding of SOI, it is true, but there is also the need for a specific SME perspective, and this for two reasons. First, in many countries SMEs are the backbone of the economy and thus the sheer cumulative importance of SMEs matters for sustainable development. SMEs (defined as companies with less than 250 employees) make up more than 90% of all businesses in the EU-27 and contribute roughly 64% of the industrial pollution in Europe (Schmiemann 2008; ECEI 2010). Therefore, on the path to sustainable development, SMEs are seen as crucial 'contributors' (Spence and Lozano 2000; Jenkins 2004; Perrini 2006; Preuss and Perschke 2010) and, further, a *critical mass of sustainable SMEs* is considered a necessity (Luetkenhorst 2004; Spence *et al.* 2008).

Second, SMEs differ significantly from larger companies with regard to their innovation efforts—they 'are not little big firms' (Welsh and White 1981; Tilley 2000). These differences cover both advantages and disadvantages in the context of sustainability (Vyakarnam *et al.* 1997; Spence and Lozano 2000; Spence and Rutherfoord 2001; Spence *et al.* 2003; Jenkins 2004; Moore and Spence 2006; Perrini 2006; Bos-Brouwers 2009; Preuss and Perschke 2010) and are often referred to as 'SME peculiarities' (Del Brio and Junquera 2003). The most important advantage of SMEs in the context of innovation is their ability to respond quickly to customer as well as market demands and to act more entrepreneurially given an owner-manager structure and fewer bureaucratic processes. Disadvantages of SMEs include resource constraints (personnel, knowledge and capital) and the absence of formal structures and strategies.

Based on Schumpeter's idea of 'creative destruction', innovation literature often argues that new entrants (i.e. small companies) are generally more likely to innovate radically while incumbents are dependent on the acquisition of entrants as they often fail to develop and commercialise such innovations themselves (Christensen and Bower 1996; Spencer and Kirchhoff 2006; Henkel *et al.* 2010). While this focus on the advantages of small companies is probably a simplification, it is also accepted that there is only a small number of very innovative small companies while most are much less so (Spencer and Kirchhoff 2006). In other words, small companies, and SMEs more broadly, seem to capitalise in different ways on the SME peculiarities, which demonstrates that they are a very heterogeneous group. This is also borne out by a multi-case study analysis by Noci and Verganti (1999) which has found that not all SMEs have the same attitudes to and behaviours concerning SOI, *and* that these are rather contingent on internal factors (resources, strategic attitude) and the external competitive arena (e.g. uncertainty, speed of change). They differentiate between three major strategic patterns ranging from rather compliance-oriented to more proactive stances (cf. Schaltegger 2002 for a comparable typology): *reactive environmental strategy* (which reacts to external stimuli, e.g. regulations); *anticipatory green strategy* (which times the strategy in such a way that a competitive advantage can be realised); and an *innovation-based green strategy* (in which environmental issues lead to innovation-based solutions, e.g. new green technologies).

SMEs belonging to the innovation-based green strategy seem to overcome the disadvantages stemming from SME peculiarities while fully leveraging their advantages and are thus able to engage in both incremental and radical SOIs (Noci and Verganti 1999; Bos-Brouwers 2009). It is this type of SME which is dealt with in the literature on sustainable entrepreneurship and ecopreneurship (Schaltegger 2002; Schaltegger and Wagner 2008). Although it would be interesting to study it further, the larger part of SMEs seem to act according to reactive or anticipatory strategies, so that the remainder of this chapter is devoted to these latter strategies (Del Brio and Junquera 2003).

The discussion of the risks associated with SOI (particularly the directional risk) makes it reasonable to argue that SOI requires a more structured innovation process and, accordingly, more resources, both of which (formalisation/structure and resources) are aspects where SMEs have disadvantages. For example, SMEs are said not just to have a lower capability to engage with non-traditional stakeholders (Noci and Verganti 1999) but manage sustainability issues in a less systematic, ad hoc way (Jenkins 2004). It is thus not surprising then that the literature reveals a strong emphasis on incremental SOI in SMEs and, more specifically, a focus on cost reduction through eco-efficient processes (Noci and Verganti 1999; Del Brio and Junquera 2003; Bos-Brouwers 2009; Klewitz and Zeyen 2010). Indeed, fewer SMEs seem to engage in more radical SOI, such as developing new products (Bos-Brouwers 2009).

Based on the discussion above, we offer the following two propositions:

> Proposition A-1: With increased complexity and higher risk of SOI, SMEs are challenged to use their scarce resources efficiently and exploit effectively their entrepreneurial audacity

> Proposition A-2: Incremental and radical SOI in SMEs involves the interaction with and exploitation of external, additional sources that support the innovation process in SMEs

The types of SME focused on in this article (reactive, anticipatory-oriented) seem to be more heavily affected by the disadvantages discussed above, such as resources constraints. One possible way to offset some of the disadvantages discussed is collaboration and networking, which is described in greater detail in the next section.

Inter-organisational networks and external stimuli for SOI

In this section we describe how third-party mediated inter-organisational networks may support SMEs in overcoming barriers related to SOI which stem from disadvantages inherent in the size and type of their organisations. We first show which additional benefits SMEs can derive from participation in such a network structure. Second, we argue for the need for an external stimulus to establish such networks. In the next section, we present various intermediaries which could provide this stimulus and we explain the special role of these actors from the public sector within the network structure. The final section presents a synthesis of these aspects in the form of a conceptual framework.

Inter-organisational networks to enhance the innovation capacity of SMEs

Inter-organisational networks consist of multiple organisations (i.e. three or more) that connect via multilateral ties (Provan *et al.* 2007). Organisations may connect because the transaction costs of the individual network member are reduced (Lawrence *et al.* 2006) and the individual capacity increased. The ways in which network members are connected include information, ideas, knowledge material, financial resources, services and peer support (Clarke and Roome 1999; Provan *et al.* 2007). In their research on means to promote environmental innovation in SMEs, Biondi *et al.* (2002) emphasise the importance of effective networking and suggest that, through the combination of business networks (e.g. customers, suppliers, consumers), regulatory networks (e.g. local and national authorities) and knowledge networks (e.g. technology centres, universities), SMEs can access information on novel technologies, maintain an oversight of legal requirements and monitor their markets better. Ultimately, networks can lead to improved learning, increased social capital, sustained change and stronger innovation capacity (Powell *et al.* 1996; Cooke and Wills 1999; Roberts *et al.* 2006; Walker and Preuss 2008).

Another division of networks is into formal and informal ones. Clarke and Roome (1999) consider 'learning action networks' as rather informal networks complementing other, more formal structures. In contrast, public–private partnerships are usually more formalised. Both formal and informal networks can exist in science parks, clusters and incubators, which are strongly institutionalised through a shared space (Pittaway *et al.* 2004).

While Pittaway *et al.* (2004), in a broader definition, include networks that span all kinds of business-to-business partnership (e.g. companies, suppliers, customers, financiers), we are interested in a more narrow understanding of network, that of a horizontal network of companies, specifically SMEs, which are mediated by a public third party, as elaborated below in more detail.

Such inter-organisational networks are important in advancing an SME's *innovation capacity* for SOI for various reasons. First, collaboration may help to overcome SME disadvantages such as resource constraints (Verheul 1999; Mitra 2000). Pittaway *et al.* (2004)—based on a systematic literature review—find that the main benefits of networking include: risk sharing, accessing new markets and novel technologies, bringing products to market, bundling complementary skills, and protecting property rights. Huggins *et al.* (2010) point to the relevance of external (knowledge) networks in that companies may acquire new knowledge in this setting which they could not generate based on their own capabilities.

Second, *collaboration and partnerships*, the basis for inter-organisational networks, also play a major role in unlocking innovation opportunities as the innovation process itself is 'increasingly non-linear', 'iterative' and of 'multi-agent character' (Kline 1985; von Hippel 1988; Perkman and Walsh 2007; Lundvall 2010). Research on and practices of 'open innovation' (Chesbrough 2003) consequently show that the use of an abundance of sources (i.e. inside and outside the firm) improves the innovativeness of a company and the innovation process in general. Given the complexity of sustainability issues, SOI seems even more dependent on collaboration (Lozano 2007): it requires knowledge beyond a company's existing experience, which is often diverse and distributed (Clarke and Roome 1999; Wagner and Llerena 2008). As knowledge created in networks is more diverse (Kogut 2000), networks can thus be a key mechanism for SOI (Lawrence *et al.* 2006; Halila 2007; Jenkins 2009).

In light of the above discussion we propose:

> Proposition B-1: To offset resource constraints and strengthen their innovation capacity, SMEs can involve themselves in inter-organisational networks that provide peer support, give access to expert knowledge and establish lasting learning structures

Having pointed out the positive aspects of networks, we must not neglect the possible downside that comes with them: they may well lead to a further strain on SMEs' limited resources, as active and proactive networking requires SMEs to dedicate time and personnel to this activity. Therefore, SMEs may also need to choose and monitor carefully the effectiveness of the networks in order to avoid the dissipation of resources. Moreover, though the overall benefits may sound intriguing enough for SMEs to engage proactively in such collaboration, evidence shows that it is only the most advanced SMEs (referred to in the innovation-based green strategy earlier) that build a capability for collaboration and networking for SOI (Noci and Verganti 1999; Jenkins 2009). We thus theorise that an external stimulus given by a third party can serve as a push-factor for SMEs to collaborate and, ultimately, engage in SOI, a topic to which we now turn.

The need for external stimuli to collaborate

It is not only the building of a capacity for collaboration that makes SMEs more likely to network for SOI (Noci and Verganti 1999). Azzone and Noci (1998) further find that SMEs react especially to external stimuli from green movements, governments, regulators or other companies. A viable way to stimulate still less proactive SMEs is thus to provide an external stimulus through a third party (Gombault and Versteege 1999; Verheul 1999; Holt *et al.* 2000). Third parties are in a particularly good position to provide the necessary tailor-made support for advancing SOI in SMEs (Hoevenagel and Wolters 2000). More specifically, there is a need to *inform, consult* and *facilitate* SOI in SMEs through awareness-raising activities, technology consulting/transfer, implementation of pilot projects and other support programmes (Verheul 1999; Mitra 2000; Del Brio and Junquera 2003). Among the terms used for third parties that provide such services are change agents, intermediaries, brokers or bridgers (Howells 2006). As will be explained in more detail later, such intermediaries can be various organisational actors, including governments, nonprofits and NGOs, and semi-private (e.g. chambers of commerce) or private actors (e.g. consultancy).

Generally, the relationships between such an intermediary and companies (here SMEs) can be distinguished according to the number of parties involved (Howells 2006). One-to-one (1:1) relationships exist when a single company cooperates with the intermediary. What we are, however, interested in are one-to-many (1:n) relationships where the intermediary works within a network of companies, especially one of SMEs.

Using the above discussion, we can now put forward our next proposition:

> Proposition B-2: The more reactive behaviour an SME exhibits towards SOI, the greater the need for external stimuli through intermediaries to instigate fruitful collaborative ties

The following section will further elaborate the roles of various types of intermediary in such networks.

Types of public intermediary and their roles

Intermediaries take a central role in inter-organisational networks (Kogut 2000; Lawrence *et al.* 2006). Intermediaries are commonly understood as third-party organisations that help to achieve desired objectives (Etgar and Zusman 1982; Oudshoorn 1997; Miller and Choi 2003; Bayar 2005). They are established as they reduce search and other transaction costs (Kodama 2008). For the purpose of this section, intermediaries are defined as organisations whose objective it is to mediate between partners, transfer knowledge and more generally facilitate innovation. In order to do this, intermediaries can generally contribute to three different phases: scanning and recognition; communication and assimilation; and application (Howells 2006):

- *Scanning and recognition.* If SMEs collaborate with intermediaries, they will possibly gain a more comprehensive view of sustainability challenges, of what they entail, access to external expertise and benefit from resource exchanges (Hartman *et al.* 1999; de Bruijn and Hofman 2000; Roome 2001; de Bruijn and Tukker 2002; Hartman *et al.* 2002)

- *Communication and assimilation.* Moreover, if an SME still tends to follow a more reactive rather than proactive approach to sustainability, it can use collaborative initiatives to acquire knowledge outside organisational boundaries (Clarke and Roome 1999). Spence *et al.* (2003) support this argument from a social capital theory perspective in that SMEs might collaborate and network to gain access to and exchange relevant information. LePoutre and Heene (2006) suggest that SMEs should collaborate or seek network contacts to reduce time and knowledge constraints, increase absorptive capacity, and to gain more knowledge

- *Application.* This phase is closest to the literature on technology transfer (e.g. Rothwell and Dodgson 1992; Bozeman 2000; Buratti and Penco 2001) in that the collaboration aims at diffusion of practices and policies in the context of SOI (Battaglia *et al.* 2010). Intermediaries can for example provide the necessary external impulses, motivation and advice to initiate or continue with environmental protection (Gombault and Versteege 1999). This initial impulse could ultimately lead to more proactive behaviour of SMEs in the context of sustainability

With reference to Pittaway *et al.*'s (2004) work on networking and parties involved in the context of innovation, we are able to identify a range of actors as potential intermediaries and classify them accordingly as public, non-profit, semi-public and private intermediaries as is summarised in Figure 13.1.

Figure 13.1 **Intermediaries in inter-organisational networks**

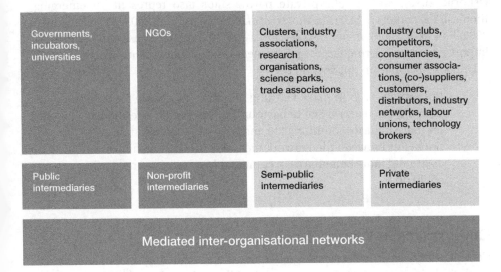

We have seen that the risks inherent in SOI (namely market and directional risk; see above), on the one hand, and the high uncertainties of potential business opportunities from SOI, on the other, can serve to explain why a larger part of SMEs might retain rather reactive stances towards SOI. Against this background, the literature reveals the importance of public (or publicly funded) intermediaries (Del Brio and Junquera 2003) and, more specifically, governments' promotion of 'business networks' (Albareda *et al.* 2007). Having access to public funds and not being profit oriented, public intermediaries can offer their service for free or at considerably lower cost than private intermediaries. Moreover, there is often an incentive for SMEs to participate in public initiatives as they may be directly related to gains in publicity as well as reputation (Klewitz and Zeyen 2010) and can lay the ground for further partnerships. Such direct benefits in the absence of high (initial) costs as well as such aspects as risk sharing (Hodge 2004) can be important factors in the face of higher risks associated with SOI. We are thus most interested in publicly mediated SME networks.

In this context we want to mention *handholding*, a further important aspect in the literature on collaboration between companies, public, non-profit, semi-public and private intermediaries. This refers to the degree to which SMEs are individually guided through the process of using support programmes that help to effectively diffuse and adopt innovation within the company (Friedman and Miles 2002). Such handholding provisions can involve the distribution of learning material, the customisation and flexibility of programme content and, more importantly, networking (Friedman and Miles 2002) as discussed in the preceding section.

When actors from the private and public sectors collaborate for mutual benefit—as is the case when public intermediaries collaborate with SMEs—this is also termed a *public–private partnership* (Kouwenhoven 1993; Akintoye *et al.* 2003; Osborne 2010). Such public–private partnerships also represent an emerging theme in the context of SOI (Martinuzzi *et al.* 2000; Malmborg 2003, 2004; La France 2005; Kolk *et al.* 2008). In our next section we will therefore discuss two of the most important public intermediaries, governments and (public) science partners.

Our conclusion from this section is:

> Proposition C-1: To make learning networks accessible for SMEs with a more reactive SOI behaviour requires public intermediaries that establish, communicate, moderate and maintain the relational ties between the network members for considerably lower costs (and more benefits) than comparable private intermediaries could do

Governments as intermediaries

Central public intermediaries are governments and regulatory bodies in general: through their power to impose new sustainability-oriented regulations they have a direct influence on some SOI-related risks and uncertainties. It is on the basis of their guiding, stimulating or regulating role that governments can become a strategic partner for SMEs (Gombault and Versteege 1999). More specifically, Meadowcroft (1999) distinguishes four types of policy tools, ranging from hard to soft law: (1) law, regulation and sanctions; (2) taxes, prices and markets; (3) normative prescriptions and persuasion; and (4) organisational engagement, negotiation and cooperation. An example of type 1 is the influence that regulators can have on the competitiveness of non-sustainable products through harsher environmental laws.

However, a closer look at possible policy tools reveals that new laws are not the only, let alone the most effective, solution to promote sustainability. Accordingly, Jenkins (2009: 34) calls for actions at the other, soft end of the continuum of policy tools, and proposes 'a supportive framework that fosters an innovative environment where SMEs can learn from each other'. Governments that act as intermediaries in SME networks aimed at awareness raising or technology transfer can be considered to fall in category 4, a soft regulation. Such public–private partnerships are only just emerging, as the 'divergent views between business and government' were traditionally considered obstacles to such a partnership (Kolk *et al.* 2008). Quite the opposite is, however, true: public–private partnerships can lead to improved relationships with local authorities (Martinuzzi *et al.* 2000; Malmborg 2003, 2004). Therefore, collaborative approaches between government and small businesses in the context of sustainability can support and stimulate SOI (de Bruijn and Hofman 2000; Hoevenagel and Wolters 2000). Some of the existing initiatives discussed in the literature are the National Cleaner Production Centers in developing nations (Luken and Navratil 2004), the Australian Small Business Support Program (van Berkel 2007) and the Austria-based ECOPROFIT initiative (Martinuzzi *et al.* 2000; Sage 2000). The ECOPROFIT initiative, for example, is based on a public–private partnership model which has spread from Austria to other countries (e.g. Korea, Italy and Slovenia) and aims to facilitate eco-efficiency innovation in SMEs. Companies that participate in this initiative are initially provided with handholding mechanisms such as learning in collaborative workshops and customised individual consultation, which facilitates the implementation of eco-efficiency innovations. Moreover, proactive intervention through the local authorities provides an external stimulus to adopt eco-efficiency innovations (Klewitz and Zeyen 2010).

On the basis of the literature reviewed, we put forward:

> Proposition C-2: Government-funded public–private partnerships offering handholding mechanisms for SMEs through networks, knowledge dissemination and customised consulting are an effective means for overcoming reactive postures of SMEs and offsetting their resource constraints

Universities and science partners as intermediaries

Universities and science partners have been considered as key sources of knowledge in knowledge-based societies (Etzkowitz and Zhou 2006). While universities and science partners can be both privately and publicly funded, in many countries (e.g. China, Germany) they are usually publicly funded (Xu and Huang 2011), which makes them important public intermediaries. Both have often been called on to move beyond their traditional role of teaching and research and interact more intensively with industry (Etzkowitz and Zhou 2006). A wide range of instruments exist to further this end, among which are research partnerships, research services, academic entrepreneurship, human resource transfer, informal interaction, commercialisation of property rights and scientific publications (Perkmann and Walsh 2007). In addition, Huggins *et al.* (2008) mention collaborative forms such as the formation of *technology transfer offices* (which administer legal processes for patenting), the creation of *science parks* (which take over consulting services or technology transfer) and the development of *outreach programmes* (to build awareness or train the industry's workforce). All these mechanisms can be arranged on a scale from high involvement (e.g. research partnerships), through medium engagement (e.g. exchange of personnel) to low engagement (e.g. technology transfer). Depending on these varying degrees of involvement, both incremental and radical innovations are possible (Pittaway *et al.* 2004), also in the context of SOI (Bos-Brouwers 2009).

With regard to SMEs, it is interesting to note that firm size has an effect on the university–industry relationship (see e.g. Cohen *et al.* 2002; Santoro and Chakrabarti 2002; Fontana *et al.* 2006). SMEs, as they are said to have a lower absorptive capacity, tend to rely on regional collaboration (Cohen and Levinthal 1990) and might thus depend more on local universities. They can benefit from the universities' infrastructure for knowledge creation through which they have access to knowledge not otherwise available because of their limited resources (Huggins *et al.* 2008). Universities in their turn are said to be wary of engagement with SMEs as knowledge transfer often does not lead to a reciprocal benefit (Huggins *et al.* 2008). As SMEs are considerably more constrained in their R&D budgets than larger firms, an important factor for the attractiveness of SMEs for universities is the existence of external funding by government (Segarra-Blasco and Arauzo-Carod 2008; Huggins and Johnston 2009). In this context, an important role as intermediaries in SME networks is also played by science partners, who are valued for their neutral position (Pittaway *et al.* 2004; Segarra-Blasco and Arauzo-Carod 2008).

In light of the above literature we propose:

> Proposition C-3: To acquire new and diverse knowledge for SOI, SMEs can collaborate with (regional) science partners to exploit their knowledge infrastructure

After having elaborated on the role of various types of intermediary and the particular reasons which lead individual SMEs to participate in intermediary-initiated networks, we now turn our attention to the relational ties that result from the collaboration between the companies belonging to the network and the mediating intermediaries.

Towards a framework for inter-organisational networks for SOI in SMEs

From the above discussion of SOI characteristics, SME peculiarities for SOI, benefits of inter-organisational networks and the potential role of public intermediaries, we can now develop a framework for SOI in SMEs. As can be seen from Figure 13.2, the framework makes explicit the structure and relational ties of publicly mediated inter-organisational networks and points to three central aspects. First, an intermediary can affect, initiate and stimulate the creation of an inter-organisational network. To this end, the preceding discussion highlighted two possible collaborative relationships for SOI: via a governmental body (innovation path A in Fig. 13.2) or via a university (innovation path B in Fig. 13.2). Second, depending on the type of intermediary—public, semi-private or private—a specific form of collaboration is the result: for example, a governmental body might instigate relational ties between an SME and itself; this would be the public–private partnership model. Third, the SMEs involved in a collaborative relationship (bi-, tri- or multipartite) can also connect to other SMEs and form a horizontal network, with the intermediary—regardless of type—building the centre of the network.

Overall, it becomes clear that, in third-party mediated inter-organisational networks, collaboration occurs in two directions: first, the collaboration between the intermediary and the individual SMEs and, second, the inter-organisational collaboration between the SMEs themselves, that is, collaboration in the horizontal network.

Further research

We are planning to conduct further research into the learning process for SOI in SMEs, with a special focus on fruitful relational ties with external partners. Further investigation, for instance, into the role of universities might be especially interesting: within the logic of the learning economy, it is above all universities that can provide know-how (skills and capability), know-why (general principles and laws), know-what (facts) and know-who (collaborative relationships) knowledge (Charles 2006). Given the great relevance of knowledge as a key resource for companies (Cohen and Levinthal 1990; Grant 1996), research into the types and sources of knowledge beneficial for SOI would seem to be particularly worthwhile. In the case of universities as intermediaries, another research path leads to models that describe a 'triple helix' relationship (see Etzkowitz et al. 2000; Etzkowitz and Zhou 2003, 2006) between government, university and industry. Etzkowitz and Zhou (2006) argue that in such collaboration polyvalent knowledge is created which is theoretical, practical, marketable and open. Bearing in mind their need for highly

Figure 13.2 **Framework for publicly intermediated innovation paths**

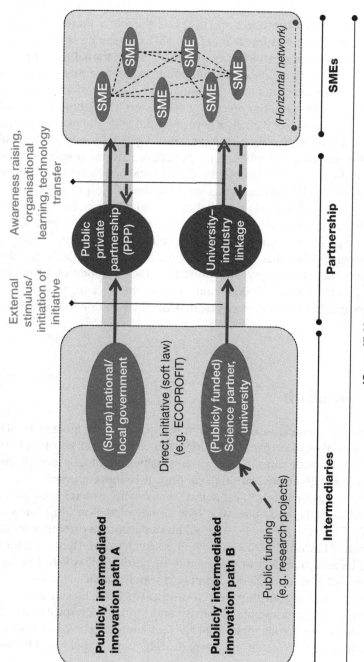

specialised and customised knowledge, this might be especially interesting for SMEs in their learning process for SOI.

Another research path could focus on intermediaries beyond governmental bodies and science partners. NGOs, for example, may also proactively mediate inter-organisational SME networks, as is often the case in multi-stakeholder collaborations. As research indicates (Manring 2007; Kolk *et al.* 2008), most of these networks are tripartite rather than bipartite; that is, networks consist of actors from more than two sectors (e.g. governments, industry, civil society) and thus considerably differ from the networks which are the focus of this contribution. Additionally, professional associations and trade/industry associations are often initiators of company networks (Pittaway *et al.* 2004) and may thus present an external stimulus for SOI (Simpson *et al.* 2004; Lawrence *et al.* 2006). Sometimes this is the case when they are 'activated by governmental interventions, or threats thereof' (Östlund 1994), so that it may be said that the trade associations' role of proactive mediation is closely linked to government actions.

Furthermore, mention must be made of the difficulties (i.e. costs and critical aspects) of collaborative relationships. Among these are hidden agendas, bargaining, free-riding and incompatible or conflicting interests (see Lozano 2007), all of which should receive more attention to ensure that mediated networks will yield the desired results for SOI in SMEs. In addition, given the heterogeneity of SMEs in terms of size and sector, the case for more research into the actual fit of network ties is no less powerful: what needs investigation is the extent to which networks can afford to be merely sector specific or need to benefit from diverse sector affiliation.

Conclusion

SOI comprises manifold business opportunities (such as cost benefits through eco-efficiency, product differentiation and new markets), on the one hand, but also considerable market and directional risks, on the other. In order to fully leverage the benefits of SOI, SMEs need to find ways to control for these latter risks. Based on the literature, we have presented a potential solution consisting of two interconnected mechanisms, inter-organisational networks and public incentives through which public intermediaries may provide an external stimulus for SOI in SMEs. The initiation of an inter-organisational network consisting of a group of SMEs (and the public intermediary itself), may then facilitate collaborative approaches of innovation and diffusion. Such collaboration is important for two reasons: it helps to overcome SME resource constraints and it responds to the need for diverse sources of knowledge inherent in SOI. It is of course also clear that SMEs only benefit from collaboration as long as the costs of networking do not exceed its benefits. Publicly intermediated networks for SOI are a promising field of research which would profit greatly from further conceptual and empirical studies.

References

Akintoye, A., M. Beck and C. Hardcastle (eds.) (2003) *Public–Private Partnerships: Managing Risks and Opportunities* (Oxford, UK: Blackwell Publishing).

Albareda, L., J. Lozano and T. Ysa (2007) 'Public Policies on Corporate Social Responsibility: The Role of Governments in Europe', *Journal of Business Ethics* 74.4: 391-407.

Azzone, G., and G. Noci (1998) 'Seeing Ecology and "Green" Innovations as a Source of Change', *Journal of Organizational Change Management* 11.2: 94-111.

Battaglia, M., L. Bianchi, M. Frey and F. Iraldo (2010) 'An Innovative Model to promote CSR among SMEs Operating in Industrial Clusters: Evidence from an EU Project', *Corporate Social Responsibility and Environmental Management* 17: 133-41.

Bayar, G. (2005) 'The Role of Intermediaries in Corruption', *Public Choice* 122.3/4: 277-98.

Biondi, V., F. Iraldo and S. Meredith (2002) 'Achieving Sustainability through Environmental Innovation: The Role of SMEs', *International Journal of Technology Management* 24.5–6: 612-26.

Birkinshaw, J., G. Hamel and M. Mol (2008) 'Management Innovation', *Academy of Management Review* 33.4: 825-45.

Blomquist, T., and J. Sandström (2004) 'From Issues to Checkpoints and Back: Managing Green Issues in R&D', *Business Strategy and the Environment* 13.6: 363-73.

Bos-Brouwers, H. (2009) 'Corporate Sustainability and Innovation in SMEs: Evidence of Themes and Activities in Practice', *Business Strategy and the Environment* 19.7: 417-35.

Bozeman, B. (2000) 'Technology Transfer and Public Policy: A Review of Research and Theory', *Research Policy* 29: 627-55.

Buratti, N., and L. Penco (2001) 'Assisted Technology Transfer to SMEs: Lessons from an Exemplary Case', *Technovation* 21: 35-43.

Charles, D. (2006) 'Universities as Key Knowledge Infrastructures in Regional Innovation Systems', *Innovation: The European Journal of Social Science Research* 19.1: 117-30.

Chesbrough, H. (2003) *Open Innovation: The New Imperative for Creating and Profiting from Technology* (Cambridge, MA: Harvard Business School Press).

Christensen, C., and J. Bower (1996) 'Custom Power, Strategic Investment, and the Failure of Leading Firms', *Strategic Management Journal* 17: 197-218.

Clarke, S., and N. Roome (1999) 'Sustainable Business: Learning Action Networks as Organizational Assets', *Business Strategy and the Environment* 8.5: 296-310.

Cohen, W., and D. Levinthal (1990) 'Absorptive Capacity: A New Perspective on Learning and Innovation', *Administrative Science Quarterly* 35.1: 128-52.

Cohen, W., R. Nelson and J. Walsh (2002) 'Links and Impacts: The Influence of Public Research on Industrial R&D', *Management Science* 48: 1-23.

Cooke, P., and D. Wills (1999) 'Small Firms, Social Capital and the Enhancement of Business Performance through Innovation Programmes', *Small Business Economics* 13: 219-34.

Cooper, R. (2001) *Winning at New Products: Accelerating the Process from Idea to Launch* (Cambridge, MA: Perseus, 3rd edn).

De Bruijn, T., and P. Hofman (2000) 'Pollution Prevention in Small and Medium-sized Enterprises: Evoking Structural Changes through Partnerships', *Greener Management International* 30: 71-82.

De Bruijn, T., and A. Tukker (eds.) (2002) *Partnership and Leadership: Building Alliances for a Sustainable Future* (Dordrecht: Kluwer).

Del Brío, J., and B. Junquera (2003) 'A Review of the Literature on Environmental Innovation Management in SMEs: Implications for Public Policies', *Technovation* 23.12: 939-48.

Dyllick, T., and K. Hockerts (2002) 'Beyond the Business Case for Corporate Sustainability', *Business Strategy and the Environment* 11.2: 130-41.

ECEI (European Commission Enterprise and Industry) (2010) 'SMEs and the Environment in the European Union', Denmark, ec.europa.eu/enterprise/policies/sme/business-environment/files/main_report_en.pdf, accessed 1 March 2011.

Elkington, J. (1998) *Cannibals with Forks: The Triple Bottom Line of 21st Century Business* (Gabriola Island, BC: New Society Publishers).

Etgar, M., and P. Zusman (1982) 'The Marketing Intermediary as an Information Seller: A New Approach', *The Journal of Business* 55.4: 505-15.

Etzkowitz, H., and C. Zhou (2003) 'Innovation in Innovation: The Triple Helix of University–Industry–Government Relations', *Social Science Information* 42.3: 293-337.

Etzkowitz, H., and C. Zhou (2006) 'Triple Helix. Triple Helix Twins: Innovation and Sustainability', *Science and Public Policy* 33.1: 77-83.

Etzkowitz, H., A. Webster, C. Gebhardt and B. Terra (2000) 'The Future of the University and the University of the Future: Evolution of Ivory Tower to Entrepreneurial Paradigm', *Research Policy* 29: 313-30.

Fichter, K., and N. Paech (2004) *Nachhaltigkeitsorientiertes Innovationsmanagement: Prozessgestaltung unter besonderer Berücksichtigung von Internet-Nutzungen; Endbericht der Basisstudie 4 des Vorhabens* [Sustainability-Oriented Innovation Management. Process Design under Consideration of Internet Usages. Final Report of Study 4 of Sustainable Markets Emerge] (Berlin/Oldenburg, Germany: University of Oldenburg).

Fichter, K., S. Beucker, T. Noack and S. Springer (eds.) (2007) *Entstehungspfade von Nachhaltigkeitsinnovationen: Fallstudien und Szenarien zu Einflussfaktoren, Schlüsselakteuren und Internetunterstützung* [Paths of Emergence of Sustainability Innovations; Case Studies and Scenarios to Impact Factors, Crucial Actors and Internet Support] (Stuttgart: IRB Verlag).

Figge, F., T. Hahn, S. Schaltegger and M. Wagner (2002) 'The Sustainability Balanced Scorecard: Linking Sustainability Management to Business Strategy', *Business Strategy and the Environment* 11.5: 269-84.

Fontana, R., A. Geuna and M. Matt (2006) 'Factors Affecting University–Industry R&D Projects: The Importance of Searching, Screening and Signaling', *Research Policy* 35.2: 309-23.

Friedman, A., and S. Miles (2002) 'SMEs and the Environment: Evaluating Dissemination Routes and Handholding Levels', *Business Strategy and the Environment* 11: 324-41.

Gombault, M., and S. Versteege (1999) 'Cleaner Production in SMEs through a Partnership with (Local) Authorities: Successes from the Netherlands', *Journal of Cleaner Production* 7: 249-61.

Grant, R. (1996) 'Toward a Knowledge-Based Theory of the Firm', *Strategic Management Journal* 17: 109-22.

Halila, F. (2007) 'Networks as a Means of Supporting the Adoption of Organizational Innovations in SMEs: The Case of Environmental Management Systems (EMSs) based on ISO 14001', *Corporate Social Responsibility and Environmental Management* 14.3: 167-81.

Hansen, G., and H. Spitzeck (2010) *Stakeholder Governance: An Analysis of BITC Corporate Responsibility Index Data on Stakeholder Engagement and Governance* (Cranfield, UK: Doughty Centre for Corporate Responsibility).

Hansen, E., F. Grosse-Dunker and R. Reichwald (2009) 'SI Cube: A Framework to Evaluate Sustainability-Oriented Innovations', *International Journal of Innovation Management* 13.4: 683-713.

Hansen, E., M. Gomm, A. Bullinger and K. Möslein (2010a) 'A Community-based Toolkit for Ride-sharing Services: The Case of a Virtual Network of Ride Access Points in Germany', *International Journal of Innovation and Sustainable Development* 5.1: 80-99.

Hansen, E., M. Sextl and R. Reichwald (2010b) 'Managing Stakeholder Collaboration through a Community-Enabled Balanced Scorecard: The Case of Merck Ltd, Thailand', *Business Strategy and the Environment* 19.6: 387-99.

Hansen, E., A. Bullinger and R. Reichwald (2011) *Innovation Contests for Sustainability-oriented Product Innovation: Findings from a Worldwide Shoe Innovation Contest* (Lüneburg, Germany: Centre for Sustainability Management).

Hartman, C., P. Hofman and E. Stafford (1999) 'Partnerships: A Path to Sustainability', *Business Strategy and the Environment* 8: 255-66.

Hartman, C., R. Hofman and E. Stafford (2002) 'Environmental Collaboration: Potential and Limits', in T. de Bruijn and A. Tukker (eds.), *Partnership and Leadership: Building Alliances for a Sustainable Future* (Dordrecht: Kluwer): 21-40.

Henkel, R., T. Rönde and M. Wagner (2010) 'And the Winner Is—Acquired: Entrepreneurship as a Contest with Acquisition as the Prize', *CEPR Discussion Paper No. DP8147* (London: Centre for Economic Policy Research).

Hockerts, K. (2003) *Sustainability Innovations, Ecological and Social Entrepreneurship and the Management of Antagonistic Assets* (Dissertation; Bamberg, Germany: Difo Verlag, University St Gallen).

Hockerts, K. (2009) 'CSR-Driven Innovation: Towards the Social Purpose Business', Denmark, www.csrinnovation.dk, accessed 5 March 2011.

Hockerts, K., and R. Wüstenhagen (2010) 'Greening Goliaths versus Emerging Davids: Theorizing about the Role of Incumbents and New Entrants in SE', *Journal of Business Venturing* 25.5: 481-92.

Hodge, G. (2004) 'The Risky Business of Public–Private Partnerships', *Australian Journal of Public Administration* 63.4: 37-49.

Hoevenagel, R., and T. Wolters (2000) 'Small and Medium-Sized Enterprises, Environmental Policies and the Supporting Role of Intermediate Organisations in the Netherlands', *Greener Management International* 30: 61-69.

Holt, D., S. Anthony and H. Viney (2000) 'Supporting Environmental Improvements in SMEs in the UK', *Greener Management International* 33: 29-49.

Howells, J. (2006) 'Intermediation and the Role of Intermediaries in Innovation', *Research Policy* 35: 715-28.

Huggins, R., and A. Johnston (2009) 'The Economic and Innovation Contribution of Universities: A Regional Perspective', *Environmental Planning C* 27.6: 1,088-106.

Huggins, R., A. Johnston and R. Steffenson (2008) 'Universities, Knowledge Networks and Regional Policy', *Cambridge Journal of Regions, Economy and Society* 1.2: 321-40.

Huggins, R., H. Izushi and D. Prokop (2010) 'University–Industry Networks: Interactions with Large R&D Performers', paper presented at the *Opening Up Innovation: Strategy, Organization and Technology Conference*, London, June 2010.

Jenkins, H. (2004) 'A Critique of Conventional CSR Theory: An SME Perspective. How can small and medium enterprises embrace corporate social responsibility?' *Journal of General Management* 29.4: 37-57.

Jenkins, H. (2009) 'A "Business Opportunity" Model of Corporate Social Responsibility for Small- and Medium-sized Enterprises', *Business Ethics: A European Review* 18.1: 21-36.

Kemp, R., J. Schot and R. Hoogma (1998) 'Regime Shifts to Sustainability through Processes of Niche Formation: The Approach of Strategic Niche Management', *Technology Analysis & Strategic Management* 10.2: 175-95.

Klewitz, J., and A. Zeyen (2010) *The Role of Intermediary Organizations in Eco-efficiency Improvements in SMEs: A Multi-Case Study in the Metal and Mechanical Engineering Industries in Germany* (CSM Discussion Paper; Lüneburg, Germany: Centre for Sustainability Management).

Kline, S. (1985) 'Innovation is not a Linear Process', *Research Management* 28.4: 36-45.

Kodama, T. (2008) 'The Role of Intermediation and Absorptive Capacity in Facilitating University–Industry Linkages: An Empirical Study', *Research Policy* 37: 1,224-40.

Kogut, B. (2000) 'The Network as Knowledge: Generative Rules and the Emergence of Structure', *Strategic Management Journal* 21: 405-25.

Kolk, A., R. van Tulder and E. Kostwinder (2008) 'Business and Partnerships for Development', *European Management Journal* 26.4: 262-73.

Kouwenhoven, W. (1993) 'The Rise of the Public Private Partnership: A Model for the Management of Public–Private Cooperation', in J. Kooiman (ed.), *Modern Governance: New Government–Society Interactions* (London: Sage): 119-30.

LaFrance, J., and M. Lehman (2005) 'Corporate Awakening: Why (Some) Corporations Embrace Public–Private Partnerships', *Business Strategy and the Environment* 14: 216-29.

Lang-Koetz, C., S. Beucker and D. Heubach (2009) 'Estimating Environmental Impact in the Early Stages of the Product Innovation Process', in S. Schaltegger, M. Bennett, R. Burritt and C. Jasch (eds.), *Eco-Efficiency in Industry and Science: Vol. 24. Environmental Management Accounting for Cleaner Production* (Dordrecht, Netherlands: Springer): 49-64.

Lawrence, S., E. Collins, K. Pavlovich and M. Arunachalam (2006) 'Sustainability Practices of SMEs: The Case of NZ', *Business Strategy and the Environment* 15.4: 242-57.

LePoutre, J., and A. Heene (2006) 'Investigating the Impact of Firm Size on Small Business Social Responsibility: A Critical Review', *Journal of Business Ethics* 67: 257-73.

Lozano, R. (2007) 'Collaboration as a Pathway for Sustainability', *Sustainable Development* 15: 370-81.

Luetkenhorst, W. (2004) 'Corporate Social Responsibility and the Development Agenda: The Case for Actively Involving Small and Medium Enterprises', *Intereconomics*, May/June 2004: 157-66.

Luken, R., and J. Navratil (2004) 'A Programmatic Review of UNIDO/UNEP National Cleaner Production Centres', *Journal of Cleaner Production* 12.3: 195-205.

Lundvall, B. (2010) 'Introduction', in B. Lundvall (ed.), *National Systems of Innovation: Toward a Theory of Innovation and Interactive Learning* (London/New York: Anthem Press): 1-17.

Malmborg, F. (2003) 'Conditions for Regional Public–Private Partnerships for Sustainable Development: Swedish Perspectives', *European Environment* 13: 133-49.

Malmborg, F. (2004) 'Network for Knowledge Transfer: Towards an Understanding of Local Authority Roles in Regional Industrial Ecosystem Management', *Business Strategy and the Environment* 13: 334-46.

Manring, S. (2007) 'Creating and Managing Interorganizational Learning Networks to Achieve Sustainable Ecosystem Management', *Organization & Environment* 20.3: 325-46.

Martinuzzi, A., E. Huchler and B. Obermayr (2000) 'EcoProfit: Promoting Partnerships between Small and Medium Sized Enterprises and Local Authorities', *Greener Management International* 30: 83-96.

Meadowcroft, J. (1999) 'Cooperative Management Regimes: Collaborative Problem Solving to Implement Sustainable Development', *International Negotiation* 4: 225-54.

Miller, C., and J. Choi (2003) 'Advertising and Knowledge Intermediaries: Managing the Ethical Challenges of Intangibles', *Journal of Business Ethics* 48.3: 267-77.

Mitra, J. (2000) 'Innovation and Collective Learning for Innovation in Small Businesses', *Education & Training* 42.4/5: 228-36.

Mont, O. (2002) 'Clarifying the Concept of Product-Service System', *Journal of Cleaner Production* 10.3: 237-45.

Moore, G., and L. Spence (2006) 'Small and Medium-Sized Enterprises and Corporate Social Responsibility: Identifying the Knowledge Gaps. Editorial', *Journal of Business Ethics* 67.3: 219-26.

Noci, G., and R. Verganti (1999) 'Managing "Green" Product Innovation in Small Firms', *R&D Management* 29.1: 3-15.

Osborne, S. (ed.) (2010) *Public–Private Partnerships* (New York: Routledge).

Östlund, S. (1994) 'The Limits and Possibilities in Designing the Environmentally Sustainable Firm', *Business Strategy and the Environment* 3.2: 21-33.

Oudshoorn, N. (1997) 'From Population Control Politics to Chemicals: The WHO as an Intermediary Organization in Contraceptive Development', *Social Studies of Sciences* 27.1: 41-72.

Paech, N. (2005) 'Richtungssicherheit im nachhaltigkeitsorientierten Innovationsmanagement' [Directional Security for Sustainability Oriented Innovation Management] in K. Fichter; N. Paech and R. Pfriem (eds.), *Theorie der Unternehmung. Nachhaltige Zukunftsmärkte. Orientierungen für unternehmerische Innovationsprozesse im 21. Jahrhundert [Theory of the Firm: Sustainable Markets of the Future. Orientation for Entrepreneurial Innovation Processes]* (Marburg, Germany: Metropolis): 327-52.

Perkmann, M., and K. Walsh (2007) 'University–Industry Relationships and Open Innovation: Towards a Research Agenda', *International Journal Management Reviews* 9.4: 259-80.

Perrini, F. (2006) 'SMEs and CSR Theory: Evidence and Implications from an Italian Perspective', *Journal of Business Ethics* 67: 305-16.

Pittaway, L., M. Robertson, A. Kamal, D. Denyer and A. Neely (2004) 'Networking and Innovation: A Systematic Review of the Evidence', *International Journal of Management Reviews* 5–6: 137-68.

Powell, W., K. Koput and L. Smith-Doerr (1996) 'Interorganizational Collaboration and the Locus of Innovation: Networks of Learning in Biotechnology', *Administrative Science Quarterly* 41.1: 116-45.

Preuss, L., and J. Perschke (2010) 'Slipstreaming the Larger Boats: Social Responsibility in Medium-Sized Enterprises', *Journal of Business Ethics* 92: 531-51.

Provan, K., A. Fish and J. Sydow (2007) 'Interorganizational Networks at the Network Level: A Review of the Empirical Literature on Whole Networks', *Journal of Management* 33.3: 479-516.

Rennings, K. (2000) 'Redefining Innovation: Eco-innovation Research and the Contribution from Ecological Economics', *Ecological Economics* 32.2: 169-336.

Roberts, S., R. Lawson and J. Nicholls (2006) 'Generating Regional-Scale Improvements in SME Corporate Responsibility Performance: Lessons from Responsibility Northwest', *Journal of Business Ethics* 67.3: 275–86.

Roome, N. (2001) 'Conceptualizing and Studying the Contribution of Networks in Environmental Management and Sustainable Development', *Business Strategy and the Environment* 10.2: 69-76.

Rothwell, R., and M. Dodgson (1992) 'European Technology Policy Evolution: Convergence towards SMEs and Regional Technology Transfer', *Technovation* 12.4: 223-38.

Sage, J. (2000) 'Continuous Learning and Improvement in a Regional Cleaner Production Network', *Journal of Cleaner Production* 8: 381-89.

Santoro, M., and A. Chakrabarti (2002) 'Firm Size and Technology Centrality in Industry–University Interactions', *Research Policy* 31: 1163-80.

Schaltegger, S. (2002) 'A Framework for Ecopreneurship: Leading Bioneers and Environmental Managers to Ecopreneurship', *Greener Management International* 38: 45-58.

Schaltegger, S., and R. Burritt (2005) 'Corporate Sustainability', in H. Folmer and T. Tietenberg (eds.), *The International Yearbook of Environmental and Resource Economics 2005/2006: A Survey of Current Issues* (Cheltenham, UK: Edward Elgar): 185-222.

Schaltegger, S., and M. Wagner (2008) 'Types of Sustainable Entrepreneurship and Conditions for Sustainability Innovation: From the Administration of a Technical Challenge to the Management of an Entrepreneurial Opportunity', in R. Wüstenhagen, J. Hamschmidt, S. Sharma and M. Starik (eds.), *Sustainable Innovation and Entrepreneurship* (Cheltenham, UK/Northampton, MA: Edward Elgar): 27-48.

Schaltegger, S., and M. Wagner (2011) 'SE and Sustainability Innovation: Categories and Interactions', *Business Strategy and the Environment* 20.4: 222-37.

Schaltegger, S., C. Herzig, O. Kleiber, T. Klinke and J. Müller (2007) *Nachhaltigkeitsmanagement in Unternehmen. Von der Idee zur Praxis: Managementansätze zur Umsetzung von Corporate Social Responsibility und Corporate Sustainability [Sustainability Management in Companies: From the Idea to Practice: Management Concepts to Realize Corporate Social Responsibility and Corporate Sustainability]* (Berlin/Lüneburg, Germany: BMU, econsense & CSM, 3rd edn).

Schmiemann, M. (2008) *Enterprises by Size Class: Overview of SMEs in the EU* (Luxembourg: Office for Official Publications of the European Communities, epp.eurostat.ec.europa. eu/cache/ITY_OFFPUB/KS-SF-08-031/EN/KS-SF-08-031-EN.PDF, accessed 1 March 2011).

Segarra-Blasco, A., and J. Arauzo-Carod (2008) 'Sources of Innovation and Industry–University Interaction: Evidence from Spanish Firms', *Research Policy* 37.8: 1,283-95.

Sharma, S. (2002) 'Research in Corporate Sustainability: What Really Matters?' in S. Sharma and M. Starik (eds.), *Research in Corporate Sustainability: The Evolving Theory and Practice of Organizations in the Natural Environment* (Cheltenham, UK: Edward Elgar): 1-30.

Simon, M., S. Poole, A. Sweatman, S. Evans, T. Bhamra and T. Mcaloone (2000) 'Environmental Priorities in Strategic Product Development', *Business Strategy and the Environment* 9: 367-77.

Simpson, M., N. Taylor and K. Barker (2004) 'Environmental Responsibility in SMEs: Does it Deliver Competitive Advantage?' *Business Strategy and the Environment* 13.3: 156-71.

Spence, L., and J. Lozano (2000) 'Communicating about Ethics with Small Firms: Experiences from the UK and Spain', *Journal of Business Ethics* 27.1/2: 43-53.

Spence, L., and R. Rutherfoord (2001) 'Social Responsibility, Profit Maximisation and the Small Firm Owner-Manager', *Journal of Small Business and Enterprise Development* 8.2: 126-39.

Spence, L., R. Schmidpeter and A. Habisch (2003) 'Assessing Social Capital: Small and Medium Sized Enterprises in Germany', *Journal of Business Ethics* 47: 17-29.

Spence, M., J. Gherib and O. Biwolé (2008) 'A Framework of SMEs' Strategic Involvement in Sustainable Development', in R. Wüstenhagen, J. Hamschmidt, S. Sharma and M. Starik (eds.), *Sustainable Innovation and Entrepreneurship* (Northampton, MA: Edward Elgar): 49-70.

Spencer, A.S., and B.A. Kirchhoff (2006) 'Schumpeter and New Technology Based Firms: Towards a Framework for how NTBFs Cause Creative Destruction', *International Entrepreneurship and Management Journal* 2.2: 145-56.

Tilley, F. (2000) 'Small Firm Environmental Ethics: How Deep Do They Go?' *Business Ethics: A European Review* 9.1: 31-41.

Vellejo, N., and P. Hauselmann (2004) *Governance and Multistakeholder Processes* (Winnipeg, Manitoba: International Institute for Sustainable Development).

Verheul, H. (1999) 'How Social Networks Influence the Dissemination of Cleaner Technologies to SMEs', *Journal of Cleaner Production* 7.3: 213-19.

Van Berkel, R. (2007) 'Cleaner Production and Eco-efficiency Initiatives in Western Australia 1996–2004', *Journal of Cleaner Production* 15.8/9: 741-55.

Von Hippel, E. (1988) *The Sources of Innovation* (New York: Oxford University Press).

Vyakarnam, S., A. Bailey, A. Myers and D. Burnett (1997) 'Towards an Understanding of Ethical Behaviour in Small Firms', *Journal of Business Ethics* 16.15: 1,625-36.

Wagner, M. (2009a) 'The Links of Sustainable Competitiveness and Innovation with Openness and User Integration: An Empirical Analysis', *International Journal of Innovation and Sustainable Development* 4.4: 314-29.

Wagner, M. (2009b) 'Innovation and Competitive Advantages from the Integration of Strategic Aspects with Social and Environmental Management in European Firms', *Business Strategy and the Environment* 18: 291-306.

Wagner, M. (2010) 'Corporate Social Performance and Innovation with High Social Benefit: A Quantitative Analysis', *Journal of Business Ethics* 94.4: 581-94.

Wagner, M., and P. Llerena (2008) *Drivers for Sustainability-Related Innovation: A Qualitative Analysis of Renewable Resources, Industrial Products and Travel Services* (Working Paper; Strasbourg, France: Bureau d'Economie Théorique et Appliquée).

Walker, H., and L. Preuss (2008) 'Fostering Sustainability through Sourcing from Small Businesses: Public Sector Perspectives', *Journal of Cleaner Production* 16: 1,600-609.

Warhurst, A. (2001) 'Corporate Citizenship and Corporate Social Investment Drivers of Tri-Sector Partnerships', *Journal of Corporate Citizenship* 1: 57-73.

Welsh, A., and J. White (1981) 'A Small Business is Not a Little Big Business', *Harvard Business Review*, July/August 1981: 18-32.

Wüstenhagen, R., J. Hamschmidt, S. Sharma and M. Starik (eds.) (2008) *Sustainable Innovation and Entrepreneurship* (Cheltenham, UK: Edward Elgar).

Xu, K., and K. Huang (2011) 'Giving Fish or Teaching to Fish? An Empirical Study for the Effects of Government R&D Policies', *Proceedings of the Academy of Management 2011 Conference*, San Antonio, Texas, 12–16 August 2011.

14

Sustainability-improving innovation
Empirical insights and relationships with sustainability-oriented entrepreneurship

Marcus Wagner and Eva-Maria Lutz
Julius-Maximilians-University of Würzburg, Germany

Sustainability-improving innovations (in the following abbreviated to sustainability innovations) and sustainability-oriented entrepreneurship need to be linked and analysed jointly to embrace their wider and longer-term impacts. Chapple *et al.* (2011), for example, argue that startups especially can benefit from network effects in regional clusters because their innovation activities are often realised in industries with high human capital intensity. In contrast, bigger incumbents mostly innovate in capital-intensive sectors. Beyond this, an agglomeration of knowledge in regional innovation systems is resulting from the presence of diverse interacting actors, including research institutions and universities. According to Chapple *et al.* (2011), the empirical influence of local markets on innovating sustainable products is much greater than the impact of spatial closeness of universities, whereas the growth potential of startups increases when closely located to universities. Beyond this, governmental intervention from regulations and standards to incentive programmes and networking strategies can stimulate sustainability innovation but the efficient combination of such instruments depends on regional conditions.

Previous studies concerning sustainability-oriented entrepreneurship, which empirically apply the typology introduced in the following show that older and very small as well as very big firms without environmental management systems are less likely to be classified as 'sustainable entrepreneurs' (Wagner and Schaltegger 2010). Furthermore, being classified as a 'sustainable entrepreneur' is largely not a matter of firm size (Wagner 2009a) beyond the negative association between firm size and radicalness of innovation that is well established in innovation economics in general (Schumpeter 1934; Wagner 2009b). Also, firms from different industry sectors have the same likelihood to be categorised as 'sustainable entrepreneurs' (Wagner and Schaltegger 2010). Additionally, a complementarity between sustainability-oriented smaller and younger firms and the larger incumbents with their market opening effect for sustainability innovations can be identified (Schaltegger and Wagner 2011). Finally, regions put different emphasis on different fields, usually focusing on certain techniques and aspects, which constitutes an important link to cluster theories. For example wind or solar energy technologies have not been the focus of innovation activities in all regions, but only some, with others having a different focus.

Fundamentally, what distinguishes sustainability-oriented entrepreneurship (Walley and Taylor 2002) from entrepreneurship in general is a close orientation towards sustainability aspects, driven by, on the one hand, internal motivation (Wagner 2011) and, on the other hand, external structural impacts such as regulations or economic incentives. In the following, first, the concepts of sustainability-oriented entrepreneurship and sustainability innovations are theoretically separated. Second, based on empirical case study analysis, an indicators system is developed in order to evaluate and compare sustainability-oriented firms and innovations, which is afterwards applied in additional case studies in order to validate it.

Concepts of sustainability-oriented entrepreneurship and sustainability innovations

In the following, we focus on sustainability-oriented entrepreneurship. Although aspects such as long-term orientation and future relevance of innovation are only partly considered here, the framework may well be extended to a more general approach which is by now beyond the scope of the analysis.

Since corporate social responsibility (CSR) can cause or enable innovations with high social benefits and a significant association between CSR activities and subsequent innovations with high social benefits has been shown empirically (Wagner 2010), these as well as more narrowly defined eco-innovations are included in the considerations to follow.

Theory-based identification of categories for sustainability-oriented entrepreneurship

Depending on how much emphasis is put on sustainability aspects within the corporation's strategy, different types of sustainability-oriented entrepreneurship can be distinguished; the categorisation of sustainable behaviour is based on two dimensions: one assesses the influence of firms on special market segments and the other dimension captures the level of integration and implementation of ecological and social issues within core business activities (Schaltegger and Wagner 2011). Further differentiation can be made along both dimensions. Figure 14.1 shows on the vertical axis a scale by means of which the priority of ecological and social issues as business objectives is evaluated. The horizontal axis in Figure 14.1 captures the level of a firm's influence on different market segments and volumes. Depending on the innovation activities and their competitiveness, firms may move from left to right on this horizontal axis. The ability and probability to enter new market segments is positively correlated with business performance as a whole.

Sustainable entrepreneurship implies on the one hand the supply of sustainability innovation and products to the mass market and on the other hand that sustainability is embedded in core business activities (Schaltegger and Wagner 2011). Hence sustainable entrepreneurs contribute most to sustainable development. Ecopreneurship (Schaltegger and Petersen 2001) is in this a predecessor to sustainable entrepreneurship. The major difference between both categories is that 'ecopreneurs' pursue the realisation of environmental improvements as core business and are less focused on social objectives. Furthermore 'institutional entrepreneurship' is also similar to 'sustainable entrepreneurship' but has a stronger focus on utilising and changing institutions in assisting a move towards the mass market than on the level of innovation (Schaltegger and Wagner 2011). A further important type of entrepreneurship is 'sustainability innovation in a niche', whose main characteristic is a focus on research and development and a small market. Based on this specialisation, this type of firm can position itself in the market successfully and stay competitive, because in comparison to bigger, established firms, it can better serve individual needs, which is frequently also not profitable for big companies. In particular, the development of environmentally friendly products and services is also central to their mission. Consequently, client groups consist of customers who have a higher willingness to pay for such products (Schaltegger and Petersen 2001).

Firm activities are referred to as 'traditional social entrepreneurship' if social requirements are regarded as a core objective of business, whereas firms focusing on the 'management of environmental and social challenges and opportunities' give only medium priority to sustainable requirements but influence different market segments (niche, mass market, market and society). Finally, lowest priority is given to the business objectives of integrating ecological and social issues by the group of firms identified as 'administration of social and environmental requirements' (Schaltegger and Wagner 2008, 2011). With reference to the latter two categories,

Figure 14.1 **Categories and development steps of sustainability-oriented entrepreneurship**

Source: based on Schaltegger and Wagner 2011

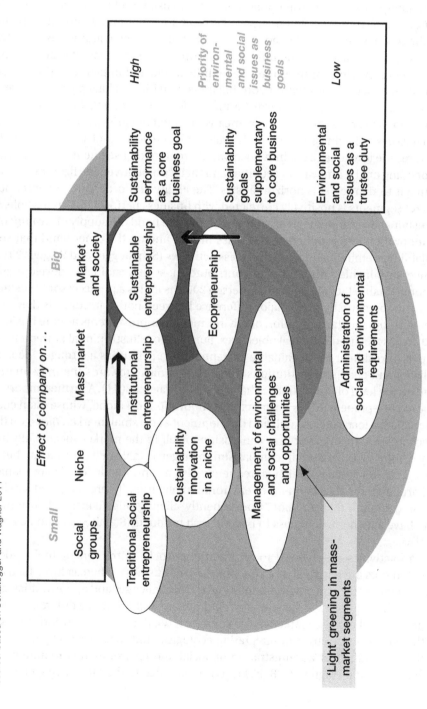

a current trend of 'light' greening in mass market segments can be observed, for example in the food retail sector. Based on these categories, companies and projects will be assigned to the main types, sustainable entrepreneur, sustainability innovation in a niche and socio-environmental managers in the case study part of this paper; their main characteristics are summarized in Table 14.1.

Table 14.1 **Characteristics of categories based on Figure 14.1**

Source: based on Wagner and Schaltegger 2010

Socio-environmental managers	Sustainability information in a niche	Sustainable entrepreneurs
Environmental or social challenges are administered rather than managed	Sustainability is central effect	Sustainability as a core goal of their activities; pull the whole market towards sustainability
Concentration on implementation of given regulations and standards	Niche market orientation	Business success through sustainability performance is a core goal of activities
Focus on a niche if sustainability is a more central goal of the enterprise		

Characteristics of sustainability innovations

Owing to society's and companies' increasing awareness of the importance of sustainability innovations, a comprehensive definition is needed. Reid and Miedzinski (2008: 1) in this respect propose to define such innovation as:

> the creation of novel and competitively priced goods, processes, systems, services, and procedures designed to satisfy human needs and provide a better quality of life for everyone with a whole-life-cycle minimal use of natural resources (materials including energy and surface area) per unit output, and a minimal release of toxic substances.

A similar, but more concise definition is proposed by the EIO Eco Innovation Observatory (2010: 10), based on statistical work of EUROSTAT and the OECD: 'Eco-innovation is any innovation that reduces the use of natural resources and decreases the release of harmful substances across the whole life-cycle'. Innovations can further be differentiated by their level and whether processes, products or services are affected.

Environmental aspects stand to the fore when eco-innovations are characterised. This includes all projects of product and process innovations which consider environmental aspects and whose purpose it is to comply with environmental policy guidelines. Eco-innovations can be implemented in diverse fields: for example, inside corporations, policy, private households, organisations and associations.

Figure 14.2 Influencing factors for sustainability innovations and their interaction

Source: extended from Rennings 2000

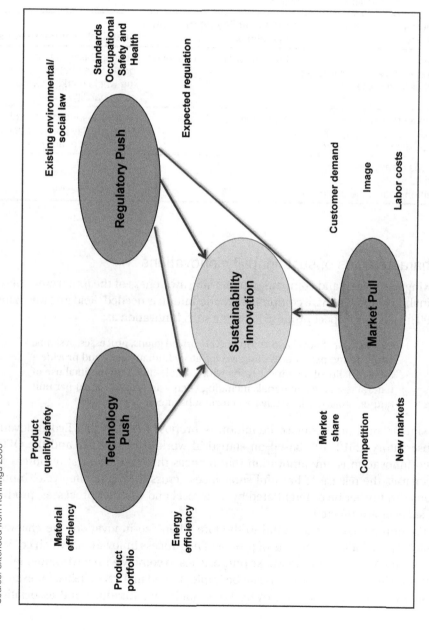

Decisive factors in this respect are the development and implementation of new methods, processes or products which focus on considering environmental aspects (Rennings 1998).

One important factor affecting sustainability innovation is the technological determinant. For instance, such a technological trend is represented by continuously increasing energy efficiency. Market influences, especially demand side and consumer preferences, are a further component. In addition to this, major influence is exerted by regulation which may trigger and accelerate innovations or push diffusion of already implemented innovation (see Fig. 14.2). Financial incentives such as governmental subsidies and tax reliefs also support sustainable or eco-innovation. Broadly, product innovations are mostly driven by market demand in terms of both the development of new products and the improvement of existing products. Conversely, regulatory requirements are more important for process innovations because they often initiate the development of these (Rennings 2000). Figure 14.2 summarises the three different determinants and shows their interaction, especially the moderating effect that regulation often has on market pull and technology push.

The link between sustainability-oriented entrepreneurship and level of sustainability innovations

Besides an integrated consideration of different sustainability aspects, an analysis of the link between (different) types of sustainability-oriented entrepreneurship and the level of sustainability innovation is necessary to be able to assess the sustainability potential of products or processes. From Figure 14.3 it becomes clear that the more strongly innovation affects knowledge or already existing system structures and the more extensively the existing relations of market and actor relations are influenced, the higher the sustainability potential of this innovation and the more the innovation is related to sustainability-oriented entrepreneurship. This means that the latter can mainly be expected in the three fields to the (upper) right in Figure 14.1 and not in the field at the bottom left (which is where mainly established firms can be expected to be active).

From Figure 14.3 it also becomes implicitly clear that more comprehensive sustainability innovations often imply the involvement of a larger number of actors (which is a special case of changes in the relations of actors and organizations).

Figure 14.3 **Link between sustainable entrepreneurship and level of sustainability innovations**

Source: based on Konrad and Nill 2001

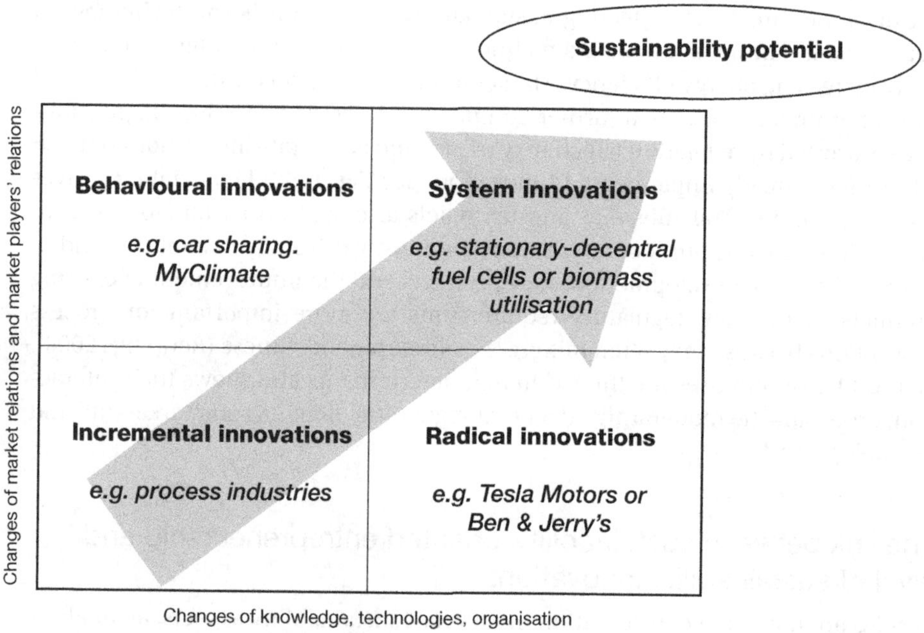

Changes of knowledge, technologies, organisation

The role of networking especially in the context of cluster structures has been highlighted more recently by Porter (1990), who renewed the attention directed to the importance of regional business clusters in a sector. Different cluster mechanisms that can be distinguished when considering the effectiveness of such agglomerations have, however, already been proposed much earlier. This concerns, for example, the spatial proximity of suppliers, customers or research institutions which promotes direct spillover effects and the dissemination of specific knowledge (Marshall 1920). Additionally, when assessing the economic performance of clusters, the converging effect within this cluster has to be considered. The competition within a cluster for input factors increases with persistence and size of the agglomeration. The number of established corporations increases as well, which in turn raises entry barriers for startups. Consequently, this process of convergence leads to decreasing growth rates of startups with age and size of clusters. This effect notwithstanding, a higher share of startups can occur in dense and strong clusters by considering convergence effects due to complementarities, although possible indirect cluster effects are not clearly separable (Porter 2003; Porter *et al.* 2010). Thus a regional focus on industries (e.g. plastics, textiles) also depends, among other things, on the type of competition (based on cost versus innovation-based). The strength and focus of spatially close clusters in turn depend on complementarities and overall regional competition.

As stated, the existence of clusters and the presence of intensive networking are especially relevant for successfully developing and implementing sustainability innovations. Thus sustainability innovations are especially suited for networks and clusters because they aim at a relatively higher planned level of innovation. Hauschildt (2004) as well as Hauschildt and Salomo (2005), who examine the dimensions of innovation success and consider their link to the level of innovation, identify direct and indirect technical effects, direct and indirect economic effects and other effects (e.g. environmental and social effects). With regard to sustainability innovations, these latter other effects are intended and thus constitute additional requirements which renders networking and clustering more relevant.

As means to achieve a great ecological and social reach of innovations, Konrad and Nill (2001) identify requirements such as complementary changes, appropriate usage and broad application possibilities. This means that technological-organisational changes alone are not sufficient, but changes of relations between markets and market players are necessary. Since sustainability innovations often require more coordinated activities in research and development, distribution and disposal, they benefit particularly from networking (Karl and Müller 2004). This implies a particular role of networking for sustainability innovation (and as a special case of this of course also eco-innovations) which shall also be illustrated in the following section on empirical analyses based on a case study of the Bavarian cluster programme.

Empirical analysis of sustainability innovations and sustainability-oriented entrepreneurship

Against the background of the above-mentioned insights, the following section uses different approaches (especially case studies, third-party evaluation of indicators) to empirically analyse sustainability innovation and sustainability-oriented entrepreneurship and their linkages as outlined above.

Relevance of networking for sustainability innovations: the Bavarian cluster programme and the Umwelttechnologische Gründerzentrum (UTG) Augsburg

The Bavarian state government initiated the Bavarian cluster programme in 2006 in order to support a directed cluster formation in certain future technology domains. This initiative pursues the constitution and promotion of 19 clusters in 21 selected sectors in the period 2006 to 2011. The programme focuses on networking and cross-linking of technology-oriented and technology-specific business incubators and technology centres. The most relevant fields of technologies in this context are new materials, chemistry, nanotechnology, energy technology and environmental technology. The Bavarian concept builds on the implementation of the cluster idea of linked producers, suppliers, services and related institutions (chambers of industry and commerce, universities, universities of applied sciences) located within a short distance of each other to improve interaction: for example through supply and demand relationships.

With a special focus on environmental technologies, the environmental cluster of Bavaria (Umweltcluster Bayern) is mainly involved in the sectors of waste and recycling, water/effluents and alternative energies (in particular waste and bio-mass energy). Furthermore, the environmental cluster is member of a European-wide network of environmental technology clusters (EcoCluP), which links more than 3,500 corporations and 430 research institutions from ten EU countries (Anon 2011).

One of the business incubators within the Bavarian cluster programme is the UTG Augsburg, a business incubator specialising in environmental technology. In order to empirically identify the central characteristics of sustainability innovations and large and eco-innovations in particular, the UTG was analysed in more detail, especially also with regard to the role of regulation. Following this, an evaluation scheme for the categories of sustainability-oriented entrepreneurship introduced above has been developed and was subsequently validated by applying it to three case studies. The evaluation scheme in a next step can be applied to individual ventures in clusters or incubators (such as the firms in the Bavarian environmental technology cluster or the UTG Augsburg) which can assist a more in-depth poten-tial analysis.

The UTG Augsburg GmbH is one of 400 business incubators in Germany, located in Bavaria and founded in 1998. With a strong focus on ecology, the business areas of the around 40 startups in it range from alternative energies to various environ-mental technologies (e.g. waste, water/effluents, noise, recycling) and biotechnol-ogy. The incubator, with its specialisation in environmental technology, is unique in Europe. Measures to evaluate the contribution to sustainability of these inno-vations are, though, difficult to define. For example, while intensively used in the energy sector, tools such as life-cycle assessment are too technology-specific to yield comparable measurements across industries. However, individual entrepre-neurs might use such tools as a marketing instrument. The mean residence time of the more than 100 firms supported so far at the UTG is 4.7 years. This period, however, varies across sectors. For example, IT startups stay for two to three years whereas environmental technology firms remain in the UTG for about eight years. In general, time-to-market of new technologies is about ten years (Hehl 2010).

Concerning financial aspects, the young firms profit from cost advantages in the business incubator due to relatively low rents and flexible contract conditions. Con-sidering the funding situation of the approximately 1,000 firms located in Bavarian business incubators, most of them follow a long-term strategy (Hehl 2010). One of the structural factors which Walley and Taylor (2002) identified to be decisive for sustainability-oriented entrepreneurship is regulation and legislation. Their influence on sustainability innovation in general and especially more narrow eco-innovations has been widely discussed during recent decades. Proponents of more stringent environmental regulation and legislation argue that these may foster innovations by forcing the firm to investigate novel areas and approaches which in turn can enhance its competitiveness (Porter and van der Linde 1995). Opponents of this point of view fear, however, that such regulations act just like another burden for companies. Though laws may increase eco-efficiency by innovations they may also negatively affect the competitive situation and imply additional costs. In any case, however, regulations seem to have a certain influence on firms' innovation activities, yet the right form of regulation seems to be essential for positive effects on competitiveness.

The literature reviewed during the process of developing the indicator/evaluation scheme for sustainability-oriented entrepreneurship and sustainability innovation supports the notion of regulations being a crucial factor (Wagner 2011). For instance, energy standards are beneficial in triggering environmental innovations, but safety regulations can be a hindrance to their diffusion. In order to find a regulatory optimum, on the one hand the detrimental effects of regulations have to be avoided at best. Positive innovation impulses from regulation should be maximised at the same time. Overall, it seems that the hindering effect is strongest and most harmful in the case of radical innovation. Additionally, there is evidence that regulations play an important role for diffusion of eco-innovations. For example Volvo first introduced the catalytic converter only in the United States because of tightened regulations. Following similar regulations in Sweden, it introduced the new technology there, too.

Further aspects especially related to startups concern internal factors as well as other external factors. Internal factors that can influence startup performance are their motivation (for-profit versus for-benefit), the level of innovation and their orientation towards sustainability as a whole. Besides regulations and the funding situation of startups, other important external factors are the sustainability orientation of whole nation-states and its growth effects. These additional aspects are in need of further analysis in future.

Development and validation of an evaluation scheme for sustainability-oriented entrepreneurship and sustainability innovation

Based on the first part of the empirical analysis, an evaluation system was designed and validated to assess sustainability-oriented entrepreneurship and sustainability innovations. Since no indicator system is considered applicable in general, a project-based evaluation scheme was developed. The intention of this scheme was to identify single projects that are rated as particularly innovative, efficient and successful and which could serve as an exemplary model or benchmark. Therefore, the evaluation scheme is divided into six different categories as follows: five categories relate to the three sustainability dimensions 'ecology' (two categories), 'economics' (one category) and 'society' (two categories); the sixth category, 'innovation', is focused on the most important innovation aspects such as novelty, state of the art and subjective judgement of future relevance for processes and products. Based on these categories, a further differentiation into 19 different indicators is done (Fig. 14.4). These indicators are then weighted according to their relevance for sustainability aspects, based among other things on the first part of the analysis.

Figure 14.4 **Evaluation scheme for sustainability-oriented entrepreneurship**

Evaluation plan (system of indicators)
- Evaluation of
  - Sustainable entrepreneurship
  - Sustainable innovations
- Six categories
  - Environment (2 aspects)
  - Economy (1 aspect)
  - Social (2 aspects)
  - Innovation (i.e. novelty, state of the art, future relevance)

⇒ 190 indicators, weighted based on sustainability relevance

Indicators particularly relevant to sustainable development are weighted with a value of three. Energy savings, reduction of material consumption, recyclability of materials, reduction of environmental and climate-damaging substances are indicators which reflect a project's level of environmental performance. They also relate to the integration of environmental aspects as a core business objective. Consequently, these indicators are assigned triple weight. Product life-cycle effects and resources utilised are also indicators representing the ecological dimension but they are only assigned double weight. The reason for this medium weighting is that greater importance is attached to the sustainable character and benefit for society of a product or process than to the product life-cycle. The indicator 'resources utilised' is relatively difficult to measure. For instance, a corporation abandons hydraulic oil in operating a wood splitter but uses clear water hydraulic systems instead. Although this method is environmentally sound and energy is saved under certain circumstances, the resource 'water' is nonetheless a good that is going to be made even scarcer in future. However, to account for the increasing usage of environmentally more benign resources this indicator is also assigned double weight.

The economic dimension is part of the sustainability triangle and therefore also an important pillar. But one has to act on the assumption that economic aspects are the main motivation of most innovations and therefore often automatically considered. A sustainability or eco-innovation is characterised by simultaneously considering ecological and social performance alongside economic performance.

Therefore, the indicator 'financial profitability' receives only single weight. 'Improving competitiveness' can in turn positively affect the situation of employees and working conditions and this dimension is accordingly assigned double weight. The indicator 'win–win results' refers to the joint achievement of cost saving and environmental impact reduction, which carries double weight because it simultaneously considers the economic and ecological dimensions.

'Meeting societal needs' and 'significant benefit to society' are an important part of any definition of sustainability (Wagner 2010). Therefore these two indicators in the social dimension are assigned triple weight. The indicators 'safeguarding employment' and 'providing new jobs' also fall in the social dimension and are assigned double weight. The reason for this is that a lower number of individuals are affected by these criteria, because even securing several thousands of jobs accounts for only a fraction of the individuals that constitute entire nations and societies.

As concerns the innovation dimensions, triple weight was assigned to indicators 'state of the art' and 'subjective judgement of future relevance'. While in principle the indicator 'level of innovation' should have the same weighting, from a sustainability perspective, the novelty of a process or product should not be overrated because a small change can have potentially enormous effects. Consequently, this indicator is assigned double weight. The 'project status' is by the same token important in order to judge the idea's potential of actually being realised. Therefore, double weight was assigned to this indicator. Finally, the indicator 'future improvements possible' was assigned only single weight since future developments are difficult to predict and any evaluation is thus rather subjective.

This evaluation scheme and indicator system was validated by applying it to three case studies which were subjected to an evaluation based on this system. The three cases below were specifically chosen since Kofink (2010) had already classified them based on the typology presented in Figure 14.1. Evaluation by means of this indicator system was based on information from this earlier classification as well as on additional research. The ratings are explained in the following:

The company Starfort supplies products such as wood splitters, high-pressure cleaners, glass crucible locks and sofas made of tree trunks. The distinctive feature of the products is that Starfort replaces oil-hydraulic cylinders with water-hydraulic systems. The company strives to meet ambitious environmental standards with this measure and was also able to enhance the mechanical engineering performance of its products. Starfort has also completely banned strong colours based on environmentally problematic dyestuffs and instead only uses biological coatings for the equipment produced. Given its niche market orientation and integration of sustainable aspects into core business activity, this company is rated as a firm pursuing sustainability innovation in a niche.

Second, the firm Ecorecycling Felderer focuses on the usage of environmentally friendly filter methods and development of novel cleaning methods for process and irrigation water. These filter systems are applied Europe-wide to small and large fruit plantations and fruit processing. Further research and application areas of

Ecorecycling Felderer are water treatment, pool water electrolysis and soil analysis. These new technologies have gathered a significant market share for which reason the company is categorised as sustainable entrepreneurs.

Finally, the company Mila focuses on the production and supply of ecologically produced and environmentally sound dairy products. The firm has achieved important environmental improvements in the production process, namely the reduction of phosphates in cleaning agents, the reduction of CO_2 emissions and of heat losses through better insulation of hot water pipes. Besides this, by purchasing milk from more than 3,500 mountain farmers, Mila supports regional environmental protection and development. With a focus on the dairy products market and implementation of several environmental requirements the firm is characterised as a socio-environmental manager (Kofink 2010).

Figure 14.5 **Analysis results of case studies based on the evaluation scheme**

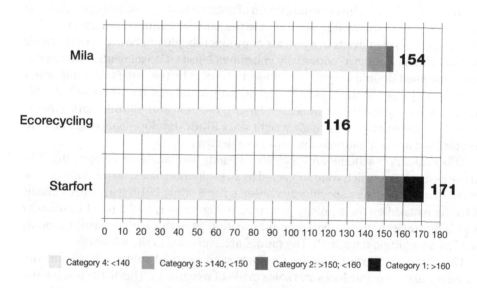

The values for the three projects from the above evaluation scheme vary between 116 and 171 (see Fig. 14.5). For a more detailed analysis values were divided into four score categories (see Fig. 14.6). One project is assigned to category four (< 140), no project is assigned to category three (> 140; < 150) and one project is assigned to the second category (> 150; < 160). The project Starfort, with the highest rating of 171 points, shows high values in the evaluation categories 'level of innovation of product or process' as well as 'novelty' specifically because of the technical process changes. Ecorecycling, representing a 'sustainable entrepreneur', achieved the lowest score in this indicator system. The reason for this could be that an error of judgement may exist, but the categorisations of Kofink (2010) are not explained in detail so that it is difficult to establish if this is the case. On the other hand, in the

Figure 14.6 **Types of sustainable entrepreneurship**

Source: based on Schaltegger and Petersen 2001 and Schaltegger and Wagner 2011

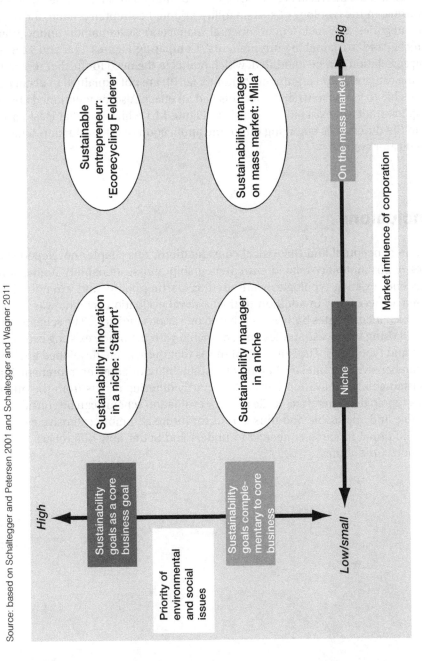

above matrix (Fig. 14.1) there exists an implicit trade-off to the degree that a higher market penetration inevitably implies some 'dilution' of sustainability objectives (as is also witnessed by the 'light' greening trend observed in many mass market segments.

As part of the validation of the evaluation scheme with the case studies, the two dimensions of the matrix in Figure 14.1 are also examined in detail for the three case study firms. In the typology of sustainability-oriented entrepreneurship, the three main categories are 'socio-environmental managers', 'sustainability innovations in a niche' and 'sustainable entrepreneurs'. Comparing Figures 14.5 and 14.6 no strong correlation can be identified, which points to the need for further research. Since the categorisation arguments of Kofink (2010) are not explained in detail it is not possible to assess to what degree this had an effect. Also, as mentioned above, an implicit trade-off exists in the matrix of Figure 14.1 which could at least partly explain the differences emerging out of the application of the evaluation scheme and indicator system.

Conclusions

Based on conceptual and theoretical considerations, this chapter developed categories of sustainability-related entrepreneurship and sustainability innovation. To this end, existing typologies were used as starting points and extended and adjusted as necessary. In addition to this, a novel evaluation scheme was developed which incorporates both aspects based on various indictors. The scheme was validated using three case studies and compared with the other, existing categorisations and typologies. The outcome of this is that the scheme developed enables a comprehensive and valid evaluation of sustainability-oriented entrepreneurship and sustainability innovation but leads to partly differing results from the other, existing typologies. Therefore, while the new evaluation scheme can be considered as reliable and applicable and thus a basis for future and more extensive evaluations, additional research is needed to understand better how differences in the evaluation come about.

References

Anon (2011) *Umwelt-Technologie und Energie in Bayern* (Munich: Media Mind GmbH).

Chapple, K., C. Kroll, T.W. Lester and S. Montero (2011) 'Innovation in the Green Economy: An Extension of the Regional Innovation System Model?' *Economic Development Quarterly* 25.1: 5-25.

EIO (Eco Innovation Observatory) (2010) *Methodological Report* (Brussels: Europe Innova).

Hauschildt, J. (2004) *Innovationsmanagement* (Munich: Vahlen).

Hauschildt, J., and S. Salomo (2005) 'Je innovativer, desto erfolgreicher?' *Journal für Betriebswirtschaft* 55: 3-20.

Hehl, W. (2010) 'Die bayerische Clusterstrategie und die Rolle des Umwelt-Technologischen Gründerzentrums Augsburgs (UTG)', presentation at the *Julius-Maximilians-University, Würzburg*, 17 November 2010.

Karl, H., and A. Möller (2004) 'Kooperationen zur Entwicklung von Umweltinnovationen: Marktendogene Kooperationsdynamik und wirtschaftspolitische Kooperationsförderung', in J. Horbach, J. Huber and T. Schulz (eds.), *Nachhaltigkeit und Innovation* (München: Ökom): 191-218.

Kofink, L. (2010) 'Nachhaltigkeit und Unternehmertum, Fallstudien aus Südtirol, Institut für Regionalentwicklung und Standortmanagement', presentation at the *Kompetenzforum Regionalmanagement 2010*, Ingolstadt, 21 October 2010.

Konrad, W., and J. Nill (2001) *Innovationen für Nachhaltigkeit, Ein interdisziplinärer Beitrag zur konzeptionellen Klärung aus wirtschafts- und sozialwissenschaftlicher Perspektive* (Berlin: Institut für ökologische Wirtschaftsforschung).

Marshall, A. (1920) *Principles of Economics* (London: Macmillan).

Porter, M.E. (1990) *The Competitive Advantage of Nations* (New York: Free Press).

Porter, M.E. (2003) 'The Economic Performance of Regions', *Regional Studies* 37: 549-78.

Porter, M.E., and C. van der Linde (1995) 'Toward a New Conception of the Environment–Competitiveness Relationship', *Journal of Economic Perspectives* 9.4: 97-118.

Porter, M.E., M. Delgado and S. Stern (2010) *Clusters and Entrepreneurship* (Boston, MA: Harvard Business School).

Reid, A., and M. Miedzinski (2008) *Sectoral Innovation Watch in Europe: Eco-Innovation* (Brussels: Europe Innova).

Rennings, K. (1998) *Towards a Theory and Policy of Eco-Innovation-Neoclassic and (Co-) Evolutionary Perspectives* (Discussion Paper 98-24; Mannheim, Germany: Centre for European Economic Research, ZEW).

Rennings, K. (2000) 'Redefining Innovation: Eco-innovation Research and the Contribution from Ecological Economics', *Ecological Economics* 32: 319-32.

Schaltegger, S., and H. Petersen (2001) *Ecopreneurship: Konzept und Typologie* (Lüneburg, Germany: Centre for Sustainability Management (CSM); Lucerne, Switzerland: Rio Management Forum).

Schaltegger, S., and M. Wagner (2008) 'Types of Sustainable Entrepreneurship and Conditions for Sustainability Innovation: From the Administration of a Technical Challenge to the Management of an Entrepreneurial Opportunity', in S. Sharma, M. Starik, R. Wüstenhagen and J. Hamschmidt (eds.), *Advances on Research in Corporate Sustainability* (Boston, MA: Edward Elgar): 27-48.

Schaltegger, S., and M. Wagner (2011) 'Sustainable Entrepreneurship and Sustainability Innovation: Categories and Interactions', *Business Strategy and the Environment* 20.4: 222-37.

Schumpeter, J.A. (1947) 'The Creative Response in Economic History', *Journal of Economic History* 7: 149-59.

Wagner, M. (2009a) 'Eco-entrepreneurship: An Empirical Perspective Based on Survey Data', *Advances in the Study of Entrepreneurship, Innovation and Economic Growth* 20: 127-52.

Wagner, M. (2009b) 'Erfolgsfaktoren für Nachhaltigkeitsinnovationen: Qualitative und quantitative Befunde', *Zeitschrift für Umweltrecht und Umweltpolitik* 2: 179-98.

Wagner, M. (2010) 'Corporate Social Performance and Innovation with High Social Benefits: A Quantitative Analysis', *Journal of Business Ethics* 94: 581-94.

Wagner, M. (2011) 'Sustainability-Related Innovation and Competitiveness-Enhancing Regulation: A Qualitative and Quantitative Analysis in the Context of Open Innovation', *International Journal of Innovation and Sustainable Development* 5.4: 371-88.

Wagner, M., and S. Schaltegger (2010) 'Classifying Entrepreneurship for the Public Good', *Journal of Small Business & Entrepreneurship* 23.3: 431-43.

Walley, E.E., and D.W. Taylor (2002) 'Opportunists, Champions, Mavericks . . . ? A Typology of Green Entrepreneurs', *Greener Management International* 38: 31-43.

About the contributors

Dr **Preeta M. Banerjee** is Assistant Professor of Strategy at the Brandeis International Business School. Recent papers on human capital in high technology and innovation shifts can be found in *R&D Management Journal, IEEE-TEM* and *Technovation*. She received her PhD from The Wharton School and her BSc from Carnegie Mellon.
banerjee@brandeis.edu

Toke Bjerregaard is a post doc researcher at Aarhus School of Business and Social Sciences. His research interests cover entrepreneurship, institutions and intercultural interaction. He has published in international and national journals and books such as *Technovation, International Journal of Entrepreneurial Venturing* and *Journal of Organizational Change Management*.
Toke@asb.dk

Esther Blom (1979) is a researcher and lecturer at the Delft Centre for Entrepreneurship at the Delft University of Technology. Her courses and her field of interest focus on sustainable entrepreneurship in an international context. She has gained a great deal of hands-on experience while working for her own foundation and social enterprise and through involvement in many projects.
E.M.Blom@tudelft.nl

Casper Boks is professor at the Norwegian University of Science and Technology in Trondheim, Norway, with a background in applied econometrics and industrial design engineering. His research interests include design strategies for sustainable behaviour and the organisational and managerial aspects of sustainable product innovation in general.
casper.boks@ntnu.no

Ivo Dewit is research assistant at the Artesis University College of Antwerp, Belgium, with a background in business studies, change management and product development. His current research focuses on increasing the efficiency of the process from early stage ideation of new products and services towards feasible market opportunities in organisations.
Ivo.dewit@artesis.be

Romano Dyerson is Senior Lecturer in Economics and Strategy at the School of Management, Royal Holloway, University of London. He gained a PhD in economics from Heriot-Watt University. Adopting a broadly research-based view approach, his research interests have focused on innovation and technological change practices in both small and large firms.
R.Dyerson@rhul.ac.uk

Timothy Galpin is Assistant Professor of Management at Colorado Mesa University, teaching strategy, leadership and entrepreneurship. His academic research is in the areas of: leading sustainable organisations, leadership effectiveness, mergers and acquisitions, and entrepreneurship. Besides his journal articles, Tim Galpin has also published three management books: *The Complete Guide to Mergers and Acquisitions*; *Making Strategy Work*; and *The Human Side of Change*.
tgalpin@coloradomesa.edu

Dr **Erik G. Hansen** is a researcher at the Centre for Sustainability Management (CSM) at Leuphana University Lüneburg, Germany. His research interests are innovation and strategic management in the context of sustainable development. Erik teaches in these fields in graduate, postgraduate and executive programmes.
erik.hansen@uni.leuphana.de   www.leuphana.de/csm

Dr **Florian Jell** has been researcher and lecturer at the Schöller Chair in Technology and Innovation Management (held by Professor Dr Joachim Henkel, Technische Universität München). His research focuses on innovation management, intellectual property management, patent strategies, entrepreneurship and venture capital. In 2009, Florian was Microsoft Fellow in the Program in Law, Economics, and Technology at the University of Michigan. He currently works as a consultant in the energy sector.
florian.jell@wi.tum.de

Ioannis Katsikis is a doctoral researcher at the Athens University of Economics and Business. He has studied innovation management and technology policy and he holds an MSc in Environmental Policy & Management, an MBA and an MPhil in Architecture and Space Planning. He has served as a business consultant to major international organisations and he has published a large number of papers in journals, edited books and international conferences.
ioannis@aueb.gr

Johanna Klewitz is a research associate at the Centre for Sustainability Management (CSM) and project manager in the Innovation Network 'Sustainable SMEs' within the EU-Project Innovation Incubator at Leuphana University Lüneburg, Germany. Her research interests are innovation and collaboration in the context of sustainable development.
klewitz@uni.leuphana.de   www.leuphana.de/csm

Otto Kroesen (1955) is Assistant Professor in Ethics and Sustainability at the Delft University of Technology. He teaches ethics, language philosophy and intercultural communication and organises and supervises internships in developing countries. His research focuses on the co-development of society, values and technology, especially in view of future strategies for developing countries, both in terms of entrepreneurship and the broader framework of governance.
J.O.Kroesen@tudelft.nl

Jakob Lauring is a professor at Aarhus School of Business and Social Sciences, Aarhus University. In recent years he has been working with intercultural interaction in culturally diverse organisations. He focuses particularly on diversity management and cross-cultural management. He has published work in journals such as *International Journal of Human Resource Management, Corporate Communication: An International Journal* and *International Business Review*, among others. He holds a Master's degree in anthropology from Aarhus University.
Jala@asb.dk

Patrick Llerena has been Professor of Economics at the University of Strasbourg since 1988. He was director and co-director of BETA and the vice-president in charge of industry and enterprise relations of the University Louis Pasteur. In addition to his teaching, his research interests lie in the theory of the firm, technology policies and the strategies of public research institutions. He has published numerous articles and books relating to these topics since 1985. He has been involved in several projects and networks funded by the EU, some of them as coordinator.
pllerena@unistra.fr

Eva-Maria Lutz was a Bachelor of Science student in economics and business administration and a student assistant at the Chair in Entrepreneurship and Management at Julius-Maximilians-University Würzburg.

Christopher Mensah-Bonsu graduated from the Technische Universität München with a degree (BSc) in management & technology at the beginning of 2011. Being part German and part Ghanaian, his interests in innovation and the developing world have their origin in childhood. While growing up in Germany and later in Canada, he was witness to his father's numerous business ventures. Christopher currently works as a consultant in the field of mobile marketing in the automotive sector.
christopher.mbonsu@googlemail.com

Fabio Musso is Professor of Management and Chairman of the MS in Marketing and Communication at Urbino University (Italy). His research interests include international strategy, CSR, marketing, marketing channels, retailing and logistics. He has more than 80 research publications in various refereed international journals/conferences and has published six books. He is Associate Editor of the *International Journal of Applied Behavioral Economics*.
fabio.musso@uniurb.it

Roland Ortt (1964) is Associate Professor of Technology Management and Director of the Delft Centre for Entrepreneurship at the Delft University of Technology, the Netherlands. His research interest focuses on the period between the first introduction of radically new high-tech products and the start of industrial production and large-scale diffusion of these products. This phase is usually erratic and chaotic: many product versions are introduced in different market segments. In this phase entrepreneurs are required to create viable combinations between customers and a mainstream product.
J.R.Ortt@tudelft.nl

Micaela Preskill graduated from Brandeis University in 2010 with a degree in economics. She has been a policy intern with Planned Parenthood Federation of America and is currently the Consumer Associate at Massachusetts Public Interest Research Group; she advocates for public transportation and product safety.
mpreskill@gmail.com

Lutz Preuss is Reader in Corporate Social Responsibility at the School of Management, Royal Holloway, University of London, where he is also the Programme Director of the MSc Sustainability and Management. He holds a PhD from King's College London in addition to qualifications from Humboldt University Berlin and the University of Reading. His research has addressed various aspects of corporate sustainability, such as interlinkages between corporate sustainability and neighbouring disciplines.
Lutz.Preuss@rhul.ac.uk

Mario Risso is Associate Professor of Management in the School of Economics at the University Niccolò Cusano and University of Rome 'Tor Vergata'. His research interests include retailing, global supply chain management, corporate social responsibility and international business.
mario.risso@uniroma2.it

Boukje Vastbinder (1982) is a researcher and lecturer at the Delft Centre for Entrepreneurship at the Delft University of Technology. Her courses and her field of interest focus on sustainable entrepreneurship. Over recent years she has gained a lot of hands-on experience while working as a product designer and a sustainable entrepreneur in many projects in developing countries.
B.Vastbinder@tudelft.nl

Elli Verhulst is research assistant and mentor at the Artesis University College of Antwerp, Belgium, with a background in product development. Her research is at the intersection of two main topics: product innovations and sustainable design implementation. The theoretical bodies underlying her research are sustainable product development and change management. Moreover, she coaches Bachelor and Master's level students in both design and research assignments.
elli.verhulst@artesis.be

Marcus Wagner is full professor and holder of the Chair in Entrepreneurship and Management at Julius-Maximilians-University Würzburg. He is an associate member of the Bureau d'Economie Théorique et Appliquée, Université de Strasbourg, and held a Marie Curie Fellowship funded by the European Commission from 2006 to 2008. His current research interests are entrepreneurship, innovation management and strategic management.

marcus.wagner@uni-wuerzburg.de

J. Lee Whittington is Professor of Management at the University of Dallas. He focuses his teaching, research and consulting in the areas of leadership, organisational behaviour and leading strategic change. His research has been published in *The Leadership Quarterly, Academy of Management Review, Journal of Management, Journal of Organizational Behavior, Journal of Business Strategy, Journal of Applied Social Psychology, Journal of Management Spirituality and Religion, Journal of Managerial Issues* and the *Journal of Behavioral and Applied Management.*

JLeeWhitt@aol.com

Index